Exceptional
Spaces

Exceptional

Spa

Essays in
Performance
and History

Edited by Della Pollock

The University of North Carolina Press

Chapel Hill and London

The paper in this book meets the guidelines for permanence
and durability of the Committee on Production Guidelines for
Book Longevity of the Council on Library Resources.

Library of Congress Cataloging-in-Publication Data
Exceptional spaces: essays in performance and history / edited by Della Pollock.
p.   cm.
Includes index.
ISBN 0-8078-2378-3 (cloth: alk. paper). — ISBN 0-8078-4684-8 (pbk.: alk. paper)
1. History — Methodology. 2. Historicism. I. Pollock, Della.
D16.E88   1998
907'.2 — dc21   97-12384
                CIP

02 01 00 99 98   5 4 3 2 1

Kay Ellen Capo, "How to Act during an Interrogation: Theatre and Moral Boundaries,"
    Soundings 70.1–2 (1987): 219–38, is reprinted here as the first part of Capo's contribution
    to this volume by permission of the author and publisher.
Kirk W. Fuoss, "Performance as Contestation: An Agonistic Perspective on the Insurgent
    Assembly," Text and Performance Quarterly 13.4 (1993): 331–49, is reprinted here by
    permission of the author and the Speech Communication Association.
A modified version of D. Soyini Madison, " 'That Was My Occupation': Oral Narrative,
    Performance, and Black Feminist Thought," Text and Performance Quarterly 13.3 (1993):
    213–32, is reprinted here by permission of the author and the Speech Communication
    Association.
A modified version of Carol Mavor, "Touching Netherplaces: Invisibility in the Photographs of
    Hannah Cullwick," Pleasures Taken: Performances of Loss and Sexuality in Victorian Photographs
    (Duke University Press, 1995), is reprinted here by permission of the author and publisher.
Joseph R. Roach, "Slave Spectacles and Tragic Octoroons: A Cultural Genealogy of Antebellum
    Performance," Theatre Survey 33.2 (1992): 167–87, is reprinted here by permission of the
    author and publisher.

Dedicated, as ever, to Frank Galati

Contents

Acknowledgments

I am grateful to my colleagues in the Department of Communication Studies at the University of North Carolina at Chapel Hill for their usual encouragement and support. I want especially to thank Bill Balthrop, Chair, for providing graduate research assistance; Chris Abernathy, John Beilenson, Lois Drabkin, and David Shaw for their painstaking help in preparing the manuscript; and Beverly Whitaker Long for her astute comments on the draft manuscript of the introduction. Many thanks, too, to Ruel Tyson and the fellows of the Institute for the Arts and Humanities at the University of North Carolina for provocative conversation, and to the College of Arts and Sciences for supplementary funding. Maura High and Stevie Champion have provided invaluable editorial assistance; thanks to Robert C. Allen and Barbara Hanrahan for initiating the project, to Pam Upton and Kate Torrey for seeing it through, and to the anonymous manuscript reviewers for their careful and helpful comments. Leah Florence, Kelly Gallagher, and Mark Olson saved me, once again, at the last minute; thanks will never be enough.

I am most happily indebted to Jacquelyn Dowd Hall for bringing me into history, and to Jane Blocker, Jacquelyn Hall, Joy Kasson, and Carol Mavor for providing a truly exceptional space in which to work and to learn. Their thoughts and spirit have been critical to every stage in the development of this project. Finally, my deepest thanks to the contributors to this volume for their thoughtful and patient work, and to Alan, Nathaniel, and Isabel — for keeping everything in perspective.

Exceptional
Spaces

Introduction

Making History Go

DELLA POLLOCK

This book is about the relationship between performance and history. Or, I should say, it is about the many relationships between performance and history that emerge when conventional distinctions between "performance" and "history" begin to blur. It is about the kinds of history made in performance and about history itself as a spectacular, performative rite. It constellates various approaches to the nexus of performance and history in an effort to understand how performance makes history *go* and what happens when history seems to *go away* — when it seems either to fade into its representations or to fall into the fragments of time.

In so doing, it is meant neither to define the burgeoning field of performance studies nor, to the contrary, to contribute to what Jill Dolan has called "contemporary theory's promiscuous citation of the performative."[1] It is meant, rather, to mark a border space, a space of interaction and possibility that, in its peculiarly dialogic, ludic, and productive dimensions, might itself be considered performative. The authors of the essays collected in this volume enter this space from various places, tracking diverse ends. Joe Roach, for instance, in his study of the "vortices" at the heart of New Orleans economies of pleasure and power, follows performance "beyond the established theatrical genres" onto a wider and rougher terrain that includes, among other things, "armed conflict and comestibles." D. Soyini Madison assumes the integration of experience and expression in the performance of life histories and pursues their implications for black feminist theory. Kay Capo begins with performance as theatrical production (or "show") and traces in the variegations of one performance a material history that, once seen, erupts into more general performativities. The book favors none and all of these perspectives. It does not represent a particular field of study or practice as much as it stages some conjunctions of the fields and practices conventionally associated with performance and history.

To the extent that the book has a disciplinary aim, it is to confound disciplinary distinctions between performance and history and to encourage such interdisciplines as performance studies and cultural studies to pursue recent developments in performance historiography. Whereas performance studies and cultural studies have tended in the past to focus on immediate and contemporary events, scholars in each overlapping area have increasingly embraced historical methodologies, problematizing those methods in turn.[2] They have struggled with the so-called problem of the "historical" to identify the interpenetrations of past and present, text and context, pleasure and power in performance practices. Drawing on distinct and overlapping resources, performance studies have not only demonstrated the impact of performance on history but also generated the working premise of this book, which is that combining performance and historical methodologies will yield substantial new insights into the structure and function of many forms of cultural production.

The essays in this volume reflect the vitality of such work. In so doing, they challenge what I think of as two of the least productive and most common approaches to the relation between history and performance: history as a constraint on the productive possibilities of performance, as the past holding back the future, and history and performance as collaborators in a kind of backward/forward motion, in a regressive course of action that Judith Butler, for one, has described as a matter of repetition that "is at once a reenactment and reexperiencing of a set of meanings already socially established; and it is the mundane and ritualized form of their legitimation."[3] Butler has, perhaps more than any other recent theorist, contributed to a sense that performance and history are linked together in deep patterns of iteration and reiteration, that performance mobilizes history through and as repetition, and that the performance of gender, for instance, is therefore at best doomed to fail history, to betray its course and dare punishment by showing the fragile temporality at its core. Butler cannot disarticulate performance and history. In her formulation, they remain entwined like sad lovers, bound to repeat themselves in slow, circling half steps while, at best it seems, their mutual distress unfolds.[4]

The essays in this volume suggest a somewhat less fetishized relation between performance and history. Without minimizing the complex entailments of action and representation in social, economic, and cultural histories, they suggest that performance draws from history its practical, analytical, critical, and theoretical capacity to make history, to make history exceed itself, to become itself even as it rages past the present into the future. They suggest moreover that, aligned with history, performance cannot be contained within "entertainment" or even "theatrical" frameworks. At once bolstered and burdened by history, performance as both a genre of practice and an analytic trope resists narrow identification with either entertainment or high art industries. It floods the chambers of insignificance, on the one hand, and preciosity, on the other, to which it is commonly dismissed. Relieved of their respective isolation within discourses of history, performance proves powerful; history proves affective, sensual, and generative. Together, they expand the performance field to include a broad spectrum of everyday practices and social structures and to raise endless questions about the role of spectacle in the production of social selves, about the status of generic performance events in protest efforts, about the nature and implications of representational agency, about the twin effects of bodily display and disappearance, about the imbrications of writing and acting historically. The essays in this volume address these, among other, questions.

In the following pages, I offer a two-part introduction to the book. The first part provides a broad, conceptual framework. It locates problems within and prospects for connecting performance and history in recent disciplinary "crises," characterizes recent approaches to the representation of history, and articulates complementary developments in theories of performance and performativity. In this opening part, I recount, in effect, one, partial story of history folding into performance and performance into history. This is not meant to be a master narrative as much as it is to indicate some of the cross- and interdisciplinary issues at stake in the dialogue represented here and to suggest its breadth. It is, moreover, meant to set the groundwork for the particular contributions made by each of the chapters described in the second part. The essays described in the second part do not, in any simple or necessarily direct way, fall out of the conceptual history offered in the first part. Rather, they take up and test the synergy of performance/history made possible by the debates around history, historiography, performance, and performativity that this first part briefly recounts. They extend, rather than reflect, those debates, demonstrating above all not only unique cross-cuts of performance and history but their correlative in combined theoretical and practical, empirical perspectives.

Problems in Performance and History

In recent years, history has faced a crisis in representation.[5] Although this crisis is in many ways general across the disciplines, it strikes hardest at those that depend most on the warrants of fact. The "objectivity question" and new developments in cultural and social history have multiplied the subjects of historical analysis and challenged the historian to take a more explicitly critical and political stance.[6] The collapse of disciplinary boundaries around issues of representation has, moreover, meant that history's neighboring disciplines have felt the tremors of its internal debates — even as those debates have been shaped by the concerns of anthropology, literary theory and criticism, and social theory. Boundaries that have for so long kept the "facts" in and the "fiction" out of history are now crossed over and traced through with such supradisciplinary questions as: What does it mean to represent the past? How have politics shaped traditions of representation? What are the appropriate objects of historical analysis (whether from the perspective of the art, literary, or social historian)? Who are the subjects of history — and are they agents or subjects only? How can the representational tactics of scholars across the disciplines restore and enable historical agency? To what extent is history writing itself an exercise in history making?

The flip side of this crisis is the challenge to fields traditionally concerned with issues of representation (fields such as art, literature, drama, and performance) to grasp their own historicity. That is, not to locate themselves within history as a linear, continuous design made up of periods and great events, but to reflect on their place within a struggle for historical preeminence, to recognize their entailments in structures, codes, and discourses of power, and to explore their concrete and often discontinuous relation with embodied (local, family, institutional) histories. Allen Feldman characterizes the difference between history and historicity as a tension between two temporal planes: the atemporal plane of legitimation and domination or "myth," and the more ephemeral plane of agency and action. For Feldman, "sites of legitimation and authorization suppress historicity through linear, teleological, eschatological, or progressive temporalities. Action, however, unfolds time as difference and as radical heterogeneity."[7] In historicity, the body practices history. It incarnates, mediates, and resists the metahistories with which it is impressed. It wrestles with the totalizing and legitimizing power of such historical tropes as *telos* and progress. The body in action makes history answer to the contingencies and particularities, or what Feldman calls the "radical heterogeneity," of everyday life. It performs its difference *in* and *from* history and so articulates history *as* difference. As John Fiske observes of the practices of everyday life:

> The body and its specific behavior is where the power system stops being abstract and becomes material. The body is where it succeeds or fails, where it is acceded to or struggled against. The struggle for control, top-down vs. bottom-up, is waged on the material terrain of the body and its immediate context.
>
> The culture of everyday life is a culture of concrete practices which embody and perform differences. These embodied differences are a site of struggle between the measured individuations that constitute social discipline, and the popularity-produced differences that fill and extend the spaces and power of the people.[8]

Historicity is, in effect, where history works itself out, in and through and sometimes against its material subjects. It is where concrete practices not only "embody and perform differences" but also contest claims for material agency.

From the perspective of historicity, history is never total: it produces contradictions and tensions that it must, in turn, continually work to overcome.

Since the late sixties, theorists have tried hard to loosen the joints of these contradictions, to release *difference* in historicity in a variety of forms, including, from a Marxist (or post-Marxist) point of view, difference as the dialectics of struggle against domination; from a poststructural point of view, difference as what Jacques Derrida calls "differance" or the instability of foundational meanings; from a feminist point of view, difference as the authority of diverse formations of race, gender, and sexuality. The spaces betwixt and between emerging differences are performative spaces. They are sites of creative practice and imaginative play. They are slippery, liminal phases, fertile with the possibility of both reviewing and revising history.[9]

Whether they like it or not, programs in the arts and humanities have been living in such critical/utopic spaces for the last twenty years or so. Charged by the renewal of historicity in new feminisms, Marxisms, and the emerging field of cultural studies, they have had to consider the implications of their favorite histories for historical practice. They have had to ask: What are the prevailing myths of art, literature, and performance? How have the stories we have told about culture (or the accumulation and articulation of the diverse practices that make up "everyday life") suppressed its historicity and so suppressed difference and the volcanic power of heterogeneity? To what extent do our histories delimit culture by characterizing it as a sphere of nonaction? To what extent do they thus indebt culture to a politics of progress and supremacy?

Much of the ensuing debate has concerned the myth of objectivity. Until recently, the prevailing story about culture was a scientific one. Drawing on the same models that have sustained history as a discipline since the late nineteenth century, departments of art and literary studies have privileged the dispassionate inquiry of the scholar. In the story they told about culture (a story often posed against anthropology's approach to culture as "a whole way of life"), the artwork/literary text was an artifact that challenged the scholar/scientist to discern and to describe its formal characteristics. The result was a diagnostic approach that culminated in the "cure" of appreciation. Accordingly, the cultural critic is a curator devoted to the preservation and display of totemic delights.

The myth of the objective object is enacted in historicity as visualism and consumption. It remakes the literal object — the book or painting or theater scene — into a figure of the powers of *sight* and the pleasures of purchase. It resists the mundane materiality of "real" objects by making of them something *special*, by making them objects-of: objects *of* cunning observation and ownership, whose value is a function *of* their relation to an expert or connoisseur. The object-of is valuable to the extent that it proves the wit of the one who owns it, even if ownership consists only in holding it for a few moments servant to a penetrating gaze (a gaze that often ascribes to the object the very characteristics it needs to seem smart and civilized). The myth of objectivity positions the artwork or event at the dead end of perspectival lines that originate with the possessive eye/I. It makes the work prove the viewer's judgment and so humiliates the work as object before the viewer's subjectivity.

In performance, this story is complicated by the performer's split role as subject and object. In the performed myth of objectivity, the materiality of the body-object and the agency of the body-subject are perilously divided.[10] In the alienation of one from the other, the subject is a subject insofar as she surveys her own body, insofar as she cuts herself off from the very thing she would own by *looking*—and by looking *good*: by observing well and by being well worth observing. By the laws of this dynamic, the body-subject "masters" herself. She appropriates her own agency to its containment, to its subjection within a matrix of looking and owning.

Like history itself, this process is not absolute. The subject/master is always at odds with herself, always escaping complete subjection in the authoritative act of subjecting herself, and always thus suggesting the possibility of alternative subject formations or self-fashionings. The historical myth of objectivity cannot wholly survive its performance in historicity. It cannot resist the erotic, affiliative promise of performance: the possibility of becoming an "other" in speaking to "others," of realizing oneself in the tongue of the other, of being transformed in the process of speaking and hearing what the feminist filmmaker Trinh Minh-ha calls "the words passed down from mouth to ear (one sexual part to another sexual part), womb to womb, body to body."[11]

Trinh calls truth and history home to the sensual dynamics of the performing body. In so doing, she romances sound. She tempts us toward the abnegation of sight and the idealization of sight's evanescent "other": sound, voice, and stories that can be *heard* precisely because they cannot be *seen*. But to yield to this romance is to reproduce the very sight/sound split on which the preeminence of sight rests. It is to posit an Eden where the subject/self no longer suffers objectification because she no longer sees even herself. Ultimately, it is to give up both the burden of the body-object and the discretion of a body-subject to a fantasy of living in a previsual, preanalytic, prediscursive space, a space in which subjectivity and objectivity no longer compete but neither does subjectivity reign—because it lacks sufficient ego to do so.[12] Surely this fantasy is only the myth of objectivity turned inside out. It signifies the final triumph of a commodifying gaze that does not really care what form effacement takes—fetishization by sight or seduction by sound—as long as it *takes*.

But between fetish and fantasy is a widening gap. History's very dependence on mimetic illusion suggests at least the possibility of mimetic *elusion*—or the *im*possibility of finally capturing the self-subject ricocheting between one eye/I and an-other, endlessly mirrored in reciprocal looking.[13] Between subject/object and multiple subject configurations is the possibility of re-vising (reseeing) the past to include a trickster-subject who, like a troll, lives under the *faux* bridges of visualism, who cannot be fixed in sight but who lives to torment and to compel and to frustrate sight, whose shape-shifting and identity play manifests the subjective *in*-sight overseers want to own.

As it is conventionally understood and practiced, objectification immobi-lizes the body-subject. It alienates the body as a commodity/object from sub-jectivity and so alienates subjectivity from the grounds of action. In a trickster history, however, the gaze is inevitably partial and the body-subject exceeds its determinations as object. I do not want to minimize the power of seeing or of being un/seen. But in even the most extreme instances, it may yet be possible to turn sight back on itself and to make mastery face its own regressions in the chipped and cracking mirror of history.

I was intrigued, for instance, by one report of visibility politics (of oppo-nents vying to control who and what is seen) at a scheduled protest by Opera-tion Rescue, the extremist pro-life group: "Soon, locals knew, video cameras would appear — toted by nearly every actor in the coming passion play: pro-lifers and pro-choicers taping each other, police taping both and TV news teams taping everybody. 'There's probably more money spent on camera equipment than anything else,' joked [the] Melbourne police captain."[14] The prospect of cameras turned on each other like guns at the OK Corral (I would say the prototype here is the Western rather than the passion play) suggests both the power and the limits of sight. On the one hand, because we are so prone to believe that what we see is what *is*, it positions sight as a critical agency and counteragency in the construction of facts and histories that will be the basis for ethical decision making. On the other hand, the layering of visualist strategies here parodies the power of visualism altogether. First of all, if everyone is taping, everyone is a spectator. There are no actors. There is nothing left to tape but people taping, indeed, taping themselves being taped. If all of the subjects are, then, masked by cameras, there is nothing left to see but *seeing*; nothing left to appropriate *by* seeing but the act *of* seeing. *Seeing* thus becomes its own object. It disables its own agency through repetition and appropriation, promising eventually to cancel itself out, to immobilize itself, to fix itself in its own, often deadly, sights.

Returning the gaze may be an effective means of overcoming the overseer.[15] Multiplied, it can also make a fool of itself, opening the way for an as yet unseen history, a history less in thrall to visible facts than to embodied, per-forming subjects. At the moment that sight becomes foolish, at the moment that the emperor appears naked, subjectivity gains a comic foothold on his-tory — and fluid, brazen play overtakes more sightly order and repose. The police captain opened this kind of play space when he joked: " 'There's probably more money spent on camera equipment than anything else.' " Although the titular voice of an "official" culture that itself depends on visibility to prove and to sustain itself, the police captain deflates the whole business of seeing — and the authority of sight — by joking about how much it costs. If only for a moment, he carnivalizes the commodification of sight and, by extension, the body-seen. Wittingly or not, he exposes the intersection of money power and visual power in the *cost* of camera equipment (or what might be called the arsenal of sight) and thus liberates the body-object from the codes of private ownership in which it is otherwise caught. The abortion drama enacted here originates, after all, in conflict over who owns a woman's body — and so who will oversee its reproductive functions: the pregnant woman? the father of the fetus she bears? the state? By joking about the literal investment in seeing/ owning and, indeed, in reproducing bodies-on-tape, the police captain strips the sovereign viewer of his/her grandeur. He gestures beyond visibility and the whole question of ownership toward the figure of a woman as a body-subject whose subjectivity (including her pregnancy), in all of its threatening plenitude, can never be fully seen, bought, or contained — no matter who or how much is invested in trying to do so.

At the limits of sight are the excesses of the body. Not the body as a set of primordial impulses, but the body as the desublimated subject living in and through the active, fickle, sometimes grotesque but always historical life of its material form — the body as creative agency, the body as the coursing sign of subjective life, the body as the purveyor of carnival pleasures and the means of practical power: the body of the police captain laughing, the body of a pregnant woman walking past banks of cameras to a clinic door. Among all cultural practices, performance is uniquely centered in the body and decentered by its excesses. By rites of excess, performance lights a transformative charge. It is explosive, extravagant, traumatic, and obscene. It overflows its borders, marking and filling other performances, running off unpredictably, growing exponentially. Performance as such is also inscribed by history and subject to the demands of scopic desire. It is treated as an object and made to bear the imprimatur of progress.[16] But like the in/visible woman approaching the clinic door — who is for all intents and purposes silenced by sight, who cannot be heard for being too much seen, and yet who confounds sight by her onward march, who eludes mythification by all those who would see/seize her — for and against — by *walking*, these performances seemed in some small way to exceed sight and to generate something more: more agency, more pleasure and possibility, more conflict and contention, and, above all, more room for the embodied subject to enlist the resources of historicity on her own behalf.[17]

The following essays ask how and why this kind of performative surplus occurs. They ask how such exceptionally excessive spaces are constituted and

8 **Della Pollock**

what they constitute in turn. They wonder what happens when performance literally cannot be seen — either when it achieves its surplus in the present or occurs in the past, outside the scope of witness and memory. How do we represent the unseen or beyond-seen? How do we reproduce it without reifying it in objectivist, visualist terms, without either freezing it as a scene/seen or idealizing it as unrepresentable?[18] How do we write the performing body-subject? If, as Peggy Phelan claims, "performance's being . . . becomes itself through disappearance," if performance realizes its peculiar strengths through, as I have suggested here, its trickster and carnival elusions of sight, how does, can, and should it "appear" in history?[19] Can the representation of history not only preserve but also produce a surplus? Can it resist domination by history?

Representing History

In many ways the Operation Rescue scene described above is definitively postmodern. It articulates a space of hyperrepresentation, representation folding in on itself, almost to the point that nothing can be seen but representation itself. My intention in describing this scene is neither to contribute to what might be called the mounting impenetrability of postmodern culture nor to romanticize the possibility of ever fully escaping the panoptic gaze. It is, rather, to chart the fissures in a process that otherwise tends to eclipse the historical subject — the agent in action — whose subjectivity is certainly more complex than any camera can know.

It is with the problem of recovering the agent to postmodern history in mind that I now return to modern history and the problems it poses for the representation of history, especially as it is articulated through the remnants of what must be the emblematic event of historical modernism: the Nazi Holocaust. Again, my aim here is not to write a history of the Holocaust or even to recommend forms for remembrance, but to indicate what is at stake in the representation of history and to test the limits of such representation. Surely we must tell this past. But the deluge of representation articulated in the clinic protest scene raises new questions about how we tell it. And yet with the threat of regression by representation in mind, I hesitate even to ask what we must nonetheless ask: Is there a danger of too much representation here — too many cameras? Is it possible that the repetition of the real in presentational forms may become its recurrence? Is it possible that, in holding our Nazi past up to our wondering, postmodern eyes, we might make it more invisible? Is it possible that we might cathect its power and surrender its victims and survivors alike to our own, powerful gaze?

These questions are immediate and burning: Auschwitz and Birkenau seem to be disappearing. Although the traces of Auschwitz are now visible in an on-site museum, Birkenau is crumbling into mere dust and ash, falling away into time almost as if it never existed — almost as if it were more figment than fact, almost as if it were in fact a great hoax. Indeed, so-called revisionist claims that the Holocaust was a hoax were built into the very structure of the camp. As one member of the International Auschwitz Council commented in a recent essay on the controversy surrounding what to do with the camp's deterioration: "Unlike most monuments in the world, Auschwitz was never intended to last. . . . The Germans built the camp with the intention of exterminating an entire race and then destroying all the evidence of this deed. Everything was poorly made — the barracks, the crematoriums, the paper used for documents. It is difficult to preserve something that was made to vanish."[20] The camps were grand monuments to the supremacy of the Aryan race made grander yet by their elusion of history's grasp, by their resistance to the claims of fact. As they become increasingly invisible, they dare historians to prove it. In effect, they trick history into collusion by refusing its necessary referent: material facts.[21]

So what do we do? Rebuild the monument? Reconstruct the gas chambers, delousing chambers, laboratories, and barracks? Do we resist the trick by fetishizing the visible fact, even to the extent of rehearsing in our own bodies the construction of mechanisms of genocide, for all the world to see and to enjoy as only tourists and later generations can? Though I would urgently press for measures of remembrance, I shudder at the thought of investing the camps with the capital of representation. I cannot help but think that, in this era of amusement parks, skinheads, and soap opera, to rebuild the camps — detail for detail, an eye for an eye — would appeal to the most maudlin and aestheticized of contemporary instincts (exemplified for me in the question I recently heard a couple of high school girls put to a video store clerk: "We want to cry tonight — do you have anything about the Holocaust?").[22] I can see visitors admiring the spectacle, wondering at the workmanship, maybe shedding a tear or two, maybe somewhere deep inside thrilling to the horror. Made into what it never actually was — a monument for all time, a tourist outpost, an aesthetic spectacle, Birkenau could become a fetish of itself: a reminder of the past, yes, but one of mythic stature, a relic displaced from the historicity in which it is now embedded, an object of fascination and so even approbation. To let Birkenau vanish would be the ultimate act of complicity with Hitler's plan. And yet in our haste to restore the camp we may similarly, insidiously acquit history of historicity. We may cut off the past from the very present in which Birkenau is vanishing — and cut off Birkenau from the vast range of German and Western history that made it possible in the first place — and that authorizes neighboring, ongoing genocides. By renewing its material form, we may lend its ideological forms weight.[23]

The problem the deteriorating camps pose for history — and for the representation of history — is echoed in ongoing debate about the mimetic urge in representational discourse: the desire to make the past *present*, to re-*present* it in language. Poststructural critics call such a desire naive on the grounds that, one, it presumes a relatively unproblematic "real" world or past outside of language that, two, can be easily or unproblematically embodied by it. The historian who pursues such transparent realism or naive mimeticism in the name of fact, critics charge, may reproduce (may recycle and reify) discourses of domination. From a mimetic perspective, they argue, history makes the past visible. And because, from a mimetic perspective, what is seen is what is true, history basically negates itself as representation: it becomes what it shows; it is the "truth." The value of mimetic representation for history is that it disappears into its object and so secures an illusion of objectivity. It achieves a certain transparency that makes history as told largely unassailable. And insofar as what history tells is what is, a naively mimetic history tends (or so the story goes) to buffer history "as is" from challenge or critique.

A naively mimetic approach to Auschwitz and Birkenau could, then, authorize the "truth" of the Holocaust and yet immunize that "truth" against questions as to its completeness or content. By making the past seem present in a mimetic sense, it could in fact secure the pastness, the otherness, of events crucial to understanding and acting in our historical present. It could encourage us to see the objectified events as pitiably and absolutely "not us" rather than (as perhaps Bertolt Brecht would recommend) critically "not not us" or otherwise in a vital dialectic with current conditions.[24] An aesthetics of presence may thus simultaneously license and foreclose on cultural memory and its implications for critical consciousness.[25]

How, then, can we speak the past without reproducing it? In the particular case of the Nazi death camps but also perhaps more generally, is it possible to preserve the *vanishing* — that space between the performative presence of the gas chambers and their impending absence in time? between the seductions of fact and the threat of silence? between history and historicity? Can we bypass mere mimeticism, on the one hand, and the complicities of silence, on the other, to find a way to use representation against itself? How can and should we perform the camps' looming absence? Where is the room for creative and resistive agency within the space of historical representation?

One of the foremost theorists of modern historiography, Hayden White, answered these questions with appeals to "narrativity." In his foundational work on the history as narrative in the late seventies and early eighties, he mitigated the mythic power of representation by recalling it to historicity, by historicizing the narrative construction of history. For White, modern histories are important acts of social history insofar as they narrativize the past: insofar as they endow the chronicles and annals of premodern histories with "the coherence, integrity, fullness, and closure of an image of life that is and can only be imaginary."[26] Narrativity is, for White, the means by which the "real" becomes the "true," the means by which narrated events gain moral cogency — when "the social system . . . is the source of any morality that we can imagine."[27] In other words, what is imaginary is not simply made up in excess of a real and determining social structure. Rather, it derives from the same kind of ideologies, institutions, and social practices that structure the events described. The trick of narrativity, however, lies in effacing the social foundations of historical truths and eliding any remaining gap between "reality" and "truth." Through narrativity, the historian defers social-moral meaning to the events "themselves." He or she makes historical events seem to "speak for themselves" and, in so doing, to speak the truth:

> Unlike the annals, the reality that is represented in the historical narrative, in "speaking itself," speaks *to* us, summons us from afar (this "afar" is the land of forms), and displays to us a formal coherency that we ourselves lack. The historical narrative, as against the chronicle, reveals to us a world that is putatively "finished," done with, over, and yet not dissolved, not falling apart. In this world, reality wears the mask of a meaning, the completeness and fullness of which we can only *imagine*, never experience. Insofar as historical stories can be completed, can be given narrative closure, can be shown to have had a *plot* all along, they give to reality the odor of the *ideal*. This is why the plot of a historical narrative is always an embarrassment and has to be presented as "found" in the events rather than put there by narrative techniques.[28]

"Narrativity," for White, is not the same as the histories narrated. It refers to the simultaneous appeal and insufficiency of historical narrative. It describes the ways in which desire for form is expressed in formulation — or what might be called the performance of narrative longing. The effect of narrativity as a theoretical trope is to underscore the historicist dimensions of history writing. It is to recover for critique the process by which the historian fulfills his or her desire for order in history. White poses the question of narrativity this way: "What is involved . . . in that finding of the 'true story,' that discovery of the 'real story' within or behind the events that come to us in the chaotic form of 'historical records'? What wish is enacted, what desire is gratified, by the fantasy that *real* events are properly represented when they can be shown to display the formal coherency of a story? In the enigma of this wish, this desire, we catch a glimpse of the cultural function of narrativizing discourse."[29] By focusing attention on the elements of the "imaginary," the "ideal," fantasy and desire in narrativity, White focuses us on narrative not as fiction per se but as the process of mediating and adjudicating the respective claims of social-moral structures and historical events. In pursuing the conjuncture of these two "realities," narrativity produces what we take to be historical truth.

Narrativity has consequently been a useful figure for talking about what *goes into* history as a discursive formation. But at its heart remain troubling implications for what historians have traditionally taken to be their stock in trade: the facts.[30] As White indicates in the passage just quoted, narrativity is centered in the irony that facts become facts when they are narrated as such, when they take on the culturally designated mantle of what a fact should be. Truth is itself a representation—a story—from which "real" events derive. Following on White (and his development through Paul Ricoeur), Feldman, for instance, argues: "*The event is not what happens. The event is that which can be narrated. The event is action organized by culturally situated meanings*" or what we have conventionally called truths.[31]

From the perspective of narrativity, historical action and history writing collapse into each other. The writing of history becomes the ultimate historical performance, making events meaningful by talking about them, by investing them with the cultural and political assumptions carried in language itself. What we can or want to call the truth thus becomes problematic. As Edward Said observed in 1979:

> The real issue is whether indeed there can be a true representation of anything, or whether any and all representations, because they are representations, are embedded first in the language and then in the culture, institutions, and political ambience of the representer. If the latter alternative is the correct one (and I believe it is), then we must be prepared to accept the fact that a representation is *eo ipso* implicated, intertwined, embedded, interwoven with a great many other things besides the "truth," which is itself a representation.[32]

For Said, the very notion of a "true representation" is at best ironic. The "true" representation is the one that cancels itself out as representation, that seems to refer with exquisite precision to a place beyond representation. For Said, the problem lies in recognizing that language is not as dutifully transparent as we might like it to be—and that truth (such as it is) always exists in and as representation. But beyond urging us to "accept the fact" of representational authority, Said challenges us to recognize just how dangerous it may be to cling to notions of the truth as something other than representation, as something out there, hidden, awaiting revelation by whatever means necessary. Such conventional or commonsense notions of the truth are behind scandalmongering, investigative journalism, "outing," and other forms of coercive disclosure. They, moreover, authorize the worst kinds of history and historical practice. As Page duBois argues in her reflection on classical formulations of torture and truth:

> Truth can be understood as a process, a dialectic, less recovery of something hidden or lost, rather a creation in a democratic dialogue. Truth that is produced in struggle and debate, the truth of democracy, of difference, need not be imagined as secret, as known only to a few to whom that secret manifests itself. But a hidden truth, one that eludes the subject, must be discovered, uncovered, unveiled, and can always be located in the dark, in the irrational, in the unknown, in the other. And that truth will continue to beckon the torturer, the sexual abuser, who will find in the other — slave, woman, revolutionary — silent or not, secret or not, the receding phantasm of a truth that must be hunted down, extracted, torn out in torture.[33]

Truth as that which is revealed, as that which is obscured by otherness and hidden in the recesses of representation (understood as dissimulation), subtends torture. Following duBois's argument, the ethical, practical, and political dangers at the heart of *not* recognizing the representational nature of truth are staggering.

But perhaps equally dangerous is the prospect of the "hyperreal" world that Jean Baudrillard imagined in his 1982 *Simulations*. In such a postmodern world, reality as such is so permeated by representation that all we have left are representations of representations, representations without referent or origin or, for that matter, real consequence. Baudrillard is the black hole in Said's and duBois's reclamations of truth as representation. The dereliction of the unreal in Said and duBois becomes in Baudrillard the "hyperreal" world of telenews, Euro-Disney, and computer-generated warscapes in which "facts" are supreme but facts are the effects of mechanical reproduction run wild:

> Simulation is characterized by a *precession of the model*, of all models around the merest fact — the models come first, and their orbital (like the bomb) circulations constitute the genuine magnetic field of events. Facts no longer have any trajectory of their own, they arise at the intersection of the models; a single fact may even be engendered by all the models at once. This anticipation, this precession, this short-circuit, this confusion of the fact with its model (no more divergence of meaning, no more dialectical polarity, no more negative electricity or implosion of poles) is what each time allows for all the possible interpretations, even the most contradictory — all are true, in the sense that their truth is exchangeable, in the image of the models from which they proceed, in a generalized cycle.[34]

In the marketplace of simulacra that Baudrillard described in *Simulations*, truth is displaced into the appearance of truth embodied in the ultimately random production of facts. More recently, Baudrillard mourned the ascendancy of the fact, the extent to which, in an economy of diffusion and dispersal, facts outrun history. Today, Baudrillard says, "through the impetus of diffusion, the circulative, total communication injunction, every fact, every event, is freed for itself alone: each fact becomes atomic, nuclear, and traces its trajectory in a vacuum. In order to be indefinitely broadcast, it must be broken down like an atomic particle, thereby attaining a counter-gravity thrust that can spin it out of return orbit, permanently separate it from history."

The speed with which the news (or what passes for history) is processed through transnational computer and televisual networks threatens the very coherence of language. "No human language," Baudrillard goes on, "can withstand the speed of light. No meaning can withstand acceleration. No history can withstand the centrifuging of facts *per se*." Following Baudrillard, the hypermediations and accelerations with which we met the catastrophes of World War II (a war "saturated" with history) left history suspended somewhere between the precession of the model and the supercession of the fact: between the determination of facts by cultural discourses and the dispersion of those same facts by electronic transmission. History, for Baudrillard, is trembling just beyond the grasp of culture, at the threshold of randomness. History has, it seems, exceeded itself. It has ceased to exist not because there is no more violence or because events have stopped occurring but because narrative has become impossible, since narrative is, "by definition (re-citing), the possible recurrence of a sequence of meaning."[35] Without sequence and the promise of recurrence it provides (enacted, of course, in its repetition and re-presentation as story), there is, for Baudrillard, no meaning or finality to history. There is no history.

And without history, there is no action. There is motion and process and change but there is no agency. We are atomized in time, less real than facts, spinning in sound bites, unable to catch onto the scaffolding of sequence. We cannot take directive action because there is no action to take: there are no narrative norms or directives, no plans or visions, no grounds for effectiveness.

History, for Baudrillard, has disappeared into postmodern historicity. Its mythic impulse has been overtaken by radical contingency and partiality. It has gone over the edge of narrativity, past even the shaping force of desire. Lost in time, fragmented in space, its plenitude can only be simulated — and mourned. Baudrillard is in many ways nostalgic for modern historical narratives and the moral imperatives they impart. He longs for, but does not pose, an alternative to the "hot" history of World War II and the ensuing "cool" news of postmodernity. His particular simulation of the postmodern world offers, but does not resolve, the tension between these two equally untenable versions of history: history as all too present and history as emptied out, exiled, vacuous, and absent.

So where do we go from here? Could it be that Baudrillard's version of history is itself bad news? Even if we share Baudrillard's impulse, must we accept his totalizing view? Can we substantiate a postmodern history without what might very well be vain or obsolete claims to absolute truth and pure fact? Is there any *good* news about postmodernity? Is there a space between fact and fiction from which to make history? How do we make history *go* when it seems to be *going away*?

Answers to these questions have been many and varied. Most fundamentally depend on a deconstruction of the fact-fiction opposition, whether from a materialist, psychoanalytic, or pragmatic point of view. Christopher Norris, for instance, rejects Baudrillard on the grounds that he — much like the naive realist Baudrillard rejects — ignores the truth-values implicit in "fiction" and fails to account for and to respond to such real-world/postmodern travesties as the Gulf War.[36] Pursuing a slightly different vein, Trinh suggests that it is precisely the distinction between fact and fiction, story and history, that delimits history, that represses the creative possibilities in history, presuming as it does that history exists in the accumulations of the past facts. Facts are, for Trinh, the capital of conventional history. She argues instead for a history built on narrative truths, on truths that supersede fact, that restore "magicality" and vision to the historical imagination. It is on the basis and in the name of such truths that she performs theory in her 1989 collection of essays, *Woman Native Other*. Given its complex multivoicing and affective layering, I will quote her theoretical performance at some length:

> When history separated itself from story, it started indulging in accumulation and facts. Or it thought it could. It thought it could build up to History because the Past, unrelated to the Present and the Future, is lying there in its entirety, waiting to be revealed and related. The act of revealing bears in itself a magical (not factual) quality — inherited undoubtedly from "primitive" storytelling — for the Past perceived as such is a well-organized past whose organization is already given. Managing to identify with History, history (with a small letter h) thus manages to oppose the factual to the fictional (turning a blind eye to the "magicality" of its claims); the story-writer — the historian — to the story-teller. As long as the transformation, manipulations, or redistributions inherent in the collecting of events are overlooked, the division continues its course, as sure of its itinerary as it certainly dreams to be. Story-writing becomes history-writing, and history

quickly sets itself apart, consigning story to the realm of tale, legend, myth, fiction, literature. Then, since fictional and factual have come to a point where they mutually exclude each other, fiction, not infrequently, means lies, and fact, truth. DID IT REALLY HAPPEN? IS IT A TRUE STORY? . . . Which truth? the question unavoidably arises. . . . Truth. Not one but two: truth and fact, just like in the old times when queens were born and kings were made in Egypt. . . . Poetry, Aristotle said, is truer than history. Story-telling as literature (narrative poetry) must then be truer than history. If we rely on history to tell us what happened at a specific time and place, we can rely on the story to tell us not only what might have happened, but also what is happening at an unspecified time and place. No wonder that in old tales storytellers are very often women, witches, and prophets. The African griot and griotte are well known for being poet, storyteller, historian, musi-cian, and magician — all at once. But why truth at all? Why this battle for truth and on behalf of truth? I do not remember having asked grandmother once whether the story she was telling me was true or not. Neither do I recall her asking me whether the story I was reading her was true or not. We knew we could make each other cry, laugh, or fear, but we never thought of saying to each other, "This is just a story." A story is a story. There was no need for clarification — a need many adults considered "natural" or impera-tive among children — for there was no such thing as "a blind acceptance of the story as literally true." Perhaps the story has become *just* a story when I have become adept at consuming truth as fact. Imagination is thus equated with falsification, and I am made to believe that if, accordingly, I am not told or do not establish in so many words what is true and what is false, I or the listener may no longer be able to differentiate fancy from fact. . . . Literature and history once were/still are stories: this does not necessarily mean that the space they form is undifferentiated, but that this space can articulate on a different set of principles, one which may be said to stand outside the hierarchical realm of facts. On the one hand, each society has its own politics of truth; on the other hand, being truthful is being in the in-between of all regimes of truth.[37]

Trinh posits a world of "story, history, literature (or religion, philosophy, natural science, ethics) — all in one."[38] In so doing, she recovers truth from facticity for history. She refuses both the supposition of truth as part of a past to be revealed (following duBois, assuming that representation gets in the way) and the precessional model of fact/truth/image run amuck. She refuses both modernist fact/fiction, past/present divisions and postmodern fragmenta-tions. She does not abandon truth as much as she rejects its identification with fact, its subjugation under the rule of fact. For Trinh, truthfulness emerges within and between "all regimes of truth." Truth is politically relative and antistructural. Truth is, in effect, most true when it refuses the inscriptions of either fact or fancy, truth or falsehood, following instead a course of magical (dis)belief. (I have perhaps no more vividly felt the magic at the heart of Trinh's formulation of story/history than I did the other day as I listened to a friend respond to her four-year-old's question, Was the helium balloon we were watching drift into the sky *really* going to 'Balloonia'?"—a sort of balloon heaven they had read about in a storybook. "Balloonia is a pretend place," my friend advised. "But the balloon is *really* going there.")

Oral historians (among others) shift the emphasis from fact to the experience of fact. They favor the messy, subjective life of the historical agent rather than his/her more "objective" accomplishments or conditions.[39] In so doing, oral history opens a great vista of postmodern agency, embracing the lives of those whose accomplishments might not be the stuff of conventional history, but whose agency thrives in the tactical politics of everyday living. The achievements of oral history suggest a postmodern history made up of small stories or what Lyotard calls "petit récits": history relieved of pretensions to a "master narrative," history as a somewhat humbler quilt of many voices and local hopes.[40]

But such developments have also led others to ask just how far the deconstruction of the fact-fiction opposition has gone or can go. Joan Scott, for instance, argues that in much counterhistory, "experience" stands in for fact as the final referent for all claims. Apparently self-evident, visceral, unmediated discourses of experience borrow on the authority of witness: (objective) seeing and (subjective) feeling collapse in an intangible sense of having been there. Further mystified by appeals to private ownership (we slide, in effect, from "these are *the* facts" to "this is *my* experience"), experience begins to look like the accumulation of what might be called subjective facts or feeling *as* fact: details and dimensions of the life as lived reified in the form of something one incontrovertibly "has" ("an experience"). Scott argues that the discourses of experience thus reproduce the epistemologies of fact—and buffer the subject from critique, casting it now as the pure, imperturbable object-grounds of history. She proposes another kind of history: "a genuinely nonfoundational history, one which retains its explanatory power and its interest in change but does not stand on or reproduce naturalized categories." In this history, the historian operates as an interrogator who takes as his/her project "*not* the reproduction and transmission of knowledge said to be arrived at through experience, but the analysis of the production of that knowledge."[41] Following Foucault, Scott proposes historicizing history, making history the very process of challenging facticity, of posing ideology against ontology, of recognizing the political status of experience. Scott refuses the taken-for-grantedness of experience. She compels us to ask not what are the facts or what was the experience, but *whose* are they, where do they come from, and how do they operate *in* history, especially insofar as they cultivate the subjects *of* history?[42]

Scott relativizes the origins of history. In pursuing the deconstruction of "fact," she moves us from questions of representation (or the role of the narrator/historian) to questions of discursive production (the role of social structures and practices in the formation of the narrator as a telling subject). Scott (among others) shifts the terms of debate from the politics of representation to the politics of production. She nonetheless thus returns us to the problematic articulated by Baudrillard: is there no anchor for history? Is there no stable ground from which to take action? Sympathetic with Scott's ideological charge and yet frustrated by the instability at the heart of her theory and the potential for the infinite regression of history-in-theory it represents, critics like (although as different as) Susan Bordo and Robert Scholes simply cut through the cake. They insist on rhetorics of reference — or what might be called urbane (as opposed to naive) realism. They appeal quite self-consciously to a last horizon of textuality, to a place outside representation where people are in real pain and things are really wrong. The world may be a text, Scholes argues, "but it is not only a text"; at some point you have to "stop reading and throw the book at somebody."[43] For Bordo, the politics and pleasures of textuality threaten to efface "the material *praxis* of people's lives, the normalizing power of cultural images, and the sadly continuing social realities of dominance and subordination."[44] She insists on a new (or renewed) materialism in which women's bodies in particular are not semiotic "playground[s]" but cultural "battleground[s]," literally riven by the interests that stalk them.[45]

In this story/history, White, Said, and Baudrillard are the threshold theorists of postmodern history. Critics/historians writing in their wake cast history in many roles — as revelation; as narrative and story; as a contest among truth, fact, and ideology; as oral history, historicization, historical action; as the body in pain; as production; as promise; as lessons wrought in the interstices of modernity and postmodernity — all in an effort, it seems, to make the real-in-representation more meaningful than charges of mere ficticity would allow.

The authors in this book also write in the space between domination and disappearance, between history as an all-powerful "master narrative" (exemplified at the height of the modern moment in Hitler's master plan) and history as loss, fragmentation, absolute contingency (the promise of narrative and representation fallen into dust and ash). From the particular vantage of performance and performance theory, they also try to revive the historical body (stupid with facts, drunk on objectivity) in all of its gaping and glorious excess. They brace open spaces of agency in which historical subjects recover and write their own histories. They push language (in all of its forms) to unmake and to renew itself, to exceed itself, to overcome "authority's desire": to perform a surplus.[46] In so doing, these essays are themselves performative. They bring the trickster in history onto the stage of history — and challenge us to entertain him for a while.

Performativity

Many practical and theoretical currents converge on contemporary uses of performance and performativity. The currently widespread use of performance gathers its momentum from, among others, developments in folklore, anthropology, philosophy, theater, feminist theory, and literary studies. In the next few pages, I follow/recount one, rough course in the theoretical emergence of performativity. This is a selective and constructed story. I have not attempted to write a definitive history of performance but to draw into a single, interwoven narrative theoretical moves that surround and underlie the work represented here. This story is meant less to explain the essays than to suggest the coherence of their variations on performance in history, the history of performance, performance as historical agency, and history (in its many guises) as performance. It also indicates, I hope, the force of performance/performativity as a corrective to and an extension of the problems entailed in representing history articulated above.

The essays in this volume are widely divergent in method and topic. They nonetheless tend to share a fundamental sense of performance as the *doing* of language: as the literal, particular transactions of speakers and hearers at a specific site. In this sense, performance is primarily something *done* rather than something *seen*. It is less the product of theatrical invention or the object of spectatorship than the process by which meanings, selves, and other effects are produced. As such, it is also more promissory than directly effective. It is the embodied process of making meaning.

J. L. Austin initiated this sense of "performativity" in his 1955 lectures in speech act theory at Harvard, collected in *How to Do Things with Words*. Austin's most critical contribution to contemporary thinking is his distinction between the "performative" and "constative" dimensions of language use — or between saying as *doing* and saying as *stating*. Insofar as an utterance is itself a form of action, insofar as it *performs* an action that may be followed or accompanied by other actions but remains primary (such as saying "I do" in a marriage ceremony or placing a bet), it cannot be held to the standards of truth and falsehood that govern constative speech.[47] The performative utterance bypasses issues of validity and referentiality. As representation, it does not refer to action (as in "I heard them say 'I do' ") but is the action to which constative statements may refer (as in "I do!"). It is action in the form of representation (rather than, as Aristotle would have it, representation in the form of action). As such, it makes questions of fact and fiction secondary, if not entirely moot. From the perspective of linguistic performativity, asking "Is it true?" yields to "What does it *do*?"[48]

Performance occurs in context, at the moment of utterance. It tends to disappear into its effects. Because it is so ephemeral, it was dismissed in later formulations of speech act and hermeneutic theory that privileged instead what John Searle called its locutionary aspect and Paul Ricoeur hailed as its sedimentations in "text."[49] In the preference for permanence and structure that guided mid-century literary studies, performance — and its general equivalent in the performativity of speech acts — suffered a kind of "antitheatrical prejudice": distrust of its power, dismay at its popular forms.[50] But with the so-called birth of the reader in the late seventies, and the rise of such diverse strategies as reader-response criticism and performance anthropology, the line dividing the text from its "low other" — performance — began to dissolve.

Not only did cultural performances of all kinds gain new notoriety, but also texts of all kinds began to be perceived as inextricable from their performances — whether those performances occurred in the minds of readers, in critical dialogue, or in ritual enactment.[51] Conventional distinctions between performance and text — the telling and the told, the act of saying and the what is said, action and meaning — fell away in favor of a dynamic reconception of texts as inseparable from the processes by which they are made, understood, and deployed. As Michel de Certeau has said of proverbs and discourse generally, texts were increasingly seen as "*marked by* uses," as signifying above all the history of their own performance: "[T]hey offer to analysis the imprints of acts or of processes of enunciation; they signify the operations whose object they have been, operations which are relative to situations and which can be thought of as the conjunctural modalizations of statements or of practices; more generally, they thus indicate a social historicity in which systems of representations or processes of fabrication no longer appear only as normative frameworks but also as tools manipulated by users."[52]

Insofar as texts signify the "operations whose objects they have been," they evoke their place within a history of tools, uses, and action: they evoke their historicity. They, moreover, call into question the representation of representational systems as "normative frameworks," suggesting that such representations operate as myths that tend to normalize history by refusing to recognize the role of texts in and as historical action. Understood as "tools manipulated by users" rather than as either formal constructs or "normative frameworks," texts charge history with the memory and promise of their own agency. They move readers and users into a space animated by conflict, possibility, efficacy, and exchange. In this space, texts ritually *mark* (and thus effect) and *are marked by* (and thus signify) the social world enacted in, around, and through them.

They trace and are traced through with the other texts with which, in the processes of historical production, they come into intimate contact.

As an interdiscipline, performance studies has prospered on the intimacies of such contact. Drawing diversely on traditions of literary and anthropological performance, performance studies generally cedes the object-status of the text (whether understood as literary, cultural, personal, or everyday) to a sense of the text-in-performance as an always already intertextual rite — as an event that occurs *between* and *among* participants whose meanings are therefore emergent and unpredictable.[53] Performance is thus characterized by the vitality, erotics, and transformative dynamics of subject-subject exchange. Whether articulated through such media as photographs or literary texts or deployed in designated theater spaces, performance concentrates its effects in bodily trades and transfers. As Joe Roach demonstrates in his essay in this volume, it is, accordingly, a peculiarly dense site of social formation. Rather than, primarily, a specific genre of practice or speech protocol, it is the alchemy of occurrence and recurrence through which agency (otherwise so deflated within the economies of the "postmodern") emerges qualified but cogent. Displacing both narrowly idealistic (intentional) and deterministic models of act-agency with the affective, sensual, multivoiced, and multiperspectival activity of discursive exchange, performance figures agency as embodied action, as that which is generated in and as performance. The relation between agency and performance is then less tautological than homological and interdependent: agency arises in the immediacy of "restored" behaviors, in the conversion of repetition into a kind of erotic power.[54]

Performance studies is particularly indebted to resurgent interest in the work of the Russian language theorist, Mikhail Bakhtin, for this claim on agency. Bakhtin's twin mandates for "carnival" and "dialogue" provide an often-contested but, even so, generative model of embodied discourse.[55] Bakhtin shares with Austin a sense of language as a concrete, historical practice rather than, say, an abstract linguistic system or a formal achievement. But by radically historicizing the relation between the speaker and his/her audience and their respective con/texts, he moves us away from Austin's speaker-centered model toward a dialogic model in which the audience is more active than reactive, and meaning is coproduced by participants equally and powerfully invested in the outcome of their exchange. Language is, for Bakhtin, imbued with conflict, dissonance, and struggle.[56] It is both inherently unstable (always already inflected with the "otherness" to which it is addressed) and an object of contest over its meanings. In many ways, dialogue describes the necessary but impossible desire to own meaning — to appropriate it to one's own interests, to stabilize it within a single discursive con/text. In dialogue, language is forever subject to barter and raids, intersection and interception.

Relentlessly bruised, borrowed, and traded in an endless process of historical/ideological "becoming," it is essentially multivoiced/superhybrid.

Dialogue encompasses monologue. It simultaneously engages and disrupts efforts at closed and stable discourse. Not the harmless counterweight to monologue that soft liberal interpretations want to make it, dialogue is a vital force in history making because it enacts both the ideological and critical, or what Bakhtin calls the "centripetal" and "centrifugal" (the centralizing and disseminative, the colonizing and deconstructive) impulses in engaged politics.[57] The potentially combustive effect of dialogue is fueled by the irony that the harder one tries to engage an "other" in appreciation of a singular point of view, the more subject one's own point of view is to transformation by the "other." The effort to change an-other in and through dialogue redounds to the speaking self. The speaker who expresses her agency in the act of claiming rights and access to language use thus becomes the agent of her own transformation.

Of course, monologue may be and usually is asserted at the expense of dialogue. A speaker or speakers may simply deny or refuse the reciprocations of "otherness" (as in the rhetoric of Operation Rescue). Indeed, for Bakhtin, dialogue remains something of an incipient ideal. Its richness may be felt in the exceptional, literary space of the novel (although, for Bakhtin, only Dostoevsky fully meets the criteria of a dialogic novel).[58] It may also be manufactured in the process of "dialogizing" a given speech act or text.[59] That is, critics may force (or cultivate) the underlying dialogics of a text. They may discern its history as an intertext — as the residue of performative pressures and exchange, as the messy, noisy conjunction of multiple and competing voices (what Bakhtin calls "heteroglossia"). And they may engage it directly in dialogue, talking with and against it in the context of immediate historical concerns, as, for instance, Shannon Jackson does in her essay, collected here, on Jane Addams's Hull-House. Whether dialogue is understood as an inherent property of a given text or a process of critical reception, it represents the ever-present potential for language to mean something else, to betray one set of meanings for another, to slip from one context or set of relations into another's arms, taking carnival pleasure with it, laughing all the way.

It is the particular prerogative of performance to mark and assert this instability. For the narrative theorist Homi Bhabha, such instability is in fact the defining characteristic of what he calls "performativity." Bhabha focuses on the creative moment in meaning making, the moment when the story-in-history is in effect caught red-handed, not inventing the facts per se but inventing the authority from which they derive their meaning and weight. Like Bakhtin, he finds the ambivalence at the center of narrative — at its would-be "origins" — less a cause for despair than celebration (even rank romance). In fact, Bhabha characterizes it as the next best thing to an originary moment: it is, for him, a "performative" moment, redolent with possibility, productivity, and agency.

As both a word and a concept, performativity invokes White's narrativity. But in Bhabha's use, for instance, performativity takes narrativity past its logical extreme, past the point at which narrativity contradicts narrative (the point at which discerning and naming the desire for closure resist closure), toward the displacement of narrative altogether. Operating on the level of the sign rather than the sequence, performativity casts narrative signs as mines in a textual field: as heteroglossic eruptions always already about to happen. For Bhabha, performativity designates not only the inherent instability of the sign (following Derrida) but its immanent "becoming" (following Bakhtin): its place in a synchronic transfiguration of ideology roiling just below the surface of all discourse. In Bhabha, performativity is an analytic framework for *mining* the creative implications of signification embodied in the duplicity of the sign and threatened by the totalizing effects of narrative closure.

In his collection, *Nation and Narration*, Bhabha turns performativity on representations of the nation. (The nation is, for Bhabha, a key trope in the construction of global histories; his particular use of it, however, resonates with other foundational categories such as class and race.) In his introductory remarks, he notes two significant but limited advances in the critique of nationality as a signifying practice: the tendency, on the one hand, to read the nation as the ideological apparatus of state power, and on the other hand, to rehearse its utopic possibilities as "the incipient or emergent expression of the 'national-popular' sentiment preserved in a radical memory."[60] The problem is that these critical narratives are totalizing in their own right. They tell dark or hopeful stories that obscure the more complex processes by which the history of the nation is written and so delimit intervention into those processes. Bhabha revels instead in the two-faced, multiaccentual multivalence of representation itself. Assuming that the boundaries defining nations are themselves always hybrid constructions, marking at once the "outside" and the "inside" of nationality, Bhabha forces the duplicity of language that similarly contains and shuts out possible meanings. His aim, as he puts it, is

> to explore the Janus-faced ambivalence of language itself in the construction of the Janus-faced discourse of the nation. This turns the familiar two-faced god into a figure of prodigious doubling that investigates the nation-space in the process of the articulation of elements: where meanings may be partial because they are *in medias res*; and history may be half-made because it is in the process of being made; and the image of cultural authority may be ambivalent because it is caught, uncertainly, in the act of "composing" its

powerful image. Without such an understanding of the performativity of language in the narratives of the nation, it would be difficult to understand why Edward Said prescribes a kind of "analytic pluralism" as the *form* of critical attention appropriate to the cultural effects of the nation. For the nation, as a form of cultural *elaboration* (in the Gramscian sense), is an agency of *ambivalent* narration that holds culture at its most productive position, as a force for "subordination, fracturing, diffusing, reproducing, as much as producing, creating, forcing, guiding."[61]

For Bhabha, the nation is both the "agency of ambivalent narration" and its duplicitous effect. It is the half-made, twice-told image of itself making itself up, (re)creating itself in the image of cultural authority. It is itself a performance, enacted, for instance, in the Kenyan juridical commissions David Cohen and E. S. Atieno Odhiambo interrogate in their essay in this volume, or in the Soviet-Lithuanian dissident trials Kay Capo describes. Following Bhabha, nationality (or class or race or gender) is not only open to revision and re-presentation but also initiates it. It invites the reader to enter its field of composition, to trespass into previously forbidden territory and so to exercise his or her own ambivalence as both a subject and an agent within culture at its "most productive": to participate equally, even simultaneously, in the cultural dynamics of " 'subordination, fracturing, diffusing, reproducing' " and of " 'producing, creating, forcing, guiding.' "

Bhabha uses "performativity" in a distinctly theatrical sense. Indeed, the alterity Bhabha discerns in representations of the nation is perhaps nowhere more fully embodied than in the now-you-see-it, now-you-don't "magic" of the theater. What has conventionally gone under the name of theatricality is an incessant, dense, and self-conscious play of "presence," a titillating alternation between signs and the worlds they represent or make present largely by extinguishing them, by replacing them with their own spectacular nonpresence.[62] As if emboldened by their very density and number, theatrical signs display themselves as signs and so risk discrediting themselves as such. (I often think that the pleasure we take in Broadway productions is a pleasure in seeing just how far this trick will go: how big can the spectacle get before it collapses in on itself? how far can the sign bend before it loses its resilience as a sign — and breaks into a million sequins and tap shoes? In fact, this was the conceit in Giorgio Strehler's production of *The Tempest* for the 1984 Olympics Art Festival in Los Angeles: when Prospero, the ultimate master magician, gave up his wand in the final act, the entire stage apron collapsed, actors disappeared into the rubble, and audience members reportedly screamed in alarm.) In effect, the theater becomes what it is by absenting the historical "other" to which it nonetheless appeals. The more vigorously it represents its "other" the more displaced that "other" is by the presence — or, then, nonpresence — of the actor. The actor as signifier shifts to the foreground — seen but, to that very extent, as unseen and unseeable as the woman captured by the cameras at the site of the Operation Rescue protest.

In enacting this irony, the theater is like most other modes of representation. It belies its mimetic or metaphorical desire with its metonymic form. It reveals itself in its absences. Where it differs from more visualist or object-centered modes of representation is in its temporality: performance, while unrepentantly representational, operates on the plane of historicity. It unfolds in time, becoming itself even as it disappears, even as it differs from itself in the play of signification.[63] In its most romantic formulations, performance is the fluid, open-ended, processual antithesis to product and all of the visualist and consumerist implications of a product-centered orientation.[64] (Perhaps the darkest turn of such a formulation is enacted at Birkenau in the process of making invisible to history both the victims and the means of genocide.) Performance is no more free of historical determination than other "products" of a capitalist system. But by its very evanescence, it retains the mark of process and the promise of change. As does action generally, performance "unfolds time as difference and as radical heterogeneity." It opens up a field of historical possibility and contest at the same time that it re-marks the terms of its own production.

Insofar as performance is thus aligned with historicity against history, it is especially capable of disseminating cultural knowledge — of dispersing meaning in time and across difference. In this capacity, performance is increasingly understood as an important site of — even a paradigmatic trope for — cultural resistance. To wit, social scientists are turning toward performance for explanation of the dialectics of power, and theater scholars are exploring the rhetoric and politics of staged events with unprecedented vigor.[65]

The history of the theater, of course, has not always recognized or subsidized the disseminative function of performance. It has not always appreciated the performativity of performance.[66] Henry Sayre argues, in fact, that only selected works even among the most radically avant-garde actually overcome the myth-history of performance as entertainment or formal achievement and realize its temporal advantages. Sayre tends to romanticize the openness of performance and to privilege the performative in a way that reproduces the very centrist models he wants performance to erode. He also ignores the elitism always already implicit in the contemporary American avant-garde he celebrates. But Sayre's distinction between performative and assimilative structures is a useful one. Sayre distinguishes the paintings of David Salle and Eric Fischl, for instance, on the grounds that, whereas Salle's work tends to assimilate meanings to its internal structures and ambiguities, containing them within the parameters of the work, Fischl's involves its audiences in an open and necessary production of ultimately undecidable meanings. For Sayre, Fischl's paintings are performative. They require "our collaboration, amplification, [and] embellishment."[67] By positioning audience members as agents in the production of cultural meanings, they also thus position audience members as social agents, who work out their relations with each other in and through the processes of meaning making engendered by the artwork/event. The performative work fans outward. It makes of its own capacity for historicity an occasion for the articulation of difference and the re-production of cultural authority, and so for contests over value, meaning, and power.

The central irony of representation — its tendency to make absent the very thing it wishes to make present — is thus layered in performance by the ironic return of history through historicity. Indeed, it is in the moments of the most intense performative play — the moments when the gaps between signifiers and their avowed signifieds are widest — that history creeps back into (or, perhaps more accurately, out of) representation. At these moments of slippage, history shape-shifts. It appears in a variety of forms: as a marked absence, as motility within the apparently fixed terms of the sign, as ideological panic and conflict, as the very stuff of cultural production, as utopic possibility, and as an excess or overflow — as that which signification simply cannot encompass or contain. Like bursting seams, these moments invite and require intervention. They avail history through culture of change — and position the historical subject as a historical agent capable of initiating change. A third twist in the logic of performativity, then, brings us to history not as something given (the facts) or as something made (the "facts") but as the very activity of making embodied in "performance" — again, not performance in the Aristotelian sense of "representation in the form of action" but performance in the sense of action enfolded in the resources of representation and of representation as itself a form of action. In this sense, performance makes history *go* sometimes by making it seem to *go away*, by exercising its representational tactics so vigorously that history can no longer be *seen*. At this moment, at the very moment that performance seems to eclipse history, it achieves its surplus: it ruptures and rattles and revises history; it challenges the easy composure of history under the sign of objectivity. It discomposes history as myth, making of it a *scene* awaiting intervention by the performing subject.

Essays in History/Performance

The essays collected in this volume address such scenes as these. They practice history in excess of its polarization between the *facts* and the "facts," between appeals to empirical objectivity, on the one hand, and imagination, on the other. They perform in the breach, where making history sometimes means making it seem to go away, to disappear, to vanish, into representational action and interaction, or history. As I stated earlier, the aim of this book is not to define a field or practice but to pursue the challenges made to definition and disciplinarity by crossing borders conventionally dividing "performance" and "history." The essays in this volume consequently represent not only diverse but also divergent, even incompatible approaches to performance/history. They draw and yet exceed their history in White, Said, Bakhtin, and Baudrillard in their respective efforts to mine the confluence of performance and history for history, to show how, across various planes and in multiple registers, performance shapes historical interpretation, production, and imagination, and, in turn, how history gives performance its means and salience. Again, these essays do not reflect as much as they follow in the wake of the issues, theories, practices, and questions identified earlier in this essay.

The authors of the essays collected in the volume conceptualize performance as variously as they are positioned in its study. Coming from and crossing into different fields, they approach performance as a deep paradigm of social processes (Cohen and Odhiambo), a metaphor for the nation-state (Richards), a social rite (Ruth Bowman, Michael Bowman, Jackson), and a mode of tactical resistance (Fuoss, Capo). They locate performance in the objects of conventionally "high" culture: in plays (Roach), novels (Richards, Ruth Bowman), photographs (Mavor), and museum archives (Ruth Bowman, Michael Bowman, Mavor, Jackson, Buck); in the currencies of popular culture: in news stories, postcards, pornography, "humbugging," film/video (Roach, Ruth Bowman), and life stories (Madison); and in the practices of everyday life: in gendered behaviors (Davis, Mavor), discourses of consumption (Roach, Ruth Bowman, Jackson, Mavor), juridical proceedings (Cohen and Odhiambo, Capo), gossip and conversation (Michael Bowman, Jackson, Capo); in the very processes of reading and writing in which each author is engaged (Cohen and Odhiambo, Michael Bowman, Mavor, Jackson, Capo); and even in death — certainly the ultimate vanishing act (Cohen and Odhiambo, Buck). In general, they explore the ways in which performance as both a theoretical trope and a historical practice makes *spaces* out of diverse *places*, the ways in which it articulates difference *in the place of* even such seductively monolithic structures as the Louisiana Superdome (Roach), the New Jersey State Assembly (Fuoss), and the Victorian theater (Davis).

The essays are rather arbitrarily divided into five sections. The essays in the first section, "Spectacular Histories," address the performativity of history. Rather than chronicling history, they stage politics in action. They spectacularize history, evoking histories driven, policed, and yet threatened by the excesses and agencies of performance. In his essay on "Slave Spectacles and Tragic Octoroons," Joseph Roach addresses two primary performance types —

the slave auction and nineteenth-century melodrama — but locates both within "a network of common but deeply problematic enunciations — the gestures, expressions, protocols, manners, habits, and attitudes — whereby a culture remembers and reinvents not only its most public relationships, but also its most intimate ones," a network that encompasses brothel shows and Madonna videos, and comprises a long history of racism in the commercial/cultural " 'contact zone' " of New Orleans.

For Roach, history and culture reveal their complicities and contingencies in the play of everyday, staged bodies. Following Foucault, Roach writes what he calls a "genealogy of performance" — a discontinuous and deeply erotic history of the generation, transmission, and dissemination of culture in and through performance.[68] In so doing, he provides an exhilarating but potentially vexing challenge to the conventions of genre study and periodization that define much theater history. Roach's essay reflects back on the disciplinary formation of theater studies through what he suggests is the more panoramic lens of performance studies. On the other hand, it looks forward to history. It anticipates the processes of "surrogation" that connect such Circean rites as slave auctions, prostitution, minstrelsy, musical comedy, football, and rock video in a tightly wound economy of pleasure. Roach takes as his structural token the eroticized substitutions of flesh, money, and property that occurred and recurred within the "vortex" of slave market exchange. These surrogations return historically as performances of race and gender, suggesting that successive performances may occupy distinct or "new" moments in history but that none can exhaust the vortical, performative energy at the heart of New Orleans's slave culture.

In "Reading the Minister's Remains," David Cohen and E. S. Atieno Odhiambo approach history synchronically, addressing rhetorics of the present as they correspond to rhetorics of *presence*. Like Roach, Cohen and Odhiambo track the consolidation of political and performative economies, relying in part on Foucault's recommendations for "archaeologies of knowledge" and in part on those critiques of mimetic historiography (including those spearheaded by White and Said) that make suspect "official" documents and news histories that purport to transparent truth keeping.

Cohen and Odhiambo's primary concerns are the public and state narratives that emerged in the wake of the horrific and mysterious death of the Kenyan minister of foreign affairs, John Robert Ouko. In "Reading the Minister's Remains," Cohen and Odhiambo meditate on the ways in which the remains of the minister's body — found burned, broken, and shot in a grassy cove a short distance from his home — were read, and on what little remains of the minister in those readings. For Cohen and Odhiambo, the minister's body in death becomes a stage on which the state performs itself. The body itself performatively disappears into its public reckonings.[69] By investigating those readings in detail (especially as they shifted from being primarily mimetic renderings to interpretive performances of "fact"), Cohen and Odhiambo radically historicize the so-called findings in the case. They open official programs of meaning (including explanations, alibis, and excuses) to the "interstitial, intermediate, indeterminate, unfinished, moments of knowing operating within and upon" them, to narratives operating outside the official register of investigation — and so force the performative indeterminacies of state power: the contingent and necessarily partial attempts by the offices of Kenya's political culture to dominate and to deflect an emergent public discourse.

Kirk W. Fuoss's essay, "Performance as Contestation," takes up the question of how staged claims on public space, particularly in the form of parodic interventions into official discourse, are or can be effective. His answer entails challenging what have come to be called "new historicist" methods to encompass the specific, material dynamics of performed history. Arising in the late seventies and early eighties out of the study of primarily Renaissance performance texts (Shakespeare's plays, in particular), the "new" historicism was meant to correct the textualism that had characterized much of twentieth-century literary studies.[70] Emphasizing the interanimating functions of text and context, the new historicism challenged at once the formalism persisting through "new critical" and poststructural approaches to literary study and earlier or "old" (nineteenth-century) historicist constructions of history as authorial background or period landscape. Moving context into the foreground and focusing on the performative interaction of text and context, the new historicists promised an implosion of text/context divisions and increased attention to the economies of textual production and consumption. As Fuoss points out, new historicist research suggests that "texts and performances fulfill both reflective and reflexive functions, that texts and performances are both products of and producers of culture." But, as he also observes, it stops short of realizing its full promise precisely on the grounds of historical analysis. By failing to particularize the dynamics of con/textual production, it limits its discoveries to rehearsal of a general dynamic, what Fuoss calls a "product-producer dialectic."

The essays in the second section of the book, "(Dis)Playing History," address popular, historical spectacles, calling each home, as it were, to performance. They counter the collapse of high culture and high history in commodity-object orientations that, as each essay shows, span the nineteenth and twentieth centuries. Working from performance-centered perspectives, perspectives founded both in Fiske's sense that the culture of everyday life is "a culture of concrete practices which embody and perform differences" and in resistance to the curated *look* (neither looks quite like traditional scholarship and neither looks only where it is supposed to look), each recovers "high" cultural artifacts to popular traditions that contradict their status within myths of American identity. Each performs the proleptic relation of high culture to so-called low or rubbish culture, turning traditions of reading Nathaniel Hawthorne and touring antebellum homes inside out, carnivalizing each, refusing the refusal that is, as Pierre Bourdieu observed, "the starting point of the high aesthetic."[71] Each resists the exclusion of so-called low culture that constitutes high culture and legitimates high history. In each chapter, moreover, performance proves the contaminating, unraveling figure of the low on whose containment American romance and the idealization of Southern confederacy, respectively, depend.

Ruth Bowman's essay, "Performing Social Rubbish: Humbug and Romance in the American Marketplace," locates Hawthorne's novel, *The House of the Seven Gables*, within a "humbug" history, a broadscale, market economy structured by performance for pleasure and profit. The maestro of mid-nineteenth-century humbug, P. T. Barnum, was careful, as Bowman notes, to distinguish the humbug from cheap theatrics, mere fraud, or deception. Following Barnum, Bowman argues that humbugging is an entrepreneurial art requiring the delicate management of the relations between advertisement and consumption. Drawing the consumer into admiration of outrageous claims and gross misrepresentation of objects displayed, humbugging depends on "promising much, and then delivering much — even though the product itself might turn out to be somewhat different from what was advertised." Figuring the "humbug" as a quintessentially democratic art, Bowman argues furthermore that it has been no more fully realized than in Barnum's own American Museum. Here (safe from the pejorative connotations of the theater) a random mix of trained fleas and "fine art" offered the consumer/viewer the pleasure of reviewing, judging, and evaluating the status of each object. In the carnival-museum, "art was operationalized, rather than aestheticized."

Bowman counterrescues Hawthorne. She recovers him from his recovery from "humbug" cultures to the American romance tradition. Countering the tendency of literary critics to refuse the operational dynamics implicit in his work, Bowman revels in its hybridity — its carnival mix of dissembling, hoaxing, posing, and double-voiced display. In its conspicuous and yet consistently dismissed theatricality, *The House of the Seven Gables* articulates with the American Museum in a comic, ironic, sometimes grotesque parody of the very sentimentality for which Hawthorne's critics tend to praise his work.

An important contribution to nineteenth-century popular culture/literary studies, Bowman's essay is nonetheless perhaps most significant for its further articulation with contemporary documentary filmmaking. In a surprising swing from the mid-nineteenth to the late-twentieth century, Bowman demonstrates the extraordinary resilience of the antitheatrical prejudice in American identity politics. Nineteenth-century romance, she argues, surfaces in contemporary appeals to personal authenticity and sincerity. Considering the reception of two controversial documentary films, Marlon Riggs's *Tongues Untied* and Jennie Livingston's *Paris Is Burning*, Bowman wonders whether an aesthetic of experience is not the ultimate hoax, whether by refusing the humbug, "we would only end up swindling ourselves."

In his essay on "Performing Southern History for the Tourist Gaze," Michael Bowman further mines popular, historical displays for their defining contradictions. Bowman introduces the reader to the semiotics of tourism, focusing on the "spiral of semiosis" in which contemporary tourism seems caught — the process by which tourists come to resent each other as tourists, the historical site/sight is reduced to a sign of itself, and locals put themselves up for pay and display. Bowman presents the dynamics by which a historical *scene* becomes what is *seen*, and the myths of visualism, on which so much of American commercial/commodity culture depends, are reiterated at the very place that the tourist theoretically comes to know him/herself in history. The self the tourist learns, of course, is that of the tourist, cut off from history by the very gaze he/she bestows upon it.

And yet Bowman thrills to the theatricality of the tour. He finds in the excessive self-representations of the antebellum home tour a resilient counterstructure, an affective space in which his own pleasure doubles and redoubles the creative, fractured, fanciful, erotic history that plays itself out and around the objects on display, *in the place of* the plantation owner, and between participants pursuing this particularly dense passage into Southern identity formation. He dis/plays the narrativity in his own critique, enacting in his own prose the slippery facades and thresholds he finds so entrancing.

The third section of the collection, "Histories of Desire: Performing Sex and Class," concerns the correlations among performances of sex, gender, class, and nationality along three planes of production: sanitary reform in the nineteenth-century theater, the subject-sight relation or subject-subject performance entailed in viewing nineteenth-century photographs, and the (re)production of the late eighteenth-century novel as a performative gesture in its own right.

Tracy Davis's essay, "Filthy — Nay — Pestilential: Sanitation and Victorian Theaters," directly addresses the economies of place. Tracing the epidemiology of sanitation facilities in the Victorian theaters, Davis shifts attention from staged representations to the formation of gender and class identities in the place of the stage. She offers a new perspective on theater economics and hence on performance historiography by specifically avoiding the image-centered approach that has characterized much of feminist and performance criticism. Focusing instead on the social relations articulated in and through audience behaviors, Davis documents the institution of sanitary facilities in the theater and marks the ensuing stratification and consolidation of class differences. Following in the wake of the great plagues, urban flight, and massive architectural reform, purifying the nineteenth-century theater meant recovering it from contagion to patronage. As Davis concludes, "[W]hile officials documented sanitary breaches under all circumstances, prosperous patrons seemed content provided that they could recreate in the unmingled vapor of their own kind."

In "Touching Netherplaces: Invisibility in the Photographs of Hannah Cullwick," Carol Mavor similarly evokes the sensual presence of the viewer/audience member in the reconstruction of the nineteenth-century sexual identity. She refuses the spectacularity of the *seen* as such, favoring instead the complex combinations of touch, smell, figural play, and erotic pleasure that make up the performative relation between the viewer, the photographic subject, and the photographer — in this case, Mavor, Hannah Cullwick, a nineteenth-century maid-of-all-work, and her secret lover and husband, the little-known symbolist poet, Arthur Munby. Cullwick is the unseen figure in the endless photographic representations of her collected by Munby. She is the subject of excess representation in the double sense that she is fetishized by Munby and that she *exceeds* Munby's — and our — fetishizing grasp of her by her performances for and before the camera's eye. Not that she was ethereal. Not that she denied sight. In fact, she relished — sometimes perversely — the opportunities for bodily display the camera gave her. But, as Mavor observes, it was precisely her enthusiasm for performance (which included blacking her body with soot and costuming herself variously as a man, as her bourgeois mistress, as a Madonna) that confounds an objectifying gaze, that draws the viewer into the space of a complex and erotic in/visibility.

Davis's essay concerns what is not staged: the identities shaped while or because the play goes on. Mavor's theater is less visible, even invisible: it is a dynamic of relation among viewers who touch the photographs of Hannah Cullwick with both hands and eyes. A critique of place, on the one hand, and of spectatorship, on the other, both Davis's and Mavor's essays draw our eyes offstage to the formations of class and sexuality that occur when and where you are not looking, at the edges of theatrical representation and yet squarely within economies of performance and pleasure that the Victorian theater represents.

In the concluding essay of this section, "The Politics of Seduction: Theater, Sexuality, and National Virtue in the Novels of Hannah Foster," Jeffrey Richards addresses the foreclosures of the theater on sexual/gendered identity within the space of the novel. Whereas the new historicist approach that

Fuoss critiques and elaborates tends to look outward from the text to context, Richards demonstrates the implosion of context on literary representation, suggesting finally that Foster's late-eighteenth-century novels are totems of everyday gendered behaviors. As such, they emblematize early republican, American anxiety about performance, at once hailing ornate performances on the stage of everyday, social life and dismissing the theater per se. In the context of the emerging republic, the theater was a threat, a figure of instability, sensuality, ambivalence, agency, and corruption.[72] It was the place of otherness, of the alien within. As such, it had to be contained, on the one hand, by bracketing it off as a form of fashionable entertainment, an object for consumption by those who could afford it, and, on the other hand, by counterposing it with rigidly and elaborately codified performances in everyday life. Theatricality was, in effect, purified of difference and contradiction; display was purged of play. Rationalized, strictly monitored, and yet pervasive, theatricality became servant to the state. And as Richards observes through Foster, the primary figure in the state's display of its own virtue was the chaste, bourgeois woman, whose iconographic representation was contradictory, repressive, and yet not absolute.

Richards refigures Foster's work as one among many hotly contested performances within the late-eighteenth-century arena of public censure and debate. In Richards's essay, Foster reflects and claims the territory of sex/gender representation. She turns eighteenth-century theatricality back on itself, challenging — however modestly — the state's totalizing claim on representational space. As Richards describes Foster's novels, they both registered and resisted nationalist and masculinist tendencies to make the representation of women legitimate state interests. They performed within and against a history rank with residual, performative desire.

Baudrillard's postmodern history is hyperreal: image-saturated and vacuous, rank with seeing surfaces bouncing off each other. It suffers, as Baudrillard declared in the early eighties, "museumification." "The museum," Baudrillard wrote, "instead of being curcumscribed [sic] in a geometrical location, is now everywhere, like a dimension of life itself."[73] Deploying the museum as the ultimate trope of what Nancy Munn recently called "ethnographic death," Baudrillard expresses a growing presentiment that the museum has expanded not only to include but also to enclose contemporary life within protocols of display, tourism, alienation, and fetishization.[74] James Boon evokes this feeling when he writes:

> Any museum, any museum at all, makes me sad. Ethnological museums, art museums, ethnic museums, museums of these museums. Permanent museums, traveling museums, museums as travel; museums in the rough or on

the mall. Literal museums, and figurative: without walls (ambiguous or permeable, anyway), or with. Williamsburg. Books read as a museum (some of them designed to be, some not); rituals enacted as a museum. Cities. Experience itself as museum: a play of context-begging specimens, oddly captioned, regarded *de loin* or *à proche* even by the one doing the experiencing.[75]

Boon mourns the dislocations implicit in a mushrooming museum culture. The essays in the fourth section of this book, "The Museum in/as Performance: Raids and Reifications," answer his and others' despair with reserved hope. They invert the museum trope as such and turn out of its pockets and folds a peculiar vitality linked specifically to performative play. They complement recent scholarly attempts to rearticulate cultural artifacts with embodied practices of production and consumption as well as practical efforts to make museum displays interactive, often through the resources of in-house performance ensembles.[76] In so doing, they test the capacity of the museum (with or without walls) as an intensive, social *place* to become a *space*: to engage its visitors in active reformulation of their relation to the subject/objects displayed and thus at least to rehearse significant, social agency.

Shannon Jackson performs the Labor Museum at Jane Addams's Hull-House in Chicago in the body of her essay, "Performance at Hull-House: Museum, Microfiche, and Historiography." She interrogates the status of the Labor Museum as a place, placing herself in dialogic relation to it. The essay represents what might be called a participatory history, an ethnographic, geographic study of history from within its immediate contours. Haunting the rooms and passageways of Hull-House, Jackson reiterates history's own spectral desires. She traverses the grounds of the Labor Museum, looking through windows, searching microfiches, reviewing artifacts, gathering gossip, and listening for the echo of "original" performances like so many historians before her. Unlike historians before her, however, her particularly heightened, performative reflexivity holds a master narrative at bay. It holds off the modern, progressivist narrative that typically followed in the tracks she follows, substituting a dialogic, self-transforming performance of historiography for its consolidation into history.

Making the absences in earlier formulations of Chicago labor history palpably present, Jackson does not so much "deconstruct" history (leaving its fragments in an untold heap) as she does recover it to time, to the temporal plane on which she and the museum's other inhabitants, past and present, co-act. She looks through the display relations structuring the museum experience to the veiled, affecting subjectivities at its heart, shifting the very ground of understanding the museum and the history it enacts from that of seeing/being seen to making history in the ongoing interaction among museum participants in and across time. Jackson effectively defers her authority to name history (echoing what seems the endless deferral of presence along the chain of signification that includes news accounts and microfiche images), performing instead her relation to history, an uneasy relation, cross-cut and cut again with competing politics and desires.

The focus of Elizabeth Buck's essay, "Museum Author-ity," is the French fin-de-siècle artist Gustave Moreau's resistance to "state-sanctioned museum logic." Buck shows how Moreau's bequest made his housed collection a national collection (part of the *patrimoine*) and yet how, in his death, Moreau claimed unprecedented control over its signification. As Buck shows, Moreau, in a virtuosic, posthumous performance, writes into the relationship between the visitor to his home/museum and the museum collection a "disruptive dynamic" that secures for Moreau a degree of distinction he never owned in life.

Moreau effectively turns poststructural theory (even as it is embodied, for instance, in Jackson's un/naming of Hull-House history) on its head. In his pre-scriptions for his museum, the much heralded and, in this case, quite literal "death of the author" becomes the basis less for the dissemination of meaning across a vast field of readerships than for an assimilation of meaning to the painter/author's *name*. For Buck, the Moreau museum is radical in *signing* representational space (almost as if it were a very large canvas), in making it subject to the absence that Moreau's *name* makes tantalizingly present. Through this sometimes bizarre autographic practice, Buck argues, Moreau keeps the *author*-ity of his work from patrimonic appropriation.

The final section of the book, "Producing History," concerns the work of narrative *praxis*. Focusing on narrative as a way of knowing, as what the performance studies scholar Dwight Conquergood, drawing on the work of White, Bhabha, Said, and Trinh, among others, calls a search for meaning "enacted, reconfigured, tested, and engaged by imaginative summonings and interpretive replays of past events in the light of present situations and struggles," the essays in this section describe journeys across fields of ethnographic, aesthetic, and everyday production.[77]

In her essay, "'That Was My Occupation': Oral Narrative, Performance, and Black Feminist Thought," D. Soyini Madison explores the collaboration of performed narratives and narrative accounts of performance in the production of "indigenous theory." She advocates for the narrative authority of Mrs. Alma Kapper, an elderly black domestic and former sharecropper, from the twin perspectives of a scholar-critic, empowered to endorse Mrs. Kapper's history by reference to the "specialized knowledge" of a professional academic, and of a daughter and sister to the "theories of the flesh" Mrs. Kapper narrates. In Madison's formulation, Mrs. Kapper's narrative is not a naive or transparent account of experience. Nor is the experience it recounts, as Scott would argue, an end in itself, a foundational claim for identity. It is, rather, the discursive space in which Madison and Mrs. Kapper respectively and reciprocally perform.

Madison intermediates Mrs. Kapper and recent developments in black feminist theory, with the primary effect of calling the latter to account. She listens to Mrs. Kapper twice over: with the distance of the activist-scholar and the proximity of a daughter or granddaughter who, like Trinh, listens to "words passed down from mouth to ear . . . body to body," finding, feeling in their turns and pleasures the truthfulness "in-between of all regimes of truth." Criss-crossing the gaps in her own identity and in her relation to Mrs. Kapper, Madison writes history as performance, as the rites and traditions that make up much of Mrs. Kapper's life history and as the dynamics of exchange that convey it, from Mrs. Kapper's mouth to her ear, and from her ear now to her reader's eye.

The performances that Madison and Kay Capo describe are each densely multivalent. They are layered, enfolded, even encrusted in performance. Each draws together and unfolds in a multiplicity of performances, showing just how inextricable staged re-presentations are from representations in everyday, popular, traditional, and interview contexts. Each intensifies and amplifies (rather than bracketing off) their place on a continuum of performative behaviors. As a result, what is perhaps most extraordinary about the performances both Madison and Capo describe is that, as the essays indicate, they continue to fan outward, intermittently and incidentally generating additional and alternative performances in an ongoing genealogy of celebrations, restorations, stories, conversations, critique, reflections, and interventions.

The performance Capo describes in her 1987 essay, "How to Act During an Interrogation: Theater and Moral Boundaries," proves particularly extravagant in this sense, although in a more intensive than extensive way. Capo's 1987 essay comprises the first part of the last chapter of this volume. It recounts her production of a play, *Thoughts in the Margin*, based on the transcripts of a dissident trial smuggled out of Soviet Lithuania in the mid-eighties. The essay provocatively describes the problems of translating the experience documented in the transcripts, of resolving the "expressive gap" produced by cultural difference. A compelling argument for the value of just such a struggle, the essay is perhaps most important for the sequel it produces here some ten years after the originating 1983 performance.

In the second part of the chapter, "Stages of Dissent in Post-Soviet Lithuania," Capo historicizes the earlier work as she watches it unravel in the light of recent history. Caught now in the fervor of Soviet dissolution and in the grip of recent conversations with the wife of the dissident on whose trial *Thoughts in the Margin* was based, Capo performs the complicities of *Thoughts in the*

Margin with a Cold War episteme: its structural affiliations with a narrative coded red. In retrospect, the production could not outthink its context. For all its resistive intentions, it could not avoid and so help but rehearse the binarisms to which its history was so urgently disposed. In retrospect, however, it seems the production finds its feet, finds its force now in spillage across Capo's life, art, and pages. In Capo's sequel, a performance caught between two forms (trial and stage play), two languages, and two state monoliths erupts into multiple performances of nationality, gender, memory, and community. The narrative of nations in which Capo's previous production seemed caught now seems to turn inside out, the performativity Bhabha hailed boiling over its edges, with much of the pleasure Bhabha hailed, but also with the anxiety and fear that must come with yoking performativity — in all of its theoretical implications — to the material performance of everyday life.

Both Madison and Capo make the particular pleasures of performing history work. They elicit and produce performances whose power unfolds in pleasure. Their essays suggest, like others in the volume, that pleasure is rarely merely docile. That it is stubborn, transgressive, and given to excess. A subject of time and sense, performance pleasures are elusive, sly, vital, transitive. They travel almost jealously from place to place, along paths of contradiction, taking us with them (sometimes willingly, sometimes not). Erotic and grotesque, pleasure draws us toward and away from each other — and toward and away from our respective pasts. It is a multihybrid phenomenon, crossing bodies, selves, languages, genders, classes, and nationalities in confusion, anxiety, and delight. In the midst of pleasure, we are most in-bodied, most *in* difference, most in the realm of action and in between the laws of myth and structure. We are in the space of performance — a space that is, as these essays consistently show, everywhere and nowhere in history, "a place out of place," allowing, even requiring us to take further exception to the rule of "place": to subject place to *play* and to perform our *difference* from its claims.[78] It is in the name of such an exceptional space that I offer this book to you.

Notes

1. Jill Dolan, "Geographies of Learning," *Theatre Journal* 45 (1993): 430.
2. E.g., James Clifford, *The Predicament of Culture: Twentieth-Century Ethnography, Literature, and Art* (Cambridge: Harvard University Press, 1988); Michael Taussig, *The Nervous System* (New York: Routledge, 1992); and Arnold Krupat, *Ethnocriticism: Ethnography, History, Literature* (Berkeley: University of California Press, 1992).
3. Judith Butler, *Gender Trouble: Feminism and the Subversion of Identity* (New York: Routledge, 1990), p. 140.
4. Ibid., esp. pp. 128–41.
5. See, e.g., Lloyd Kramer and Donald Reid, "Introduction: Historical Knowledge, Education, and Public Culture," in *Learning History in America: Schools, Cultures, and*

Politics, edited by Kramer, Reid, and William L. Barney (Minneapolis: University of Minnesota Press, 1994), for a sense of the challenges currently facing the discipline of history, and Patrick Brantlinger, "The Humanities (and a Lot More) in Crisis," in *Crusoe's Footprints: Cultural Studies in Britain and America* (New York: Routledge, 1990), pp. 1–33, for an assessment of the "crisis" as it affects the humanities and the rise of cultural studies more generally.

6. For a more complete elaboration of the debates about the nature of historical knowledge that have troubled the profession of history since the late nineteenth century, see Peter Novick, *That Noble Dream: The "Objectivity Question" and the American Historical Profession* (Cambridge: Cambridge University Press, 1988). See also Peter Burke, ed., *New Perspectives on Historical Writing* (University Park: Pennsylvania State University Press, 1991), for a useful overview of diverse approaches and issues.

7. Allen Feldman, *Formations of Violence: The Narrative of the Body and Political Terror in Northern Ireland* (Chicago: University of Chicago Press, 1991), p. 2.

8. John Fiske, "Cultural Studies and the Culture of Everyday Life," in *Cultural Studies*, edited by Lawrence Grossberg, Cary Nelson, and Paula Treichler (New York: Routledge, 1992), p. 162.

9. On liminality, see Victor Turner, "Liminal to Liminoid, in Play, Flow, Ritual," in Turner, *From Ritual to Theatre: The Human Seriousness of Play* (New York: Performing Arts Journal Publications, 1982), pp. 20–60.

10. See, e.g., Jill Dolan's account of producing Marlane Meyer's play, *Etta Jenks*, in *Presence and Desire: Essays on Gender, Sexuality, Performance*, edited by Dolan (Ann Arbor: University of Michigan Press, 1993), pp. 99–120.

11. Trinh T. Minh-ha, *Woman Native Other: Writing Postcoloniality and Feminism* (Bloomington: Indiana University Press, 1989), p. 136.

12. The romantic preference for sound and the "presential" qualities of speech — or "phonocentrism" — is, of course, the object of Jacques Derrida's founding critique of structuralism; see Derrida, "Structure, Sign, and Play in the Discourse of the Human Sciences," in *The Structuralist Controversy: The Languages of Criticism and the Sciences of Man*, edited by Richard Macksey and Eugenio Donato (Baltimore: Johns Hopkins University Press, 1972), pp. 247–72, and, e.g., *Of Grammatology*, translated by Gayatri Chakravorty Spivak (Baltimore: Johns Hopkins University Press, 1977). Derrida's supplementation of speech by writing remains problematic, however, leading Julia Kristeva, for one, to formulate (following Lacan) a more utopic theory based on a difference between "semiotic" and "symbolic" spaces; Kristeva, *Desire in Language*, translated by Leon S. Roudiez (Oxford: Basil Blackwell, 1980). Although Kristeva's "semiotic" space is prediscursive in the specific sense that it is not yet fully coded by the "father" and exists in dialectical and potentially subversive relation to dominant sign systems, it does not collapse into the neat binarism I am suggesting here — toward which, for instance, a work like Walter Ong's *Orality and Literacy* (New York: Methuen, 1982) is prone.

13. See Peggy Phelan, "Broken Symmetries: Memory, Sight, Love," *Unmarked: The Politics of Performance* (New York: Routledge, 1993), pp. 1–33. For a substantial critique of modern Euro/Western visualism, see Martin Jay, *Downcast Eyes: The Denigration of Vision in Twentieth-Century French Thought* (Berkeley: University of California Press, 1993).

14. *Time*, July 19, 1993, p. 29, "In Your Town, In Your Face." See also Peggy

Phelan, "White Men and Pregnancy: Discovering the Body to be Rescued," *Unmarked*, pp. 130–45.

15. On the politics of returning the gaze, see, e.g., Mieke Bal, "The Politics of Citation," *Diacritics* 21.1 (1991): 25–45; Jill Dolan, *The Feminist Spectator as Critic* (Ann Arbor: UMI Research Press, 1988); and bell hooks, "The Oppositional Gaze," *Black Looks: Race and Representation* (Boston: South End Press, 1992), pp. 115–32.

16. In this way, as Mary Russo argues, excess is made to serve narratives of modernist "exceptionalism." See Russo, *The Female Grotesque: Risk, Excess, and Modernity* (New York: Routledge, 1994), esp. pp. 17–51.

17. On walking as a "spatial practice," see Michel de Certeau, "Walking in the City," *The Practice of Everyday Life*, translated by Steven Rendell (Berkeley: University of California Press, 1984), pp. 91–110.

18. This is, for instance, a problem in Stephen A. Tyler's otherwise provocative work on postmodern anthropology and ethnography in *The Unspeakable: Discourse, Dialogue, and Rhetoric in the Postmodern World* (Madison: University of Wisconsin Press, 1987), pp. 171–218.

19. Phelan, *Unmarked*, p. 148. Regarding the performative surplus of history writing, see also, e.g., Michel de Certeau, *The Writing of History*, translated by Tom Conley (New York: Columbia University Press, 1988), and Susan Leigh Foster, ed., *Choreographing History* (Bloomington: University of Indiana Press, 1995).

20. Quoted in Timothy W. Ryback, "Evidence of Evil," *New Yorker*, November 15, 1993, p. 80.

21. A definitive proof of the existence of extermination facilities at Auschwitz was recently provided by Jean-Claude Pressac, *Auschwitz: Technique and Operation of the Gas Chambers* (New York: Beate Klarsfeld Foundation, 1989). See Ryback, "Evidence of Evil," pp. 72 ff., for discussion.

22. The prospect of theme parks celebrating historical atrocities is not paranoid imagining on my part. National Public Radio (NPR) recently reported on the plans of a German entrepreneur (with the support of a major Berlin investment firm) to build a theme park in which East Germany under Communist rule would be re-created in miniature. In addition to angry shopkeepers, empty shelves, and military parades, the park would feature a Stasi prison where visitors who dared to collaborate in escape plans would be detained. According to Stephen Kinzer, reporting for the *New York Times*, the park would be designed to appeal to two groups: those who never experienced East Germany and those who remember it fondly. NPR, *Morning Edition*, November 16, 1993. As the NPR reporter observed, the image of a park founded on nostalgia and resentment of contemporary politics underscored the controversies surrounding Disney's now defunct plans to build an American history park near Manassas, Virginia.

23. For complementary analyses, see, e.g., Elie Wiesel, "Art and the Holocaust: Trivializing Memory," *New York Times Review of Books*, June 11, 1989, p. 1ff., and Philip Gourevitch, "The Holocaust Memorial Museum: One More American Theme Park," *Harper's Magazine*, July 1993, pp. 55–62.

24. The achievement of such a dialectic was Brecht's aim in "historicizing" the theater. See "A Short Organum for the Theatre," *Brecht on Theatre*, edited and translated by John Willett (New York: Hill and Wang, 1964), esp. pp. 190–91. Richard

Schechner further describes this dialectic as it relates to the nonpresential quality of acting, the extent to which an actor in performance is "not himself" and yet "not not himself"; see Schechner, *Between Theater and Anthropology* (Philadelphia: University of Pennsylvania Press, 1985), p. 3.

25. See Thomas Laqueur's provocative comparison of the critical potential of the Washington, D.C., Vietnam Memorial Wall and the Holocaust Museum: "The Holocaust Museum," *Threepenny Review* 56 (Winter 1994): 30–35. See also Steven Mullaney's analysis of how verisimilitude may actually counteract the resurgent power of remembrance and ironically turn memory into a kind of forgetting in Mullaney, "The Rehearsal of Cultures," *The Place of the Stage: License, Play, and Power in Renaissance England* (Chicago: University of Chicago Press, 1988).

26. Hayden White, "The Value of Narrativity in the Representation of Reality," *Critical Inquiry* 7.1 (1980): 23. I first came to White through Teresa de Lauretis, "Desire in Narrative," *Alice Doesn't* (Bloomington: Indiana University Press), pp. 103–57. De Lauretis clearly has more confidence in the radical implications of White's work than does, say, Tracy Davis, "Annie Oakley and Her Ideal Husband of No Importance," in *Critical Theory and Performance*, edited by Janelle B. Reinelt and Joseph R. Roach (Ann Arbor: University of Michigan Press, 1992), pp. 299–312.

27. White, "The Value of Narrativity," p. 14.

28. Ibid., p. 20.

29. Ibid., p. 4.

30. See, e.g., Gertrude Himmelfarb, "Some Reflections on the New History," American History Forum on "The Old History and the New," *American History Review* 94.3 (1989): 661–70.

31. Feldman, *Formations of Violence*, p. 14. Feldman attributes this notion generally to Hayden White, *Metahistory: The Historical Imagination in Nineteenth-Century Europe* (Baltimore: Johns Hopkins University Press, 1973); Paul Ricoeur, *Time and Narrative*, vol. 1 (Chicago: University of Chicago Press, 1984); and Paul Veyne, *Writing History: An Essay in Epistemology* (Middletown, Conn.: Wesleyan University Press, 1984).

32. Edward Said, *Orientalism* (New York: Vintage, 1979), pp. 272–73.

33. Page duBois, *Torture and Truth* (New York: Routledge, 1991), p. 147.

34. Jean Baudrillard, *Simulations* (New York: Semiotext[e], 1983), p. 32. For a complementary perspective, see Walter Benjamin, "The Work of Art in the Age of Mechanical Reproduction," in *Illuminations*, translated by Harry Zohn, edited by Hannah Arendt (New York: Schocken, 1968), pp. 217–52.

35. Jean Baudrillard, "Hot Painting: The Inevitable Fate of the Image," *Reconstructing Modernism: Art in New York, Paris, and Montreal 1945–1964*, edited by Serge Guilbaut (Cambridge: MIT Press, 1990), p. 19.

36. Christopher Norris, *Uncritical Theory: Postmodernism, Intellectuals, and the Gulf War* (Amherst: University of Massachusetts Press, 1992), pp. 55, 57, 190–91.

37. Trinh, *Woman Native Other*, pp. 119–21.

38. Ibid., p. 119.

39. See Burke, *New Perspectives on Historical Writing*, for an excellent review of oral history and other recent developments in historical writing.

40. Jean François Lyotard is generally acknowledged to have provided the seminal

analysis of the decline of the modern grand or "meta-" narrative in *The Postmodern Condition: A Report on Knowledge*, translated by Geoff Bennington and Brian Massumi (Minneapolis: University of Minnesota Press, 1984).

41. Joan W. Scott, "The Evidence of Experience," *Critical Inquiry* 17.4 (1991): 797.

42. For a succinct summary of how these issues articulate with issues in performance theory and history, see Joseph R. Roach's introduction to the essays addressing theater history and historiography in *Critical Theory and Performance*, ed. Reinelt and Roach.

43. Robert Scholes, *Protocols of Reading* (New Haven: Yale University Press, 1989), pp. 91, 105. See also Scholes, chap. 5, "Reference and Difference," *Textual Power: Literary Theory and the Teaching of English* (New Haven: Yale University Press, 1985), pp. 86–110, and new developments in "critical rhetoric," e.g., Michael Calvin McGee, "Text, Context, and the Fragmentation of Contemporary Culture," *Western Journal of Speech Communication* 54 (1990): 278: the "circle of negativism (decentering, deconstructing) should be broken. . . . I think it is time to stop whining about the so-called 'post-modern condition' and to develop realistic strategies to cope with it as a fact of human life."

44. Susan Bordo, " 'Material Girl': The Effacements of Postmodern Culture," *Michigan Quarterly Review* 29.4 (1990): 676.

45. Ibid., p. 667. See also, e.g., Judith Butler, *Bodies That Matter: On the Discursive Limits of "Sex"* (New York: Routledge, 1993).

46. Peter Hitchcock, *Dialogics of the Oppressed* (Minneapolis: University of Minnesota Press, 1993), p. 6.

47. J. L. Austin, *How To Do Things with Words* (Cambridge: Harvard University Press, 1962), pp. 4–11.

48. See Eve Kosofsky Sedgwick's critique of the heterosexual presumption in "Queer Performativity: Henry James's *The Art of the Novel*," *GLQ* 1 (1993): 2, rehearsed in her introduction, with Andrew Parker, to *Performance and Performativity*, edited by Andrew Parker and Sedgwick (New York: Routledge, 1995).

49. Paul Ricoeur, "The Model of the Text: Meaningful Action Considered as Text," in *Hermeneutics and the Human Sciences*, edited and translated by John B. Thompson (Cambridge: Cambridge University Press, 1981).

50. See Jonas Barish, *The Anti-Theatrical Prejudice* (Berkeley: University of California Press, 1981).

51. On criticism as performance, see, e.g., Henry M. Sayre, "Critical Performance: The Example of Roland Barthes," *The Object of Performance: The American Avant-Garde since 1970* (Chicago: University of Chicago Press, 1989). On reading as a performative process, see esp. Wolfgang Iser, *The Act of Reading* (Baltimore: Johns Hopkins University Press, 1978), and Stanley Fish's early work, *Self-Consuming Artifacts: The Experience of Seventeenth-Century Literature* (Berkeley: University of California Press, 1972).

52. De Certeau, *The Practice of Everyday Life*, p. 21. Here de Certeau cites L. Wittgenstein, *Philosophical Investigations* (Oxford: Blackwell, 1976), pp. 116, 48. De Certeau's claims here resonate with Kenneth Burke's specifically rhetorical theory of "Literature as Equipment for Living," *The Philosophy of Literary Form: Studies in Symbolic Action*, 3d ed. (Berkeley: University of California Press, [1941, 1967] 1973), pp. 293–304.

53. See, e.g., Richard Bauman, "Verbal Art as Performance," *American Anthropologist* 77 (1975): 290–311; Dwight Conquergood, "Poetics, Play, Process, and Power:

The Performative Turn in Anthropology," *Text and Performance Quarterly* 9.1 (1989): 82–88; and Richard Schechner, *Between Theater and Anthropology* (Philadelphia: University of Pennsylvania Press, 1985).

54. For Schechner's definition of performance as "restored behavior," see *Between Theater and Anthropology*, pp. 36–38.

55. Mikhail M. Bakhtin, *The Dialogic Imagination: Four Essays*, edited by Michael Holquist, translated by Caryl Emerson and Holquist (Austin: University of Texas Press, 1981).

56. See, e.g., Hitchcock, *Dialogics of the Oppressed*, chap. 1, for a summary and critique of weak liberal interpretations of Bakhtin.

57. Bakhtin, "Discourse in the Novel," *The Dialogic Imagination*, esp. pp. 272–75.

58. See Bakhtin, "Dostoevsky's Polyphonic Novel and Its Treatment in Critical Literature," *Problems of Dostoevsky's Poetics*, edited and translated by Caryl Emerson (Minneapolis: University of Minnesota Press, 1984), pp. 5–46. Whether it is appropriate to attribute "polyphony" to authors or genres other than Dostoevsky's novels has been the subject of considerable reflection. Though it would be impossible to cite in full the minor industry that has grown up around polyphony (as it extends to plays, poetry, short stories, popular culture, ethnography, etc.), it might be useful to note a few attempts to show its kinship with some forms of theatrical practice. See, e.g., Marvin Carlson, "Theater and Dialogism," in *Critical Theory and Performance*, ed. Reinelt and Roach; Max Harris, *The Dialogical Theater: Dramatizations of the Conquest of Mexico and the Question of the Other* (New York: St. Martin's Press, 1993); Della Pollock, "The Play as Novel: Reappropriating Brecht's *Drums in the Night*," *Quarterly Journal of Speech* 74.3 (1988): 296–309, and "Telling the Told: Performing Like a Family," *Oral History Review* 18.2 (1990): 1–36.

59. See, e.g., Dale Bauer and Susan McKinstry, eds., *Feminism, Bakhtin, and the Dialogic* (Albany: State University of New York Press, 1991); Henry Louis Gates Jr., "The Blackness of Blackness: A Critique of the Sign and the Signifying Monkey," in *Black Literature and Literary Theory*, edited by Gates (New York: Methuen, 1984), pp. 285–321; and Hitchcock, *Dialogics of the Oppressed*.

60. Homi K. Bhabha, "Introduction: Narrating the Nation," *Nation and Narration*, edited by Bhabha (New York: Routledge, 1990), p. 3. Bhabha's sense of performativity should be distinguished from, for instance, Lyotard's. For Lyotard (*Postmodern Condition*, p. 47), performativity describes the legitimizing force of language in a technosphere whereby "the performativity of an utterance, be it denotative or prescriptive, increases proportionally to the amount of information about its referent one has at one's disposal. Thus the growth of power, and its self-legitimation, are now taking the route of data storage and accessibility, and the operativity of information." See also Bhabha's more recent work, *The Location of Culture* (New York: Routledge, 1994), esp. pp. 46–49.

61. Bhabha, "Narrating the Nation," p. 3, quoting Edward Said, *The World, the Text, and the Critic* (Cambridge: Harvard University Press, 1983), p. 171.

62. See also Sayre's discussion of Barthes, "Critical Performance," esp. p. 252, and Phelan, *Unmarked*, p. 150, on the metonymic status of the performer.

63. See Phelan's remarkable ontology of performance in *Unmarked*, chap. 7, pp. 146–66.

64. Exemplified in the late seventies, e.g., in Michel Benamou, ed., *Performance in Postmodern Culture* (Milwaukee: Center for Twentieth-Century Studies, University of Wisconsin, 1977).

65. On what has been called the "performative turn" in the social sciences, see, e.g., Dwight Conquergood, "Rethinking Ethnography: Towards a Critical Cultural Poetics," *Communication Monographs* 58.2 (1991): 179–94; James W. Fernandez, *Persuasions and Performances: The Play of Tropes in Culture* (Bloomington: University of Indiana Press, 1986); James C. Scott, *Domination and the Arts of Resistance: Hidden Transcripts* (New Haven: Yale University Press, 1990); and Michael Taussig, *Shamanism, Colonialism, and the Wild Man: A Study in Terror and Healing* (Chicago: University of Chicago Press, 1987). For examples of the rhetorical turn in theater studies, see — in addition to other works cited here and as only a few examples among many — Philip Auslander, *Presence and Resistance: Postmodernism and Cultural Politics in Contemporary American Performance* (Ann Arbor: University of Michigan Press, 1992); Sue-Ellen Case and Janelle Reinelt, eds., *The Performance of Power: Theatrical Discourse and Politics* (Iowa City: University of Iowa Press, 1991); Lynda Hart and Peggy Phelan, eds., *Acting Out: Feminist Performances* (Ann Arbor: University of Michigan Press, 1993); Baz Kershaw, *The Politics of Performance: Radical Theatre as Cultural Intervention* (London: Routledge, 1992); and Randy Martin, *Performance as Political Act: The Embodied Self* (New York: Bergin and Garvey, 1990).

66. For elaboration, see, e.g., Joseph Roach's essay in this volume or Thomas Postlewait and Bruce A. McConachie, eds., *Interpreting the Theatrical Past: Essays in the Historiography of Performance* (Iowa City: University of Iowa Press, 1989).

67. Sayre, *The Object of Performance*, pp. 25–26.

68. See Michel Foucault, "Nietzsche, Genealogy, History," in *Language, Counter-Memory, Practice: Selected Essays and Interviews*, edited by Donald F. Bouchard, translated by Bouchard and Sherry Simon (Ithaca: Cornell University Press, 1977). See also Butler's critique of Foucault's aims for genealogy in *Gender Trouble*, pp. 129–30.

69. Phelan uses "reckonings" in a similar but somewhat more hopeful sense. See *Unmarked*, chap. 7.

70. For the premises of the new historicism, see Stephen Greenblatt's influential work, *Shakespearean Negotiations: The Circulation of Social Energy in Renaissance England* (Berkeley: University of California Press, 1988), and, e.g., H. Aram Veeser, ed., *The New Historicism* (New York: Routledge, 1989).

71. Pierre Bourdieu, *Distinction: A Social Critique of the Judgment of Taste*, translated by Richard Nice (Cambridge: Harvard University Press, 1984), p. 32.

72. See Barish, *The Anti-Theatrical Prejudice*.

73. Baudrillard, *Simulations*, pp. 15–16. The phrase "to museumify" is James Clifford's; see "On Collecting Art and Culture," reprinted in *The Cultural Studies Reader*, edited by Simon During (New York: Routledge, 1993), pp. 49–73.

74. Nancy Munn, "Artifacts and the Symbolization of Value in Malinowski's Iconography" (paper presented at the Conference on the Problem of the Fetish, University of North Carolina at Chapel Hill, March 28, 1992). See also Barbara Kirshenblatt-Gimblett on the museum as a "tomb with a view," "Objects of Ethnography," in *Exhibiting Cultures: The Poetics and Politics of Museum Display*, edited by Ivan Karp and Steven D. Lavine (Washington, D.C.: Smithsonian Institution, 1991), pp. 386–443.

75. James A. Boon, "Why Museums Make Me Sad," in *Exhibiting Cultures*, ed. Karp and Lavine, pp. 255–56.

76. See, e.g., Lynne Cooke and Peter Wollen, eds., *Visual Display: Culture Beyond Appearances* (Seattle: Bay Press, 1995). Note the exemplary work of the resident theater ensemble at the Canadian Museum of Civilization in Ottawa.

77. Dwight Conquergood, "Storied Worlds and the Work of Teaching," *Communication Education* 42.4 (1993): 337. Conquergood is indebted to Donna Haraway, "Situated Knowledges," *Simians, Cyborgs, and Women: The Reinvention of Nature* (New York: Routledge, 1991), pp. 183–201.

78. The phrase "place out of place" belongs to Louis Marin, *Utopics: Spatial Play*, translated by Robert A. Vollrath (Atlantic Highlands, N.J.: Humanities Press, 1984), p. 7.

Spectacular Histories

Slave Spectacles and Tragic Octoroons

A Cultural Genealogy of Antebellum Performance

JOSEPH R. ROACH

There is no arguing with pictures.
   Harriet Beecher Stowe

The economy of desire — of exchange — is man's business.
   Luce Irigaray

In recent critical theory, the word "performance" has undergone a significant expansion, some would say an inflation. As the editor's note to a 1992 issue of *PMLA* ("Special Topic: Performance") observes: "What once was an event has become a critical category, now applied to everything from a play to a war to a meal. The performative . . . is a cultural act, a critical perspective, a political intervention."[1] Theater historians will perhaps greet such pronouncements with mixed emotions. On the one hand, they may welcome the acknowledgment by the principal organ of the Modern Language Association that performance (as opposed to merely drama) can count for so much. On the other hand, they may wonder what exactly is intended by the conceptual leap that takes performance beyond the established theatrical genres to encompass armed conflict and comestibles.

In this speculative study of the representation of slave auctions as theatrical events, I want to propose a rationale for that enlarged conception of performance. My speculations follow the expansion of another arguably hyperinflated word — culture. A culture is both an actual community and an imagined one; it is a special way of doing things together and a way of insisting on the more or less compulsory "normality" of that specialness. As a theater historian, I am particularly interested in performance as a medium of cultural definition and transmission. It is clear to me that performance represents one powerful way in which cultures set about the necessary business of remembering who and what they are. Performance is also one powerful way of making them into who and what they are, and even into who and what they might someday be.

My overarching concept here is of an approach that combines the traditional study of dramatic literature and theater history with the emerging field of performance studies.[2] In that regard, I am indebted to Richard Schechner's definition of performance as "restored behavior" or "twice-behaved behavior" — (re)presentations that can be rehearsed, repeated, and readapted — and Michel de Certeau's formulation of the performative "practice of everyday life."[3] In this light, the artifacts and documents with which theater historians deal may be understood as the archival repository of restored behavior, the contrived or accidental residue not only of the "twice-behaved" behavior of the theater, but also of the performative practices of daily life as it is constructed within historic cultures.

Here I am concerned with some of the performative traditions that link the cultural politics of antebellum America to those of the present day, particularly those representing the public sale of human flesh. These traditions are inextricably linked to the interdependent economy of the circum-Atlantic world in the nineteenth century, and I have attempted to keep such broad cultural connections in mind as I examine more closely local instances — namely, the historic representations of Louisiana, especially New Orleans, a leading port city on the circum-Caribbean and the larger circum-Atlantic rim. These representations include paintings, sculptures, newspaper illustrations and accounts, slave narratives, pornography, postcards, novels, poems, cityscapes, and — as a concession to my specialty — even plays, most particularly *The Octoroon; or, Life in Louisiana* by Dion Boucicault. I am aware that when these representations depict black people, they demonstrate what Henry Louis Gates Jr. concisely sums up as "the filter of racist images that [whites] placed over the black face of humanity like a mask over an actor."[4] Indeed, that is my point about such performances. I will not examine them in detail as works of art in themselves, though that might be usefully done, but rather as nodal points in a network of common but deeply problematic enunciations — the gestures, expressions, protocols, manners, habits, and attitudes — whereby a culture remembers and reinvents not only its most public relationships, but also its most intimate ones.

What I am hoping to demonstrate by this aggregation of materials I will call a "genealogy of performance." Genealogies of performance document the historical transmission and dissemination of cultural practices and attitudes through collective representations. They excavate the lineage of restored behaviors still visible in contemporary culture, in effect "writing the history of the present."[5] In that spirit, I will focus my attention on a performance genealogy that dates (at least in its most intense form) from antebellum New Orleans, a genealogy that remains visible in the spatial organization of the city, and in the behavior that preserves it and in the behavior that is preserved by it.

This behavior encompasses the exchange of human bodies, coded by race and gender, in an expanding marketplace filled with commodities of all kinds, and the concomitant commerce in the images and representations of that exchange throughout the circum-Atlantic world. I insist on the term circum-Atlantic, as opposed to trans-Atlantic, because, as the work of Paul Gilroy and others has shown, the creation and re-creation of the Atlantic world is truly a multicultural project, forged in what postmodern ethnography recognizes as "contact zones," those frontiers of encounter and exchange especially visible in a creolized interculture like New Orleans. As Gilroy puts it in broad terms: "A new structure of cultural exchange has been built up across the imperial networks which once played host to the triangular trade of sugar, slaves and capital."[6]

The genealogy of slave market performance in the contact zone of New Orleans may be traced through three overlapping phenomena of collective behavior and cultural memory: (1) behavioral vortices, the nodes of commerce and entertainment that draw in the public to certain urban "hot spots"; (2) surrogation, the tendency to substitute one commodity for another by symbolic transfer; and (3) displaced transmission, the adaptation of historic practices to changing conditions, in which popular behaviors are resituated in new locales.

Behavioral Vortices

One potentially informative guide to the genealogy of performance is the institutional convergence of business and pleasure. The staged exhibition of bodies for the purpose of selling those bodies is an obvious enough marketing strategy. Nineteenth-century historians of slavery traced the performance genealogy of the slave market to the ancient world, in which they found detailed precedents for contemporary practice. Thus W. O. Blake's *History of Slavery* describes Athens: "On this occasion [market day] the slaves were stationed in a circle in the marketplace, and the one whose turn it was to be sold, mounted a table, where he exhibited himself and was knocked down to the best bidder. The sales seem to have been conducted precisely like those of the present day in Richmond, Charleston, New Orleans, and other cities of the South."[7]

That the Greek and Roman exhibitions included nudity or seminudity likewise lent a legitimating dignity or, at least, time-honored pragmatism (in the eyes of the buyers), to the custom of exposing and examining all the surfaces of the slave's body: "They were placed on a raised stone, or table, so that every one might see and handle them, even if they did not wish to purchase them. Purchasers took care to have them stripped, for slave dealers had recourse to as many tricks to conceal defects, as a horse-jockey of modern times." The less obvious but more enduring strategy was to use the traffic in bodies to promote the sale of other commodities as well. This technique gave slave spectacles utility as drawing cards even for the customers who "did not

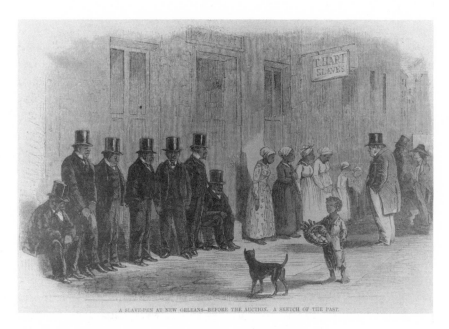

Figure 1. Slaves exhibited for sale, Exchange Alley, ca. 1860.
(*Harper's Weekly*, 1863)

wish to purchase" slaves, but who might be induced to spend their money in any number of other ways, their mimetic desire released by the eye-filling scenes of the public flesh market.

In antebellum New Orleans particularly, slave auctions proved a popular and highly theatrical spectacle. They took place in a magnificent theaterlike rotunda, designed and built for this purpose, in the St. Louis Hotel. The management provided music from a regular orchestra. Of the entertainment value of the slave auctions of the mid-1850s, the local press remarked: "Amusements seldom prove attractive here unless music is brought to the aid of other inducements to spend money."[8] The brokers also provided special theatrical costumes — formal wear for the male slaves and brightly colored dresses for the women. These are shown in an illustration from *Harper's Weekly* in which the preauction display of merchandise takes place on the street in "Exchange Alley," part of the St. Louis Hotel complex (Fig. 1). Captioned "A Slave-Pen at New Orleans — Before the Auction. A Sketch of the Past," the text and image "by a foreign artist" offer a retrospective view of slave marketing before the outbreak of the Civil War: "The men and women are well clothed, in their Sunday best — the men in blue cloth of good quality, with beaver hats; and the women in calico dresses, of more or less brilliancy, with silk bandana handkerchiefs bound round their heads. Placed in a row in a quiet thoroughfare, where, without interrupting the traffic, they may command a good chance of

Figure 2. St. Louis Hotel and Rotunda (*center left*), 1838. (Detail from aerial view of New Orleans, *Currier & Ives*, 1884; Historic New Orleans Collection, acc. no. 00.35)

transient custom, they stand through a great part of the day, subject to the inspection of the purchasing or non-purchasing passing crowd. They look heavy, perhaps a little sad, but not altogether unhappy."[9]

The apparent callousness of such accounts may be in part explained (though not in any way excused) by the very normality of the slave trade in the performance of daily life in New Orleans. The restored behavior of the marketplace created by its synergy a behavioral vortex in which human relationships could be drained of sympathetic imagination and shaped to the purposes of consumption and exchange. Under such conditions, the most intolerable of injustices may be made to seem natural and commonplace, and the most demented of spectacles "normal."

Normality does not happen by accident. Antebellum New Orleans, with the earliest American "suburb" linked to the urban hub by public transportation, was in some respects a prototypical circum-Atlantic city. In this urban plan, the Exchange complex (Fig. 2), surpassed in scale only by St. Louis

Cathedral in Jackson Square, comprised not only a commercial center but also a "ludic space," in Roland Barthes's propitious term, a crux in the semiotext of the cityscape. As Marvin Carlson has documented in *Places of Performance*, the urban confluence of pathways, nodes, and landmarks favors the theatrical and the performative.[10] I would interpret the performative space of the Exchange as a behavioral vortex of consumption and expenditure, material and symbolic. Into such behavioral vortices, the magnetic forces of commerce and pleasure suck the willing and unwilling alike. Although such a zone or district seems to offer a place for transgression, for things that could not happen otherwise or elsewhere, in fact what it provides is far more official: a place in which everyday practices and attitudes may be legitimated, "brought out into the open," reinforced, celebrated, or intensified. The "normal" thrives by exposure (and construction) through extraordinary performances. Why else dress up slaves in top hat and tails?

The behavioral vortex of the city center constitutes the collective, social version of the psychological paradox that masquerade is the most powerful form of self-expression. The vortex is a kind of permanent, spatially induced carnival. The Exchange was just such a center of cultural self-invention through restored behavior. Its promoters, ridiculing the old marketplaces of the French and Spanish colonial period (in which, under the unique Code Noir, slaves could earn the price of their freedom), touted the Exchange as the Louisianian staging point of a new circum-Atlantic empire: "We can't say how it is elsewhere, but here, the going-going-gone of the auctioneers, and the clinching 'bang' of their hammers, follow the rounds of our city and keep company with the streets, as the roll of the British drum is poetically said to follow the sun, and keep company with the hours around the world."[11] In this estimation, slave spectacles expand the centripetal "pull" of the behavioral vortex to the suburban perimeters of the metropolis and beyond.

The "eye" of the vortex, however, was the Rotunda of the St. Louis Hotel. The building was designed in 1838 by the French architect J. B. Pouilly as the anchor of one end of Exchange Alley. He conceived the alley as a mall-like promenade, cut through the French Quarter to link the Rotunda to Canal Street, a major thoroughfare of commerce and the dividing line between the Latin and Anglo-American zones of the city. The concept closely resembled a contemporary suburban shopping mall with "anchor" department stores at each end of a promenade of smaller specialty shops. Pouilly's proto-mall featured male-oriented ateliers such as tobacconists, gunsmiths, and fencing masters lining each side, mixed in with slave brokers, and leading to the imposing urban landmark of the St. Louis Hotel itself.

The hotel was a kind of homosocial pleasure dome with overlapping commercial and leisure attractions. The informative *Historical Sketch Book and*

Figure 3. Slave auction block, Rotunda, St. Louis Hotel, from a picture postcard, 1906. (Historic New Orleans Collection, acc. no. 1958.85.220)

Guide to New Orleans recalled: "This exchange not only contained the finest barroom in the city, but the principal auction mart, where slaves, stocks, real estate, and all other kinds of property were sold from noon to 3:00 P.M., the auctioneers crying their wares in a multitude of languages, the English, the French, and the Spanish predominating. The entire upper portion of the building was devoted exclusively to gambling and billiard rooms. . . . Adjoining the exchange [was] a cockpit."[12] The auction itself began with a "promenade," a kind of production number, in which the chorus of commodities paraded to the auction block (Fig. 3), led by a high-strutting master of ceremonies. According to an account in the Louisiana WPA oral history project: "Some of the traders kept a big, good-natured buck to lead the parade (of slaves to be sold) and uniforms for both men and women, so that the high hats, the riot of white, pink, red and blue would attract the attention of prospective buyers."[13]

The fancy costumes came off as the merchandise was stripped to permit close examination. In her narrative, former slave Lu Perkins recalls having been stripped at her own sale, noting that there was a practical motive for the exhibition of her upper body: "I 'members when they put me on the auction block. They pulled my dress down over my back to my waist, to show I ain't gashed and slashed up. That's to show you ain't a mean nigger." (In Louisiana it would also show if the slave had been branded with the sign of the fleur-de-

Figure 4. Unidentified artist, *Slave Auction*, 1850s. (Carnegie Museum of Art, Pittsburgh; gift of Mrs. Fitch Ingersoll, 58.4)

lis, the prescribed punishment under the Code Noir for running away.) Slaves on the block were sometimes expected to dance in order to show at once their liveliness and their docility. They also had a motive to increase their sale price: the more valuable the slave, the less willingness on the part of the master to inflict harm. In his slave narrative, James Martin recalls: "Then [the auctioneer] makes 'em hop, he makes 'em trot, he makes 'em jump. 'How much,' he yells, for this buck? A thousand? Eleven hundred? Twelve hundred dollars?' "[14]

Here resides a plausible, if as yet relatively unexplored, genealogy of performance. With music, dance, and seminudity, the slave auction, as a performance genre, might be said to have anticipated the development of American musical comedy. It certainly had important linkages to the black-faced minstrel show. These enacted the effacement of the cultural traditions of those whose very flesh signified its availability for display and consumption. But they were not the only descendants of slave auction performance art.

In terms of drawing power, the "fancy-girl" auctions, the sale of quadroons (one-quarter African-descended females) and octoroons (one-eighth African) proved an exceptionally popular New Orleans specialty, performed in an atmosphere charged not only with white privilege but also with male privilege (Fig. 4).[15] As anxious buyers bid up the price to five and even ten times that of a good field hand, the sale of relatively well-educated and relatively white

Figure 5. W. H. Brooke, *Sale of Estates, Pictures, and Slaves in the Rotunda, New Orleans*, 1854. (Historic New Orleans Collection, acc. no. 1953.149)

women into sexual bondage raised the erotic stakes higher in a public, democratic spectacle than in all but the most private pornographic exhibitions in aristocratic Europe.[16]

The compelling, even hypnotic fascination inspired by slave spectacles resides, I believe, in their violent, triangular conjunction of money, property, and flesh. In the Rotunda of the St. Louis Hotel, as it was represented by an engraving in 1854, three kinds of property go under the gavel at once: pictures on the left, real estate on the right, and slaves in the middle (Fig. 5). In the dramatic lighting of the classical, pantheonlike dome, the centrality of naked flesh signifies the abundant availability of all commodities: everything can be put up for sale, and everything can be examined and handled even by those who are "just looking." In the staging of New Orleans slave auctions, there is a fiercely laminating adhesion of bodies and objects, the individual desire for pleasure and the collective desire to compete for possession. As competitions between men, the auctions seethe with the potential for homosocial violence.

As theatrical spectacle, they materialize the most intense of symbolic transactions in circum-Atlantic culture: money transforms flesh into property, property transforms flesh into money, flesh transforms money into property.

Surrogation

One of the nineteenth-century circum-Atlantic world's greatest showmen certainly saw the dramatic possibilities of the "fancy-girl" auctions. Dion Boucicault, the Franco-Anglo-Irish dramatist, wrote the *The Octoroon; or, Life in Louisiana* (1859) around such a sensational scene. His melodrama retails the plot of Captain Mayne Reid's romance *The Quadroon; or, A Lover's Adventures in Louisiana* (1856), which was itself only one of dozens of novels, biographies, and other representations dealing with "tragic" octoroon or quadroon heroines, beginning with Hildreth's *The Slave* (1836).[17] In both Boucicault's play and Reid's novel, a rare beauty of delicate manners and mixed race, legally exposed by the foreclosure of a mismanaged plantation, finds herself auctioned off as a slave to the highest bidder, who turns out to be the mustache-twirling villain. Reid's hero rescues the quadroon, and then he marries her. Boucicault reversed the outcome for the New York version of the play: the octoroon (Zoe) takes poison moments before the letter of credit, saving the plantation, arrives. I am interested in a close reading of the auction scene particularly because it illustrates the process of symbolic substitution — of a white-appearing body for a black one, of gender difference for racial difference, and of one commodity for another — that I want to call "surrogation."

The Octoroon has recently been proposed as an exemplary work in the establishment of a new American dramatic canon, one of a small group of plays that "formed the basis for the 'Americanization' of American drama after the Civil War had come to an end."[18] I do not challenge this view, but I want to emphasize the limitations of the context in which such an argument unfolds. To my way of thinking, the connections between Dion Boucicault's play and any other works in an emerging American theatrical canon seem important mainly as they participate in the broader conception of a performance genealogy, one that acknowledges that such a work will constitute, in varying degrees, "a cultural act, a critical perspective, a political intervention." By this I do not mean simply the depiction of a general historical and cultural "background," but rather the discovery of intersecting networks of practices, attitudes, actions, and meanings, those that reside in specific cultural conditions and those that become visible by means of performance.

Boucicault's own residence in New Orleans, at the height of the spectacular slave auctions of the mid-1850s, offers an example of how the performance of everyday life may be reconstructed for the stage. He made his New Orleans debut on January 23, 1855, though his plays had long been popular in the

Crescent City before his arrival in person. Looking for a likely venue to establish a permanent company, Boucicault secured local backing and assumed the role of actor-manager-playwright of the Gaiety Theatre, which opened on December 1, 1855.[19] The big success of the season was the acting of Boucicault's wife, Agnes Robertson. She excelled in roles, often written for her by her husband, in which she could take on several different identities. In *The Chameleon*, her Gaiety debut, she played the part of an actress who impersonates three different characters to win the heart of her skeptical father-in-law to be. She followed up this role with two other star vehicles, *The Cat Changed into a Woman* and *Violet; or, The Life of an Actress*.[20] Her ability to suggest liminality (a "betwixt-and-betweenness") and the consequent instability but great attractiveness of her image made Robertson's acting style particularly amenable to surrogation, the substitution of one symbolic identity for another.

New Orleans high society welcomed Boucicault and Robertson hospitably, a source of great local bitterness after the premiere of the play that purported to show contemporary "Life in Louisiana." Boucicault could not help but observe the weird demimonde of plaçage, the Creole custom of arranging extramarital liaisons with educated mulatas: some New Orleans theaters set aside one performance a week for gentlemen and their quadroon mistresses; at these miscegenist fêtes, the managements desegregated the seating and disinvited white women.[21]

After a brief return appearance in 1857, Boucicault left New Orleans for brighter prospects in New York and London. One of the brightest of these was the chance to craft another role for Agnes Robertson—Zoe—in which she could excel in her specialty of multiple identity, a poised walk along the borders of difference, before the clarifying moments of the final tableau, when she is purified by death: "O! George, you may, without a blush, confess your love for the Octoroon!"[22] The *Daily Picayune*, drawing on accounts of the production in the abolitionist papers in the North, responded with a savagely vituperative review, headed "The Last of Mr. Boucicault," especially noting Robertson's willowy rendering of the title role as "a delicately colored young female, enwrapped in white muslin, sentiment, and poetry."[23]

The Octoroon opened at the Winter Garden Theatre in New York City on December 6, 1859, four days after the execution of John Brown. Two years later, as the Civil War raged in the United States, Boucicault took his play to London, where it initially failed because the audience rejected the unhappy ending. They could not except Agnes Robertson's death in any role. Boucicault cobbled together a new version, "composed by the Public," as he put it, "and edited by the Author," in which the octoroon revives.[24] One of the most widely reproduced illustrations of a scene from that copious archive of sensation that Michael Booth calls "Victorian spectacular theatre" appeared in the

Figure 6. *The Octoroon*, Adelphi Theatre, *London Illustrated News*, November 30, 1861. (Howard Tilton Memorial Library, Tulane University)

London Illustrated News (Fig. 6), but more than a simple spectacle, the image is a *realization* in the deep sense that Martin Meisel has imparted to that word.[25] The scene depicts a climactic moment from Act III of *The Octoroon* in which Zoe, amid the financial collapse of Terrebone Plantation, stands on a table in the mansion she once graced. It represents onstage the restored behavior of the slave auctions of the New Orleans Exchange, the transformation of cash into flesh and of flesh into property.

What happens to Zoe happens in a room filled with men, both spectators and combatants, who assemble for the purpose of selling "Estates, Pictures, and Slaves." Boucicault's placement of the public auction in the private parlor (though no doubt motivated in part by scenic economy) brings the scene of slavery "home" into the domestic sphere, a setting that middle-class audiences outside the South could also recognize. Many authors appropriated the ever-useful "mortgage melodrama" masterplot (which Chekhov warmed over in *The Cherry Orchard*), a surefire appeal to bourgeois anxieties of displacement, but the "tragic octoroon" variant substituted expendable female bodies for the foreclosed properties of the melodramatic master narrative.

What Boucicault engineers in the buildup to the auction scene is a symbolic and material linkage between the representation of race and the representation of gender. Both become commodities, but it is the scarcely visible presence of black "blood" that provides the signifier of commodification. When George ardently proposes marriage, Zoe takes her somewhat obtuse lover on a frank fact-finding tour of her body, including her extraordinary blood count:

> *Zoe*: And what shall I say? I — my mother was — no, no — not her! Why should I refer the blame to her? George, do you see that hand you hold? look at these fingers; do you see the nails are a bluish tinge?
> *George*: Yes, near the quick there is a faint blue mark.
> *Zoe*: Look in my eyes; is not the same color in the white?
> *George*: It is their beauty.
> *Zoe*: Could you see the roots of my hair you would see the same dark, fatal mark. Do you know what that is?
> *George*: No.
> *Zoe*: That is the ineffaceable curse of Cain. Of the blood that feeds my heart, one drop in eight is black — bright red as the rest may be, that one drop poisons all the flood; those seven bright drops give me love like yours--hope like yours — ambition like yours — life hung with passions like dew-drops in the morning flowers; but the one black drop gives me despair, for I'm an unclean thing — forbidden by the laws — I'm an Octoroon! (pp. 16–17)

The body of the white-appearing octoroon (played by the fascinatingly liminal Agnes Robertson) offers itself as the crucible in which a strange alchemy of cultural surrogation takes place. In the defining event of commercial exchange, from flesh to property, the object of desire mutates and transforms itself, from African to Woman: its nearly invisible but fatal blackness makes it available; its whiteness somehow makes it clean.

Such a slave spectacle is, I think, as American as baseball. Boucicault drew on a large and growing repository of images and descriptions of this pathetic and erotic scene.[26] The hostile review of the New York octoroon in the *New Orleans Daily Picayune* referred to "a delicately colored young female, enwrapped in white muslin." In the competing images of the slave auction scene, circulated in high-culture venues through easel paintings and sculptures of the period, the delicately colored young female was more often unwrapped than enwrapped. The image of Robertson's Zoe, fully clothed on the auction block, must be viewed in the context of antebellum slave sales and their representation in several popular circum-Atlantic media. In that context, Zoe would have to strip, and she would be stripped by association in the minds of the viewers, as she stepped up on the tabletop.[27]

Jean-Léon Gérôme's orientalizing *Slave Market* of 1856 stands in for many widely exhibited paintings in this genre (Fig. 7). As the prospective buyers inspect the mouth of the slave, their focus of attention displaces the gaze of the

Figure 7. Jean-Léon Gérôme, *Slave Market*, Salon, 1856. (Sterling and Francine Clark Art Institute, Williamstown, Mass.)

beholder down to the chastely depiliated pudendum. In the social semiotics of Victorian nudity, the absence of pubic hair, such as in those smoothly modeled plaster casts of classical statues that ruined John Ruskin's wedding night, signified purity. This signifier of innocence promised a body as yet untouched — acquiescent, passive, virginal, ownable — the body of a slave, the body of a child. Such a strong cultural signification marks American sculptor John Bell's masterpiece, *The Octoroon*, exhibited at the Royal Academy in 1868 (Fig. 8). The octoroon's smooth skin glows childlike and white, Bell's alabaster marble medium helping here to reinforce his message. That message seems to be that slavery is more tragic and exciting when it is suffered by innocent white women. The octoroon repines unresistingly in the almost ornamental chains of her bondage. Like Rapunzel, she sweetly, and very carefully, lets down her hair.

"The Quadroon Girl" by Henry Wadsworth Longfellow retails many of the same images but with the added narrative complication that the unnamed girl is being sold off in the front parlor by her bankrupt planter father. Three of Longfellow's twelve stanzas allow the reader to catch his drift:

Her eyes were large, and full of light,
Her arms and neck were bare;
No garment she wore save a kirtle bright,
And her own long, raven hair.

And on her lips there played a smile
As holy, meek, and faint,
As lights in some cathedral aisle
The features of a saint.

"The soil is barren, — the farm is old,"
The thoughtful planter said;
Then looked upon the Slaver's gold,
And then upon the maid.[28]

The liminal status of the quadroon girl opens up a space for erotic play even in the most earnest of abolitionist tracts, the kind of play facilitated by the duality of the subject — white and black, child and woman, angel and wench. It was through this kind of weirdly bifurcated imagery that the circum-Atlantic world viewed slavery and race in America.

To the public nudity by association in the auction scene of *The Octoroon*, Boucicault adds another erotic twist. This one amplifies the racial and gendered doubling of the octoroon by playing her off sexually against a "white" woman. Zoe stands at the apex of a compositional triangle (see Fig. 6). She is anchored on one side by the scene of gladiatorial male violence (between

Figure 8. John Bell, *The Octoroon*, Royal Academy, 1868. (Blackburn Museum and Art Gallery, Lancashire, England)

Figure 9. George Hare, *The Victory of Faith*, Royal Academy, 1891.
(National Gallery of Victoria, Melbourne)

M'Closky, the villain, and George, her boyfriend, backed up by Salem Scud-
der, the amiably murderous Yankee Jonathan). On the other side she is anchored by the neighboring plantation belle Dora Sunnyside's heaving bosom.
All those along the base of the triangle, including Dora, bid on Zoe. Dora's bid
intensifies the erotic effects of the scene by linking the two women sexually.
Dora's participation in the male-centered activity of bidding on property at
an auction makes hers a kind of breeches role, recalling that the comparable scene in the source novel, Reid's *Quadroon*, has the Dora character cross-
dress so that she can enter the Rotunda at the St. Louis Hotel to procure the
slave girl.[29]

The implicitly lesbian coupling of two women, one fair the other dark,
proliferates in the Victorian erotica of the circum-Atlantic exchange. For
instance, in a painting entitled *The Victory of Faith*, the Royal Academician
St. George Hare exploits this erotic theme in the guise of a religious painting
(Fig. 9). The otherwise puzzling title is explained by the narrative program,
which invites the beholder to believe that these nudes represent two Christian
virgins in ancient Rome, sleeping innocently together in the holding pen
of the Colisseum on the last night before their fatal rendezvous with the
lions. The presence of the (unchained) black girl, on which the grasp of the
white girl's hand insists, insinuates what the unrepresentability of pubic hair
cannot — the pressure of sexual desire from within even the whitest body. The

sexualized virgin martyr, the White Goddess, rises transcendent from the flesh of her black double.

The Victory of Faith epitomizes the interracial and sexual doubling whereby the "tragic" sale of white women displaces the representation of black slave sales, in which the generic prototypes of white culture's musical comedy predominates. The scene from Boucicault's *Octoroon* is so rich because it shows in action this process of surrogation (of white for black) and transformation (from buffo comedy to noble tragedy). Obscured in the corner of the room (Fig. 6, stage right) stand the other slaves who have been on the block earlier in the scene: Lot "No. 1" is Solon; Lot "No. 2, the yellow girl Grace, with two children — Saul, aged four, Victoria five (They get on the table)." These slaves happily celebrate their good fortune when they are sold as a family; then 'Ole Pete, the Uncle Tom character, stands on the block as Lot "No. 3," and he dances cheerfully to show how spry he is and raise his bid accordingly (pp. 27–28). But all of this is preparatory to the sale of Zoe: when she stands on the table, the tone of the scene shifts from minstrelsy to melodrama, the tragic heroine literally taking stage, pushing the comic supernumeraries off right. Even from a slave sale, black people are excluded.

To accomplish such a coup de théâtre, Boucicault must purify Zoe of her own traces of African blood. He does this by having her die by her own hand and then — miraculously — turn white. As Zoe expires, Dora reverently reports: "Her eyes have changed color"; 'Ole Pete explains, "Dat's what her soul's gwine do. It's going up dar, whar dere's no line atween folks" (p. 39). Out of the ruptured chrysalis of the octoroon's body floats a miraculous White Goddess.

Displaced Transmission

In terms of the genealogy of performance, New Orleans slave spectacles themselves undergo a process not of complete cessation, but of transformation and displacement. I believe that slavery was explicitly and officially sexualized — and thereby at least symbolically recuperated — in the development of legally sanctioned prostitution during the post-Reconstruction 1880s. Unique in the history of American "Tenderloin" or "red light" districts, the district that came to be known as Storyville was established by city ordinance, and it was included as an important hub in the new streetcar system. Its architecturally elaborate houses, built from the ground up to serve their designated purpose and marked by prominent rooflines featuring Victorian cupolas, made Storyville an important urban and even civic landmark and nodal point.

In the genealogy of New Orleanian vortices of behavior, Storyville succeeds Exchange Alley and the St. Louis Hotel, turning the principal ludic space on its axis and moving it a few blocks over, reconstituting the homosocial pleasure dome in the post-Reconstruction era of Southern Redemption and its explosive mania about race. The most prominent cupola on the skyline belonged to Miss Lulu White's Mahogany Hall, a brothel specializing in mixed-race women and heavily advertised as "The Octoroon Club." The whorehouses published directories or catalogs (such as the notorious "Blue Book") that advertised specialized sexual services in highly coded language. In their self-representation, if that is what it is, the women stress their skills as performers and their racial categories: "The beautiful Estelle Russell, now a member of high standing in Miss White's famous Octoroon Club, a few years ago one of the leading stars in Sam T. Jack's Creole Show. . . . Emma Sears . . . the colored Carmencita . . . [a]s a tamborine dancer she has no superior and very few equals. Tall, graceful, winning."[30] The photo-portraits illustrating the "Blue Books" closely resemble the Victorian theatrical visiting cards that Laurence Senelick has recently brought to light.[31] In the normalizing courtesies of business cards and consumer guides, the flesh market is once again subsumed into the "legitimate" economy of the city: at its peak, Storyville employed over a thousand people; it promoted tourism and well-controlled shore leaves for the U.S. Navy; it became, like a family dinner at Antoine's, a local tradition for some, a place for fathers to initiate their sons into a privileged "knowledge of the world" and of their own proper place in it as men.

Some Storyville brothels offered special performances, called "Circuses," three nights per week. The musical accompaniment to such entertainments remain important in the early history of jazz music (Lulu White's Mahogany Hall furniture is still in use in the reading room of the Hogan Jazz Archives at Tulane University). In one photograph, the girls gather around the piano, which is played by none other than Jelly Roll Morton (Fig. 10). According to Mr. Jelly Roll's own oral history, the staging here is more demure than usual, for the whores danced naked. The madam put up a screen between the piano and the stage, but Mr. Jelly Roll cut a hole so that he could see the Circus. The word he used to describe what he saw was "cruel": "I worked for all the houses, even Emma Johnson's Circus House, where the guests got everything from soup to nuts. They did a lot of uncultured things then that probably couldn't be mentioned, and the irony part of it, they always picked the youngest and most beautiful girls to do them right before the eyes of everybody."[32] The genealogy of New Orleans brothel performances has roots deep in representations and behaviors spawned in the slave culture of the antebellum period — and in the reconstructed memories and restored behaviors consciously evoking that period. Storyville establishments featured auctions in which young girls and even children, advertised as "Virgins," were put up on front-parlor tables and gaveled down to the top bidder.

Ernest J. Bellocq photographed many of the women in Storyville, and his fragile, haunting images suggest the performative character of the self-

Figure 10. Jelly Roll Morton plays piano at Hilma Burt's Mirror Ballroom, ca. 1904. (William Ransom Hogan Jazz Archive, Tulane University)

representation of the sex-workers. Bellocq's reclining nude portrait of a young girl (the scene restaged with Brooke Shields by Louis Malle in the film *Pretty Baby*) evokes the imagery of vulnerability and availability that also character-ized the depictions of the tragic octoroon (Fig. 11). She is the recumbent version of John Bell's statue (cf. Fig. 8), except that wherever the black or octoroon woman is absent, as she apparently is from this photograph, pubic hair tends to appear. The pose in Bellocq's photo quotes another strong tradi-tion of erotic representation in European painting, the reclining nude Venus and her clothed handmaiden, so there is an empty space in Bellocq's composi-tion that connoisseurs could reasonably be expected to fill in (Fig. 12). The image of the black woman in the upper right corner of Edouard Manet's noto-rious painting of a sixteen-year-old white prostitute, *Olympia*, insists on con-structing the linkages between the diverse flesh markets throughout circum-Atlantic culture. But as much as the image insists, its beholders erased it. The West Indian woman (identified by her headdress) became all but invisible to subsequent commentators — except to those who praised Manet for his formal compositional effects of light and shade — evidence of the success of surroga-tion as cultural displacement.[33]

In the Storyville sex circuses, other popular specialities included "dark and

68 **Joseph R. Roach**

Figure 11. Storyville prostitute. (Photo by Ernest Bellocq; Howard Tilton Memorial Library, Tulane University)

fair" lesbian acts and even displays of beastiality. The New Orleans historian Al Rose has interviewed a number of those prostitutes who lived into the 1950s and 1960s. Their histories read something like slave narratives, especially when their sexual initiation included being auctioned off like the antebellum "fancy girls." One of Rose's informants speaks unsentimentally and explicitly about her sale on the block at Emma Johnson's Circus in about 1915 or 1916, when she was about twelve years old:

> I was in the circus two or three nights a week. There was another kid my age . . . Liz. . . . We used to work together. By this time we were getting a little figure and looked pretty good . . . and neither one of us was afraid to do them things the johns liked, so we'd get a hundred a night to be in the circus. My mother was in the circus, too. She's the one who used to fuck the pony. Emma kept a stable in the yard and a colored man, Wash, used to take care of the two ponies and the horse. In the daytime me and Liz rode the ponies around the yard. . . . Ain't that something?
>
> So, Emma . . . made a speech about me and Liz and how everybody in the District knew we was virgins, even though we did all these other things and

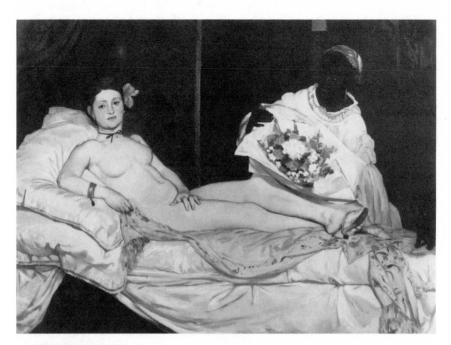

Figure 12. Edouard Manet, *Olympia*, 1863. (Musée d'Orsay, Paris)

that if the price was right, tonight was the night and she'd have an auction. Some snotty kid bid a dollar and Emma had one of the floor men slug him and throw him out in the street. One man bid the both of us in, honest to God, for seven hundred and seventy-five dollars each! A lot of johns bid, and he wasn't gonna be satisfied with just one. He bought us both. Well, we went upstairs with him. He wanted us both together, and you know how it is, we thought he ought to be entitled to somethin' for all that money, so we came on with everything we could think of, includin' the dyke act. . . . We did a dance we had worked out where we jerked ourselves and each other off.[34]

Theater historians, alert to the particulars of stage business, will appreciate the detail in which this virtuosic performance is recorded. It actually took two nights, in deference to the premature exhaustion of the patron. The "dyke act," a pornographic mainstay, signals the availability of the girls, their readiness for defloration, while reiterating their status intacta, their Sapphic innocence of other penises (Fig. 13). With their purchase comes a fantasy of their possession, an echo of the absolute ownership once possible under the old regime:

> The Slaver led her from the door,
> He led her by the hand,
> To be his slave and paramour
> In a strange and distant land.[35]

Joseph R. Roach

GOOD GOD!
The Crimes of Sodom and Gomorrah Discounted.

Figure 13. Cover story, *The Mascot*, Storyville, 1893. (Howard Tilton Memorial Library, Tulane University)

In New Orleans, the transmission of black slavery was displaced to the white variety in more direct and literal ways than in other places. As the Jim Crow laws developed, the liaisons permitted in Storyville became more rigorously segregated. Just before the district closed down in 1917, African-descended women were forbidden to work in white-only brothels.

To this day, however, the urban behavioral vortex is still propelled by energies unleashed by slavery, white and black. The question is not whether slavery still exists but whether or not people still treat each other as if it did. Reconstituted on Bourbon Street, New Orleans's more recent "ludic space," as the work of Les Wade has shown, Storyville lives symbolically in such pseudo-fleshpots and jazz joints as Lulu White's Mahogany Hall and Storyville Lounge — "Girls, Girls, Girls." These alternate with strip clubs and T-shirt emporia to resituate the homosocial pleasure zone as synecdoche for the entire city of New Orleans. This Afro-Caribbean capital, which has now somehow constructed itself as the nation's libido (i.e., "The Big Easy"), publishes some of the most bizarre promotional literature in the history of American boosterism. Les Wade found this chamber of commerce bon mot in a recent tourbook: "A corpulent hostess, patted and daubed with rouge, New Orleans reclines along the banks of the wide river, straining her corsets of convention and drawing her admirers to her with a languid gesture."[36]

In such a formulation, the city of New Orleans itself becomes the ludic space, the behavioral vortex, for the rest of the nation. If that is really so, then my theory of displaced transmission would predict that the homosocial pleasure dome must have reconstituted itself in some significant and prominent way in a vortex-inducing landmark or node. Following out the logic of my line of speculation on the genealogy of antebellum performance, I believe that it has. Roughly equidistant by only a few city blocks from the sites of both the St. Louis Exchange and Storyville, the Louisiana Superdome consummates the performance genealogy of the North American traffic in money and flesh (Fig. 14). It is the cyclonic center of mall-like avenues of shops and department stores, and at times of peak use it becomes a prime procurer of trade for prostitutes during such events as tractor pulls, trade shows, and the 1988 Republican National Convention. It is also the most prominent stage for North America's most popular national spectacle, NFL football. Such spectacles — the commodification of flesh in an economy of ever more highly specialized greed — display immensely valuable black bodies sweating for white people who still unblinkingly call themselves "owners."

In the postmodern circum-Atlantic world of late capitalism, what Paul Gilroy calls "the sound system culture" both symbolizes and embodies the syncretism whereby African, North American, Caribbean, and European forms circulate together in a plagiarized interculture. Sound system culture "re-

Figure 14. Louisiana Superdome. (Greater New Orleans Tourist and Convention Commission, Inc.)

defines the meaning of performance by separating the input of the artist who originally made the recording from the equally important work of those who adapt and rework it so that it directly expresses the moment in which it is being consumed."[37] The image of Boucicault's tragic octoroon, borne up "Like a Virgin" to displace the experience of African Americans with the image of a White Goddess, has yet to exhaust its powers of re-circulation (Fig. 15). Madonna's sixty-million-dollar contract with Time-Warner is worth pondering in the context of auctions, recycled commodities, and displaced spectacles. Flesh sells — it sells itself, and more important it sells everything else:

> They can beg and they can plead
> But they can't see the light
> It's the boy with the cold hard cash
> Who's always Mister Right
>
> For we are living in a material world
> And I'm a Material Girl.[38]

As the White Goddess, Madonna rides the crest of a dark wave of Afrocentric cultural performances. She sings their songs and dances their dances, appropriating their rhythms and in their styles. She is their surrogate. Like much of the rest of the country, the multibillion-dollar entertainment industry is

Figure 15. Madonna and her *Blond Ambition* dancers. (London Features)

built by the irregularly remunerated sweat of African Americans. They carry this culture on their backs, a fact that apparently sometimes still makes them as hard to see as they were in the slave auction scene of Boucicault's melodrama. If the words performance and culture have experienced double-digit inflation, perhaps it is because the genealogical significance and power of their interdependence in fixing the value of human exchange is now beginning to be understood. To transmit means not only to broadcast, but also to pass along through time.

Notes

1. John W. Kronik, Editor's Note, *PMLA* 107 (1992): 425.

2. Joseph R. Roach, "Mardi Gras Indians and Others: Genealogies of American Performance," *Theatre Journal* 44 (1992): 461–83.

3. Richard Schechner, *Between Theater and Anthropology* (Philadelphia: University of Pennsylvania Press, 1985), pp. 36–38; Michel de Certeau, *The Practice of Everyday Life*, translated by Steven Rendall (Berkeley: University of California Press, 1984), esp. "Walking in the City," pp. 91–110.

4. Henry Louis Gates Jr., "The Face and Voice of Blackness," in *Facing History: The Black Image in American Art, 1710–1940*, edited by Guy C. McElroy (Washington, D.C.: Corcoran Gallery of Art, 1990), p. xxix.

5. Michel Foucault, *Discipline and Punish: The Birth of the Prison*, translated by Alan Sheridan (New York: Vintage Books, 1979), p. 31.

6. Paul Gilroy, *"There Ain't No Black in the Union Jack": The Cultural Politics of Race and Nation* (Chicago: University of Chicago Press, 1987), p. 157. On "contact zones," see Dwight Conquergood, "Rethinking Ethnography: Towards a Critical Cultural Politics," *Communication Monographs* 58 (1991): 184–86. For the construction of the trans-Atlantic world in earlier periods, see Jean-Christophe Agnew, *Worlds Apart: The Market and the Theater in Anglo-American Thought, 1550–1750* (Cambridge: Cambridge University Press, 1986).

7. W. O. Blake, *The History of Slavery and the Slave Trade, Ancient and Modern* (1857; reprint, Columbus, Ohio: H. Miller, 1861), pp. 29, 50.

8. *Daily Picayune*, March 26, 1853.

9. *Harper's Weekly*, January 21, 1863.

10. Marvin Carlson, *Places of Performance: The Semiotics of Theatre Architecture* (Ithaca: Cornell University Press, 1989), pp. 10–11.

11. *Daily Picayune*, February 20, 1853.

12. *Historical Sketch Book and Guide to New Orleans and Environs* (New York: Will H. Coleman, 1885), p. 77.

13. *Gumbo Ya-Ya: A Collection of Louisiana Folk Tales*, compiled by Lyle Saxon, Edward Dreyer, and Robert Tallant (1945; reprint, Gretna: Pelican Publishing Co., 1988), p. 226.

14. *Bullwhip Days: The Slaves Remember, an Oral History*, edited by James Mellon (New York: Avon Books, 1988), pp. 291–92.

15. Eugene D. Genovese, *Roll, Jordan, Roll: The World the Slaves Made* (New York: Pantheon Books, 1972), pp. 416–17.

16. See Laurence Senelick, "The Erotic Bondage of Serf Theatre," *Russian Review* 50 (1991): 24–34.

17. Jules Zanger, "The 'Tragic Octoroon' in Pre–Civil War Fiction," *American Quarterly* 18 (1966): 63–70.

18. Heinz Kosok, "Dion Boucicault's 'American' Plays: Considerations on Defining National Literatures in English," in *Literature and the Art of Creation*, edited by Robert Welch and Suheil Badi Bushrui (Totowa, N.J.: Barnes and Noble, 1988), p. 95.

19. *American Theatre Companies, 1749–1887*, edited by Weldon Durham (New York: Greenwood Press, 1986), p. 502.

20. *Daily Picayune*, December 20, 1855, January 14, 1856.

21. John A. Kendall, *The Golden Age of New Orleans Theatre* (Baton Rouge: Louisiana State University Press, 1952), pp. 38–39.

22. *The Octoroon; or, Life in Louisiana* (1861; reprint, Miami, Fla.: Mnemosyne Publishing Company, 1969), p. 40. Subsequent citations of this edition will be given in the text.

23. *Daily Picayune*, December 24, 1859.

24. John A. Degen, "How to End *The Octoroon*," *Theatre Journal* 27 (1975): 170–78.

25. Michael Booth, *Victorian Spectacular Theatre* (London: Routledge, 1981); Martin Meisel, *Realizations: Narrative, Pictorial, and Theatrical Arts in Nineteenth-Century England* (Princeton, N.J.: Princeton University Press, 1983).

26. See Hugh Honour, *The Image of the Black in Western Art*, vol. 4, part 1, "Slaves and Liberators"; part 2, "Black Models and White Myths" (Cambridge: Harvard University Press, 1989).

27. See Tracy C. Davis, "The Spectacle of Absent Costume: Nudity on the Victorian Stage," *New Theatre Quarterly* 20 (1989): 321–33.

28. Henry Wadsworth Longfellow, "The Quadroon Girl," in *The Complete Poetical Works* (Boston: Houghton, Mifflin, 1902), p. 28.

29. Captain Mayne Reid, *The Quadroon; or, A Lover's Adventures in Louisiana* (New York: Robert M. De Witt, 1856), pp. 308–9.

30. Lulu White's "Octoroon Club" brochure, quoted in Al Rose, *Storyville, New Orleans* (Tuscaloosa: University of Alabama Press, 1974), p. 126.

31. Laurence Senelick, "Eroticism in Early Theatrical Photography," *Theatre History Studies* 11 (1991): 1–50.

32. Alan Lomax, *Mister Jelly Roll: The Fortunes of Jelly Roll Morton, New Orleans Creole and "Inventor of Jazz"* (New York: Duell, Sloan, and Pearce, 1950), p. 127.

33. Albert Boime, *The Art of Exclusion: Representing Blacks in the Nineteenth Century* (Washington. D.C.: Smithsonian Institution Press, 1990), pp. 2–4. See Hollis Clayson, *Painted Love: Prostitution in French Art of the Impressionist Era* (New Haven: Yale University Press, 1991), pp. 6, 16.

34. Quoted in Rose, *Storyville*, pp. 149–50.

35. Longfellow, "The Quadroon Girl," p. 28.

36. Les Wade, "New Orleans French Theatre and Its Cultural Containment: The Origins of Bourbon Street Burlesque," forthcoming in *L'Annuaire théâtral: Revue d'histoire et de recherche.*

37. Gilroy, *"There Ain't No Black in the Union Jack,"* p. 165.

38. Madonna, "Material Girl," from *Like a Virgin* (1985).

Reading the Minister's Remains

Investigations into the Death of the Honourable Minister

John Robert Ouko in Kenya, February 1990

DAVID WILLIAM COHEN & E. S. ATIENO ODHIAMBO

On Thursday evening, February 15, 1990, the *Voice of Kenya* radio and television services issued an astonishing announcement: "The family of the minister for foreign affairs and international cooperation, Dr. Robert Ouko, has reported that the minister left his Koru home [in western Kenya] last Tuesday, February 13, in the morning, and has not been seen since. Could Dr. Ouko please contact his family or the nearest police station? Any member of the public who might have any information as to the minister's whereabouts should report to the nearest police station."

The next day President Daniel arap Moi issued additional statements,[1] including one formally announcing the death of his minister of foreign affairs:

> It is with profound sorrow that I have to announce the death of the Honourable Robert Ouko, minister for foreign affairs and international cooperation and member of parliament for Kisumu Town.
>
> On learning of the report of his disappearance on Wednesday, the government mounted an intensive search for Dr. Ouko, using all means at its disposal.
>
> Dr. Ouko's partly burnt body was discovered today six kilometres away from his Koru home in circumstances which at the moment suggest foul play.
>
> Further investigations are being conducted into the death of the Hon. Dr. Ouko but I would like to assure the public that anyone who may be associated with this horrible event will most certainly be apprehended and brought to justice.

Within hours of President Moi's February 16 statement, amid interpretations of early government announcements that seemed to reckon Ouko's death a suicide — and with the eruption of civil disturbances across Kenya and a rising tide of popular anger — the president invited a team from Great Britain's Scotland Yard to investigate Ouko's death. The British team, under the direction of Detective Superintendent John H. B. Troon, began its work on February 21, undertaking its own pathological examination just before Ouko's body was moved, on February 23, from a Nairobi funeral home to the town of Kisumu and then to Koru for burial on February 24. The Scotland Yard contingent completed its investigation in mid-June 1990. After a lengthy standoff with the attorney general of Kenya over the proprieties of transmittal, Troon, on Monday, September 20, 1990, delivered — into the hands of a still reticent, virtually reclusive, attorney general — a final (sealed) report dated August 28.[2]

The Scotland Yard investigation was one of five major inquiries into Ouko's death to date, the first having been begun by the Kenyan Criminal Investigation Department (CID) and Special Branch after the discovery of Ouko's disappearance. There also were several lesser inquiries. Among the major probes was the lengthy prosecution of Jonah Anguka, a former district commissioner, on charges of murdering Robert Ouko.

Emphasizing from the beginning his interest in communicating the circumstances of Ouko's death to the Kenyan people, President Moi nevertheless decided to withhold Scotland Yard's findings from the public. Over the months of the Yard's active investigation, followed by further months of waiting for the presentation and release of the report, there was enormous speculation in the press at home and abroad, as well as in the streets, bars, buses, and taxis of Kenya, about the discoveries of Scotland Yard. Indeed, every Kenyan newspaper was preoccupied with the case for several years. Over and over, some publications played up the grizzly details of the corpse. Others, particularly the weekly and monthly journals, saw the evolution of the Ouko investigation in the context of human rights and multiparty campaigns, essentially putting the government itself on trial concerning its ability to carry out an independent and successful investigation.

The *Nairobi Law Monthly* was a key player, carrying a number of stories critical of the government over the two years following the tragedy. The *Monthly* had an almost surreal relationship to the circumstances surrounding Ouko's death, for — on the minister's last full day on earth — the journal's celebrated and imprisoned editor, Gitobu Imanyara, was presented the Robert F. Kennedy Prize in Human Rights by Ethel Kennedy and Kerry Kennedy Cuomo, who went to Nairobi to present the award to Gitobu when he was not allowed to travel to the United States to receive it. A number of those later implicated in Ouko's death were lunching with the Kennedys in Nairobi just thirteen hours before his disappearance.

On October 2, 1990, with the Scotland Yard report still withheld from the public and with rumors and controversy spiraling, President Moi appointed a judicial commission of inquiry, under the chairmanship of Justice John Evans Gicheru of the Kenyan Court of Appeals, to investigate Minister Ouko's disappearance and death.[3] Over a 246-day period, the commission took evidence from 172 witnesses, meeting openly and being reported extensively in the press. But the Gicheru Commission was dissolved by the president on November 26, 1991, and an "official account" of its work was never released. Moi then called for intensive police investigations leading to indictments and prosecutions.

On the same day President Moi dissolved the Gicheru Commission, several prominent and powerful individuals—Jonah Anguka, district commissioner, Nakuru; Nicholas Biwott, minister of industry; and Hezekiah Oyugi, permanent secretary in the Office of the President, who was responsible for provincial administration and internal security—were arrested. These detentions followed on the heels of a host of others, including many witnesses deposed by the commission, who were picked up by the police in the last days of the Gicheru hearings. Among those detained during that new wave of arrests was George Oraro, senior counsel to the Ouko family (the immediate family, not the extended one), who had represented it before the Gicheru Commission. The arrest of Oraro was recognized by commission members as part of an accelerating campaign to intimidate and undermine them. Of those apprehended in 1991, only Jonah Anguka was ultimately tried for Ouko's murder. Formally charged in December 1991 and ordered to stand trial in May 1992, he was released when a mistrial was declared in December 1993 and then reindicted within minutes of that decision. Anguka was finally acquitted in July 1994. Also cleared were Hezekiah Oyugi, who died in August 1992, and Nicholas Biwott, who ran as a candidate for the governing party, KANU, and won election to Kenya's Seventh Parliament. In the years since the dissolution of the Gicheru Commission, there have been numerous calls for a fresh inquiry.

Inquiries

There are, obviously, different possible approaches to the death of Dr. Robert Ouko. Most inquiries have sought to determine "who did it" and what motives underlay the disappearance and murder. Our study of the case takes an entirely different direction. The interest here is in examining the processes of investigation, including the complex programs of knowledge production, both official and public, as revealed in the texts produced within and around the various inquiries.[4] There are archaeologies of knowledge in the Ouko case as they build through specific moments and sites of investigation, revelation, and cover-up, of how what is "known" at a particular moment is constituted in its own sociology and politics, informing, enforcing, and enabling a next moment as inquiries of various shapes, sizes, and capacities have proceeded. By locating the study of knowledge within such a detailed examination of its constitution, formulation, articulation, and reception, it is possible to identify, recontextualize, and represent programs of knowledge production, both public and official. A close analysis of the workings of interest and institution within the movements of knowledge into different forms and formulations, *and over time,* reveals the interstitial, intermediate, indeterminate, unfinished moments of knowing operating within and upon official programs of construction of findings, critiques, answers, explanations, excuses, and alibis.

The issues surrounding the disappearance and death of Robert Ouko, along with the multiple investigations, have left a massive record of public interpretation and debate, reflected in extraordinary press coverage, in the investigative reports produced by Scotland Yard and the Kenyan police, in the thirteen-month proceedings of the judicial commission of inquiry, and in the records of Jonah Anguka's prosecution for murder. Taken together, these materials reveal the openings and closures between the speakable and the unspeakable in different contexts, between the workings of "official" and "public" knowledge. Such proceedings as the Gicheru Commission in Kenya, the Warren Commission in the United States, and the Goldstone Commission in South Africa are infused with a double sense of gravity: the definition of core, formal, official questions and the privileging of an official epistemology. With a commission of inquiry one is powerfully drawn — practically subjected — to the terms and languages of the official exercise — "Was there a gunman on the grassy knoll?" "Was the wound an exit wound?" "How many shots were actually fired?" — missing the opportunities to read a more complex world of practice, routine, meaning, language, power, and interest out of such massive and unique sources, and avoiding the questions that Adam Ashforth and others have asked regarding what such commissions of inquiry are *actually about*.[5]

The texts — for example, the testimony and examination of the Kenyan physician Oluoch — provide portraits of power in Kenya that surpass in many respects the portraits produced by a generation of political scientists. As Ashforth has shown, commissions of inquiry such as the Gicheru Commission are intensely political.[6] In commentary on the Gicheru inquiry, the *Nairobi Law Monthly* at an early stage postulated the notion that Kenya was, essentially, governed by "commissions of inquiry,"[7] anticipating readings of the end-of-apartheid Goldstone Commission as a state within a state in South Africa and forcing attention to the nearly century-long history of commissions of inquiry in the organization of the political landscape of East Africa.[8] Ashforth's grim comparison of the work of state commissions of inquiry to the work of state torture establishes an all-too-baroque stage on which the Ouko saga was enacted:[9] Ouko, a frightened prey, dragged from his home; a beaten and broken living body, stilled by a bullet through the brain; a blood-soaked corpse moved from the site of torture and killing to Got Alila; the prone corpse bathed in diesel fuel, set alight, and left to burn and smolder; months later the readings of the tortured body become the core text of the state inquiry.[10] The investigations of Robert Ouko's death inevitably became within Kenya — and also to a certain extent abroad — examinations of the Kenyan state, deeply involved throughout the Ouko episode with the ongoing multiparty and human rights campaigns in the country. Discourses on Ouko's disappeared and found body came to constitute a means of speaking about the state — in Kenya and, indeed, in Africa generally — in expressive and powerful, as well as novel and highly detailed, ways.[11]

Although the Kenyan state figures prominently in the Ouko inquiries, the Ouko materials are empty of explicit talk of sovereignty and nationalism. In fact, a national frame of reference is tested by observations of power organizing itself, not so much in Nairobi as along the many conduits connecting international agencies, foreign corporations, and Kenyan officials. And as the results of inquiries into Ouko's death in Kenya overlapped with investigations of Mafia-influenced government corruption in Italy, one caught a glimpse of a well-seated transnational or international episteme. The records of both cases are full of extraordinary detail concerning international contracting, finance, transnational clientelism. Terms like "neo-colonialism" seem to have no purchase or value against the play of detailed and thickly textured practices of managing state administrations, development projects, foreign investments, consultations, commercial agencies, bank accounts, and the like. One is hardly surprised by the revelations of corruption; but one is surely taken aback by the highly conventionalized and naturalized, or systematized, practices by which powerful men in Kenya have sought to extend their power and amass their wealth. But what was virtually unremarkable to coteries of journalists, university lecturers, IMF experts, diplomats, and government officials themselves became poison in the hands of Minister Robert Ouko.

Attending to the deeper history of this phenomenon — commissions, that is, not state torture or political murders — raises the important question of how the "commission of inquiry," in formalizing official inscriptions of already existing public knowledge, shrinks the distance between "revulsion" and "consent" in public comment. While Jürgen Habermas's theorization of a "public sphere" may help one recognize the workings of print journalism and media in the motivation for immense interest in an earlier litigation (the S. M. Otieno case),[12] the Central European models do not translate well into Kenyan experience, perhaps most profoundly because of the descent of contemporary Kenya from an invasive and predatory colonial state, but also because of the absence of an idea of a "private sphere" in the Kenya of President Moi's discourse. In addition to seeing the Ouko episode as permitting an examination of public sphere and civil society models in a late-twentieth-century Kenya context, the challenge for the moment is in discerning the practices, programs, discourses, and theories (seated within Kenya) through which Kenyans locate, constitute, operationalize, reproduce, comprehend, represent, and theorize distinctive fields of political interest, and thereby create and test notions of governance and consent.[13] Those in Kenya, South Africa, the United States, Japan, Italy, and France who demand "official inquiries" into truth qualities of what is already understood, averred, known, or comprehended — turning, if possible, convictions into convictions — are, after all, actively engaged in, first, constructing the grounds and terms of consent, and, second, agreeing to those terms. How or why, following a question posed by Tim Burke, do "discursive communities — gathered around conspiracies, disappearances, assassinations, or martyrdoms — all indisputably 'know' *the* truth about the event, though they dispute powerfully the specifics of that truth. . . . [A] compelling question [is] . . . *why* such communities then insist that the state formally and officially confirm that truth."[14]

It is this very contradiction that impels such inquiries forward, a demanding community forcing into existence a Gicheru Commission. Inevitably, as both observers and practitioners in this further intervention in the Ouko episode, the community stumbles into the global phenomenon of "never finished" inquiries such as those into the death of Robert Ouko or John F. Kennedy and what they mean for the present and future of nations. Here, it seems, the programs of *consent* embedded in public appeals for official instantiation of public knowledge are intrinsically related to public *dissent* in regard to the hearing or reading of official productions of knowledge — a critical piece of the late-twentieth-century dissolution of the nineteenth-century nation-state into the "nation-against-the-state."

These extraordinary inquiries have produced extraordinary materials, and they provide views not only of the extraordinary events that led Robert Ouko to his death but also of an "everyday world" of appointment books, business travel, letters of understanding, social conversations, and telephone calls, through which ministers of state maintained their responsibilities and house-maids maintained routines of order and security. The materials produced by the layers of investigations into the Ouko murder provide an unequaled text on Kenyan society — for example, on the operations of a household, on the meaning of time within the schedules of the days and the weeks, on the spa-tialities of farm and household work, on the geography of security and risk, on the constitution of office life, on friendship and affection, and on marriage and trust. What are the meanings to be drawn from Minister Ouko asking his housemaid — at 10:30 in the evening — for a key to an exterior security gate? Or from reports of Ouko *sitting next* to President Moi for eight hours on a flight between London and Nairobi after Ouko was said to have infuriated the president by upstaging him at a February 2, 1990, press conference during an "unofficial visit" to Washington, D.C.? How does one interpret the fields of meaning surrounding Moi's order to Ouko to put aside his official duties and return to his Koru farm and *take a rest*?

Reading the Found Body

On Friday morning, February 16 [1990], at approximately 10:30 A.M., the burnt remains of the body of Hon. Dr. Ouko were found by a search party lying in the bush six kilometres away from his Koru home. The following items were found near the body: a super-dip jerrican, Hon. Ouko's Somali-sword and walking stick. Near Hon. Ouko's head on the right, near the right hand was a .38 special revolver with one empty cartridge in it. This revolver has been confirmed by the chief firearms licensing officer, Central Firearms Bureau, as the one the minister was licensed to possess. About three to four metres from his burnt body a polythene bag containing well folded socks and a pair of jeans, a kitenge shirt, a leather jacket in whose pocket were four rounds of ammunition and some shs. 450 were found. All these were confirmed by the maid as belonging to Dr. Ouko. A box of matches and a torch which was still on but dimly were lying next to the body on the left side. The ground immediately around Hon. Ouko's body was charred. The body was identified beyond doubt by the following persons: Mr. Barrack Mbajah . . .

From a Government of Kenya official statement of February 19, 1990, in *The Weekly Review*, February 23, 1990

It is difficult to conceive that the little grassy opening which is almost surrounded by thickets of wild guava and other plants near the foot of a small hill known to the local people in Koru, Kisumu District, as Got Alila, has acquired a historic and sinister significance since Friday last week. It is in that small, almost circular, grassy patch, hardly four kilometres from his large farm house perched on another small hill, that the badly charred body of the late Kenyan minister for foreign affairs and international co-operation, Dr. Robert John Ouko, was discovered on the fateful Friday, February 16, after his mysterious disappearance on Tuesday, February 13, and the frantic search that ensued. The spot where Ouko's mortal remains were found still bears the marks of the horrifying occurrence, despite the many thousands of human feet that have trodden the place since, and the rains that have lashed the area in recent days. A blackened patch of grass, roughly equally and nearly formed in the shape of an adult human body, marks the exact spot where Ouko's body was immolated. Directly above the spot, a singed branch of a guava shrub seems to point to the possibility that the minister's body was burned by fire that did not, however, spread to surrounding grass or shrubs.

"The Scene of the Crime," *The Weekly Review*, February 23, 1990

The body lay on its back with most of the trunk destroyed by fire. The face and head had escaped burning and was easily identified. A torch owned by the minister's driver Joseph Otieno (of which the minister had temporarily borrowed) lay beside his left leg in the off position. Behind and to the right of his head lay his .38 five chambered, revolver, with one spent round at the twelve o'clock position. Approximately 3–4 feet to the right of the body was a plastic 6 litre white jerrycan with the top open. A matchbox containing several matches lay nearby.

Approximately 15 feet to the west of the body lay a walking stick, holster, jerrycan top, pair of Wellington boots, a plastic bag containing one pair of socks, jeans and a shirt. One leather jacket containing in the pockets four live rounds .38 ammunition, one pair of glasses and cash Shs. 400. Most items were subsequently identified as belonging to the minister. . . . The body was examined at the scene by Dr. Jason Ndaka Kaviti MB, ChD, DMJ (Path) the Kenyan State Pathologist. . . . He did ascertain at the scene that the late minister had a through and through bullet wound to the head. The entry wound being 8 cm above the right ear, and exit being 6 cm about the left ear. He also observed a fracture of the right tibia and fibula which in his first statement, he attributed to heat, but in an additional statement mentions other causes, could have been application of a blunt or sharp force.

From the Scotland Yard report produced before the Gicheru Judicial Commission of Inquiry by Detective Superintendent John H. B. Troon, in *The Standard*, December 4, 1991

(1) Cause of death was by a firearm wound to the head which occurred in life. (2) The burning of Ouko's body [is] . . . consistent with burns . . . during the post-mortem period. (3) There are no indications that the deceased body was on fire whilst he was alive. (4) The heat damage indicates a slow but intense fire which caused severe burning to the back of the trunk, abdomen and to a lesser degree to the limbs. (5) There was no indication that the deceased had been on fire whilst in an upright position. (6) There was no evidence to confirm that the firearm entry wound was a contact wound. (7) The wound was not in the usual position for a suicidal gunshot. (8) The amount of skull damage was more severe than one would normally associate with a standard .38 special round. A slightly more powerful round could produce the injury. (9) The distribution of the blood flow over the

deceased's face as seen in the photographs taken of the deceased at the scene indicate that the head had been moved after the fatal injury had occurred and within 6 hours of death. (10) He would have lost consciousness immediately the firearm wound was inflicted and would have lost all muscular activity at that time. (11) The compound fracture of the deceased's right ankle was caused in life and was consistent with a heavy fall or blow.

> From the summary by Detective Superintendent John H. B. Troon of the findings of the postmortem performed by Dr. Iain West, MB, Ch.D, FRC, Path. DMJ, a Home Office (U.K.) forensic pathologist, of Guys and St. Thomas Hospitals, London, from the presentation of the Scotland Yard report to the Gicheru Judicial Commission of Inquiry, in *The Standard*, December 4, 1993

Gicheru: His legs, how were they?
Shikuku: One of them was broken but I can't remember —
Gicheru: Was it broken or snapped?
Shikuku: Broken. (The witness demonstrates.)
Gicheru: You saw his hands?
Shikuku: I also saw but they were burnt.
Gicheru: How much were they burnt?
Shikuku: They were burnt, the fingers could not be seen.
Gicheru: Could you still see the bones of the hands?
Shikuku: The flesh was there but had dried up . . .

> Extract from the examination of Paul Shikuku, "herdsboy," by the Gicheru Judicial Commission of Inquiry on November 21, 1990, as reported in the *Daily Nation*, 22 November 1990

These five "readings" of the found remains of Robert Ouko suggest the range of public and official accounts of the body and the site of its discovery. One might well speculate that thousands of individuals "read" Ouko's body from the time he left or was taken from his house at Koru on the night of February 12, 1990, to the occasion of the public viewing of his body in an open coffin at Moi Stadium, Kisumu, on Friday, February 23, and his burial at Koru on Saturday, February 24.[15] In the official investigations into Ouko's disappearance and murder alone, more than twenty people spoke or were examined at length on the found remains. They included Paul Shikuku, the "herdsboy," who was reported to be the first person to find the body — he had noted something burning at a distance on February 13 and had returned to the site three days later, on the sixteenth. Harris Otieno Ouma, a farm employee, reported to the Gicheru Commission that on February 13 Paul Shikuku had brought his attention to the burning corpse, and that he could see the smoke from two hundred meters away: "The smoke was not much. The smell was like that of roasted meat. I don't eat meat and its smell makes me feel like vomiting. I left the place and started grazing towards home."

Other individuals interviewed included Inspector James Owino Gendi of the administrative police, who had joined a police search for Minister Ouko in the area near Ouko's home, and who reported that the remains found resembled the minister. Corporal Charles Nzomo of the Koru Police Station was one of the party of four policeman to discover the body on February 16, though twice Nzomo had given statements saying that he had found it on the fifteenth. Geoffrey Paul Warman, a Ph.D. in material science and a scientist at the Metropolitan Police (Scotland Yard) Forensic Science Laboratory, examined some evidence from the remains and from the scene by use of electron microscopy. Superintendent Vincent Martin Wamalwa, the Kisumu Deputy Officer Commanding Police Division, told the Gicheru Commission he was of the opinion that the scene of discovery of the remains might have been faked. And Dr. Joseph Hannington Oluoch, a private physician in Nairobi and Robert Ouko's personal doctor, represented the Ouko family during the postmortem examinations carried out in Nairobi by Dr. Kaviti and Dr. West.

The readings of the found remains constitute an immense and peculiar body of texts, but it is both the quantity of texts and their peculiar quality that suggest the value of an extensive program of reading and analysis. As noted, more than twenty individuals provided their readings of the remains to one inquiry or another, and, like the *Weekly Review* account above, the daily and weekly papers in Kenya published their own reporters' and editors' readings of the remains. Most of those who testified were examined multiple times, their testimonies being given in different contexts over as long as two years. Charles Nzomo, for example, provided numerous statements to various proceedings, including four statements within a two-month period.

The inquiries, with multiple counsel, assign particular interest to observed contradictions within the serial testimonies of many witnesses. As text, they assume different narrative forms. Some are contingent on examination by counsel; others are readings into a tribunal of reports drafted in laboratories and offices. Some statements were available to the public (and therefore to all potential readers of the remains) within a day of the testimony, through the press, through radio and television broadcasts, and through open and public hearings, whereas others were privileged and contained within ongoing investigations, only to be released — and sometimes only in summary form — in published reports of the investigation. Some are referential, that is they pick up on earlier testimony by the speaker or by another witness. Some are summaries rendering the testimony or witness of others. Within much of the testimony and within the examinations by counsel, there are attempts to locate what materials an individual might have seen or had access to at a particular point of speaking.

There are issues of vision, of how the scene of discovery was reconstituted and narrated as a "seen scene" by various witnesses. One witness may have viewed the scene from no closer than two hundred meters; another may have read it from the observations made by electron microscopy in a London laboratory. And as the succession of inquiries proceeded, the official and public "readers" of the found remains (like the present "readers") developed a more sophisticated control of the "props" on the stage of the Got Alila site: the jerrican, the walking stick, the handgun, the torch, the leather coat, the smoke, the smell, the guava branch, the match, the sock, the burned earth, the posture of the body, and so forth. Rummaging through the thirteen-month proceedings of the Gicheru Judicial Commission of Inquiry, one might be excused for detecting a shift from an inquiry in which witnesses were sought who could "restage" the scene to an inquiry in which the veracity, capacity, and interests of a witness could be thoroughly evaluated by reference to how successful they were in managing the "props" intrinsic to the emergent narrative.

One may also, with presumably a large section of the Kenyan public, move beyond the forensic questions enabled by the close look at Ouko's mutilated corpse toward a comprehension of the poetics and dramaturgics of the body's transfiguration as a state and nation to see how the dead body, and the inquiries over and into it, themselves animate and enable, and also shape and constrain, a new social and political reckoning — new political programs, democratization in all its varied dress, new forms of consciousness, new forms of critique and self-critique — much as the S. M. Otieno litigation, an earlier subject of study, was not only expressive and diagnostic but also constructive of a nation.[16] One may also see, or judge, how the very indeterminacies of the readings and revisions of readings of the facts of Ouko's mutilated body may enable a comprehension of the indeterminacies of power, or what might be called "the incomplete dialectics of experience."

Who Was Ouko? A Debate over Representation

At least five distinct narratives of Ouko's demise have been published in media outside of Kenya. They have genealogical and thematic connections. And they share or work off some common evidentiary material. One may note their separate as well as their common development and observe the modes of production of these narratives as historical representations; one may also undertake a closer analysis of the emplotments and languages of their narratives. To take an example, the logic adopted in the narrative published in the November 1991 *Family Mirror* of Tanzania is one that, through its language, assigns a substantial agency to Robert Ouko himself. The unnamed author writes: "Through errors of omissions [*sic*] and commission the late Kenya's Minister of Foreign Affairs and International Co-operation, Dr. Robert John Ouko caused his murder on February 12, 1990."[17] The *Mirror*'s narrative reaches back to 1983. Whereas it wraps its version of the story around the notion of Ouko's agency (as if he caused his own death), most other accounts situate Ouko in a complex of relationships — personal, political, national, and international — that are seen to ground the motivations of *those others* who would see him dead and *those others* who would see his death avenged or his murderers prosecuted. The quality of Ouko's relationships with kin, spouse, friends, colleagues, ministerial associates, and business partners are not easily read. One issue concerns Ouko's identities as brother, husband, father, and son, understood in the context of his identity as a member of a clan in a broader Luo setting and as a Luo in a wider national setting.

Ouko's death was reported by President Moi as we were finishing the manuscript that appeared in 1992 as *Burying SM*, a book-length study of the complex public and judicial debates in Kenya in 1986 and 1987 over the disposition of the remains of the criminal lawyer S. M. Otieno. Corinne Kratz, one of the scholars invited to produce a critical commentary to be published with the book, briefly took up one section of the emergent crisis surrounding the investigation of Robert Ouko's death. In her contribution,[18] drafted as the Gicheru Commission began its work, Kratz discussed the proposition then being debated in Kenya as to whether Ouko's Ominde clan had a standing in the proposed investigation of his death. The clan's argument built upon arguments presented during the S. M. Otieno litigation, which we had been studying since early 1987.

The presence of the Ominde clan in the work of the Gicheru Judicial Commission of Inquiry is one intriguing issue in the Ouko case. Another is the involvement of Justice Richard Kwach of the Court of Appeals as one of the commissioners. Kwach had represented the Umira Kager clan in its legal struggle with Wambui Otieno over the body of her late husband, S. M. Otieno. Kwach, whose unexpected appointment by Moi to the Court of Appeals came after the conclusion of the Otieno case, surprised many observers of the Ouko investigation by seeming to give encouragement to a widening and deepening of the inquiry, and to hold resolute against the demands of government officials that their testimony be presented in camera.

The Ominde clan was ultimately successful in its claim for standing and came to be represented and to actively participate in the Gicheru inquiry through the work of one of Kenya's legal stars, Dr. Ooko Ombaka. The Ominde presence in the proceedings of this judicial commission was motivated by tensions between members of the clan and Ouko's immediate family.[19] Throughout the Ouko inquiries, those who claimed an identity with Ouko did in specific contexts visit upon his body competing narratives and interpretations of his history, of his life, situating the effect of these interpretations — based on emotions and interests — within the proceedings of the Gicheru inquiry.[20]

The Surveillance of Men

In examining the debates in Kenya in 1986–87 over the disposition of the remains of S. M. Otieno, we were drawn to the arguments of Patricia Stamp that the struggle for the body of a dead man, "SM," was, essentially, a struggle over the control of the person of a living woman, Wambui Otieno, SM's widow. Although Stamp's reading of the case, published in *Signs* nearly a year before the appearance of our book, was powerful and influential, it was also effectively the same constrained position that Wambui Otieno herself exercised outside the courts but withheld within them.[21] Both Wambui's perorations on the steps of the high court and Stamp's arguments in *Signs* are exemplars of feminist discourse that create power by exposing how women are constituted and subjected as a category, and how male authorities, professionals, doctors, academics, and clan leaders participate in the construction of women as category, as gender, as subject, as commodity.

In developing a reading on the Otieno case, we were taken by the work of the radical German filmmaker Helke Sander, particularly her film *The Germans and Their Men*, in which — from a feminist perspective — Sander turns her camera from the question of what men do to women to the question of what men do. *The Germans and Their Men* explores the category of "men" itself: how the very fabric of male consensus and solidarity is woven in unconscious, unself-conscious ways; how men operate as a category, a corporation, a gender, even as they deny any consciousness of the fabric of this construct. Sander demonstrates how the construction of the male gender proceeds and how it is revealed in everyday life — through the uncommon interrogation and the surveillance of men by a most acute woman filmmaker — and suggests that the very power of men may lie in their denial of any regard of their own gendered behavior. Beginning with Sander's surveillance program, *Burying SM* looked at the cast of lawyers and judges as well as a philosopher and a grave digger — all men — who paraded proudly as esteemed professionals through the proceedings.

With respect to the Ouko materials, it is possible to extend these observations to men — detectives, doctors, drivers, farm laborers, herdsmen, house servants, journalists, judges, lawyers, ministers, parliamentarians, party officials, pathologists, politicians, security guards, and a president — who have collectively constituted this extraordinary record on the subject of Robert Ouko's death. But the record on Ouko is not only a record of *men*. Selina Aoko Ndalo Were, whom the press constantly identifies as Robert Ouko's "maid," constructs her own identity as a person, as a servant, and as a woman among those with whom she worked and lived and the ways in which the members of the Gicheru Commission, and its various counsel, constructed her identity within the proceedings of the official inquiry. Selina Aoko was one of the last people in Robert Ouko's household to see him alive;[22] she is also reckoned as the person to whom Ouko would assign his last semblance of trust when he could not trust officials of the government with the knowledge that he had assembled. In an important way, in his final days and hours, Robert Ouko constructed Selina Aoko in a structural opposition to Moi's regime if not also in opposition to members of his own family.

Although Selina, the custodian of Ouko's very being, was drawn into this critical and powerful oppositional role, one all the more complex for the deferential attitude she managed in regard to the minister, she sees herself — in the retrospective view from within the commission of inquiry — as powerless among the people "of the village" and, in particular, in respect to Minister Ouko's security guard, the administrative policeman Zablon Agalo Obonyo, because "he [Obonyo] is a man." But whereas Selina Aoko situates Obonyo as commanding power over her (the trusted protector of the minister of foreign affairs), the commission members look at Obonyo, the guard, as a person of no reliability or worth, too proletarian to command authority over the knowledge of the household and the affairs of important men like Ouko.

These complex — and incongruent — constructions of persons, and of men and of women, among them Selina Aoko, Agalo Obonyo, Ouko, and the commission, force a reappraisal of the typical modes of the constitution of identities within gender studies. The "oppositions" here may be far more complex than those of opposed sexualities, and they do not resolve themselves into simple, binary fields of identity and status. Where is the logical and powerful ground for the complex constructions of identity and personhood that Selina Aoko, in testimony and under examination, reveals for her own circumstances, work, life, and self-regard?

Locks and Keys: "A New Locus for Living"—and Also Dying

Given the discrepancies in the reporting of Ouko's death, one might well wonder how to find Got Alila — the much-reported site where his body was discovered. President Moi, in his official announcement of Ouko's death, locates Got Alila "six kilometres away from his Koru home," whereas the Troon report says that it is "some 2.8 kilometres west of his Koru Farm complex."

One of the most sensational narratives of the murder holds that a helicopter crew, variously from Israeli intelligence or Kenyan, was attempting to drop Ouko's body into the nearby River Nyando, where it would wash out into Lake Victoria and disappear forever, but that, it being nighttime, the crew missed the river and dropped the corpse on land at Got Alila. This narrative requires a more complex plot, given that few helicopter pilots would fly a burning corpse across the Kenyan landscape; its twist is that it proposes a second attempt to cover up the murder and the fact of Ouko's identity (the first being the botched attempt to dump the body) by setting the corpse ablaze. Such an account is firmly grounded in what is broadly recognized in Kenya as the utility and prominence of helicopters, and also from time to time Israelis, in state security. The helicopter narrative unfolds into an array of speculations concerning whether or not all parties to the murder were agreed that the body of Ouko should be, or should not be, found and identified.

The intersections of various theories of the crime and various geographies of the neighborhood of Got Alila are only a few of the questions to be asked about the spatialities of life and death of ministers of state in western Kenya. Of the thousands of pages of testimony and reportage from the investigations, a great part of the documentation revolves around spatial dimensions of the last hours of Robert Ouko's life, the activities of members of his immediate and extended family, of his friends and visitors, and of his employees. The texts together constitute an "ethnography" of a farm, within what we depicted in our 1989 book *Siaya* as a new Luo *habitus*: the sugar belt in western Kenya, in which civil servants and professionals plant sugar on their land by telephone and travel to their farms on the weekend to establish a third life, neither in Nairobi and its suburbs nor at the "home" of their birth in the old Luo homelands, but rather in these new freehold spaces, which have been termed "the Kenyatta Bequest." In *Siaya* we noted, however, that "what the proprietors usually find is that the telephone brings them news that planting, cutting, transport and the work force on their lands are badly disarranged. Many have come to see the absentee farm as unlikely to succeed, but the farm remains for most an avocation, and in some senses is being transferred slowly from fully productive land, to a reserve for precious capital, to new status, and to a new locus for living."[23]

In his testimony to the Scotland Yard team, Ouko's storeman, Philip Ogutu, one of fourteen employees on his Koru farm, related that at about 2:00 A.M. on Tuesday, February 13, he was awakened by Ouko's chicken man, Erasto Olang, and was told that the minister wanted the key to the store. Ogutu went with Olang and gave the minister the key. Minister Ouko was concerned, Ogutu narrated, about the welfare of five hundred newly delivered chicks on the cold nights of February and wanted to find additional heating bulbs to install in the chicken house. But Minister Ouko did not want his workers to accompany him into the store, and in the event no additional bulbs were to be found. All the workers on the farm testified that it was well known that no spares were kept. Ogutu related that he himself then went to bed, and that at about 7:00 A.M. Olang handed back the key. When Ogutu checked "his" store, he found the door shut, though the padlock was not closed.

In the records of the inquiries, one notes the highly detailed textualization of locks and keys on the night of Robert Ouko's disappearance, as servants and others — through layers and layers of testimony over more than two years — have spoken of their duties and responsibilities in the Ouko household and on the farm at Koru, and as successive interpreters have sought to unlock certain meanings or intentions from these discourses on locks and keys. Morning and evening routines of attaching padlocks to both the pedestrian and automobile gates at the upper and lower ends of the compound were represented as customary practices, and meanings were attached by direct witnesses and interpreters to what were portrayed as departures from these routines.[24] The securing of the door to Ouko's chicken house was seen as procedural, as were the routines of closing up the house and locking certain interior doors overnight. The domestic and working spaces of the farm were, the sources suggest, ordered around routines of when gates and doors were opened and closed and around which employees at what periods of the day and night were expected to maintain control over essential keys and specific spaces. There is certainly much that can be learned of contemporary Kenyan society if one chooses to look across the grain of these accounts at the detailed workings of such naturalized routines of management, duty, work, temporality, and spatiality — the normative and axiomatic — through which Robert Ouko transited from a productive and living, yet frightened and cornered, body to an enabling and productive, yet decidedly dead and mutilated one.

These highly compartmentalized routines of work and management at Koru were raveled with ideas concerning danger and security. On the one hand these routines appear to have devolved from programs of security introduced on the European farms of Kenya during the Mau Mau Emergency; on the other, they seem continuous with the compartmentalized arrangements of work and security in the offices of leading ministers of the Kenyan government.

With Ouko's corpse, and its highly textualized reincarnation, comes an opportunity to see the constitution of state power in the almost innocent and everyday realms of appointments, bank deposits, commercial deals, contracts, conversations, franchises, and friendships, as well as locks and keys. That the Ouko record locates such activity not only at Koru, Naivasha, and Nairobi but also in Amsterdam, Milan, Rome, and Washington moreover shifts attention to an enlarged, international or transnational, locus for further investigation of the constitution of the late-twentieth-century Kenyan state and society.[25]

Recognizing what Natalie Zemon Davis, Carlo Ginzburg, Le Roy Ladurie, Jean-Claude Schmitt, and others have achieved in wresting reconstructions of culture and society in the past from the documents left behind by inquisitions and other institutions of investigation, we find an opportunity to examine recent and present Kenya through a comparable lens. Continuing our interest in the "anthropology of shadows," we do not mean by this simply bringing into view "offstage" action.[26] Rather, the challenge is to comprehend the "work" or "force," as well as the emergent and shifting rules and constraints, of the active representational and interpretative programs already under way concerning the meanings of asking for a key, sitting beside the president, and being told to go home and take a rest.

The arguments surrounding the investigations of Ouko's death, and the associated demands for a further tribunal, were important elements of the multiparty campaigns running up to the December 1992 elections and in the election aftermath. These calls for a new or reconvened commission of inquiry have an ironic quality: on the one hand, it would be next to impossible to offer to a new commission a credible history of the four days February 12–16, 1990; on the other, what happened over those four days is already *too well known* to *too many parties* throughout Kenya, in the United Kingdom, and elsewhere. What is situated and centered is not so much the events of the four days, but the already constructed knowledge of that period — in all its variegated authority and reliability — operating on the Kenyan political landscape.

In his 1984 *Power in the Blood*, David Sabean produced a remarkable and comparable model for such a multilayered reading of serial accounts of a single "event," the May 9, 1733, death of Pastor Friederich Wilheim Breuninger of Württemberg.[27] Reading across the grain of a variety of village, state, and ecclesiastic sources, Sabean sought "to understand how events, issues, and struggles were experienced, to consider the dialectic between external reality and the notions which people had to grasp that reality with."[28] The "reality" of the Ouko episode — the disappearance, murder, inquests, investigations, conspiracies, and cover-ups — is similarly, thickly enraveled with the available interpretive means of grasping that reality. It was the struggle of Troon and his investigators and the struggle of Gicheru's commissioners to make transparent so much of these otherwise dense layers of interpretive regard. Nevertheless, within the constrained and mannered setting of the commission of inquiry — with its concern for the "props" of Ouko's demise and of his body's discovery — this regard made it possible to speak the unspeakable: to observe that a disappeared and mutilated body had become a surface on which to inscribe readings of the state and of the nation.

Notes

Mark Auslander, Keith Breckenridge, Tim Burke, Catherine Burns, Matt Cenzer, Carolyn Hamilton, Amanda Majisu, Tim Marchant, Kim Lane Scheppele, Keith Shear, Ben Soares, Lynn Thomas, and Luise White commented most valuably on earlier drafts of this essay, as did students and faculty at the University of Michigan, Stanford University, and members of the 1993–94 Institute for Advanced Study and Research in the African Humanities in Evanston, Illinois. This earlier work, written by David William Cohen under the title "Unspeakable Bodies," attempted to define the ongoing larger project into which *this* version attempts to situate one *body* of sources: the multiple and varied readings of Robert Ouko's found remains and the site of their discovery. In 1993 staff of the Program of African Studies, Northwestern University, helped assemble documentation on the Gicheru Judicial Commission of Inquiry, 1990–91, from transcripts published in *The Daily Nation* (Kenya).

1. President Daniel arap Moi of Kenya (Friday morning, February 16, 1990): "I wish to express my sadness and grave concern on the sudden disappearance of my minister for foreign affairs and international co-operation, the Hon. Dr. Robert Ouko. As soon as I received this information on Wednesday, February 14, 1990, I directed that the government machinery be deployed to trace his whereabouts. I wish to assure members of the public that at the moment my own security personnel are applying maximum effort to achieve this intention. Meanwhile, every member of the public who has any information which might help in tracing his whereabouts is requested to report to the nearest police station. This government is committed to protecting the life of each and every Kenyan and no effort will be spared achieving this intention. The public will be informed as soon as further progress is made on [the] investigation."

2. The Scotland Yard team, under the direction of Superintendent Troon, took 235 statements from witnesses. Although the Troon Report, as it came to be called, was not published as a single document, it was — in November 1991 — read into the Gicheru Commission's proceedings by Troon himself and aides, and from this the report appeared serially in *The Standard* during December 3–11, 1991. From the first days of investigation up through Troon's appearance before the Gicheru Commission — seventeen months — the Yard investigations were subject to "informed reports," "premature publication," rumors, accusations of leaks, and other forms of access and dissemination (and also "divination"), which brought multiple and diverse renderings into "public view" in Kenya as well as abroad.

3. In his statement creating the commission, Moi announced: "It is the resolve of my government that all available legal avenues be invoked to help us determine this issue, which is of great concern and importance to all peace-loving Kenyans. I have therefore given consideration to all available alternatives and come to the conclusion that the most effectual manner of proceeding further on the above matter is to appoint a judicial commission of inquiry."

4. We are *not* interested in establishing ourselves as some privileged authority capable of educing the "true facts" of what happened to Robert Ouko between the night of February 12, 1990, when he was last seen alive, and February 16, 1990, when a police-organized search party found his body. We, as authors, have no skills as forensic scientists, are not detectives, and do not wish to undertake the most effective and not-so-effective investigative work that has already been done by the Scotland Yard team, the Kenya Police, and the panel of the commission of inquiry. We are — to make the point directly — uninterested in "solving" this case and do not presume that close reading of the texts of the various investigations will permit a "solution."

5. Ashforth remarks that "the representation of Truth produced by Commissions of Inquiry are an important institutional form in modern states through which the parameters of 'responsible' political action and debate are constructed. . . . [T]he questions facing those who would seek to understand commissions of inquiry concern the ways in which this 'truth' of State is constructed through public inquiry. . . . [A]nalysis of these dimensions of commission work . . . can reveal some of the discursive formations underlying State power: ways of speaking about social life which make possible the work of organizing political subjection." Adam Ashforth, "Reckoning Schemes of Legitimation: On Commissions of Inquiry as Power/Knowledge Forms," *Journal of Historical Sociology* 3.1 (March 1990): 17.

6. See ibid, pp. 1–22; see also Adam Ashforth, *The Politics of Official Discourse in Twentieth-Century South Africa* (London: Oxford University Press, 1990).

7. Chris Mburu, "A Government by Commissions of Inquiry and Probe Committees," *Nairobi Law Monthly* 37 (October 1991): 27.

8. If there were a comic side to the Gicheru Commission, it was in its members waking up one morning to discover that, just as it was focusing on the controversies and scandals surrounding the failure to complete new plans to finish the Kisumu Molasses Plant as integral to the investigation of Robert Ouko's death, President Moi announced the formation of another commission of inquiry, this one to examine the Kisumu Molasses project.

9. Ashforth, "Reckoning Schemes," pp. 10–11.

10. Of course, Kenyans noted the paradox of what many have recognized as a governmental self-inquiry. Oginga Odinga observed in 1991 that "[i]t is an insult to the intelligence of Kenyans to set up a commission of inquiry to clear the same mess it has created." See *Nairobi Law Monthly* 37 (October 1991): 27.

11. The present text on the Ouko investigations is an early offering of a series of approaches, arguments, and programs of reading. It is a work-in-progress as well as a program statement for lines of inquiry that might be further developed. It will eventually be integrated with our other writings on the topic, and we foresee a process of coauthoring extending for two or three years — our previous method (continuous conversations between us concerning expanding drafts) will hopefully still be workable. Although the tactics of reading and coauthoring may be clear at this point, the topics that will draw our separate and collaborative attention remain to be defined. But there are, clearly, a few issues small and large that have attracted our attention; some are fresh and almost unformed, some carry over from the S. M. Otieno project.

12. Jürgen Habermas, *The Structural Transformation of the Public Sphere*, translated

by Thomas Burger from the 1962 German original (Cambridge: MIT Press, 1989); David William Cohen and E. S. Atieno Odhiambo, *Burying SM: The Politics of Knowledge and the Sociology of Power in Africa* (Portsmouth, N.H.: Heinemann, 1992).

13. This continues some of the insights that David Parkin educed from research in Kenya a decade and a half ago. See Parkin, *The Cultural Definition of Political Response: Lineal Destiny among the Luo* (London: Academic Press, 1978).

14. Timothy J. Burke, personal communication, March 31, 1993.

15. Those "reading" the body would have included, of course, individuals involved in the disappearance and murder of the minister.

16. In *Imagined Communities: Reflections on the Origin and Spread of Nationalism* (London: Verso, 1991), rev. ed., p. 10, Benedict Anderson observes that "it may be useful to begin a consideration of the cultural roots of nationalism with death, as the last of a whole gamut of fatalities." Though Anderson sets up such a discussion, the book hardly proceeds past a few suggestive associations. In *Burying SM*, we note that one of the enabling features of the case that occasioned a national debate over the disposition of S. M. Otieno's remains was that SM was both present and absent, centered in discourse, positioned to be spoken for, but unable to speak. Likewise, the broad and intense national speculation and interpretation centered on the last three to five hours of Robert Ouko's life were only possible in the context of a corpse present, which was also the absent witness.

17. *Family Mirror*, no. 66, Premier Issue, November 1991, p. 1.

18. See Cohen and Odhiambo, *Burying SM*, p. 102.

19. Relationships among the circle of Robert Ouko's kin were subject to considerable investigation and speculation through all of the inquiries. Marital difficulties and extramarital affairs were considered at various points to be possible motives or contexts for Ouko's murder. Observed or alleged tensions between Robert Ouko and his brother Eston Barak Mbajah were considered an appropriate pretext (by the Kenyan police) for Mbajah's arrest, interrogation, and detention. Detective Superintendent John Troon, the head of the Scotland Yard team, observed in his final report that Mbajah was beaten and tortured while in custody. Mbajah and Troon both speculated that someone feared that Mbajah had passed important and dangerous information to the Scotland Yard team. Mbajah's sworn affidavit, dated September 23, 1991, which was submitted to the Gicheru Commission, contains a remarkable account of the circumstances leading to and following his brother's murder. It has been published in the *Nairobi Law Monthly* 38 (November 1991): 21–23.

20. At a more general level, one may note what appears to be the almost seamless quality of crises and debates in Kenya developing around a long lineage of contested corpses extending back, according to another of our critics, John Lonsdale, into the late nineteenth and early twentieth centuries. See Lonsdale's commentary in Cohen and Odhiambo, *Burying SM*, pp. 109–10.

21. Patricia Stamp, "Burying Otieno: The Politics of Gender and Ethnicity in Kenya," *Signs* 16.4 (1991): 808–45.

22. As a consequence, Selina Aoko has been interviewed, examined, and cross-examined multiple times (as well as arrested in 1991) over, to date (1997), five major investigations.

23. David William Cohen and E. S. Atieno Odhiambo, *Siaya: The Historical Anthropology of an African Landscape* (London: James Currey, 1989), p. 55.

24. To suggest that this is a minor, technical issue is to miss the point of how widely known across Kenya were these details about the locks and keys. A year after the murder one headline blazoned news of a report that Robert Ouko may have, after all, routinely carried a key to one of his doors.

25. If Ouko has been said by some to have signed his death warrant by his behavior in January and February 1990 in Washington, D.C., a comparable delegation of President Moi and key ministers to London in 1979 established another Luo and another minister, Isaac Omolo Okero, as a surviving humorist of international ministerial junkets. See Cohen and Odhiambo, *Burying SM*, pp. 84–85.

26. Cohen and Odhiambo, *Siaya*, pp. 111–28.

27. David Sabean, *Power in the Blood: Popular Culture and Village Discourse in Early Modern Germany* (Cambridge: Cambridge University Press, 1984), pp. 147–63.

28. Ibid., p. 146.

Performance as Contestation

An Agonistic Perspective on the Insurgent Assembly

KIRK W. FUOSS

Since the rise of new historicism in the early 1980s, performance scholars increasingly invoke a product-producer or culture-performance dialectic in which performance is viewed as simultaneously a product of the culture out of which it emerged and a producer of the very culture in which it participates. Louis Montrose's "Shaping Fantasies" illustrates the growing tendency to invoke a product-producer dialectic. He writes, "*A Midsummer Night's Dream* is, then, in a double sense a creation of Elizabethan culture: for it also creates the culture by which it is created, shapes the fantasies by which it is shaped, begets that by which it's begotten."[1] Critics such as Montrose deny the exclusively documentary function of texts and performances, arguing instead that texts and performances fulfill both reflective and reflexive functions, that texts and performances are both products of and producers of culture.

The product-producer/culture-performance dialectic is valuable in underscoring the mutual action of culture and performance on one another; however, because the dialectic applies to all performances, its value for discriminating among diverse performance phenomena is limited at best. Moreover, although new historicists have popularized the culture-performance dialectic, they have not provided an accompanying analytical framework for particularizing the performance contestation entailed by this dialectic. On the contrary, new historicists remain decidedly taciturn with regard to the methods employed to arrive at their conclusions.

My purpose in this essay is to sketch the broad outlines of an agonistic analytical framework that will aid performance scholars in their attempts to particularize the specific forms of contestation operating in individual performances. In order to realize this goal, I begin by describing a particular cultural performance — the Workers' Alliance of America's (WAA) 1936 seizure of the New Jersey State Assembly — and then explore the contestation occurring within this performance, identifying three dimensions of performance contestation: the direction of effectivity (whether the performance maintains or subverts status quo relations of power), the mode of effectivity (the strategies through which this directional movement is transacted), and the spheres of contestation (the levels at which these strategies are operationalized, whether textual, spatial, or conceptual).

A number of assumptions are implicit in the agonistic framework. First, cultural performances make things happen that would not have happened in that way, to that extent, in that place, at that time, or among those persons had the cultural performances not occurred. In short, cultural performances are not merely objects of aesthetic contemplation but more importantly sites of sociopolitical competition. Second, cultural performances move the social formation in which they occur and of which they are a part in one of two directions, either toward a further entrenchment of status quo values and relations of power or toward a loosening of status quo values with a redistribution of status quo relations of power. Third, this directional movement occurs as a result of strategies that human agents operationalize, and, further, these strategies operate either in the cultural performances themselves or in ancillary activities related to them, such as talking about performances prior to or after their occurrence.

Before I proceed, one final introductory comment needs to be made. Although this essay employs as its primary example a protest performance, the areas of inquiry highlighted by the agonistic perspective operate not only in performances designed to resist the status quo but also in performances designed to perpetuate it. Accordingly, the significance of this essay lies not so much in what it reveals about protest performance per se but in its potential to sharpen our ability to analyze the contestatory nature of all performances, even those performances that try very hard to mask their political agendas.

The WAA Seizure of the New Jersey Assembly

When the New Jersey State Assembly reconvened on April 20, 1936, after a three-day recess, the state government had run out of relief appropriations and turned relief back over to the local governments, most of which were in no better financial shape. David Lasser, spokesperson for the WAA, an organization of unemployed persons and relief workers, warned legislators that "they were sitting on a volcano," threatened that "tens of thousands will camp at the State House if something is not done about the relief situation," and argued that if the legislators could not find a solution to the relief crisis, they should resign and let others take their places.[2] This suggestion drew cheers from Alliance members seated in the gallery. The following afternoon, Roy Cooke — an unemployed vaudeville actor and the state chair of the New Jersey WAA — addressed the legislators: "Appropriate two million dollars at once. If you don't, we'll give you a real demonstration and right soon."[3] Two hours later, having taken no action on the relief issue, the Assembly voted to recess until

Monday, April 27. As house speaker Marcus Newcomb banged his gavel, Ray Cooke and nineteen other Alliance members moved to the floor of the legislative chamber and slipped quietly into the assemblymen's seats, announcing their intention to occupy the chamber until the legislators reconvened to act on the relief crisis.

Word of the occupation quickly spread, and within hours fifty of the sixty seats in the assembly were occupied.[4] Members of the Women's Auxiliary of the WAA brought in donated food and tobacco, transforming the speaker's table into a makeshift cafeteria.[5] As night approached, only two bulbs in the press boxes at the rear of the chamber illuminated the scene, and after sitting in the near dark for two hours, the beleaguered occupants petitioned the State House police chief for additional light. At 8:30, four bulbs in the huge overhead chandelier were lit.[6]

Having been granted illumination, John Spain marched to the front of the chamber, sat down in the speaker's seat, picked up and banged the speaker's gavel, and announced that the house was in session. In response, some of those positioned in the house leaned back, put their feet on the desks, and began puffing imaginary cigars and reading newspapers — as one source put it, "as indifferent to what was going on in the House as true gentlemen of the Assembly."[7] Spain responded:

> I'm glad to see that some of us know how real legislators act, but this is at present, an assembly of the Workers' Alliance, not the gathering of the bunch of miserable buffoons that you usually witness in this building. So let's show whoever's watching that we know how to conduct ourselves in a way the gentlemen of the Assembly don't know how to do, like decent people, like workers. . . . It is up to us . . . to show the state that there are people who can sit in this building and legislate honestly and intelligently — even though it's never been done before. Let's make the people of this state recognize what kind of people they have elected here by showing them what kind of people they should have elected.[8]

Alliance members sat up, moved their feet from the desks, and put away their newspapers. For several hours, bills that had been considered by the New Jersey legislators were reconsidered by those now occupying the chamber. After debating and defeating a proposed sales tax on the grounds that it taxed the very persons it was designed to aid, the demonstrators passed an income tax and a corporate tax bill, as well as a resolution limiting the work week to a maximum of thirty hours.[9]

Having depicted their ideal legislature, "Speaker" Spain directed those gathered in the assembly to shift to a depiction of the actual legislature. Alliance members donned Harvard accents, used a vocabulary so pompous that what they said seemed perfectly congruent with the way they said it, and referred to one another as "the gentleman from ——," bowing to each other as they did so. They seldom listened as others spoke but frequently posed for imaginary and real reporters in the press boxes.[10] They appointed each other roles such as Majority Leader Lawrence Cavinato, Speaker of the House Marcus Newcomb, and Minority Leader Grant Scott. At one point, Alliance member William "Schnozzle" Schroeder rolled a cigarette while imitating the oratory of actual Majority Leader Lawrence Cavinato. In the midst of his impersonation, he paused, momentarily stepping out of the Cavinato role to critique his own performance. "Something's wrong here," he noted. "The Majority Leader should use tailor-made cigarettes."[11]

After settling on their roles, the members proposed and debated resolutions, passing one bill that doubled their salary and another that turned "the Delaware and Raritan Canal over to the relief clients, letting them catch fish for their meals."[12] In the course of consideration of the first of these bills, John Spain, acting as assembly speaker Marcus Newcomb, looked up to the gallery where just hours before he and his cohorts had sat and warned imaginary WAA members: "Any more demonstrations, and the sergeant-at-arms will have to clear the gallery."[13] While performing consideration of the canal bill, the following interchange apparently ridiculing the parliamentary form of discussion transpired:

> *1*: Will the gentleman from Burlington submit to a question?
> *Speaker*: Will the gentleman from Burlington submit to a question?
> *2*: I will if it's not too technical.
> *Speaker*: He will if it's not too technical.
> *1*: Isn't it true that you have a brother-in-law who is third vice-president of a fishing supply company?
> *2*: Mr. Speaker! I have never been so insulted in all my life! . . . He can't insinuate that I am personally interested in seeing this bill passed! . . . He can't insinuate that I am interested in anything that goes on in this place! And now will the gentleman from Hunterdon submit to a question?
> *Speaker*: Will the gentleman from Hunterdon submit to a question?
> *1*: I will.
> *Speaker*: He will.
> *2*: Are you a citizen?[14]

In addition to targeting the parliamentary form of discussion, the demonstrators repeatedly articulated their perception of the actual legislators' perception of themselves (i.e., the unemployed and relief recipients). One demonstrator-as-legislator argued against turning the canal over to the unemployed, warning: "Give them a fingernail and they'll want your arm up to your shoulder. We must teach them to rely on themselves."[15]

By Wednesday morning, the number of protesters outnumbered the assembly seats and the arrival of entire families necessitated that some protesters take up positions in the gallery. One local newspaper reported that throughout Wednesday "State House officials straggled in to watch what they called 'the show'" and that one spectator — an unnamed legislator who slipped into the gallery — assessed the scene as follows: "These are not the really hungry people. These are agitators and should go out and go to work."[16] Although the governor met with WAA representatives for two hours Wednesday afternoon, no action was taken to redress the relief crisis.

Thursday brought fresh drama to the demonstration. A civil service exam had been scheduled for the assembly chambers, and after State House officials attempted unsuccessfully to persuade the squatters to take up residence temporarily in one of the committee rooms, a compromise was reached. Demonstrators were granted use of the senate chambers for the day with the understanding that after the civil service exam was completed, they would be free to return to the assembly chamber.[17] The change of venue resulted in changes in the number and names of the dramatis personae, as well as in deportment. The *New York Times* reported that "'Speaker' Spain of the Assembly became 'Mr. President' and the session was called to order. . . . The meeting, in keeping with its new surroundings, was carried on with more decorum than in the Assembly. Since the senate has only twenty members, all but twenty of the group took their places in the gallery to act as spectators and applaud."[18]

The session began with the demonstrators burlesquing the real senators. Impersonating the actual senators, they reconsidered a bill that had been debated and defeated the week before that would have cut the senators' salaries in half. Urging that the bill be passed, one "senator" contended, "It'll look as though we're trying to help out in the crisis, and that'll make us go over great with the relief clients. . . . Even Presidents have been known to use this stunt."[19] Later, when the demonstrators performed as ideal legislators, they passed a five-million-dollar emergency appropriations bill by a margin of 24 to 0 despite the presence of only twenty "senators."[20]

By Friday morning the demonstrators were once again in the assembly chamber, alternately enacting actual and ideal legislation, and the day appears to have been relatively uneventful. On Saturday, the governor released a statement justifying his refusal to approve emergency appropriations: "Already there is grave danger that the constitutional ban against creating debt has been violated. Without the vote of the people, the state has no power to borrow money or to create debts of any kind except for war purposes, to repel invasions, or to suppress insurrection."[21] Within minutes the demonstrators passed a resolution and sent it to the governor: "Whereas, since the Governor advises that the Constitution gives him power to create indebtedness to repel invasions and insurrections: Therefore be it resolved: That the group of citizens now invading the State Assembly chamber in the State House at Trenton do hereby inform the Governor of the state of New Jersey that an insurrection is in progress against the State legislature for failure to provide relief funds."[22]

Those opposed to the WAA seizure became more vociferous on Saturday than they had been earlier in the week. Assemblyman Horace Bogle told the press he had proof that the demonstrators were not actually unemployed but were instead being paid $4.50 for each day they participated in the demonstration.[23] Assemblyman J. Parnell Thomas suggested to the governor in a telegram that the "mob of occupation [was] under Communist leaders" and that "the present show at the State House is being deliberately staged to build a case for new taxes." The telegram concluded: "If you don't care to exercise your authority [i.e., have state police clear the demonstrators out of the chambers], I then suggest you feed the crowd caviar and chocolate eclairs."[24] On hearing of the telegram, the demonstrators picked up the eclair motif, passing a resolution challenging Thomas to select any of the demonstrators above the age of three for a fight to the finish with cream puffs.[25] That evening, Trenton residents appear to have had an unforeseen theater offering. One local newspaper reported that "for several hours, curious spectators, some of them in evening clothes, watched the members enact parliamentary scenes. . . . As the hour approached midnight, the crowd of spectators increased. They stood behind the glass barricade, their faces pressed tightly against the glazed surface, watching with intense interest the antics of the 'legislators.' "[26]

Sunday, after being compared to "good samaritans" in a sermon by a local clergyman, the demonstrators returned to their legislative duties.[27] One of the more interesting resolutions of the day appropriated a thousand dollars "to permit Governor Harold G. Hoffman and Mayor Frank Hague of Jersey City to go to Alaska and survey the Alaskan salmon, its life, loves and tax problems, so the New Jersey legislature will be free to do its duty without outside influence."[28]

Monday evening the regular assembly was scheduled to reconvene, and the demonstrators spent much of that day negotiating whether they would leave the chamber, whether they would have the right to speak during the assembly session, and whether they would be allowed to return to the chamber floor after the session was completed. By late Monday afternoon, negotiators agreed that all but five of the demonstrators would retire to the gallery, that only one of the delegation remaining on the floor would be allowed speaking privileges, and that following the session the demonstrators could once again take up position in the chamber.[29] When the assembly was called to order at 7:30, between 5,000 and 7,000 persons were present in and outside the State House.[30]

Shortly into the assembly session, WAA spokesperson Ray Cooke was allowed the privilege of the floor, which he used to respond to Thomas's assertion that the demonstration was being staged by communist agitators. His response: "I am here to say that he is a liar."[31] The assembly's response was a gag rule. By a vote of 55–5, Cooke was denied speaking privileges.[32] Two resolutions were debated during the course of the evening. Frank Osmers put forth a resolution calling for a full investigation of the demonstrators' identities.[33] Another legislator moved that the resolution be tabled, and the movement to table the resolution passed. The evening's second resolution demanded that the governor "censure those persons responsible for permitting this unwarranted insult to the dignity of this House and Sovereign State and take suitable steps to prevent a repetition of similar occurrences in the future."[34] Although this resolution was adopted, State House police did not restrain the demonstrators from returning to the chamber floor when the assembly, after an hour, recessed until Wednesday evening.[35]

Once back in the chamber, WAA demonstrators passed a resolution calling for the formation of a Farm-Labor Party to represent the laborers' interests in the upcoming November elections.[36] The Farm-Labor Party became the keynote of the final two days of the WAA seizure. After the Wednesday evening session adjourned and the demonstrators were not permitted to return to the floor of the chamber, a final session of the insurgent assembly was held in the gallery, where the following resolution was approved: "Whereas, we have held the halls of legislature for a period of nine days; and Whereas, the regular assembly has been thoroughly exposed by the Workers Alliance as an impotent, inefficient tool of the public utilities, banks, and big industries; Be it therefore resolved: that the Workers Alliance divorce itself entirely from the State machine of finance and capital and adjourn immediately to prepare a State machine of its own."[37] With the approval of this final resolution, the nine-day old WAA's insurgent assembly came to a close.

An Agonistic Perspective on the Insurgent Assembly

This section advances an agonistic analytical framework designed specifically to fix the investigator's attention on performance as a site of struggle. Adopting the agonistic framework foregrounds questions such as: How does a performance maintain or subvert existing social relations? Whom does a particular performance serve? How does it serve them? How does a performance engage in communal identity politics — that is, how does it enact and argue for particular construals of categories such as "us" and "them," "insider" and "outsider," "ally" and "opposition," "community" and "other"? Employing the agonistic framework involves analysis of three dimensions of performance contestation: the direction of effectivity, the mode of effectivity, and the spheres of contestation. The term "effectivity" is employed to underscore the argument that cultural performances have effects, that they make things happen that would not have happened in that way, to that extent, in that place, at that time, or among those persons had the cultural performances not occurred.

Analysis of the first dimension involves discerning whether the direction of effectivity of the performance is ideological or resistant or both. Although all performances are ideological, not all performances are ideological. The apparent contradiction of this statement disappears as soon as neutral and critical construals of ideology are differentiated. When construed neutrally as a system of beliefs and assumptions possessed by an individual or group, ideology functions as a universal condition with no outside, no other; however, when construed critically as the perpetrator/perpetuator of systematic asymmetries of power, ideology functions as a particular rather than universal phenomenon — one whose others are resistance and opposition.[38] Thus, although all performances are ideological when ideology is construed neutrally, a performance may or may not be ideological when ideology is construed critically. Performances possessing an ideological direction of effectivity perpetuate existing patterns of domination, whereas performances possessing a resistant direction of effectivity subvert or challenge existing patterns of domination. The pigeonholing tendency implicit in these categories is mitigated by the recognition of multiple axes of domination (e.g., gender, class, race, sexual orientation). Once multiple axes of domination are accounted for, a performance may be ideological along one axis yet resistant along another. A performance, likewise, may be ambivalent along any single axis, being neither clearly resistant nor ideological.

Analysis of the second dimension of contestation — the mode of effectivity — involves specification of the strategies through which the directional movement is transacted. Richard Terdiman underscores the importance of studying the mode of resistance, noting that "it is critical to provide as precise an account as can be derived . . . of [the counter-discourse's] mode of relation, its specific tactic of opposition to the adversary it projected for itself. Such accounts constitute a map. For in their opposition to the dominant, counter-discourses function to survey its limits and its internal weaknesses."[39]

Analysis of the third dimension — spheres of contestation — involves specification of the levels at which the contestation occurs. At least three spheres exist: textual, spatial, and conceptual. In the discussion and analysis that follow, I define and focus predominantly on the spheres of contestation as they are the centerpiece of the agonistic framework I am advancing. It is, after all, at the various spheres of contestation that particular strategies (i.e., modes of effectivity) are operationalized in order to move the social formation in particular directions (i.e., the direction of effectivity).

Textual Sphere of Contestation

Of the three spheres of contestation, the one most frequently focused on in existing scholarship is the textual sphere. The textual sphere of contestation refers to the struggle among competing symbolic practices at both the intratextual and intertextual levels. Intratextual contestation refers to the contestation among symbolic practices within a performance and is roughly equivalent to what Mikhail Bakhtin calls "internal dialogism," the struggle among the various discourses incorporated within a single text to overpower, discredit, and displace one another. Intertextual contestation refers to the way an individual performance (with its particular intratextual configuration) competes with other performances and other types of texts (with their particular intratextual configurations).[40]

One way to begin analysis of the textual sphere of contestation in the WAA demonstration is by accounting for the multiple performance postures employed. Throughout the demonstration, WAA members assumed three distinct performance postures: (1) Alliance members as worker-legislators considering resolutions addressing the relief crisis, (2) Alliance members as worker-legislators considering resolutions addressing the actual legislators, and (3) Alliance members as actual legislators.

The first performance posture engaged Alliance members as ideal worker-legislators considering resolutions that addressed the relief crisis. I refer to this posture as *demonstrative* performance because it operates in the fashion of the "how-to" and the exemplary and because a tone of seriousness pervades the performance. The core of this posture is that demonstrators enact legislators who represent workers' interests and who debate resolutions that respond to the relief appropriations crisis. Examples of bills voted on while this posture was adopted include the Tuesday evening defeat of a proposed sales tax on the ground that it taxed the very persons it was designed to aid and the passing on Tuesday evening of an income tax and a corporate tax bill. The resolutions that emerged within the demonstrative performance posture followed the formal, semantic constraints ("Whereas . . . Therefore, Be It Resolved . . .") of legislative resolutions but differed primarily in content. The income tax and corporate tax bills passed on Tuesday evening, for example, maintained the stylistic features of actual legislative resolutions while simultaneously reversing previous electoral decisions made by the actual legislators. Given the available information on this historical event, it is difficult to tell whether the traditional parliamentary form of discussion was employed in debating the resolutions and, if so, how tightly or loosely it was followed.

The second and third performance postures are both types of *remonstrative* performance. Etymologically, "remonstrate" is derived from the Latin "monstrare," meaning "to point out, show." Interestingly, "monstrare" also functions as the derivative root of "monster." The second and third postures function respectively "to show" and "to point out" what the WAA perceived as a monster. In both postures the dominant mode is ridicule, but the ridicule is transacted differently in each.

The remonstrative posture that *points out* the monster involves enacting the act of ridiculing. In this posture, as in the demonstrative posture, Alliance members enact the role of worker-legislators. Unlike the demonstrative posture, however, here worker-legislators do not consider resolutions responding directly to the relief crisis but instead consider resolutions responding to the actual legislators, and the dominant mood is mock-seriousness. One resolution passed while this performance posture was assumed appropriated a thousand dollars "to permit Governor Harold G. Hoffman and Mayor Frank Hague of Jersey City to go to Alaska and survey the Alaskan salmon, its life, loves and tax problems, so the New Jersey legislature will be free to do its duty without outside interference."[41] A second resolution passed while this posture was adopted challenged Assemblyman J. Parnell Thomas, who had earlier accused the demonstrators of being paid $4.50 for participating in the demonstration, to select any of the demonstrators above the age of three for a fight to the finish with cream puffs.[42]

The remonstrative performance posture that *shows* the monster involves enacting the object of ridicule by impersonating the actual politicians who failed to act on the relief crisis. If a tone of seriousness seems dominant in the demonstrative posture, here the mood is doubly inflected — the mood is serious, but it is, more importantly, mock-serious. Here we are in the realm of phony accents, pompous vocabularies, and parliamentary protocol (e.g., "Will the gentleman from Burlington submit to a question?" "Will the gentleman from Hunterdon submit to a question?"). The primary objects of ridicule in this posture are the actual legislators, and the dominant mode of effectivity is parody.

Much of the contestation transacted at the textual level in the WAA demonstration centers on communal identity politics. Not surprisingly, the construals of the categories "us" and "them" inscribed in WAA cultural performances differed markedly from those circulated by their opponents. The actual legislators situated themselves as the "duly constituted representatives" of the people of New Jersey and vilified the WAA demonstrators as lazy and shiftless communists.[43] In contrast, the WAA demonstrators situated themselves as champions of the common man and vilified the actual legislators as political insiders who by virtue of their "insider" status were "outsiders" to the community of ordinary citizens.

Cultural performances staged by WAA demonstrators redefined the relationship between extant political parties, construing the relationship between Democrats and Republicans as one of complicitousness rather than opposition. Spain initiated this argument in his opening statements on the first night of the demonstration when he described the relief crisis as "something our predecessors have played around with for months, and something they have made no real effort to solve because it wasn't in their best interests to solve it."[44] When "Speaker" Spain requested that the demonstrators role-play the actual legislators, the demonstrators immediately divided into factions and factions within factions. As performed by the Alliance members, however, these factions were less the outcome of real differences than the means for realizing the shared goal of postponing legislative action on the relief crisis until after the election. The supposed alterity of the political parties with regard to one another was inscribed within WAA cultural performances *as a deceptive performance* purposefully engaged in by legislators from both parties in order to mask their more fundamental commonality, a commonality that set them apart from relief clients.

One of the more interesting struggles at the textual sphere centers on the way in which the demonstrators subverted the legislators' derision of the WAA. The demonstrators did this not by denying the legislators' derisive comments but by incorporating them into a performance posture that undermined the validity of the claims. For example, when WAA members parodied the actual legislators, they included, as a part of this performance, the legislators' derision of themselves. This occurred when Spain, portraying the assembly speaker, threatened to clear imaginary Alliance members from the gallery if there were any more outbursts, as well as when, during debate over an appropriations bill in the senate, an Alliance member-senator protested that the bill was "for a bunch of trouble-makers who don't want jobs because they don't want to get up in the morning."[45] In this manner, the derision aimed at the self by the hostile other is both recognized and contained in a performance of the hostile other that is itself derisive. In effect, the derision of one's self becomes the object of derision, and the insulted self is invited to laugh at the slight by contextualizing it in the frame of a laughable other.

Spatial Sphere of Contestation

The spatial sphere of contestation focuses on the politics of space. David Harvey, a postmodern geographer, contends that space "gets treated as a fact of nature, 'naturalized,' through the assignment of common sense everyday meaning."[46] That space is not merely a container in which human action transpires but instead simultaneously a product and producer of action has become a rallying cry of a growing number of theorists who focus on the politics of place. Edward Soja, for example, warns that "we must be insistently aware of . . . how relations of power and discipline are inscribed into the apparently innocent spatiality of social life, how human geographies become filled with politics and ideology."[47] Similarly, Henri Lefebvre contends that "space has been shaped and molded from historical and natural elements, but this has been a political process. Space is political and ideological. It is a product literally filled with ideologies."[48]

Analysis of the spatial sphere of performance contestation involves analysis of the politics of theater spaces. In *Performance Theory*, Richard Schechner contends that theaters are created by "writing on" space, and this insight is echoed in Sally Harrison-Pepper's analysis of street performers' transformation of city space into theater place: "Like a palimpsest, an ancient parchment repeatedly erased and written upon over the centuries, . . . the square [a site popular with street performers] has thus become a kind of 'laminated space,' with multiple meanings and activities layered upon it."[49] Harrison-Pepper's example of marginalized and often outlawed street performers underscores the contestatory nature of writing on space in a way and to an extent that Schechner's example of primitive hunting bands does not. In advanced capitalist societies, the space that is written on by performers has (more often than not) already been written on, and the authors of the earlier writing are not always excited by the prospect of having their text defaced and refaced by new inscriptions.

Consideration of the spatial sphere of performance contestation involves analysis of (1) the location of theaters in space, (2) the deployment of space in theaters, and (3) the representation of space in performances. Analysis of the location of theaters in space involves answering questions about what spaces get utilized as performance spaces, where these spaces are in relation to spaces reserved primarily for other uses, and whether the use of the space for performance is sanctioned or nonsanctioned. Analysis of the deployment of space in theaters involves answering such questions as how does the architecture of the theater affect audience members' relationships to one another (e.g., gender, racial, and class segregation; presence or lack of lobbies) and to the performers (e.g., proximity of performers and audience members; proscenium, thrust, theater-in-the-round; degree of separation of theaters into house, stage, and backstage areas). Analysis of the representation of space in performance involves answering such questions as how does the spatial representation put forth in the performance reproduce or diverge from existing cultural uses of space.

Two major struggles occurred at the spatial sphere of contestation in the WAA seizure of the New Jersey State Assembly: a battle to renegotiate the boundary between domestic and political space and a battle between the influential and the latent environment. Alliance members' attempts to renegotiate the boundary between domestic and political space took place on two fronts and in two directions. Demonstrators in the assembly chamber domesticated the political space for the nine days of their stay: desks became beds, law books became pillows, and the speaker's table became a makeshift cafeteria. The staging of the demonstration within the legislative assembly immediately set into motion a visual rhetoric, highlighting the sharp difference between the world of the assemblymen who normally occupied the space and the world of the relief clients who took up temporary residence there. While demonstrators inside the State House were domesticating the political space of the assembly chamber, other demonstrators were politicizing domestic space by periodically targeting assemblymen's homes for picketing and demonstrations.

A second battle at the spatial level centers on what Stanford Anderson calls the influential and latent environment. The influential environment is the dominant or realized function of the space. The latent environment includes nonrealized potential functions of the space. Central to Anderson's analysis of these is his concept "resiliency." Resiliency refers to the degree of adaptability of an environment for multiple purposes.[50] The WAA seizure of the assembly represents a battle by Alliance members to realize a latent environment in an environment with little resiliency, a space whose resiliency is limited by a firmly entrenched influential environment. In the influential environment of a legislative chamber, Alliance members realized the latent environmental possibility of using the space as a theater.

That the legislative chamber was temporarily transformed into a theater, however, is only half of the story. The other half is that the latent theatrical environment was then employed to re-present the displaced influential environment. The assembly chamber (influential environment) was transformed into a theater (latent environment) that was then used to re-inscribe and comment on the displaced influential environment. By thematizing the displaced legislative chamber within the latent theater, a doubling effect is put into operation in which the assembly chamber functions simultaneously as the container and the contained. Moreover, by employing three different performance postures to re-present the legislative function of the assembly, a sense that it-could-be-otherwise/it-doesn't-have-to-be-this-way is introduced.

Before I proceed to the conceptual sphere, one final note regarding the spatial sphere warrants comment. Unlike the sessions of the mock assembly where racial and class segregation appears not to have been employed, during the actual legislative sessions that twice interrupted the mock assembly, the various communities that together comprised the audience were physically separated in such a manner that while they simultaneously watched the same performance, they did so separately. During the Wednesday evening session, for instance, the spectators were split into three groups with each group having its own physical space. The reporters and photographers filled the press box at the rear of the assembly chamber. State House officials, New Jersey state senators, their friends and family members took up residence in a gallery that had been reserved especially for them. The remaining gallery was filled largely by relief workers and unemployed persons who had occupied the chamber throughout the weeklong ordeal, as well as by additional persons who had traveled to Trenton to lend support to the demonstrators.

The section of the chamber occupied by WAA members and supporters appears to have followed the "WAA Declaration of Principles" — namely, that the WAA is open to all workers "regardless of race, creed, color, sex, nationality, or political belief."[51] Of the two galleries, only the WAA's was racially integrated.[52] During sessions of the actual New Jersey Assembly only men occupied the floor of the legislative chamber. During sessions of the WAA insurgent assembly, the floor of the legislative chamber housed women and children as well as men. The performance staged by the WAA included not only male, mock legislators but also children and women. Although it is unclear whether women assumed roles as mock legislators, it is known that women actively participated in the WAA demonstration. A Trenton newspaper reports that on Saturday, April 25, long after their children had climbed onto the desks and gone to sleep, "the women remained in their chairs. They refused to go home and took an active part in the debate."[53] Contestation at the spatial sphere centered not only on the activities that transpired in the assembly chamber but also on who engaged in those activities. The very presence of white and black working-class women, men, and children in a space usually reserved for upper-class, white males is itself contestatory.

Conceptual Sphere of Contestation

The struggle that transpires at the conceptual sphere occurs at a metalevel and focuses on the strategic deployment of the concept "performance." Central to the conceptual sphere is a twofold analysis: first, an analysis of "performance" as an example of what W. B. Gallie has termed an "essentially contested concept" (ECC) and, second, an analysis of the operation of what Jonas Barish has termed the "antitheatrical prejudice."

ECCs are concepts "the proper use of which inevitably involves endless disputes about their proper uses on the part of their users."[54] That "performance" is an ECC has been implied by Paul Gray and overtly stated by Mary S. Strine, Beverly Long, and Mary Frances HopKins.[55] To the extent that different construals of performance invoke different evaluative criteria, the contestation referred to here is not just over which phenomena get designated as performances but also over which phenomena, once designated as performances, get evaluated as "good" and "bad" performances.

A second form of conceptual contestation centers on the analogical deployment of the concept "performance" to discredit phenomena by making them seem less than true or larger than life.[56] "My students know how to perform political correctness" exemplifies the use of a performance analogy to make a phenomenon seem less than true. "He made a spectacle of himself" exemplifies the use of a performance analogy to make a phenomenon seem larger than life.

In the WAA demonstration, the primary contestation at the conceptual sphere centers on antitheatrical prejudice, with WAA opponents and proponents arguing that the "real" performance occurs in different places. WAA opponents attempted to construe the entire demonstration as a performance. Consider, for example, the following charges: "these are not really hungry people," "the present show at the State House is being staged to build a case for new taxes," and "the demonstrators are being paid $4.50 per day." This interpretation of the events at Trenton is epitomized in an editorial in the *Trenton State Gazette*: "All these are by no means unemployed workers. There are some with a consistent record of aversion to employment, others with a chronic urge for publicity, and a few to whom the novelty of the idea of living in the State Capitol has a somewhat natural appeal."[57] Even more pointedly, J. Parnell Thomas argued that "the present show at the State House is being deliberately staged to build a case for new taxes."[58] Months after the seizure had ended, Joseph Kamp was still portraying WAA demonstrations as performances: "The same stunt [occupation of a public building] was tried a few weeks later at the Chicago City Hall, but after attempting to take possession of the mayor's office, the marchers were dispersed with tear gas. In St. Louis, they were more successful when, in September, a march converged on the Council Chamber and held possession for several days. Now, the Alliance repeats previous Communist performances in staging a march on Washington."[59] The entire demonstration, WAA opponents argued, was a sham, a scam, an attempt by charlatan agitators to dupe the public.

The WAA situates "real" performance in a markedly different position, and this situating is inextricably linked to the presentation of multiple performance postures. Whereas demonstrative performance operates in the subjunctive mood presenting the hypothetical rather than the actual, the remonstrative depiction of the actual legislators operates in the indicative mood, ostensibly representing the real, the actual, the existent. Ultimately, however, these two postures are staged by the WAA in such a way that the hypothetical of demonstrative performance becomes more real and less feigned than the remonstrative depiction of the actual legislators. This reversal is accomplished in a number of ways. First, the actual assemblymen are depicted stereotypically as larger than life and, consequently, as less life-like. Second, the actual assemblymen are depicted as consciously performing or feigning concern for the little person. Recall, for example, the demonstrator-as-"senator" who argued for a pay cut, noting that accepting the reduction "will make us look as though we're trying to help out in the crisis, and that'll make us go over great with the relief clients. . . . Even Presidents have been known to use this stunt."[60] Third, the presentation of parliamentary procedure as akin to vaudeville shtick ("Will the gentleman from Hunterdon submit to a question? Will the gentleman from Hunterdon submit to a question? I will. He will.") makes this particular remonstrative posture seem more put-on than the demonstrative performance of the hypothetical legislative exemplars.

Although proponents and opponents of the WAA demonstration position "performance" in different places, both groups appear to do so for similar reasons. Opponents of the WAA demonstration identify the entire protest as a performance in order to induce the public to believe that the persons involved are faking their hardships, are not really as bad off as they would have the public believe. Similarly, WAA demonstrators identify the actual assemblymen as performers who fake their concern for the "little man" in order to dupe the public into voting for them. Both sides charge the other side with performing, hoping to capitalize on the public's equation of performance with mimesis (faking) rather than kinesis (making).

To summarize, analyzing the role of contestation in cultural performance involves considering at least three dimensions of performance contestation: the direction of effectivity (whether the cultural performance maintains or subverts status quo values and relations of power), the modes of effectivity (the strategies through which the maintenance or subversion is transacted), and the spheres of contestation (the levels at which these strategies are operationalized, whether textual, spatial, or conceptual). As the application of the agonistic framework to the WAA seizure of the New Jersey Assembly illustrates, the framework enables performance scholars not only to argue that a particular performance is contestatory but more importantly to specify the nature, direction, and sites of contestation.

In the case of the WAA demonstration in Trenton, unemployed persons and relief clients used performance to challenge the state legislators' failure to act on the relief appropriations crisis. At the textual sphere, WAA demonstrators engaged in a variety of performance postures, including parodic sendups of the actual legislators as well as enactments of ideal worker-legislators. At the spatial sphere, two battles transpired: a battle to renegotiate the boundary between domestic and political space and a battle between the influential legislative environment and the latent theatrical environment. When WAA members inside the chamber used desks for beds, law books for pillows, and the speaker's table as a makeshift kitchen, they domesticated the political space of the legislative chamber; conversely, when WAA members outside the chamber targeted legislators' homes for periodic demonstrations, they politicized the domestic space of the home. The transformation of the legislative chamber into a theatrical space where white and black working-class women, men, and children enacted their protest against the upper-class white, male legislators was also contestatory insofar as this transformation involved nonsanctioned agents using the legislative space for nonsanctioned purposes. At the conceptual sphere, the primary contestation centered on the antitheatrical prejudice, with WAA proponents and opponents arguing that the "real" performance occurred in different places. While WAA opponents attempted to construe the entire demonstration as a performance and thereby discredit it, the WAA attempted to use performance to construe the actual legislators as performers, thereby discrediting them.

Particularizing Performance Contestation

The past two decades have witnessed the emergence of a growing body of scholarship that addresses the political aspects of performance. Performance scholars not only write about the politics of performance more frequently than twenty years ago, they also conceptualize the politics of performance in a fundamentally different manner. Writing in 1975, Michael Kirby contended that "theater is political if . . . it is intentionally concerned with government, . . . [if it] is intentionally engaged in or consciously takes sides in politics."[61] In contrast, when Mary S. Strine writes of "the politics of asking women's questions," she casts a much broader net, equating politics with the production, reproduction, and circulation of personal and social values.[62]

Although performance scholars have focused increasingly on the political aspects of performance, much performance scholarship nevertheless has stopped short of embracing a view of performance as inherently contestatory. The analytical framework outlined in this essay, rooted as it is in an agonistic view of performance as inherently contestatory, promises a number of advances for performance studies scholarship.

First, the agonistic view of performance avoids the tendency to view performance as representing or containing conflict rather than engaged in conflict. The agonistic framework recognizes that performances represent conflict but goes on to insist that, to the extent that the same conflict can be represented in different ways and for different purposes, the representation of conflict is itself conflictual. Or, to put the matter differently, performances leak, and, as a result, that which is inscribed *in* performances — including conflict — does not remain on the stage but rather seeps into the house, into the lobby, into the streets, and into the more encompassing culture in which the performance occurs.

Second, the analytical framework proposed here simultaneously essentializes and particularizes performance contestation. Unlike some strains of contemporary performance scholarship that view only performances that work against the grain of the status quo as contestatory, the agonistic view of performance recognizes that the status quo does not passively maintain itself but instead is actively maintained by agents whose interests are served by the status quo distribution of power. Just as performances that attempt to foment social change oppose the hegemonic normalizing and naturalizing of the status quo, so also performances that attempt to maintain and solidify the status quo oppose those forces intent on upsetting or at least unsettling status quo relations of power. By arguing that hegemonic performances oppose the redistribution of power and that resistant performances oppose the retrenchment of status quo relations of power, the agonistic framework essentializes performance contestation: all performances are essentially contestatory.

To argue that performance is essentially contestatory, however, does not mean that all performances transact their contestation in the same way, toward the same end, or with the same effects. The analytical framework I have outlined is grounded in the assumption that all performances are contestatory, but it aims at particularizing performance contestation by offering scholars a topoi to guide their analyses of specific performance practices.

It is no longer sufficient for performance scholars to maintain that all performances are shaped by and shape social contexts. Instead, we need to engage in microanalyses geared toward uncovering the specific modalities through which the culture-performance dialectic operates in specific performances. Hopefully, the framework for analyzing how performances instantiate contestation that I have proposed in this essay will prove a useful starting point in this process.

Notes

1. Louis Montrose, "Shaping Fantasies: Figurations of Gender and Power in Elizabethan Culture," in *Representing the English Renaissance*, edited by Stephen Greenblatt (Berkeley: University of California Press, 1988), p. 56.

2. "Luxury Tax Loses Again," *New York Times*, April 21, 1936, p. 4.

3. "Capitol Relief Siege Brings Demand for Special Session," *Trenton Evening Times*, April 22, 1936, p. 2.

4. "Jobless Begin Capitol Siege," *Trenton State Gazette*, April 22, 1936, p. 1.

5. "Jobless Take Over Jersey Assembly," *New York Times*, April 22, 1936, p. 1.

6. " 'Army of Unoccupation' in State House," *Trenton Evening News*, April 22, 1936, p. 1.

7. George Breitman, *The Trenton Siege* (n.p: Le Matro Press, 1936), p. 15.

8. Quoted in ibid., p. 15.

9. Ibid., pp. 15–16.

10. Ibid., pp. 17–18.

11. "Governor Refuses to Help Needy without New Taxes," *Trenton State Gazette*, April 23, 1936, p. 1.

12. Breitman, *The Trenton Siege*, pp. 18–19.

13. Ibid., pp. 17–18.

14. Based on a narrative account in ibid., p. 20.

15. Ibid., p. 19.

16. "Governor Refuses," p. 1.

17. "Senate Balks as House Gets Call to Meet on Relief Snarl," *Trenton Evening Times*, April 23, 1936, p. 2.

18. "Jersey Assembly Heeds Relief Call," *New York Times*, April 24, 1936, p. 6.

19. Breitman, *The Trenton Siege*, p. 23.

20. "Senate Balks," p. 2.

21. "Jobless Assembly in Trenton Votes State of Revolt," *New York Times*, April 22, 1936, p. 1.

22. Ibid.

23. "Mercenary Crusaders?" *Trenton State Gazette*, April 26, 1936, p. 6.

24. "Legislative Tax Action Compelled by Campers," *Sunday Times Advertiser*, April 26, 1936, p. 1.

25. Breitman, *The Trenton Siege*, p. 28.

26. "Alliance Moves to Sue Thomas," *Sunday Times Advertiser*, April 26, 1936, p. 2.

27. "Cleric Praises Jobless' Cause in New Jersey Capitol Sermon," *Washington Post*, April 27, 1936, p. 1.

28. "Unemployed Groups Mobilize for March on State Capitol," *Trenton Evening Times*, April 27, 1936, p. 2.

29. "Jersey Assembly Opens in Uproar," *New York Times*, April 28, 1936, p. 3.

30. Breitman, *The Trenton Siege*, p. 29.

31. "Jersey Assembly Opens," p. 3.

32. "Jersey Jobless Again Camping at State House," *Washington Post*, April 28, 1936, p. 9.

33. *Minutes of the Votes and Proceedings of the Hundred and Sixtieth General Assembly of the State of New Jersey* (Trenton: Macrellis and Quigley, 1936), pp. 697–98.

34. Ibid., pp. 698–99.

35. "Jersey Jobless," p. 9.

36. "Rumpus Kicked Up in Assembly," *Trenton State Gazette*, April 28, 1936, p. 1.

37. "Five Republicans Rule New Jersey Relief," *New York Times*, April 30, 1936, p. 1.

38. John B. Thompson, *Ideology and Modern Culture: Critical Social Theory in the Era of Mass Communications* (Stanford, Calif.: Stanford University Press, 1990), p. 7.

39. Richard Terdiman, *Discourse/Counter-Discourse: The Theory and Practice of Sym-*

bolic Resistance in Nineteenth-Century France (Ithaca: Cornell University Press, 1985), p. 68.

40. Mikhail M. Bakhtin, "Discourse in the Novel," *The Dialogic Imagination: Four Essays*, edited by Michael Holquist, translated by Caryl Emerson and Holquist (Austin: University of Texas Press, 1981), pp. 275–301.

41. "Unemployed Groups," p. 2.

42. Breitman, *The Trenton Siege*, p. 28.

43. *Minutes*, p. 698.

44. Breitman, *The Trenton Siege*, p. 15.

45. "Senate Balks," p. 2.

46. David Harvey, *The Condition of Postmodernity: An Enquiry into the Origins of Cultural Change* (Oxford: Basil Blackwell, 1989), p. 203.

47. Edward Soja, *Postmodern Geographies: The Reassertion of Space in Critical Social Theory* (New York: Verso, 1989), p. 6.

48. Henri Lefebvre, "Reflections on the Politics of Space," translated by Michael J. Enders, in *Radical Geography: Alternative Viewpoints on Contemporary Social Issues*, edited by Richard Peet (Chicago: Maroufa P, 1977), p. 341.

49. Richard Schechner, *Performance Theory* (New York: Routledge, 1988), p. 156; Sally Harrison-Pepper, *Drawing a Circle in the Square: Street Performance in New York's Washington Square Park* (Jackson: University of Mississippi Press, 1990), p. 53.

50. Stanford Anderson, "People in the Physical Environment," in *On Streets*, edited by Stanford Anderson (Cambridge: MIT Press, 1978), pp. 6–7.

51. Quoted in John Spain, Introduction to *The Trenton Seige*, by Breitman, p. 5.

52. Ibid.

53. "Alliance Moves," p. 2.

54. W. B. Gallie, *Philosophy and Historical Understanding* (New York: Schocken, 1964), p. 158.

55. Paul Gray, "The Uses of Theory," *Text and Performance Quarterly* 11.3 (1991): 271–72; Mary S. Strine, Beverly Long, and Mary Frances HopKins, "Research in Interpretation and Performance Studies: Trends, Issues, and Priorities," in *Speech Communication: Essays to Commemorate the 75th Anniversary of the Speech Communication Association*, edited by Gerald Phillips and Julia Wood (Carbondale: Southern Illinois University Press, 1991), pp. 191–201.

56. Jonas Barish, *The Antitheatrical Prejudice* (Berkeley: University of California Press, 1981).

57. "Agitators Have Their Uses," *Trenton State Gazette*, April 25, 1936, p. 6.

58. "Jobless Assembly," p. 1.

59. Joseph Kamp, "Hunger March on Washington," *Commonweal*, February 5, 1937, p. 402.

60. Breitman, *The Trenton Siege*, p. 23.

61. Michael Kirby, "On Political Theater," *Drama Review* 19.2 (1975): 129.

62. Mary S. Strine, "The Politics of Asking Women's Questions: Voice and Value in the Poetry of Adrienne Rich," *Text and Performance Quarterly* 9.1 (1989): 24–41.

(Dis)Playing History

Performing Social Rubbish

Humbug and Romance in the American Marketplace

RUTH LAURION BOWMAN

In his 1865 publication, *The Humbugs of the World*, P. T. Barnum suggested: "It would be a wonderful thing for mankind if some philosophic Yankee would contrive some kind of 'meter' that would measure the infusion of humbug in anything. A 'humbugometer' he might call it. I would warrant him a good sale."[1]

Motivated more by curiosity than philanthropy or profit, I have sought to contrive a particularly refined humbugometer that would be able to detect both the overall infusion of humbug in a thing, as well as more specific gradations of humbug contained within a thing. In particular, I felt that a humbugometer would be especially useful in helping to understand the baffling bamboozle and persistent puffery that keeps popping up in those texts associated with the American romance tradition. For more than a century now, critics have puzzled over the question of why a writer such as Nathaniel Hawthorne would so cavalierly pollute the purity of his artistic masterpieces with cheap theatrics, outrageous displays, as if he were "an entertainer on the stage who must improvise in order not to lose his audience."[2] Taking Hawthorne as a test case, I eagerly hooked up my humbugometer to *The House of the Seven Gables* and found that Richard Chase's worst fears were confirmed: the text was rife with humbug. Indeed, subsequent experiments showed that Hawthorne's canon as a whole had an exceedingly high humbug factor. But what did this mean? What had I found? What *is* humbug?

In various dictionary definitions and colloquial usages, of course, "humbug" is associated with deceit, fraud, or imposture. To Barnum, however, the self-proclaimed "Prince of Humbugs," the term had a more positive — and more conspicuously theatrical — meaning: " 'humbug' consists in putting on glittering appearances — outside show — novel expedients, by which to suddenly arrest public attention, and attract the public eye and ear . . . there are various trades and occupations which need only notoriety to insure success, always provided that when customers are once attracted, they never fail to get their money's worth. If, however, after attracting crowds of customers by his unique displays, a man foolishly fails to give them a full equivalent for their money, they never patronize him a second time, but they very properly denounce him as a swindler, a cheat, an imposter; they do not, however, call him a 'humbug.' "[3] For Barnum, then, humbug is not — or at least not just — the perpetration of a fraud, hoax, or deception, but rather a savvy entrepreneurial strategy, an advertisement, designed to attract the attention of the public. But it was not enough simply to draw customers and take their money, Barnum insisted: the humbug, unlike the cheat or the swindler, always gave them "a full equivalent for their money." The art of humbug lay in promising much and then delivering much — even though the product itself might turn out to be somewhat different from what was advertised.

If we understand humbug, therefore, as a function of the relationship between the promotional framing matter — the advertisements or "puffs" — and the objects displayed, then we may appreciate how delicate an operation it is to manage. Barnum was prolifically inventive in devising puffs that were only marginally related to the material reality of the objects advertised. But, according to Richard Herskowitz, to see them merely as gross misrepresentations is to miss the achievement, for Barnum's real skill was "his elaboration of methods of making misrepresentation tolerable to the consumer," his ability to solicit "the spectator's democratic participation in deceptive image-making." As "a metamessage about a deceptive relationship," Herskowitz concludes, humbug was both "a call to action" and "an occasion for contemplating the showman's ingenious trickery."[4] Barnum had it both ways, apparently: he could make false or exaggerated claims about his products, and then when the audience came to discover the deception, the reflexive aspect of the humbug would kick in to say, "But wasn't this a clever bit of image-making?" Consequently, when Barnum asserted that "the bigger the humbug, the better the people will like it," he was speaking not only of the great pleasure some people derive from being conned, tricked, or hoaxed — though there was that, certainly — but also of the audience's appreciation for the showman's ability to perform a feat that it had judged to be preposterous, outrageous, or impossible.[5]

It is tempting to read Barnum's humbugging as Herskowitz does — that is, as a form of popular culture pedagogy akin to modern advertising: a practice that teaches people to want things they did not know they wanted, and, worse, to experience their own manipulation and exploitation as an aesthetic pleasure. The danger of such a reading, however, is that it transforms Barnum into a rude prototype of today's slick Madison Avenue wizards, inviting us to comprehend and dismiss him in one stroke: we understand the aestheticization of the commodity environment, whereas Barnum's poor "suckers" did not. But, of course, that simply is not true. Not all people valued humbug to the same extent as Barnum, nor was everyone content to sit back and enjoy Barnum's theatrics. In 1867 the *Nation* perceived the danger of humbug quite clearly when it wrote that humbug "eats out the heart of religion and morality . . . , and . . . if it were to spread, might easily end in presenting us with a community regular in its praying and singing, and decent in external crust, but in which all below was rottenness and uncleanness."[6] Though it is true that Barnum himself was loathed and despised by many and suffered many personal attacks, the writer for the *Nation* suggested that the real danger was not so much Barnum himself as what he represented: a virulent strain of hypocrisy and theatricality that might be picked up by the body politic and develop into a social epidemic.

Given the nature of humbug as it has been outlined thus far, it would appear that the user's interpretation of humbugometer-data will depend very much on whether the user *values* humbug, values "glittering appearances" and "outside show"—in other words, values conspicuous theatricality and artifice. In Barnum's cosmology, humbug was good. Not only did it make him rich; it also, or so he claimed, provided a kind of social therapy. But for others who fear or mistrust theatricality, who want an "external crust" that truthfully replicates the internal core, humbug is bad, equivalent to vulgarity, rubbish, moral and social decay. In light of the forty-one million visitors who, between 1841 and 1868, made Barnum's five-storied New York City monstrosity, his American Museum, the most popular attraction of its kind, it is no wonder that Barnum felt that he was providing his public with a desired, even necessary, product. But if we discount the profit motive of humbug, we need to consider Barnum's more complicated and controversial claim that humbug is socially therapeutic and ask why his exhibits were so popular.

According to Neil Harris, Barnum knew perfectly well that "the qualities that had made [him] rich might make humanity unhappy."[7] The Jacksonian ethos of enlightened self-interest helped foster a social climate of aggressive individualism and competitive materialism where, as Barnum put it, "Everyone expected to be cheated, if it was possible."[8] Barnum's "commerce of roguery" was a spectacular—though by no means unique—example of how the principles of democratic individualism could be turned to serve private interests and ambitions.[9] But there was also the danger of eroding the social confidence needed to prevent the whole democratic experiment from collapsing in chaos. As Karen Halttunen has shown, the figure who best embodied these contradictory tendencies in the young republic was the Confidence Man/Yankee, who, like all tricksters, was a thoroughly ambiguous figure: "On the one hand, he was mercenary, hypocritical, philistine, an evil genius of duplicity whose sharp practices exploited the confidence placed in him by his fellow men. But on the other hand he was thrifty, industrious, ascetic, 'a cracker barrel mentor, a Romantic rustic given to apothegms on trust in oneself, in one's fellow man, and in the benevolence of "Natur.' " . . . [H]e was not simply a confidence man, but a 'man of confidence,' uniquely suited to represent the

American nation in an age of democratic patriotism, romanticism, and expanding capitalism."[10] Barnum worked hard to cultivate a public image of himself as a savvy, hardheaded entrepreneur — the Universal Yankee — but he also wanted to be seen as public-spirited, a generous benefactor to his nation and its people, a "man of confidence."

As Harris shows, Barnum pursued the latter task in several ways.[11] Essentially, though, Barnum's view of humbug as social therapy derived from his ideas about the function of entertainment, conspicuous theatricality, and exaggerated advertisements in a society grown suspicious and cynical from the constant pressures of money getting and competition. Barnum felt that humbug offered a much-needed social lubricant or safety valve for a society that had declared war on the arts of illusion in favor of a social performance governed by the imperatives of practicality, self-discipline, self-improvement, and industry. In other words, humbug offered the public a brief reprieve or "blow-off" from the anxieties and pressures of the quotidian social performance.

At the same time, however, while Barnum's puffed-up ploys sought to ease the stress people experienced in the growing American marketplace, it is important to recognize that his humbugs succeeded, not as a counterforce, but because they made use of or "worked" the very same myths, values, and beliefs that gave rise to and supported the new democracy. Essentially, humbug worked to restore social confidence by trusting the spectator to render a competent judgment of the truth or falsity, the value or worth, of the objects or products displayed. Barnum's humbug directed itself toward the much-celebrated "common man," manipulating the era's faith in self-interest, self-improvement, and competition.

Harris argues that humbug was an art based on an "operational aesthetic" — "a delight in observing process and examining for literal truth."[12] It was an art of manufacturing controversy in a culture that valued debate, derived pleasure from learning about how things worked, and placed its trust in the common sense of the common man. As Harris notes, Barnum always "relied on his audience for his taste" and, in so doing, theatricalized "an approach to experience that equated beauty with information and technique, accepting guile because it was more complicated than candor."[13] Because "he understood that American audiences did not mind cries of trickery; in fact they delighted in debate," Barnum's hoaxes and exhibits were usually arranged so as to provoke debate over what was real or genuine, as well as over the processes by which the exhibit had been fashioned.[14]

Barnum's preferred, and most notorious, method of humbugging was to manufacture controversy via "planted" exposés or press reports (many of which he would write himself) questioning the scientific validity of a particular exhibit he was advertising. His elaborate campaign prior to displaying the

"Fejee Mermaid," a dried-up, black-looking fish with parts of a monkey sewn onto it, pressed all the right buttons as his humbug took full advantage of the nation's popular fascination with and ongoing debate over the relationship between Science and Nature/Creation. In response to the onslaught of "expert" opinions, opposing reports, scientific pamphlets, and newspaper puffs, the public came to the museum to decide for itself. Barnum's humbugs said, in effect: "I don't know whether it's genuine or not, and the experts disagree. I leave it to the public to decide." And come they did: within "the first four weeks of the mermaid's exhibition, museum receipts almost tripled."[15]

Though some people undoubtedly were taken in by such things as the Fejee Mermaid, others were not. Even so, they rarely felt cheated but instead took pleasure from the act of seeing through the deception. As Harvey Root explains, "[T]here is no doubt that large numbers got no little egotistical pleasure from the idea that some of Barnum's exhibits were deceptions, but that *they* could distinguish between the real and artificial. . . . The public enjoyed matching its wits against those of the showman in an effort to detect any misrepresentation, and most people at the time looked upon the whole matter much as they did the performance of a prestidigitator whose reputation depended upon his ability to fool them."[16] Further, the pleasure of seeing through the deception was compounded by the spectators' delight in discussing the relative cleverness or crudeness of an object's construction and of Barnum's own humbugging process. Primary to Barnum's definition and use of humbug, then, is his view of the consumer public not as inept or passive, a victim position that is used by critics to support the charge of humbug as exploitation, but as shrewd and savvy marketplace opponents who, in paying to see the puffed-up exhibits, purchased the right to pit their skills of detection—their education and judgment—against the Master Hoaxer of mid-nineteenth-century America.

Less spectacular evidence of Barnum's ability to successfully decode and implement the tastes and values of his audience is his promoting and providing the middle-class family with a safe and fairly respectable arena for "blow off" behavior. Like our contemporary family amusement centers and theme parks, Barnum's American Museum offered a carnival-like atmosphere protected by "safe" moral and physical boundaries. Parents who would never dare set foot in a "house of satan," a theater, much less expose their children to its unhealthy atmosphere, felt comfortable in the "museum" context, even though Barnum's museum featured its own in-house theatrical company. The motley mix of historical artifacts and curiosities, living and stuffed animals, freaks and wax figures, food and souvenir vendors, as well as the scientific demonstrations, melodramas, musical reviews, magic acts, and minstrel shows staged in the "Lecture Room" were "all in an atmosphere, as the proprietor promised, free from the noxious fumes of 'segars' and rum, and . . . 'improper' characters."[17] Furthermore, because "fine art" was displayed alongside tomahawks and trained fleas, the viewer's distrust, dislike, or fear of the more abstract aspects of "high" art was replaced by the pleasures of evaluating the object's "cost, age, detail, and rarity. . . . Beauty, significance, spiritual values, could be bypassed in favor of seeing what was odd, or what worked, or was genuine."[18] In the museum context Barnum created, art was operationalized, rather than aestheticized.

As I noted in the beginning of this essay, Hawthorne has been criticized for much the same reason that Barnum was, for practicing a kind of outrageous duplicity. Henry James helped to establish this line of criticism early on by calling attention to the opposition between allegory and realism in Hawthorne's texts. In James's view, Hawthorne always was seeking to find a way to express profound spiritual truths, but for some reason—James suggests, of course, that it was the relative thinness of American culture — he was unable to find an adequate material basis in reality that would serve as a vehicle to express those truths. Consequently, Hawthorne's "spirituality" seems almost to lapse at times into physical comedy; his reductive allegories work so hard to be profound that it is almost embarrassing. In short, while James recognized that Hawthorne wanted to write about society, wanted to address the public, wanted to enter the cultural marketplace, he felt that Hawthorne usually ended up by wandering off into an allegorical cloud-cuckoo-land.[19]

Interestingly enough, Hawthorne's own assessments of his work say much the same thing. His prefaces are filled with what appear, on one level, to be devastating critiques of his shortcomings as a writer. Not only does he "confess" his inability to convey his allegorical meanings in a realistic narrative; he also draws attention to his "inability" to communicate anything at all of substance: "How little have I told! — and, of that little, how almost nothing is even tinctured with any quality that makes it exclusively my own! Has the reader gone wandering, hand in hand with me, through the inner passages of my being, and have we groped together into all its chambers and examined their treasures or their rubbish? Not so. . . . So far as I am a man of really individual attributes, I veil my face; nor am I, nor have ever been, one of those supremely hospitable people, who serve up their own hearts delicately fried, with brain-sauce, as a tidbit for their beloved public."[20] Although Hawthorne's irony here seems transparent, critics commonly condemn him precisely for withholding those "tidbits," for "veiling his face," for speaking through masks rather than speaking the language of his "heart." In addition to Chase, who compared Hawthorne to an entertainer, others have fixed him with such epithets as "magician," "rogue," and "dissembler."[21] A common by-product of these charges is that the spectacle in Hawthorne's fiction is stripped away, criticized, or reworked into new interpretive allegories — as if spectacle itself were unworthy of study, as if it were irrelevant in comparison to "brain-sauce."

In general, Hawthorne's "dissembling" is usually interpreted in one of three ways: as a symptom of his psychological tics or obsessions, as an indication of his stylistic faults as a writer, or as evidence of his desire to be "popular." Consequently, whereas James himself suggested that "Hawthorne always knew perfectly what he was about," many critics who followed him tend to make Hawthorne the victim of his veil wearing, rather than an active user of those veils.[22] As a result, Hawthorne is given no credit for his jester attire and is reconstructed as an entirely earnest fellow who was betrayed by his artistic limitations, his unconscious, or by the demands of the "oppressive" marketplace.[23] In so rescuing Hawthorne from his own theatricality, his romances continue to meet what appears to be *our* need for a visionary but victimized artist-on-the-fringe, the marginal figure who turns out to be oh-so-central in revealing the cultural, material, or spiritual poverty of the United States. Such readings work very well to uphold the pervasive myth of the American romance, but they drain Hawthorne's texts of their celebratory aspects, glittering spectacles, crude narrators, stupid jokes, middle-class values, humbug.

In *The House of the Seven Gables*, Hawthorne humbugs his reader in at least three ways. First, he promises a moral. Second, the moral is dramatized using codes the nineteenth-century reader knew well. Third, the romance is funny.

Basically, the romance concerns itself with how three questionable and related deaths in the fictive past affect the nineteenth-century Pyncheon household in the fictive present. The first death occurred in the early colonial period, when the powerful Colonel Pyncheon, desirous of the "obscure" Matthew Maule's land, accused Maule of being a warlock, saw him executed on the scaffold, and thereafter laid claim to Maule's property. After erecting a seven-gabled house on the ill-gotten land, Colonel Pyncheon dies, apparently by choking on his own blood. In the more recent past, the original crime is compounded when the colonel's descendant, Judge Jaffrey Pyncheon, frames his own cousin, Clifford, for the curious death of their uncle and thereby inherits the Pyncheon fortune. The bulk of the romance tells the story of the last remaining relics of the Pyncheon clan, placing the now-released but enfeebled Clifford, his elderly sister Hepzibah, and their young country cousin, Phoebe, in the house and at the mercy of the judge, who resides on his own rural estate. The Maule contingent is secretly represented by the daguerreotypist, Holgrave, who boards at the old Pyncheon home. By the end of the romance, the history of Pyncheon criminality has been made public, the "evil" Judge Pyncheon has died, and the surviving characters have abandoned the decaying old house and moved into the judge's newer country home where, presumably, they will live happily ever after. Or will they?

What troubles many critics about this ending is that it appears to contradict the "moral purpose" Hawthorne advertised in the preface to the romance: " — the truth, namely, that the wrong-doing of one generation lives into the successive ones ... and [the author] would feel it a singular gratification, if this Romance might effectually convince mankind . . . of the folly of tumbling down an avalanche of ill-gotten gold, or real estate, on the heads of an unfortunate posterity, thereby to maim and crush them."[24] With this moral in mind, critics commonly center the text's authority in the character of Holgrave, whose initial status as a progressive democrat, social reformer, and artist is equated with Hawthorne. Consequently, Holgrave's conversion to a more conservative, bourgeois life — married to Phoebe Pyncheon and living in the country estate of the deceased Judge Pyncheon — is perceived as inconsistent with the character's (and author's) avowed moral and political stance. Furthermore, it is not altogether clear how this "happy ending" puts an end to "Maule's curse," how it atones for the sins of the past. In his 1851 review, E. P. Whipple complained that the "integrity of the original conception" is destroyed by the "contrived" conclusion.[25] More recently, Michael Gilmore claimed that Holgrave's "action betrays his calling as an artist of the legendary and is precisely analogous to Hawthorne's contrivance of a happy ending" in hopes of commercial success.[26] In both cases, Hawthorne's final product is found lacking in terms of his original promise, his "humbug" is proclaimed to be a swindle.

In his recent study, Richard Millington challenges this popular reading of the romance by relocating its moral center. Instead of relying on the Holgrave-as-Hawthorne link, Millington argues that the romance is primarily concerned with "what it means to speak from the center of a community" and, in so doing, "transform that center in the very act of occupying it."[27] The challenge facing the characters in the text is how to reestablish the community's moral center when the community's main legacy is a historical cycle of treachery, ill-gotten wealth, and death. The "romantic" solution, of course, would be to kill off all the Pyncheons in a grand gesture of atonement and to have Holgrave light out for the territories, get back to nature, meet some Indians, and so forth. Hawthorne chose a different resolution, one that advocates rebuilding a "communal consensus" out of those extant social codes that give "a culture its center of gravity."[28] Hence, as the heavily encoded "progressive democrat," Holgrave, moves closer to his opposite, the heavily encoded "domestic female," Phoebe, they each move closer to the moral "key" of the romance, which is, Millington concludes, "a marriage between . . . domestic values and action in the world at large." It is this marriage, rather than the individuals alone, which resists "the authoritarian and construct[s] a community that can sustain its inevitable encounter with the economic and social forces that will unmoor it."[29]

Millington's study is helpful in providing us with a more positive assessment of what Hawthorne actually does in the romance. Instead of chastising him for what he did not do — provide a grand, dramatic resolution to the sins of the past — Millington looks at the more homely image of community represented at the end of the romance in order to decipher its moral center. Where Millington and I disagree is in our understanding of what that community looks like, of what its moral center consists, and how it is put together. Whereas Millington sees the new communal consensus as an effect of the Holgrave-Phoebe marriage, I see the marriage as an effect of other causes. A major factor that accounts for our different readings is our understanding of the comic and grotesque elements in the text. To put it simply: I value humbug; Millington does not.

One example of this is Millington's discussion of chapters two through four of the romance, which depicts the elderly Hepzibah, who, "after sixty years of narrowing means," must "step down from her pedestal of imaginary rank" and open a cent-shop on the ground floor of the old house.[30] These early chapters are devoted to Hepzibah's "overpoweringly ridiculous" first day, with the narrator providing a detailed account of a "mildewed piece of aristocracy" turned shopkeeper: "There, again, she has upset a tumbler of marbles, all of which roll different ways, and each individual marble, devil-directed, into the most difficult obscurity that it can find. Heaven help our poor old Hepzibah, and forgive us for taking a ludicrous view of her position! As her rigid and rusty frame goes down upon its hands and knees, in quest of the absconding marbles, we positively feel so much the more inclined to shed tears of sympathy, from the very fact that we must needs turn aside and laugh at her!"[31] In passages such as this one, Millington detects two different voices struggling over the representation of "our poor old Hepzibah." Agreeing with Richard Brodhead's view that " 'the cruel humor' " of the first narrative voice " 'is supplemented by . . . a more omniscient narrator who is privileged to know the interior of Hepzibah's heart,' " Millington argues that the first "inanely aggressive" voice "can only represent Hepzibah by misrepresenting her," whereas the second, and prevailing, voice asserts "the significance of everyday life despite the triviality or grotesqueness of its surface." In sum, Millington concludes that Hawthorne sets these "voices" in opposition in order to illustrate to the reader how "a communal voice" must educate "itself out of bluntmindedness into perspicacity."[32]

It is not that a more sympathetic, serious, sometimes sentimental, tone or mode of expression is not used in this and other sections of the *House*. It is, and often. But, by devaluing the broadly comic, vulgar, and parodic mode of expression that Hawthorne uses here and throughout the romance, Millington seems to suggest that the new moral consensus cannot tolerate the trivial and grotesque aspects of everyday life unless these are scrubbed clean, rendered "perspicacious." In other words, he posits that Hawthorne used a parodic-travestying voice in the romance as something of a straw man: he makes fun of Hepzibah only to show us in the end that making fun of people is not a very nice thing to do.

As Mikhail Bakhtin has taught us, however, double-voiced discourse such as Hawthorne's cannot be domesticated quite so easily as Millington suggests. Parody, jokes, and laughter are always corrosive, threatening, or destabilizing, working both to "ridicule the straightforward, serious word in all its generic guises" and to provide a comic, critical alternative to it.[33] Instead of viewing Hawthorne's parodic-travestying modes of expression as antithetical to the reeducation of the community, Bakhtin would have us see them as integral to the reeducation of the community. For Bakhtin, this objective or telos is best represented in the figure of the clown or fool. He writes: "[T]he masks of the clown and the fool (transformed in various ways) come to the aid of the novelist. These masks are not invented. . . . They are linked with the folk . . . the chronotope of the public square and with the trappings of the theater. All of this is of the highest importance for the novel. At last a form was found to portray the mode of existence of a man who is in life, but not of it, life's perpetual spy and reflector; at last specific forms had been found to reflect private life and make it public."[34] Hawthorne's narrator works in just this way. In the case of Hepzibah, for example, he offers us an enticing view of Hepzibah's private life, demonstrating a powerful sympathy for her frailty and her reduced circumstances. But he also finds the scene — poor old Hepzibah crawling around on the floor after her marbles — to be extremely funny. By permitting himself to turn away and laugh at her, he manages to find a way of making her private life public, but without falling into the trap of sentimentality. Laughter exposes the cult of sentimentality and the self-indulgent spilling of "brain-sauce" as farcical impostures.

In *The House of the Seven Gables*, the serio-comic telos or "moral center" is evident not only in Hawthorne's clownish narration, but also in a character within the text, the "patched philosopher," Uncle Venner.[35] Uncle Venner is usually overlooked by readers and critics of the romance. Insofar as he is a "minor" character, tangential to the central drama going on inside the house, this is understandable. Ironically, though, Venner is also a concrete example of what gets purged or shoved aside in our conception of the American romance. On one level, Venner is a prototypical "Yankee" and country bumpkin. He is a clown or fool, a bit of comic relief, and thus disposable. On another level, however, his presence and what he represents pollutes, destabilizes, and pokes fun at any tendencies the romance might have toward erecting some sort of fixed social, aesthetic, and moral center. As the embodiment of parody and humbug,

Venner undermines and offers an alternative to Holgrave and Phoebe's Eden in Suburbia.

A literal and figurative "man of patches," Venner is described as "a miscellaneous old gentleman, partly himself, but, in good measure, somebody else; patched together . . . of different epochs; an epitome of times and fashions."[36] Venner is a walking, talking American Museum. Although he appears only sporadically throughout the tale, each of his appearances works like Barnum's museum to initiate debate, to provoke controversy, to raise questions. In effect, Venner operationalizes the romance by asking the reader to consider how his philosophy differs from that of the other characters and how his presence affects the overall meaning of the tale.

The principal philosophical battle depicted in the romance pits the progressive democrat, Holgrave, against the exploitative capitalist, Judge Pyncheon. Venner's actions appear unrelated to this grand philosophical debate. Rather than working to accumulate riches or proselytize for social reform, the old man goes "his rounds, every morning, to gather up the crumbs of the table and overflowings of the dinner-pot, as food for a pig of his own."[37] And, on his retirement to what he calls "his farm" (actually, a government-funded workhouse), Venner hopes to "make a feast of the portly grunter, and invite all his neighbors to partake of the joints and spareribs which they had helped to fatten."[38] Venner's conception of democracy as a feast or party built from scraps and leftovers offers a comic alternative to Holgrave's desire to rebuild democracy by tearing down the "lifeless institutions" of "the moss-grown and rotten Past" and the judge's efforts to preserve those institutions by "trampling on the weak, and, when essential to his ends, doing his utmost to beat down the strong."[39]

Venner's seemingly low and unthreatening status enables him to gain access to and insinuate his authority over the ideological battleground that is the house. Not only does Uncle Venner outlive the powerful Judge Pyncheon and secure enough authority to warrant his being the last character seen on the romance's stage, he also has a significant impact on Holgrave's reeducation. It is Venner's daguerreotype, after all, that Holgrave displays at the entrance to his studio, and it is the old man who instigates Holgrave's betrothal to Phoebe. Indeed, as the narrator succinctly points out, "[Holgrave's] error lay, in supposing that this age, more than any past or future one, is destined to see the tattered garments of Antiquity exchanged for a new suit, instead of gradually renewing themselves by patchwork."[40]

By the end of the romance, the death of Judge Pyncheon facilitates the final victory of Venner's patchwork philosophy in the image of community that Hawthorne represents. Because the old house analogues the dead or fixed nature of the judge, it is categorically left to him. The death also bestows on

Clifford, Hepzibah, Phoebe, and, "through her, that sworn foe of wealth and all manner of conservatism — the wild reformer — Holgrave," the riches of the past.[41] If the *House* is read under the common prescriptives of the American romance, Holgrave should have been repulsed by the materialistic and conservative bent of the new arrangement and, in visionary transcendence, gone elsewhere. If denied his freedom from the oppressive sins of the past, he should have died. Instead, Holgrave opts to spend the remainder of his life living with a nice young woman in a nice house in the nice suburbs of Salem.

Who can blame him?

But this elegant estate in the Eden of Suburbia is not occupied by Adam and Eve alone. Instead, Adam and Eve are accompanied by an eccentric uncle, a rusty aunt, the ancestral chickens, and, yes, Uncle Venner. This patched-together assembly marks, as Michel de Certeau might say, "*a way of using imposed systems*" to "redistribute . . . space."[42] The movement of the patchwork family into the judge's country estate does not reject or transform the "dominant order," of course, nor does it atone for all the sins of the past. What it does suggest, however, is that social reformation may be a bit messier than certain moral fictions would have us believe. As the narrator puts it, "No great mistake, whether acted or endured, in our mortal sphere, is ever really set right."[43] Hawthorne's parodic reversal of presumed expectations "demonstrates," as Bertolt Brecht writes, "the insufficiency of all things, including ourselves" — in this case, our tidy little morals.[44] Instead, the family is asked to "make do" within the "joke of contradiction." By means of a somewhat messy display of what sits underneath the pure ideals, illusions, and myths of the American House, Hawthorne's romance refuses the charm of Beauty and urges his reader into an arena where the patched ideas of a clown are highlighted. As with the visitors to Barnum's museum, the characters are not taught what to learn. Rather, they learn how to speak, and in a more messy register. As the "sagacious" neighbor Dixey observes, it is " 'Pretty good business! . . . Pretty good business!' "[45]

By suggesting in the preceding discussion that Hawthorne's actual practice of romance resembles Barnum's humbug more than it does our canonical view of American romance, I should perhaps make it clear — in case it is not already — that I see this as a good thing and not — as many of Hawthorne's critics have done — as evidence of his artistic gaffes or psychological peculiarities. Like Barnum, Hawthorne was highly accomplished at working the relationship between the "puff" of romance and the material reality of the objects, characters, and actions he displays. And though critics since Henry James have called attention to the discrepancies that often result from Hawthorne's humbugging, they have usually interpreted such things as evidence of Hawthorne's shortcomings.

It is my argument that Hawthorne made use of the spectacular, the theatrical, the comic, the grotesque, and the vulgar throughout his work to subvert the tendency, on the part of his readers or critics, to sentimentalize or romanticize his romances. Indeed, I would suggest that he used these discursive modes in much the same way that Barnum did: to provoke debate — debate over the very "romantic" solutions that his texts seem to propose. Hawthorne's texts always entice us with the hope or promise of a romantic solution to our social ills — of a new community redeemed from the sins of the past, of a new moral code built from a marriage of contending social-historical forces, of a more authentic life where the truths of the heart could be expressed fully. But they also subvert that desire by demonstrating the insufficiency of any fixed or finalized solution to our problems, by calling attention to the inescapable gulf that exists between our desire for profound allegorical meanings or spiritual truths and the crude materiality of our social existence. Even so, with private life or personal experience made laughable by public-izing it, with romance carefully circumscribed as a ludicrous imposture, there is still ample scope for living in the acceptance of human weakness, frailty, and imperfection.

American literary and cultural history has always displayed a deep ambivalence toward conspicuous theatricality and artifice, outward shows, glittering appearances, and humbug, even though such practices have always been popular staples of American cultural creativity. Consequently, although our history is filled with examples of conspicuous theatricality and exaggerated forms of representation, it is also marked by equally vigorous strains of antitheatricalism or antirepresentationalism, which stress the importance of constructing more "authentic" forms of speech and behavior that would erase the line between being and seeming. This ambivalence is best exemplified in the way we have learned to oppose the two terms I have discussed in this essay: humbug and romance. My purpose has been to show that any contradiction or opposition that one might be tempted to see between humbug and romance is based on certain misconceptions, not only about how Hawthorne actually practiced romance, but also about what humbug meant, how *it* was practiced, in the nineteenth-century cultural marketplace. To dismiss humbug as simple deceit, fraud, or imposture is to ignore its function in the public sphere, where it worked to operationalize a common form of cultural criticism. And to ignore Hawthorne's use of humbug in his own romances is to perpetuate an asocial or "romanced" idea of those romances. Yet, although Barnum and Hawthorne were critical of the desire for an "authentic" speech devoid of theatricality and artifice, that desire is still evident in today's cultural marketplace, particularly in those texts that favor an "evocative," experiential voice as a way to question (or evade) the problematic conventions of historical representation.

In July 1991 the Public Broadcasting Service (PBS) aired, as part of its *P.O.V.* (Point of View) series, the experimental/documentary film *Tongues Untied*. In this film, director/writer/performer Marlon Riggs seeks to destroy the stereotypic social codes that have marked the black, male homosexual as a monster and, in turn, isolated him from the American experience and its modes of expression. In his well-crafted mosaic of personal narratives, poems, songs, dances, and visual imagery, Riggs's "tribe of warriors and outlaws" appear on camera to speak passionately of their feelings and experiences as a way to explore and, perhaps, escape the suppressed cultural space into which black gay males have been confined.

In his review of *Tongues Untied*, Howard Rosenberg praised the film and its message, even though he feared that it might "nourish homophobia even as it seeks to drive a spike through its heart." Unfortunately, though, Rosenberg seems unable to explain *why* the film might "nourish homophobia," except to suggest that viewers would be unduly influenced by all the controversy surrounding the film's airing. This was not the fault of the "award-laden" film, Rosenberg argues, but of the narrow-mindedness of those "conservative tongues" who pressured PBS to remove the film from its schedule because of its subject matter ("black men loving black men"), its "pornographic" imagery, and its "obscene" language. In this, Rosenberg implies that the more outrageous words and images employed in the construction of the film are justified by the "correctness" of the film's overall message.[46]

What is disturbing about Riggs's film, as well as Rosenberg's review of it, is that there is nothing particularly disturbing about it at all—that a film that understands itself to be "revolutionary," both in form and content, should be so ordinary in its use of standard, romanticized performance modalities.[47] Certainly, Riggs's evocation of his experiences as a black gay male strives to challenge rather than placate (some) viewers and their expectations. But, as the artful images, fragments, and vignettes pile up, the uninterrupted harmony of Riggs's "challenging" voice becomes monotonously fixed. There are few, if any, disruptive contrasts, alternative views, voices, or images, that, were they included, might in fact have facilitated and activated the movement of Riggs's collective into the problematic and messy marketplace from which he feels he has been outcast. Instead, Riggs exploits the very few images of his "others" (black women, white men) in order to celebrate himself and his community, to dwell on his pain, pride, doubt, and experience.

This exploitative mode of expression does not, I suspect, represent Riggs's intent. Indeed, a confessional and self-reflective search for "my reflection . . . my passage back home," the lifting of "my burden," and the evocation of his pain, pride, doubt, and knowledge better characterize his purpose. Riggs may not want to placate viewers, but he does not seem interested in talking to them, either. As his title implies, having been silenced for so long, he wants simply to speak; he does not want to debate but to monopolize the conversation (for the length of the film, at least). As Bill Nichols points out, the film refuses to give us "the usual sociological evidence about the problems of identity and self-esteem"; nor does it adopt a classic problem/solution expository structure; instead, "the film tends to accumulate impressions and evidence but without subordinating them to a controlling argument."[48] Although this quality invites us to see the film, as Nichols does, as essentially "open" or "dialogical," the film itself is not dialogic, at least in Bakhtin's sense of the term, for the viewer is put in the position either of having to accept the film's sentiments as an authentic expression of one individual's or one group's racial and sexual self-hood, or of rejecting it altogether. Like so many other "evocative" forms of rhetoric and performance today, *Tongues Untied* appears to have abandoned persuasion as an end, has given up on the possibility of forging a more gen-uinely democratic assembly, because it assumes that the audience is already polarized or divided by irreconcilable attitudes, beliefs, or values.

In another recent film, *Paris Is Burning*, director Jennie Livingston focuses her camera on the staging of drag balls in Harlem clubs between 1987 and 1989. In the film, the balls are represented as highly competitive events in which Latino and African American male gays, transsexuals, and transvestites costume themselves in such a way as to represent the social performances of certain recognizable, contemporary social "types" (e.g., preppies, yuppies, debutantes, soldiers). These types are then displayed in spectacular prom-enades, "voguing," before what appears to be a largely inclusive audience of ball participant-observers. Trophies go to those performers who best replicate the various social types in costume and presentational style, although in the latter case there is plenty of room for stylized free play. Outer form, showy dis-play, spectacle, and artifice are, it appears, extremely valuable qualities within this specific subcultural event.

Although a considerable portion of the film is devoted to images of these events, the film also devotes approximately half its time to interviews with various participants and "stars" of the ball subculture, most of which are shot in the conventional "talking heads" documentary style. In some cases, the interviewees function as informants, telling us about the meaning or signifi-cance of some element of the subculture's speech or behavior; in other cases, they talk about their own lives. In comparison to Riggs's film, this one appears to have been made rather crudely. The film refuses to "aestheticize" the balls or the participants: neither the balls nor the interviews are lit, framed, or set as art; nor does the film comment on what it shows with voiceover narration. Consequently, the filmmaker's attitudes and intentions must be deciphered mainly from the construction of the montage, the way that scenes of the balls are edited together with the interviews. The main effect of the montage is to construct an objective image of the filmmaker that "says," in effect: "Here's what I saw and heard. I'm not sure what it's all about. You decide." And, for the most part, reviewers have decided that the film offers a sympathetic or neutral representation of the ball subculture.[49]

Other critics, however, have rebuked Livingston precisely on the grounds of her seeming objectivity. In a scathing review, bell hooks criticizes Livingston for her decision to show the balls at all, rather than concentrating solely on the personal narratives of her informants, as the "yuppie-looking, straight-acting, pushy, predominantly white folks in the audience" will tend to see these events as entertaining or "funny."[50] Like other forms of "objective" colonialist rhetoric, hooks argues, Livingston's film placates middle-class white heterosexual viewers by transforming black "ritual" into entertaining "spectacle."[51] That is, "the sustained focus on elaborate displays at balls diffused the power of the more serious critical narrative" embodied in the "true life stories and testimonies" offered in the interviews.[52] Finally, because many performers in the film mimic an idealized version of the social performances of successful white women, hooks claims that the film offers "a graphic documentary portrait of the way in which colonized black people (in this case black gay brothers, some of whom were drag queens) worship at the throne of whiteness, even when such worship demands that we live in perpetual self-hate, steal, lie, go hungry, and even die in its pursuit."[53] In short, "Livingston does not oppose the way hegemonic whiteness 'represents' blackness, but rather assumes an imperial overseeing position that is in no way progressive or counterhegemonic."[54]

Although hooks is reacting partly to the film itself and partly to the positive responses to it by audiences and reviewers, she is also somewhat critical of the balls and ball participants. Instead of humbugging themselves with drag balls, hooks says, black gays and lesbians should "break through denial" and "confront and accept ourselves as we really are."[55] As Peggy Phelan pointed out, however, it is precisely this longing for an "authentic" racial and sexual identity — a selfhood unleashed from the restrictive codes of representation — that the spectacle of the balls works to critique. Although the ball participants express that desire, their performances "stage its perpetual failure."[56] Finally, because the participants have experienced that failure in performance, their attitudes toward the construction of the illusion of gender are tinged with an irony that, as I read it, is all the more powerful for Livingston's decision *not* to impose her own irony or reflexivity onto the film.[57] Moreover, because this ironic knowledge develops from the experience of an exaggerated, highly theatrical performance style, it is difficult to accept hooks's curious conflation of "theatricality" and "denial." And insofar as spectacular forms of *mis*representation have often served as important means for managing inter- and intra-cultural communication, it would be presumptuous of us to recommend that black gays, or any other group, abandon such forms.[58]

Perhaps it is true, as Phelan suggests, that *Paris Is Burning* accepts too easily the conventions for representing otherness found in ethnographic/documentary film for it to take full advantage of the "radical epistemology" of cross-dressing performed by its subjects.[59] And perhaps it is true, as well, that viewers will miss or ignore the radical "message" of the balls and see them as exotic entertainments, as hooks argues. But what should Livingston have done instead? What strategies are available now for representing people, their experiences, and our encounters with them, now that contemporary theory has given the lie to so many forms of representation?

If it is true that representation is always an assertion of power, a way of domesticating "otherness" and normalizing "difference," one that sacrifices embodied knowledge and situated experience in favor of disembodied knowledge and abstract conceptualizations, then one option might be to abandon representation altogether in favor of the evocative, experiential mode of expression featured in Riggs's *Tongues Untied*. So far, however, it has been easier to talk about such things than it has been to produce them, and it is far from clear how evocation "defamiliarizes commonsense reality in a bracketed context of performance, evokes a fantasy whole abducted from fragments, and then returns participants to the world of commonsense — transformed, renewed and sacralized," as Stephen Tyler claims.[60] Nor is it clear how such performances might restore or augment our social confidence. Sitting around trying to tell "our own" stories — a lot of emperors without any clothes — perhaps we would only end up swindling ourselves.

Both Phelan and hooks suggest another option when they posit that Livingston's film might have been saved from its appropriative, hegemonic functioning if she had quit posing as an ethnographer/documentarist, had spoken reflexively about her own status as "outsider" (white woman/lesbian), and had confessed her inability to say or know anything authoritative about the events or persons depicted in her film. However, as Paul Rabinow has argued, such recommendations seem historically naive about Western epistemological traditions.[61] As Brecht and many others — Barnum and Hawthorne, for example — have shown us, the reflexive option does not resolve the problem of authority so much as it creates new ones. In today's cultural marketplace, especially, demonstrating one's reflexivity is, more often than not, a device used to *establish* one's authority rather than to disown it.

Furthermore, such recommendations seem historically naive about American cultural, literary, and performance traditions, as well. We find an intriguing parallel to current debates over the politics of representation in nineteenth-century efforts to resolve the problems of representation by developing a code of sincerity. Barnum, Hawthorne, and others understood that attempts to fashion a national or personal ethos on antitheatrical or antirepresentational premises was highly problematic, and that efforts to build a social character by cultivating inner realities at the expense of outward appearances had the ironic effect of promoting, rather than retarding, hypocrisy. As Karen Halttunen has shown, Americans discovered, much to their chagrin, that appearances were becoming *more* important to personal success and less reliable as indicators of personal character: hypocrisy paid off, and in a society that valued what "worked" or paid off, "the problem of hypocrisy revealed a serious crisis in urban middle-class norms of social conduct."[62]

If the cult of sincerity and sentimentality that developed during the middle decades of the nineteenth century can be viewed as an attempt to develop a new code for scripting a social performance to resolve the question of hypocrisy, I would suggest that humbug worked in an analogous way at the level of "reading" social performances. That is, humbug was a form of cultural performance enacted to the rituals of the quotidian social performance. Because it was such a conspicuous, reflexive metacommentary on the sincerity/hypocrisy dilemma, humbug allowed its audiences to test and refine their skills as readers of the social text. Consequently, although humbug has often been interpreted as exploiting and undermining social confidence, it may be interpreted at another level as helping to restore social confidence by trusting the spectator to render a competent judgment of the truth or falsity, the value or worth, of the objects or products displayed in the cultural marketplace.

Notes

1. P. T. Barnum, *The Humbugs of the World* (New York: Carleton, 1865), p. 159.

2. Richard Chase, *The American Novel and Its Tradition* (Baltimore: Johns Hopkins University Press, 1957), p. 83.

3. Barnum, *Humbugs of the World*, p. 20.

4. Richard Herskowitz, "P. T. Barnum's Double Bind," *Social Text* 2 (Summer 1979): 134, 133, 140.

5. Quoted in Neil Harris, *Humbug: The Art of P. T. Barnum* (Chicago: University of Chicago Press, 1973), p. 168.

6. Quoted in ibid., p. 190.

7. Ibid., p. 214.

8. Quoted in ibid., p. 12.

9. Ibid., p. 10.

10. Karen Halttunen, *Confidence Men and Painted Women: A Study of Middle–class Culture in America, 1830–1870* (New Haven: Yale University Press, 1982), p. 31.

11. See Harris, *Humbug*, chap. 8. Much of the following account is indebted to Harris's superb study.

12. Ibid., p. 79.

13. Ibid., pp. 229, 57.

14. Ibid., pp. 61–62.

15. Ibid., pp. 63–64.

16. Harvey W. Root, *The Unknown Barnum* (New York: Harper and Brothers, 1927), pp. 312–13; emphasis in original.

17. A. H. Saxon, Introduction to *Selected Letters of P. T. Barnum*, edited by Saxon (New York: Columbia University Press, 1983), p. xiv.

18. Harris, *Humbug*, p. 79.

19. Henry James, *Hawthorne* (1879; reprint, New York: Harper, 1907). See esp. pp. 41–50, 60–64, 111–14.

20. Nathaniel Hawthorne, Preface to *Mosses from an Old Manse*: The Old Manse," in *Tales and Sketches*, edited by Roy Harvey Pearce (New York: Library of America, 1982), p. 1147.

21. Granville Hicks, *The Great Tradition: An Interpretation of American Literature since the Civil War* (1933; reprint, Chicago: Quadrangle Books, 1969), p. 6; R. W. B. Lewis, *The American Adam: Innocence, Tragedy, and Tradition in the Nineteenth Century* (Chicago: University of Chicago Press, 1955), p. 115; Kenneth Marc Harris, *Hypocrisy and Self-Deception in Hawthorne's Fiction* (Charlottesville: University Press of Virginia, 1988), p. 141. Hawthorne's duplicity is also a prominent theme in D. H. Lawrence's *Studies in Classic American Literature* (1923; reprint, Harmondsworth: Penguin Books, 1977), chaps. 7–8. J. Hillis Miller provides a more positive reading of Hawthorne's strategy of "veiling" in his "De-Facing It: Hawthorne and History," in *Hawthorne and History*, edited by Martin Heusser and Harold Schweizer (Cambridge, Mass.: Basil Blackwell, 1991), pp. 46–132.

22. James, *Hawthorne*, p. 47.

23. Robert Clark, *History, Ideology, and Myth in American Fiction, 1832–52* (London: Macmillan, 1984), p. 122.

24. Nathaniel Hawthorne, Preface to *The House of the Seven Gables*, in *Novels*, edited by Millicent Bell (New York: Library of America, 1983), p. 352.

25. Edwin Percy Whipple, [Review of *The House of the Seven Gables*], *Graham's Magazine* 38 (Spring 1851): 467–68. Reprinted in *Hawthorne: The Critical Heritage*, edited by J. Donald Crowley (New York: Barnes and Noble, 1970), p. 201.

26. Michael T. Gilmore, *American Romanticism and the Marketplace* (Chicago: University of Chicago Press, 1985), p. 109.

27. Richard Millington, *Practicing Romance: Narrative Form and Cultural Engagement in Hawthorne's Fiction* (Princeton: Princeton University Press, 1992), p. 106.

28. Ibid., p. 120.

29. Ibid., p. 152.

30. Hawthorne, *The House of the Seven Gables*, p. 383.

31. Ibid., pp. 385, 398, 383.

32. Millington, *Practicing Romance*, pp. 110–11.

33. Mikhail M. Bakhtin, *The Dialogic Imagination: Four Essays*, edited by Michael Holquist, translated by Caryl Emerson and Holquist (Austin: University of Texas Press, 1981), p. 52.

34. Ibid., p. 161.

35. Hawthorne, *The House of the Seven Gables*, p. 598.

36. Ibid., pp. 486, 405.

37. Ibid., p. 404.

38. Ibid., p. 598.

39. Ibid., pp. 506, 458.

40. Ibid., p. 507.

41. Ibid., p. 621.

42. Michel de Certeau, *The Practice of Everyday Life*, translated by Steven Rendall (Berkeley: University of California Press, 1984), p. 18.

43. Hawthorne, *The House of the Seven Gables*, p. 621.

44. Quoted in Joel Schechter, *Durov's Pig: Clowns, Politics, and Theatre* (New York: Theatre Communications Group, 1985), p. 39.

45. Hawthorne, *The House of the Seven Gables*, p. 626.

46. Howard Rosenberg, "'Untied' Sets Conservative Tongues Wagging," *Arizona Republic*, July 16, 1991, p. C-6.

47. Riggs's last voiceover comment in the film is, "Black men loving black men is *the* revolutionary act." Bill Nichols discusses many of the formal elements of the film in his essay, "'Getting to Know You . . .': Knowledge, Power, and the Body," in *Theorizing Documentary*, edited by Michael Renov (New York: Routledge, 1993), pp. 186–88. Nichols notes simply that "Rigg's [*sic*] work evades categorization" — at least in terms of standard or experimental documentary conventions.

48. Nichols, "'Getting to Know You . . .,'" pp. 187–88.

49. See, e.g., Vincent Canby, "Paris Is Burning," *New York Times*, March 13, 1991, p. C-13; Georgia Brown, "Paris Is Burning," *Village Voice*, March 19, 1991, p. 54; and Essex Hemphill, "Paris Is Burning," *Guardian*, July 3, 1991, pp. 10–11.

50. bell hooks, "Is Paris Burning?," *Black Looks: Race and Representation* (Boston: South End Press, 1992), p. 149.

51. Ibid., p. 152. See also Peggy Phelan, "The Golden Apple: Jenny Livingston's *Paris Is Burning*," *Unmarked: The Politics of Performance* (London: Routledge, 1993), p. 102.

52. hooks, "Is Paris Burning?," p. 154.

53. Ibid., p. 149.

54. Ibid., p. 151.

55. Ibid., p. 156.

56. Phelan, "The Golden Apple," p. 103.

57. See also Linda Williams, "Mirrors Without Memories: Truth, History, and the New Documentary," *Film Quarterly* 46.3 (1993): 21 n. 2.

58. Cf. Barbara Kirshenblatt-Gimblett, "Objects of Ethnography," *Exhibiting Cultures: The Poetics and Politics of Museum Display*, edited by Ivan Karp and Steven D. Lavine (Washington, D.C.: Smithsonian Institution Press, 1991), pp. 428–30. Kirshenblatt-Gimblett describes how in recent folklife programs folk performers have been en-

couraged to abandon many of the performance conventions they have developed for presenting themselves to themselves or outsiders in favor of an "ascetic aesthetic" — a minimalist performance style that will signal to the audiences of outsiders that the program organizers have found a genuine, authentic folk performer. In light of Kirshenblatt-Gimblett's analysis, we should ask whose interests would be served by hooks's recommendation that gays abandon the theatrical forms such as Livingston documents in favor of "confronting themselves as they really are."

59. Phelan, "The Golden Apple," p. 103.

60. Stephen Tyler, "Post-Modern Ethnography: From Document of the Occult to Occult Document," in *Writing Culture: The Poetics and Politics of Ethnography*, edited by James Clifford and George E. Marcus (Berkeley: University of California Press, 1986), p. 126.

61. Paul Rabinow, "Representations Are Social Facts: Modernity and Post-Modernity in Anthropology," *Writing Culture*, pp. 234–61.

62. Halttunen, *Confidence Men and Painted Women*, p. 50.

Performing Southern History for the Tourist Gaze

Antebellum Home Tour Guide Performances

MICHAEL S. BOWMAN

Jesus, the south is fine, isn't it.
It's better than the theatre, isn't it.
     William Faulkner, Absalom, Absalom!

Today, critics from diverse ideological camps argue that societies invariably reconstruct their pasts and rewrite their cultures, rather than faithfully record or preserve them, in order to serve the needs of the present. For many, the critical question now is whether newer forms of historical and cultural reconstruction, especially those associated with tourism and other forms of commercialized leisure, represent something more insidious than business-as-usual. If it is true, as recent performance studies researchers have argued, that culture is a set of social and political boundaries that are marked and contested in performance, then we might ask what happens to culture when the performances people give are determined, in part, by the interpretive framework of tourism, or what John Urry calls "the tourist gaze."[1]

Tourism is a popular and pleasurable leisure pursuit, of course, but it is also a complex form of communication and performance. The multinational tourist industry, with its tremendous infrastructural support system in the form of elaborate communications technologies and transportation networks, enables millions of people to move relatively efficiently from place to place around the world and provides facilities for them to be housed and entertained. Mass tourism has had the positive effect of democratizing travel and of eroding certain class distinctions and hierarchical relations that derived from and were enacted by travel. Although travel and tourism are still markers of status, distinctions are usually based on *where* or *how* one travels and not on the older distinction between those who could and those who could not travel. Finally, in many parts of the globe tourism has become synonymous with "development," providing both the rationale and the means for construction or renovation projects that will produce environments for tourists. Assessing the consequences of tourism — especially its impact on how culture is produced and represented in performances-for-others — offers fertile ground for performance studies research.

For the last couple of years, I have been engaged in a project loosely centered on the enactment of southern identity in certain sites of cultural production involving practices regularly, though by no means exclusively, carried out for tourists — guided tours, of course, but also foodways and cuisine, as well as more overtly theatrical forms like festivals and carnival (Mardi Gras). By "sites," I mean specific areas developed or framed for one or more of the domains of tourism: ethnic, cultural, historical, environmental, or recreational.[2] This includes such attractions as museums, heritage or folklife centers, historical buildings and districts, nature preserves and parks, as well as shopping areas, hotels, and restaurants. The primary geographic domain in which I have traveled — owing mainly to limitations imposed by my bank account — is southern Louisiana. However, I have traveled to other places, too, and these other travels are not irrelevant to the project.

This essay will concentrate primarily on one of these sites, the antebellum plantation home, and will serve, I hope, as a preface to some of its problems. At the very least, the essay has a framing theme — the exoticization (and eroticization) of the South that, as Faulkner knew, is so pervasive in the theatricalization of the South (both academic and popular), as well as in the specific activities and sites where tourists and southerners gather and interact. But it also argues that attention to the performance elements of tourist productions might revise our impressions of tourism's regressive function.

As John Frow recently noted, most of the discourse on tourism — both academic and nonacademic — follows one of three analytically distinct paths.[3] The first is based on a distinction between travel and tourism, where the latter is construed as a vulgar, "mass" culture variant of the former. Daniel Boorstin's essay, "From Traveler to Tourist: The Lost Art of Travel," anticipates the later, though more fashionable, work of Umberto Eco and Jean Baudrillard by describing tourism as a self-enclosed, self-perpetuating system of illusions, "pseudo-events," and prepackaged experiences that tourists gullibly consume, even though real, authentic culture and experience are all around them, free as the air.[4] Tempting though it has been to dismiss Boorstin's critique as a snobbish attempt to reconstitute the class distinctions that tourism helped unravel, he is too discerning a thinker and historian not to notice that democratizing travel has altered the experience of travel. Boorstin's essay expresses a sense of historical belatedness and cultural attenuation: because tourism has made travel familiar and unthreatening, the kinds of experiences it enables have become familiar and unthreatening, too. We like to look on tourism as an adventure, but we also depend crucially on the very conveniences that seem to kill off adventure and make travel today seem ordinary, routine, mundane.

Today, tourist agencies offer prepackaged, even pre*lived* (as in television ads for cruises), experiences. Tourism is also pre*scribed* to the extent that wherever one goes there will be too many guidebooks. And those who do venture forth find that a mass-produced, plastic culture of schlock and tourist kitsch proliferates everywhere. Since the end of World War II, all that remains is what Bill Buford calls "a monoculture of mass consumerism, package-holidays and the extraordinary imperialism of the American hamburger" — and, of course, the postmodern photo op, like those depicted in Don DeLillo's *White Noise*, where busloads of tourists take snapshots of each other taking snapshots of the most photographed barn in America.[5] Finally, there is the rise of "Banana Republicanism," which has transformed adventure or risk taking into commodities that have more to do with status anxieties than with an interest in other cultures, and where the adventure of travel has been replaced by the adventure of wearing uncombed cotton or wool products imported from independent artisans.[6]

Whereas this line of critique stresses tourism's inauthenticity, semiotic studies of tourism have promoted a view of tourism as a flight *from* inauthenticity toward some place, some time, or some Other that is presumed to be more authentic than what we find in our everyday lives. Dean MacCannell identified the problem in his 1976 study, *The Tourist*: "Sightseeing is a kind of collective striving for a transcendence of the modern totality, a way of attempting to overcome the discontinuity of modernity, of incorporating its fragments into unified experience."[7] As Jonathan Culler noted, the distinction between the inauthenticity of one's own life and the presumed authenticity of some Other is "a powerful semiotic operator within tourism."[8] In Culler's terms, tourism is persuasive mainly because it promises an "escape from semiosis" — while simultaneously obscuring the fact that the "authentic" escape or getaway is always already semiotically mediated:[9] "The paradox, the dilemma of authenticity, is that to be experienced as authentic it must be marked as authentic, but when it is marked as authentic it is mediated, a sign of itself, and hence lacks the authenticity of what is truly unspoiled, untouched by mediating cultural codes. . . . The authentic sight requires markers, but our notion of the authentic is the unmarked."[10] Semiotic studies of tourism have been most effective in deciphering this paradox at the heart of the enterprise. But from this paradox, several others follow, and consideration of these produces a rather dismal view of tourism's social consequences.

First, there is the phenomenon that MacCannell calls "touristic shame," or the tendency of tourism to alienate people both internally and externally. Everyone hates tourists; even other tourists hate tourists. Consequently, tourism must promote "a rhetoric of moral superiority" that will permit tourists to imagine themselves as less "touristy" than each other.[11] Several months ago, I had dinner with a couple of friends from my graduate school days, and after several moments of the obligatory "tell-about-the-South" chitchat, one of them began to tell the other about New Orleans and what a fabulous place it is to visit. She concluded her brief travelogue by saying, "If it weren't for all the tourists, it'd be perfect." In this episode, several features of the touristic code as explained by MacCannell are evident: (1) that New Orleans — like Paris or the Grand Canyon — is, "of course," one of those places that everyone "really must see"; (2) that the touristic consensus over what must be seen — which is truly international — is used often to constitute hierarchies in interpersonal relations, setting the "have seens" apart from the "have not seens"; and (3) that within the tourist site itself, the touristic code works to create hostility, as each tourist perceives others like him- or herself as impediments or enemies of the perfect tourist experience. Frow suggests that the inherent bad faith of the tourist performance not only makes it an easy target for criticism; it also creates disillusionment and melancholy among those who perform the role.[12]

The second paradox is perhaps even more troubling. For once we recognize the semiotic character of tourist productions, we begin to see the "difficulties of appreciating otherness except through signifying structures that mark and reduce it."[13] Part of the difficulty is the traditional hermeneutic problem of how to understand the Other without reducing him/her/it to the categories of our own understanding. In semiotic terms, however, the constitutive role of representation in producing the touristic Other/object also has the effect of turning that Other/object into a sign of itself. Highway signs, plaques, guidebooks, brochures and pamphlets, snapshots, postcards, ashtrays, T-shirts — such markers and reproductions of the "real," "authentic," or "original" sight not only serve an important semiotic function in framing the sight for tourists. They also work to transform the sight into a simulacrum of itself — that is, the sight comes to resemble itself. Mount Rushmore, for example, is so familiar to us from professional and amateur photography that it seems to be nothing more than another, though bigger, reproduction of itself. The logical conclusion to this chain of supplementarity is when the relations between sight and marker become inverted, so that the sight itself either becomes obliterated by, irrelevant to, or a signifier of its own markers.[14] As MacCannell argues, the semiotic confusion between marker and sight that often occurs in tourist productions makes it virtually impossible to construct otherness, because "every nicely motivated effort to preserve nature, primitives and the past, and to represent them authentically contributes to an opposite tendency — the present is made more unified against its past, more in control of nature, less a product of history."[15]

The third, or "postmodern," moment in this spiral of semiosis occurs when it becomes necessary, in order to make "a convincing display of honest honesty," for tourist sights/sites to be constructed as plausible representations of themselves.[16] In Chadds Ford, Pennsylvania, for example, John Dorst shows us a community struggling to become the image of itself made popular by the work of Andrew Wyeth.[17] Tourists go to Chadds Ford expecting to see the widely circulated Wyeth images of the area, and the residents know that economic loss would result if they and their surrounding environment failed to live up to those images, failed to *be* like paintings. Critics of the heritage industry in Great Britain have identified similar effects of that nation's emphasis on historical tourism, producing what might be described as "Ye Merrie Olde-ing" of major segments of the country and its population.[18] As Jonathan Raban noted, "nowhere outside Africa were the tribespeople so willing to dress up in 'traditional' costumes and cater for the entertainment of their visitors. . . . The thing had become a national industry. Year by year, England was being made more picturesquely merrie."[19]

All over the globe, indeed, traditional tribal cultures or recent ex-"primitives" have been transformed by tourism into what MacCannell calls "performative primitives."[20] The economic imperatives and opportunities that tourism opens up and represents enable various tribes, ethnic groups, or formerly primitive peoples to earn a living by charging tourists to look at their social or everyday life performances, as well as their sacred rituals. As MacCannell quips, most remaining hunter-gatherers can now add "motion picture actor" and "tour guide" to their resumés. He surmises that with a good agent, a corporate sponsor, and the proper promotion and handling, the Masai of Kenya could conceivably earn a handsome income simply by *acting Masai* in perpetuity.[21]

The postmodern moment has effected a significant transformation in the structure of tourism itself and, more importantly, in the politics and poetics of culture. The problem for many areas affected by tourism today is analogous to that of Chadds Ford: of trying to live up to their own imagery. According to Barbara Kirshenblatt-Gimblett and Edward Bruner, this latest phase of tourism represents a shift from the traditional questions of authenticity to questions of authentication: "who has the power to represent whom and to determine which representation is authoritative?"[22] For those who study culture, the focus on questions of authentication has drawn attention to how representational conventions informing the production of history, nature, ethnicity — "otherness" — as objects of knowledge reinforce (or alter) hierarchical or exploitative relations of power.[23]

During the last decade or so, a considerable body of criticism has accumulated that suggests that, at one level of analysis (and of the "practice" of tourism), history and culture are most commonly reconstructed or rewritten in terms of a conservative cultural politics that works to elide controversy or debate, as well as variations or differences in class, race, gender, ethnicity, and so on, in favor of producing myths of consensus, stability, and reconciliation. As Michael Kammen recently noted, in the United States, at least, the principal message extolled in hundreds of local histories and tourist productions alike is captured in that familiar slogan, "a tradition of progress."[24] Michael Wallace put the matter more bluntly still in his influential reading of Henry Ford's Greenfield Village when he suggested that this popular historical museum says, in effect, that life was better in the good old days — and it has been getting better ever since.[25]

This "message" is minimally readable to anyone literate in the design and layout of a historical site — which, thanks in part to tourism, includes just about everyone with a modest education and income. Certainly, this readability may be minimal indeed, especially for novices or newcomers. And because the processes of cultural-historical production and transmission in the United States tend to be decentralized, ad hoc, diffuse, and relatively noncoercive, the potential for misreadings or aberrant decodings of the oppositional or negotiated sort may be all the greater.[26] Nevertheless, there are still some basic features of content, design, and presentation to help make sure that visitors get the message.

At first glance, antebellum plantation homes would seem to epitomize this tendency of historical and cultural tourism to produce ameliorative images of the past. After all, what better example could one find to support Walter Benjamin's claim that all the great cultural treasures of the past are also monuments to barbarism and oppression?[27] How is it possible, then, for such places to be transformed from icons of a slavocratic ideology into pleasant places to spend a Sunday afternoon? During the Civil War, Union soldiers (and, to be sure, the newly freed slaves) could hardly be restrained from blowing such places to smithereens or burning them to the ground.[28] To them, there was no ambiguity about the symbology of the plantation Big House, nor could such symbology be ameliorated by aesthetic considerations.

Today, however, stories about (or physical traces of) antisouthern or antislaveholder rage are usually inflected so as to convey images of another kind of barbarism, one that was anti-art or anticulture. Such images are extremely useful and effective in the production of the antebellum home as heritage or culture or art or architecture. Each production poses the question: Can you believe there were once people who wanted to destroy these beautiful homes? And it is difficult to walk away without giving thanks that the damn Yankees never got their hands on *this* place.

The most peculiar gap or silence in the antebellum home tour is in relation to the "peculiar institution" itself. For whatever reason — by accident or design — the world the slaves made has all but disappeared from most of the homes I have visited. Of course, it is true that the material and verbal culture of the slaves (and the poor whites) was made of less durable stuff than that of the slaveholding class of merchants and planters. Consequently, the absence of slave cabins and other semiotic remnants of slave culture on most sites is perfectly understandable, "natural" even. There are exceptions, of course: at a couple of sites, extant slave cabins have been restored and made over into quaint gift shops and restaurants; and some homes feature a reconstructed cabin or two to suggest how they looked and where they were situated in relation to the Big House. But none of the tours I have seen has ever been guided out there — suggesting, implicitly and actually, that history stops at the threshold of the Big House.

The slaves themselves are commonly represented in the tour guide narratives — if at all — through the euphemism, "servant," or else they are transformed into abstractions with passive voice constructions such as, "The cooking was done . . . ," or "The house was built. . . ."[29] In a couple of places, they go so far as to show us how the cooking "was done" in the eighteenth or nineteenth centuries — with white, female costumed interpreters. The experience can be disconcerting at times: although "everybody knows" that southern plantations had slaves, visitors sometimes feel compelled to do a perception check by asking, "Did they have slaves here?" or "How many slaves did they have here?"

At this level, antebellum plantation homes often seem to legitimize an ideology that works to reproduce a hegemonic discourse that goes back to the Old South. But instead of serving the interests of a slaveholding class of planters and merchants, it serves the interests of a class of professionals whose business is the control of information, meanings, values, and images within and across cultural lines. These are the promoters and managers of an official display and the mediators of an official imagery. We are not concerned here with identifiable individuals, of course, but with a more general and anonymous apparatus, a style of production, a discourse that manages to be "traditional" and "postmodern" at the same time.

In Louisiana, home builders and contractors are sometimes called "storymakers," which is suggestive of how the structures themselves are conceived as more than merely wood and brick and mortar and plaster:[30] they are the narratives of communities and generations and social systems. Efforts to preserve older, historic structures may be read as part of an effort to preserve these "stories," these older structures of social relations.[31] Though some of the earliest organized efforts at historic preservation may be traced back to the antebellum South itself (the Mount Vernon Ladies' Society), the major efforts have occurred since the 1920s, when Colonial Williamsburg, Charleston's historic district, and the French Quarter received their initial support. As

David Goldfield notes, such efforts were instrumental in bringing together two formerly antagonistic groups — the boosters and the preservationists — by demonstrating that "the past" could be good for business.[32]

By the end of the nineteenth century, many of the antebellum homes and plantations across the South had been abandoned or were disintegrating — mainly because the plantation economy had been shattered by the Civil War, Emancipation, and Reconstruction. Many of the old planters had died, of course, but others (or their descendants) had simply moved into the cities or away from the region altogether.[33] With the collapse of the plantation economy and the decay of the buildings themselves, a whole system of social and cultural performances was also threatened. For such homes were the very gathering places, the theaters, where a set of social roles could be grandly and satisfyingly performed.

In 1931 the women of the Natchez (Mississippi) Garden Club inaugurated a whole new tourist genre, the pilgrimage, to help stimulate interest in and finance the preservation of the city's collection of antebellum homes. The metaphor of "pilgrimage" is noteworthy, in part, because it supports the anthropological commonplace that tourism is the modern world's equivalent of the sacred journey.[34] More importantly, though, the metaphor of pilgrimage is an *argument*. According to James Fernandez, such metaphorical arguments are persuasive because they "provide images in relation to which the organization of behavior can take place."[35] Pilgrimage is what Fernandez would call a "performative metaphor," as the figural organization of behavior in the metaphor actually does "pass over into performance."[36] The performative consequences of pilgrimages are to mobilize local, national, and even international participation in the maintenance of a set of social and cultural performances centered historically around the antebellum homes and plantations.

In several places throughout the South, "preservation" and "pilgrimage" involve not only the restoration of the houses and other artifacts of material culture, but also the pageantry and spectacle of the antebellum period, the recreation of a whole mise-en-scène, and the reconstitution of hierarchical social relations in newer, more "benign" forms, such as tourist bureaus, garden clubs, and the like. And though there are exceptions, the union of preservationists and boosters has worked mainly to preserve the social and economic interests of an overwhelmingly white, professional, upper or upper-middle class. Some of the social consequences of this have been the gentrification of neighborhoods, government subsidies (in the form of tax relief or grants) for the improvement of individually or corporately held properties, the displacement or forced relocation of people, and the burden of higher taxes for those who remain.[37]

In Louisiana, as elsewhere on the Caribbean rim, the plantation style ideology of the old slaveholding days is returning in the form of what MacCannell calls "plantation style tourism," where "the rhetoric of ethnic relations changes to create the impression of progress while older forms of repression and exploitation are perpetuated beneath the surface."[38] A handbook devoted to local development of tourism in Louisiana begins with the statement: "Tourism means money."[39] The manual does not tell us how much or for whom, but it is tremendously instructive in showing how the rhetoric of economic development, jobs, heritage, and community pride can be used to solicit free or cheap labor. In the name of tourism, exploitative or inegalitarian social relations are reproduced and naturalized.

Investigations into the political economy of tourism raise serious questions about its benefits for the people whose social and cultural performances are now the attraction. The collapse of oil prices during the early eighties was devastating to Louisiana's economy, and by the mid-eighties tourism had become the state's only growth industry.[40] Yet, although there was a dramatic increase in tourist expenditures during the eighties, it is difficult to say how much of that trickled down to the people themselves. Certainly, most of the tourist spending would have been on airline tickets, hotel accommodations, and food, very little of which would stay on site. Moreover, whatever new jobs were created by Louisiana's tourist boom were almost certainly entry-level, minimum-wage service positions.[41] Having been squeezed out of higher-paying jobs in the petrochemical industry, Louisiana's citizens are now being squeezed for symbols to market to tourists—one effect of which is to squeeze them back into the menial positions they had traditionally occupied.

As MacCannell suggests, it is also difficult to explain how ethnic or historical tourism improves the lives of the residents of the state.[42] Certainly, some of the newer attractions, such as the Aquarium of the Americas in New Orleans, can be enjoyed by locals as much as by tourists. But if, as a representative of a local minority or ethnic group, you *are* the attraction—as is the case in Louisiana's promotion of its Cajun culture—it is difficult to discern how you might benefit from becoming an attraction or how you might learn anything about yourself. When it is your house or your labor or your entertainments that tourists come to see, one should imagine that they would be more of an inconvenience than anything else.

When southern Louisiana's various "ethnic" groups were first drawn into the global economy, they were enslaved or poorly paid, discriminated against on the basis of skin color, language, and religion, and segregated socially and physically. Now, we are to understand that they will benefit from tourism. Perhaps they will. The rhetoric of tourism typically emphasizes the growing self-consciousness and self-determination of minorities, ethnic groups, or formerly oppressed peoples; it aims to correct or fill in gaps in the historical record; and it stresses the unique contributions of such groups to the larger culture. But a major point of concern is whether such progressive aims can be realized through the discursive framework of tourism—a discourse that promotes structurally social relationships that are likely to be ephemeral and superficial, or filled with envy, mistrust, and even hatred.

In addition to their ideological or cultural myth-making function, all tourist sites are obliged, as well, to perform a ritual of differentiation that conveys a sense of uniqueness or specialness about the site. I see this as a performance project because it requires the predication of a more complex, localized, and contingent affective relation to the tourist site/production than does the more common scenario of tourist sites as "arenas for ideological assertion."[43] In one way or another, all tourist productions may "say" the same thing. But I do not think one need refute this in order to concentrate instead on the ways that particular tourist sites/productions strive to become "special" in the lives of those who visit them.

Like other cultural texts, antebellum plantation homes present us with an interpretive dilemma. On the one hand, such buildings have been crucial in shaping our conceptions of southern history and culture; on the other, our conceptions of southern history and culture frequently interfere with our ability to develop a more accurate historiography at such sites.[44] No matter how well-intentioned or historically accurate a given antebellum home tour may be, it must compete with other forms of popular history—such as historical romance novels, Hollywood films, television miniseries, glossy coffee-table picture books, and Gothic, anecdotal collections with such titles as *Ghosts Along the Mississippi*—which continue to exert a tremendous influence on many Americans' (and foreigners') perceptions of the antebellum South and its plantation homes. Consequently, it is actually quite difficult to "see" an antebellum plantation home as something other than an essentializing or totalizing sign for something else: we see the essence of the Old South, or we see the whole of the Old South from the metonymic fragment. Thus, antebellum homes must strive to differentiate themselves, in part, to combat the tourist's judgment that "if you've seen one, you've seen them all."

Certainly, because many of the homes are now operated as businesses, there is an economic motive at work here. But we cannot derive commentary on their function, tourists' responses to them, or their own performances of "difference" solely on the basis of this economic rationale. Antebellum homes are not fixed or consistent or permanent. They are always getting face-lifts, changing their images, and so on. And they have to struggle against the image-changing forces of nature itself—floods, fires—that threaten to face-lift them right out of business. At every possible level of analysis—and there are many of them—antebellum homes are constitutively paradoxical. At one level, they are obviously, monolithically ideological and seem very often to be paradigms of false consciousness. But when you try to argue with them, they dissolve at any one point into an openness and indeterminacy that might suit any critic's fantasies about the counterhegemonic meanings and pleasures of the polysemic text.

Tamar Katriel argues that every tour guide performance enacts a more or less explicit contest between a site's official or consensual narrative of itself and alternative or oppositional versions of that story through which various audiences, or the performers themselves, may challenge the home's authorized narrative. Katriel reveals that attention to the dialogic character of such performances "highlights their role in a larger cultural struggle over forms of collective representation."[45] In the typical home tour performance, the manifest content of the tour guide's narrative is built out of a series of short, often disconnected, anecdotes about the house's design, construction, and furnishings; about the lives of those who owned the house or visited it; and about how certain design features and material artifacts can be made to "speak" about a general "way of life" in antebellum Louisiana. Because many of these anecdotes are represented as little mysteries—"Do you see this? Do any of you know what it is? Can you imagine what it was used for?"—and because the structure of the tour as a whole usually progresses from the frontstage regions of the house to the backstage regions, the rhetoric of the tour works to reinforce the aura surrounding the antebellum period, while at the same time permitting visitors a privileged look behind it or through it: life really was better in the Old South, and it has been getting better ever since. When performers and audiences share the same orientation to the "storymaking" that continues to create the house, the whole tour can become a ritualized enactment of certainly widely held views of southern and U.S. history.

But what happens when performers and audiences do not share the same enthusiasm for storymaking or the "proper" ritual attitude toward the past? Two moments or images from my own field experience may help to illustrate the point I want to make. The role of antebellum home tour guide is performed by a wide range of individuals—young and old, male and female, volunteers and paid employees; typically, though, the guide is a middle-aged woman. Yet the most "interesting" performances to me are the ones given by *young* women. To illustrate, I will present the first image by reproducing a passage from a journal entry written after one of my visits. At this particular site, the women who served as tour guides were costumed, as they often are, in a kind of generic "Southern Belle" fashion.[46] And while some of the women were older, forty-ish to sixty-ish, many of them appeared to be quite young—high school or college age, perhaps. The group I was in was led by one of these girls:

I love these girls. They are so adorable with their little dolly-dresses and their cute little southern accents. I love the way they walk. I love the way they talk. I followed this girl around the house—up and down the stairs, into those tacky little rooms—and didn't hear a word she said. I didn't care: I would have followed her anywhere. She could have asked me to do anything for her. I just wanted to hug her. I just wanted to take care of her. I just wanted to take her home and put her on my mantle.[47]

That is one image.

The second one occurred a few moments later during the same visit. After completing the tour, I entered the gift shop along with most of the other members of my group. (That's where the tour ends, of course.) As I was standing at the counter flipping through the postcards, the sales clerk opened a door behind the counter that led to a kind of backstage area—a combination storage room and green room, it appeared to me. The young woman who had just led my group through the home was in the room. I watched her. She hiked up her dress, sat down on a little bench, and kicked off her shoes. Then she pulled out a pack of Marlboros. She lit a cigarette, inhaled deeply, and grumbled to the clerk, "Fuckin' tourists."

That is the second image. What do I do with them? How do I reconcile them? More disturbing, perhaps, how do I reconcile my response to them? Which "girl" did I prefer? Which one did *she* prefer? Impasse. Paralysis. Bewitchment?

In the course of subsequent observations of and interactions with some of these women, I have found that the powerful combination of acquiescence and attack that I encountered on that occasion frequently operates at other levels than the separation of frontstage and backstage personae. Most commonly, it enters the performance in the form of a flat, affectless delivery style. Initially, I was inclined to interpret such features as evidence of the performer's lack of talent, as if she were incapable of producing the kind of spontaneity—that illusion of the first time—that conventional performer training has taught us to value. After having seen a number of these performers, many of them more than once, I am more inclined now to see this feature as a deliberate tactic, as yet another manifestation of the "fuckin' tourists" sentiment, and also as a form of opposition to the imperatives of having to act like a Southern Belle, of being transformed into performative versions of a stereotypical southern woman.

Frequently, the performer's resistance to the imperatives of the tourist production enters the content of the speech, as well—albeit in a somewhat disguised fashion. One informant told me, for example, that it is not uncommon for the tour guides to "make up" portions of the stories they tell, to extemporize some fanciful, or patently ludicrous, narrative about an artifact or piece of furniture, or to offer their own southern versions of the "George Washington slept here" legend. In some instances, to be sure, such exercises are performed for the tour guide's own amusement, to ward off boredom, as a personal tour de force, as a private joke, or even for the entertainment of her fellow tour guides. In other cases, though, it appears to be another version of the "fuckin' tourists" sentiment—that is, the "damn Yankees" sentiment. At one home, there used to be an unspoken rule to the effect that if a tour were being given, say, to a busload of Ohioans, then the guides would extemporize new stories about any of the furnishings that may have come from the northern states. So, for example, if a chandelier had been made in Philadelphia or Chicago, then the guide would say that it had come from France and would spin out some fanciful story about a world-famous foundry in Paris, a long and arduous journey across the Atlantic and up the Mississippi, and perhaps an episode to illustrate the cunning or courage it took to save the item from the depredations of the Yankees.

In situations such as these, the experiential context of the performances is characterized more by ambiguity or antagonism than by consensus, and I do not believe that such ambiguity or antagonism is unusual or idiosyncratic. Indeed, ambiguity, resistance, opposition, and even antagonism are ever-present and palpable features of many tours, even though such things are rarely articulated in the actual content of the tour guide's narrative or during question-and-answer sessions. Once offstage, both the guides and the tourists are able to speak of these things, as in the instances described above; onstage, however, a sense of decorum or "interactional delicacy," as Katriel calls it, seems to shield tour guides and audiences from each other: the former may modify their messages slightly when faced with audiences of Yankees or foreigners or African Americans, and the latter will refrain from openly challenging or criticizing the performer.[48] In short, the public transcript of the antebellum home tour, as James Scott might call it, is almost always a respectable performance, but the hidden transcript is another matter altogether.[49]

The critical question is whether the experiential ambiguity of such encounters can effect the kind of intellectual or moral ambiguity that could provoke a more critical orientation to the tourist production—and whether the techniques of spectacle in tourism, especially its increasing objectification of locals or "natives" into performative versions of themselves, are as inherently regressive as many critics believe. The answer to such questions depends very much, I think, on how we understand the performance aspects of tourism. The task of analyzing particular discourses and sites of tourism involves, on the one hand, participation in the event as tourist/audience/reader/consumer, sharing in the perceptions, sensations, emotions, and ideas generated in a given performance (which, of course, can be negative, as well as positive). On the other hand, it involves the attempt to fashion a position from which we can distance ourselves from those sensations so that we might speak as other-than-tourist—standing back from or outside the performance so as not to be absorbed by our own absorption in it. The latter mode has been characteristic of most anthropological and sociological studies of leisure and tourism to date, and it has given us a rather depressing view of tourism's social semiotic functioning. But the former mode is becoming increasingly more common today in performance and cultural studies, and it has helped us to see a more optimistic outcome. In addition to Katriel's work, for example, Elizabeth Fine and Jean Haskell Speer have shown how the experiential context of a tour guide performance sometimes creates a kind of liminal experience — an experience where both the guides and the visitors may temporarily escape their prescripted roles — that has the potential to open up alternative endings to the tour itself, and also to foster interpersonal relations between tourists and guides that can generate other forms of feeling and experience than those of mistrust, jealousy, or loathing.[50]

There is more research to be done in this area, of course, but here I only want to make the point that, at the very least, an analysis of tourist productions ought to adopt initially a pose of ambivalence toward its objects rather than a condescension toward them — or an astonishment before them. Ambivalence allows a thinking of the relations between contradictory states. It is a "pose," of course, a performance — but one that is probably more appropriate to the "everyday" experience and practice of tourism itself. Above all, it does not eliminate the moments of discontent — of anger, frustration, fear, boredom, fatigue — that accompany the pleasures of tourism. Criticism and tourism both are minimally a performance of discontent with "the everyday" and with wide-eyed acceptance or celebrations of the everyday as "the way things are." Like good cultural critics everywhere, tourists often proceed by staring long and hard at the people, places, objects, and activities they encounter, and not infrequently they become absorbed in or enchanted by the sights they see. But tourism also permits the possibility of rejecting what is seen; it includes moments of sharpened focus, narrowed gaze — of skeptical assessment as well as wide-eyed wonder.

Notes

1. See, e.g., Joseph Roach, "Mardi Gras Indians and Others: Genealogies of American Performance," *Theatre Journal* 44.4 (1992): 461–83. I am indebted to John Urry, *The Tourist Gaze: Leisure and Travel in Contemporary Societies* (London: Sage, 1990), for this notion of the gaze.

2. Valene L. Smith, Introduction to *Hosts and Guests: The Anthropology of Tourism*, 2d ed., edited by Smith (Philadelphia: University of Pennsylvania Press, 1989), pp. 4–6.

3. John Frow, "Tourism and the Semiotics of Nostalgia," *October* 57 (1991): 127–31. See also Urry, *The Tourist Gaze*, pp. 7–15, and Jonathan Culler, "The Semiotics of Tourism," in *Framing the Sign: Criticism and Its Institutions* (Norman: University of Oklahoma Press, 1988), pp. 153–67.

4. Daniel Boorstin, *The Image: A Guide to Pseudo-Events in America*, 25th anniversary ed. (1987; reprint, New York: Vintage, 1992), pp. 77–117.

5. Bill Buford, Editorial, *Granta* 10 (1984): 5; Don DeLillo, *White Noise* (New York: Viking-Penguin, 1985), pp. 12–13.

6. Stephen Tatum, "Adventure in the Fashion System," *Western Humanities Review* 43 (1989): 5–26. I am indebted to Michael Kowalewski's discussion of these issues in his "Introduction: The Modern Literature of Travel," in *Temperamental Journeys: Essays on the Modern Literature of Travel*, edited by Kowalewski (Athens: University of Georgia Press, 1992), pp. 1–16.

7. Dean MacCannell, *The Tourist: A New Theory of the Leisure Class* (1976; reprint, New York: Schocken Books, 1989), p. 13.

8. Culler, "The Semiotics of Tourism," p. 159.

9. Ibid., p. 167.

10. Ibid., p. 164.

11. MacCannell, *The Tourist*, pp. 10, 9.

12. Frow, "Tourism and the Semiotics of Nostalgia," pp. 146–49.

13. Culler, "The Semiotics of Tourism," p. 167.

14. In addition to Culler and Frow, see Georges van den Abbeele, "Sightseers: The Tourist as Theorist," *Diacritics* 10.4 (1980): 2–14.

15. MacCannell, *The Tourist*, p. 83.

16. Ibid., p. 128.

17. John D. Dorst, *The Written Suburb: An American Site, An Ethnographic Dilemma* (Philadelphia: University of Pennsylvania Press, 1989). See also MacCannell's recent study, *Empty Meeting Grounds: The Tourist Papers* (New York: Routledge, 1992), which also focuses on this third, or "postmodern," phase of tourism.

18. See, e.g., Bob West, "The Making of the English Working Past: A Critical View of the Ironbridge Gorge Museum," in *The Museum Time-Machine: Putting Cultures on Display*, edited by Robert Lumley (London: Comedia-Routledge, 1988), pp. 36–62.

19. Jonathan Raban, *Coasting* (London: Picador, 1986), pp. 194–95; quoted in Urry, *The Tourist Gaze*, p. 106.

20. MacCannell, *Empty Meeting Grounds*, p. 26, et passim.

21. Ibid., pp. 18–19.

22. Barbara Kirshenblatt-Gimblett and Edward M. Bruner, "Tourism," in *Folklore, Cultural Performances, and Popular Entertainments: A Communications-Centered Handbook*, edited by Richard Bauman (New York: Oxford University Press, 1992), p. 304.

23. See, e.g., Barbara Kirshenblatt-Gimblett, "Objects of Ethnography," in *Exhibiting Cultures: The Poetics and Politics of Museum Display*, edited by Ivan Karp and Steven D. Lavine (Washington, D.C.: Smithsonian Institution Press, 1991), pp. 386–443.

24. Michael Kammen, *Mystic Chords of Memory: The Transformation of Tradition in American Culture* (New York: Alfred A. Knopf, 1991), pp. 13–14.

25. Michael Wallace, "Visiting the Past: History Museums in the United States," *Radical History Review* 25 (1981): 73.

26. Kammen, *Mystic Chords of Memory*, p. 14.

27. Walter Benjamin, "Theses on the Philosophy of History," in *Illuminations*, edited with an introduction by Hannah Arendt, translated by Harry Zohn (New York: Schocken Books, 1969), p. 256.

28. Civil War histories are filled with such accounts, and they have become a common motif of tour guide performances, especially in those areas contiguous with the Mississippi River (where Union gunboats liked to use the homes for target practice) and those areas occupied by the armies of Grant and (especially) Sherman. Charles Royster offers a vivid account of how and why such destruction was practiced in his description of the burning of Columbia, South Carolina, in February 1865; see his *The Destructive War: William Tecumseh Sherman, Stonewall Jackson, and the Americans* (New York: Alfred A. Knopf, 1991), chap. 1.

29. Thomas A. Greenfield noticed a similar phenomenon in the tours given at Thomas Jefferson's Monticello; see his "Race and Passive Voice at Monticello," *Crisis* 82.4 (1975): 146–47.

30. Joseph A. Arrigo and Cara M. Batt, *Plantations: Forty-four of Louisiana's Most Beautiful Antebellum Plantation Homes* (San Francisco: Lexicos, 1983), n.p.

31. See Michael Bommes and Patrick Wright, " 'Charms of Residence': The Public and the Past," in *Making Histories: Studies in History-Writing and Politics*, edited by Richard Johnson, Gregor McLennan, Bill Schwarz, and David Sutton (London: Hutchinson, 1982), pp. 253–301.

32. David R. Goldfield, "Historic Preservation," in *Encyclopedia of Southern Culture*, edited by Charles Reagan Wilson and William Ferris (Chapel Hill: University of North Carolina Press, 1989), p. 626.

33. See Edward L. Ayers, *The Promise of the New South: Life After Reconstruction* (New York: Oxford University Press, 1992), pp. 24–25, 457–58 n. 51.

34. See, e.g., Nelson H. Graburn, "Tourism: The Sacred Journey," in *Hosts and Guests: The Anthropology of Tourism*, 2d ed., edited by Valene L. Smith (Philadelphia: University of Pennsylvania Press, 1989), pp. 21–36.

35. James W. Fernandez, *Persuasions and Performances: The Play of Tropes in Culture* (Bloomington: Indiana University Press, 1986), p. 7.

36. Ibid., p. 20.

37. MacCannell's term for this "postmodern community planning" is "Nouvelle Racism" or "Racism Lite"; significantly, though, MacCannell's analysis draws on the example of Orange County, California, which should disabuse us of any fantasies that such practices are confined to the South. See MacCannell, *Empty Meeting Grounds*, pp. 103–4.

38. Ibid., pp. 174, 178.

39. *Louisiana Open House Handbook* (n.p: n.d.), p. 1.

40. Louisiana Office of Tourism, *Master Plan, 1987–1990* (Baton Rouge: Department of Culture, Recreation, and Tourism, n.d.), p. 4.

41. The Louisiana Office of Tourism recuperates this aspect of tourism's economic structure in the rhetoric of its Master Plan by saying that "the travel product is still an export commodity, is a 'clean' industry, *still employs* minorities and entry level workers, contributes to state and local tax bases and demands very little from government to produce those benefits" (*Master Plan*, p. 5; emphasis added).

42. MacCannell, *Empty Meeting Grounds*, p. 175.

43. I borrow this phrase from Tamar Katriel, "'Our Future Is Where Our Past Is': Studying Heritage Museums as Ideological and Performative Arenas," *Communication Monographs* 60.1 (1993): 70. I should hasten to add that Katriel, too, believes that the ideological functioning of heritage museums tells only part of the story.

44. See Jessie Poesch, "Architecture," in *Encyclopedia of Southern Culture*, edited by Charles Reagan Wilson and William Ferris (Chapel Hill: University of North Carolina Press, 1989), pp. 55–57, and Michael W. Fazio, "Historiography of Southern Architecture," in *Encyclopedia of Southern Culture*, pp. 79–80.

45. Katriel, "'Our Future Is Where Our Past Is,'" p. 71.

46. The generic "Southern Belle" costume worn by the younger women resembles a prom dress, usually with features that suggest metonymically the older forms of costuming of the antebellum period. Some of the homes still feature performers who wear more authentic period costumes, usually for special events.

47. Journal entry, February 15, 1992.

48. Katriel, "'Our Future Is Where Our Past Is,'" p. 72.

49. James C. Scott, *Domination and the Arts of Resistance: Hidden Transcripts* (New Haven: Yale University Press, 1990).

50. Elizabeth C. Fine and Jean Haskell Speer, "Tour Guide Performances as Sight Sacralization," *Annals of Tourism Research* 12 (1985): 73–95.

Histories of Desire

Performing Sex and Class

Filthy — Nay — Pestilential

Sanitation and Victorian Theaters

TRACY C. DAVIS

The flushing water closet, an invention of late Elizabethan England and first patented in 1775, was slow to be incorporated into British public buildings.[1] Though planned for the Haymarket opera house of 1778, the first water closets documented in a theater were at the Pantheon in 1793.[2] The prevalence of chamber pots in drawing rooms and even dining rooms in eighteenth-century Britain (so as not to take guests away from the conversation) suggests that there might be little compunction for using such conveniences in the boxes of theaters.[3] Audiences had been bringing chamber pots to public entertainments since the days of Imperial Rome,[4] and presumably they continued to do so, or just relieved themselves on the spot, as is implied by the lead lining ordered in 1837 for "the Floor between the front seat and front of the Gallery . . . to prevent Nuisances" at the Theatre Royal Newcastle.[5] Before assigned seating became the norm in pits and galleries, patrons queued for hours, then stormed in and scrambled for a place. Under such packed circumstances, chamber pots were probably not a viable option (not because of squeamishness over privacy but because getting pots in and out would have been difficult) and vacating a seat in order to go relieve oneself — assuming that there was somewhere to go — meant losing the seat. The 1848 Public Health Act required fixed sanitary arrangements in every home in England, but this did not mean trapped or even flushing fixtures,[6] and in no way obligated buildings for public assembly, such as theaters, to incorporate sanitary facilities or, if they were there, to keep them clean. We should not underestimate the odiferous consequences in poorly ventilated buildings, where the fumes of gaslight mingled with bodies and clothing not subject to late-twentieth-century Westerners' strictures on frequent washing. Any modern actor who has ever experienced gastrointestinal distress as a symptom of stage fright, any woman who has ever spent an entire intermission queuing in the washroom, and any traveler who has ever gasped in passing a third world public toilet, take note.

Varying degrees of sanitary measures were undertaken by individual theater entrepreneurs, and this essay focuses on the provision of sanitary facilities in order to bring about new perspectives on performance historiography and theater architecture by linking audiences to aesthetic changes and economic motivations to epidemiological arguments that were thrashed out in the mid-Victorian period. There was always and inevitably a need for sanitary facilities, especially since theaters sold drinks during the intervals, and with the constant consumption of refreshments in music halls the need must have been even more acute. But what did audiences do in their presence or absence, and how does this everyday behavior suggest new ways of answering lingering questions about the experience of nineteenth-century theatergoing, about class and gender, as well as about other circumstances of the theater relative to the culture that it served, contained, and embodied?

One of the primary motivations for sanitary reform was the appearance, for the first time in Europe, of typhoid and cholera, respectively, in the late 1820s and 1831. The 55,000 English deaths in the 1849 cholera epidemic emphasized the necessity for widespread action; in the next outbreak, 1854, 4.5 percent of London's population perished. Technically, the Sanitary Act of 1866 gave powers to order cleansing and disinfecting of buildings, but it was not invoked with regard to theaters. The powers of the Local Government Board (under the Public Health Act of 1891) were not adopted when recommended to the London County Council by the Medical Officer of Health in 1891 or again in 1899. To his distress, the provision and ventilation of theaters' water closets was never brought into line with requirements for factories, or even mines, during the course of the nineteenth century.[7]

Though the scientist William Budd suspected the existence of microorganisms in disease pathology as early as 1849, John Snow developed his theory that cholera was transmitted through contaminated water in the late 1850s, and the medical profession generally accepted microorganisms as the agents of disease around 1868, their existence was not proved until 1883 and bacteriology was not properly established until the mid-1890s.[8] And though we now know that cholera can be transmitted person to person but is almost always (like typhoid) contracted through contaminated water, the public health measures did little to directly curtail the spread of disease prior to 1870, and contagionist theory (later supported by proof of microscopic disease-producing organisms) only slowly won out over miasmatology. The various miasmatic theories that prevailed through most of the century entailed the belief that corrupted air that degenerates becomes "sticky," and that this "sticky" air is what infected people. The formula of "dirt → smells → miasma → pestilence" meant that odor was the chief indication that disease might be lurking.[9] Among infected communities, British authorities invoked quarantine and prevention programs that were virtually unchanged since the last bubonic plague.

In 1854 London saw 10,675 deaths from cholera. In half of all cases, death occurred within hours of the onset of diarrhea and vomiting. Regular theater inspection reports commencing in 1855 — the same year that cholera raged around Poland and Broad Streets (Soho), Gordon Square (Bloomsbury), and Wardour Street (leading from Oxford Street to Leicester Square),[10] all close by the precincts of the West End theater district — reveal that some theaters had urinals, but facilities for women were less common (see Appendix).[11] Police reports on the "nuisances" committed in the absence of indoor or outdoor urinals in the vicinity of some theaters make for compelling reading as among the most graphic instances of publicly enacted indecencies in Victorian culture.[12] In buildings with facilities, provision was less than adequate; the second Canterbury Hall, for example, catering on a Saturday night to "trades people, and their wives, working men, lads, and girls" of the Lambeth neighborhood, offered three water closet compartments for the stalls — a typical number, too, for theaters in the 1890s — and regularly "at the interval which takes places about 1/2 past 9 there are sometimes 50 or 60 people waiting in a row outside the lavatory door waiting their turn to go in."[13]

Not even in the 1900s could it be taken for granted that both sexes could be accommodated in all parts of the highly class-stratified (or class-exclusive) theaters, never mind accommodated adequately in proportion to their numbers, which helps explain why, apart from the desire to prevent deaths during fires or panics, separate entrances and internal segregation were so important.[14] In more ways than one, the segregation that kept gallery from box holders or stalls from pit came to be regarded not just as a matter of the privileges that came to some via economic stratification, but a variable governing life or death.

What I wish to add to the well-traversed scholarship about the improved fireproofing of theatrical property is another variable on the regulators' minds that concerned a growing awareness of scientific principles of hygiene.[15] Throughout the nineteenth century, even when privies were present they were sometimes so offensive-smelling that they could barely be used. Many theaters were impregnated with the stenches of what, proverbially, only ragpickers touched. Standards of sanitation were unrecognizable by modern Western standards. At the capacious Theatre Royal Covent Garden, which had at least some flushing water closets, the other privies were emptied a total of twice a year from 1822 to 1827, as often as the chimney flues were swept.[16] According to cash books for the Royal Lyceum Theatre in Macclesfield, the so-called night soil was removed at most once a year in the 1850s and 1860s.[17] By 1886 civic regulations at Exeter firmly stipulated that "the several Lavatories and Urinals in the Theatre shall be properly and effectually cleansed once at least in each and every week during which the building is used for public performances,"[18] but the crowds and neglect in London were much greater, and thus the problem was more severe. In 1864 the Lord Chamberlain acknowledged the importance of providing properly ventilated water closets and urinals on every floor, preferably "self-acting (Turner's patent), and that water be laid on the urinals on the same plan as adopted at Railway Stations generally" (i.e., automatic flushing and ventilation through a window to the outdoors), but this was unenforceable.[19]

The following year the Lord Chamberlain's officers (the Examiner of Plays, whose usual duties consisted of licensing scripts, and the Inspector of Theatres, a pro tem appointment of an architect prominent in theater design) began to visit every part of London's theaters, not just attending primarily to the auditoria and stage houses. They recommended a host of inexpensive remedies including the application of water, lime-whitening, and the introduction of fresh air, rarely to any avail.[20] Nevertheless, they inveighed that "[a] third of the Dressing Rooms inspected this year may, without exaggeration, be called nurseries of fever. . . . Floors constantly damp, ceilings and walls begrimed with dirt; atmosphere charged with gas, passages reeking with sulphuretted hydrogen, windows which either will not open, or are never opened, [and] rooms without windows and without any mode of escape for vitiated air are serious blemishes in every House devoted to public entertainments."[21]

It is not entirely clear whether they were reacting to foul privies or what performers and staff resorted to in the absence of water closets. The Examiner of Plays, William Bodham Donne, a classical scholar, wrote privately to his daughter: "All last week visiting Theatres. The heat, dirt, dust, smells, horrible. I never had such a job. We took in the dressing-rooms this year. Talk of Ireland and pigsties — they are Dutch cleanliness compared to some of these rooms. I have been sick and dizzy half-a-dozen times a day. I have imported into our own house several varieties of biting and stinging insects."[22] Thirty years later, one of his successors, Edward Pigott, was also being made ill by the annual inspections and begged to be excused from the ritual: "It is not only that I have always felt entirely superfluous, and useless and ignorant, and good for nothing . . . but that I have suffered in health from the fatigue & bad air, and have generally carried away from the Inspection a cold & cough which have aggravated my chronic bronchial catarrh, and spoilt any good effects of my holidays, when I should have been laying in a stock of health for the winter."[23] Of course, this describes circumstances that employees and audiences endured daily.

A successful inspection was necessary to renew the annual license. Despite the personal discomfort experienced by the inspectors and their frequent notations of horrendous conditions, renewals were virtually always granted. It was in the interest of the employees of the Lord Chamberlain to keep as many theaters on their books as possible, for they divided the fees received from licensing among themselves as a supplement to their Queen's List salaries. At the Strand Theatre in 1858, for example, though it was noted that there were no gallery urinals, the pit urinals were not connected to running water, the water closets' drains were not trapped, and the sewers were woefully inadequate, the Lord Chamberlain backed down from requiring necessary repairs because the lessee, Louisa Swanborough, would be unlikely to want to undertake major repairs to her landlord's property until she took a long lease, and so to avoid causing her hardship he granted the license monthly.[24] By the mid-1870s the Examiner of Plays could almost double his salary by this method.

Thus, the sincerity of the whole operation of inspecting has to be called into question. But though I would have scant evidence indeed if I doubted the accuracy of the written reports, it should be mentioned that at most fifteen minutes were spent inspecting each building (cellar, stage, gallery, roof, auditorium, foyers, and all means of egress) including the time spent traveling between appointments. Consequently, I suspect that, if anything, the reports probably chronicle the most glaring atrocities rather than cataloging the fullest possible range of indiscretions, inclining toward understatement rather than hyperbole. This haste may also explain the weight given to foul urinals (facilities exclusive to men) rather than lavatories (which strictly speaking means a sink, but when referred to separately from urinals usually alludes to provision for women) because there was one less door between the urinal and the common space than between the water closet and the retiring room, bar, promenade, dressing room, carpenter's shop, or auditorium. In their haste, it is easy to imagine the inspectors relying on their sense of smell to guide them through each building, toward or away from stenches depending on their inclinations to report various kinds of transgressions in a given year. In 1876, after his retirement, Donne commented on the proposed written "Rules for Theatres Licensed by the Lord Chamberlain" and noted that "I suppose it would be indecent to mention W.Cs. and urinals, and perhaps these matters may be left to the annual inspectors."[25] In other words, keeping the rules unwritten gave the examiners complete latitude to diagnose and prescribe. By 1878 the inspectors had given up insisting on adequate provision of privies, focusing instead only on those that were foul. By this time, of course, the Metropolitan Board of Works also had acquired jurisdiction, and as a government rather than a Crown agency its specifications had to be obeyed, for it could sue in court; this took the onus off the Lord Chamberlain's Office to reform even what it knew to be foul and allowed its officers to collect the fees with a clearer conscience.

The annual inspections were done in late August or early September, the slowest season in the theatrical year but also when fever incidents peaked and the need for vigilance was most pressing. Many of the theaters were dark; lessees took advantage of the lull in business to undertake an annual cleaning, however superficial. Thus, theaters were generally being seen at their best, after a period of vacancy or when they were least besieged by the public. At any rate, this is likely of the better theaters, for the slack period followed the London season when Society had migrated to the country for the latter part of summer. The less prestigious theaters did business all year round, but the heat discharged from gas lighting could be particularly unpleasant in the late summer, so patronage may have slackened seasonally for reasons of comfort as well as the extra hours of work available for many in East End trades. The humbler theaters were certainly seen at their worst: in the hottest season of the year, when water pressure was lowest and at a point when the manager's financial resources were invariably depleted and the incentives and the means to effect improvements were least prevalent.

Concern for audiences long predated concern for the theaters' employees, and though the standards specified for workers were out of synch with other industrial sectors, the movement to instill and (eventually) enforce standards for the audiences' health is resonant with some of Britain's largest public works schemes: the embankment of the Thames, Bazalgette's drainage plans, and the invention of the public toilet.[26] Though the complaints reveal much about this commercial sector's halting acceptance of sanitary standards, they also show much about the social history of odor, linking behaviors of private hygiene in this quintessential public space to anxieties related to the ascendant class system, and showing the impetus for change coming not from regulatory agencies but from patrons. The arrival of Asiatic cholera in Britain in 1831, recurring in several severe outbreaks mid-century, and the presence of typhoid since the late 1820s, remaining endemic but periodically flaring to epidemic proportions, made fulfillment of the sanitary ideal a particularly acute problem in the growing metropolis. Theaters, occasionally shut in the sixteenth and seventeenth centuries because they allowed the assembly of contagious persons, could be said in the Victorian era to actually create disease.

V. Cholerae (like salmonella typhi) thrived in "hot and humid weather, a water supply capable of being repeatedly and grossly contaminated by sewage, and a relatively poor population crowded together in insanitary conditions," or at any rate this is what we now know.[27] Cholera and typhoid's etiology as understood in most of the nineteenth century dictated that although public assembly per se should not be discouraged, the circulated air within a place of public gathering was highly suspect. Whether according to contagionist or miasmatic principles, not only cleanliness but also the organization of auditorium space appears to have been thought instrumental in controlling the spread of disease. In 1866 Britain's commissioners to the International Sanitary Conference in Constantinople sent home a dispatch explaining that "cholera is a disease transmissible from man to man . . . mainly, though not exclusively, through the discharges from the stomach and bowels, which may pollute air or water, and thus bring the infection within range of a large number of persons, without the necessity of actual contact." This insight explains why, formerly, its passage seemed so obscure and "the connecting link of infection was absent."[28] While they advised "that there is no reason to suppose that cholera is communicable by actual contact between individuals," proximity sufficed: "when infected articles or places are shut up and excluded from free air, they preserve their dangerous qualities for an indefinite length of time . . . the freer the exposure to ventilation, the more rapidly they become innocuous."[29] For William Budd in 1856, "the sewer may be looked upon . . . as a direct continuation of the diseased intestine" in the transmission of typhoid; the escape of sewer gas, like the miasma resulting from poor plumbing, was considered deadly.[30]

When the cholera recurred in London in 1849, 1854, and 1866, and typhoid flared in 1856 and 1861–68, there was reason to be particularly suspicious of theatrical neighborhoods (see Tables 1 and 2). Though the morbidity and mortality rates from cholera in theatrical parishes were approximately one-third less than London's average, and the percentage of mortality was greater than average in middle-class residential districts, the population density of the theatrical neighborhoods slightly exceeded the metropolitan average and certainly represented the densest districts commonly encountered by the middle classes. Typhoid mortality was consistently greater for residents of the theatrical neighborhoods, though with the death of Prince Albert in 1861 and near death of the Prince of Wales in 1871, all Britons considered themselves at risk. Associating the epidemics with the theatrical areas was logical given the prevalent understanding about methods of transmission. Thus, the theaters' hygienic and architectural optimization of miasmas fully justified suspicion.

An 1847 decree from the Metropolitan Commission of Sewers forbade the use of 200,000 cesspits beneath London homes, including the "cesslakes" of wealthy neighborhoods pocked with active as well as disused pits. What had formerly been cradled in earthen dugouts, albeit often overflowing through the floorboards, was compelled to be emptied into the rudimentary sewer system for delivery to the Thames. Thus, paradoxically, it was improved household sanitation (and especially the flushing water closet) that precipitated the crisis, not just because of the cross-infection from bacterially contaminated water closets, but because the discharge of effluents formerly dealt with in local cesspits newly went into the sewers and thence to the river, transforming the Thames into the greatest open sewer in the nation and a major hazard to public health. The majority of London's theaters surrounded the river,[31] whose effluvia ran upstream from Woolwich to Chelsea twice a day on the summer tides. At high tide, the pollution was swept backward into the few

TABLE I.

Cholera Statistics for Selected London Parishes, 1832

Theatrical Parishes	Mean Density per Acre	Morbidity Rate per 10,000	Mortality Rate per 10,000	Fatality Rate (%)
West End				
Strand	154	114	32	29
Holborn	230	45	12	28
St. Giles	212	119	53	45
Covent Garden	200	58	35	60
St. Martin's	92	25	14	54
West End average	177.6	72.2	29.2	43.2
East End				
Shoreditch	111	16	8	53
Whitechapel	192	137	92	67
East End average	151.5	76.5	50	60
Surreyside				
Lambeth	24	64	38	60
Average	151.9	72.3	35.5	49.5
Selected Middle-Class Residential Parishes				
Kensington	8	18	13	76
Hanover Square	53	21	13	59
Fulham	5	14	5	33
Islington	12	16	10	65
Hackney	9	2	2	100
Camberwell	6	77	37	49
Clapham	9	27	17	63
Average	14.6	25	13.9	63.6
London average (48 parishes)	145.3	101.8	54.5	51.3

Source: Michael Durey, *The Return of the Plague: British Society and the Cholera, 1831–1832* (Dublin: Gill and Macmillan, 1979), pp. 68–69.

TABLE 2.

Typhoid and Typhus Statistics for Selected London Parishes, 1851–1900

Mortality per 100,000 Population

Theatrical Parishes	1851–60	1861–70	1871–80	1881–90	1891–1900
West End					
Westminster*	87	81	32	23	27
Holborn	78	100	30	19	16
St. Giles	93	100	23	19	13
West End average	86	94	28	20	19
East End					
Shoreditch	132	120	34	20	16
Whitechapel	106	135	42	39	13
East End average	119	128	38	30	15
Surreyside					
Lambeth	76	85	35	25	12
Average	94	102	34	25	15
Selected Middle-Class Residential Parishes					
Kensington	61	54	21	22	10
Islington	77	76	32	24	13
Hackney	83	71	33	27	13
Chelsea	77	70	29	16	13
Hampstead	65	31	20	19	11
Average	73	60	27	22	12
London average (33 parishes)	87	89	30	18	12

Source: W. Luckin, "Typhus and Typhoid," in *Urban Disease and Mortality in Nineteenth-Century England*, edited by Robert Woods and John Woodward (London: Batsford Academic and Educational, 1986; New York: St. Martin's, 1986), pp. 108–9.
*Includes parishes of St. George Hanover Square, Westminster, St. Martin's, St. James's, and Strand.

sewers that existed, closing the outlets and forcing sewage back into ditches, cellars, streets, and yards. Thus, the theatrical neighborhoods were undeniably fetid in good weather. Theaters are not normally classed among the industries releasing noxious smells — tanning, pulpmaking, and bone boiling are generally in another league — but the human dimension of theater (thousands of bodies confined together for the duration of an event) suggests that, in addition to being located in noxious neighborhoods, they produced offensive odors indoors as a residual product of consumption. The Strand, Her Majesty's, and Lyceum are among the West End theaters singled out for comment along these lines in 1858.[32] The prosperous classes had, by the mid-Victorian period, mainly vacated the ancient residential districts of metropolitan London in favor of the more fragrant suburbs to the north, west, and south, where Thomas Cubitt had provided excellent drains, but they returned to Westminster for their dramatic entertainments. Logic dictates that attracting their custom should have been an enormous economic incentive for reform, but the relatively remote Queen's Theatre in Charlotte Street (later the Prince of Wales's under Marie Wilton) was the only house to exhibit commendable standards by 1860.

In 1858, as early as July 8, the Examiner of Plays remarked that Parliament was prostrate, and the legal district centered on Chancery Lane was also closing down. It was the year of the Great Stink:

> The Thames is so pestilential that Hon. Members are fain to speak, holding their noses, and many of them are laid up with sickness so they purpose closing the session. The Lord Chief Justice shut up his Court lately, as neither his Lordship, the jury nor the Bar could stand the odour; and we only want a Bishop to catch the typhus fever to persuade the public that the river needs scouring. It is to be hoped that one at least of those holy men will die for his country's good, or next year we shall be lying all like frogs at the edge of a dry-pond, gasping, on our backs.[33]

Indeed, 1859 was even worse. The weather conspired to make the situation as bad as possible by the beginning of July: "The watermen do not remember at the same season such a long continuance of east winds as we have had: this prevented the water from passing as it would otherwise have done to the sea. The small amount of rain by reducing the quantity of water inland had also an injurious effect, and a body of putrid liquid, which was daily becoming more and more intense, was kept floating between Woolwich and Chelsea."[34] Traveling on the Thames from Chelsea to Deptford midday, a journalist noted that "the smell was bad enough to produce in us a nausea which lasted several hours."[35] By August 20, diphtheria raged and some cholera cases were known. Like most summers, the farmers who daily hauled in hay and hauled out manure from London's horses and other livestock were preoccupied on their land. Dung accumulated and flies thrived. Opposite a dairy on the upper end of Drury Lane where thirty to forty cows were shut in, "the effluvium was sickening."[36] On a day in mid-September, "From early morning, in the northern suburbs of London, the sky was of a leaden deadly hue. Towards the more dense part of the town the haze was thicker. No sunshine made its way from this blighting mist, yet the heat was oppressive; the leaves of the trees did not move; the smoke from chimneys rose lazily, almost perpendicularly from its source."[37]

As far away from the Thames as the Marylebone Theatre, a house that was, in this period, still attracting a cross section of the public, conditions were dire by the first of September:

> There is neither urinal nor w-c for the use of Gallery. The wc for Pit, being placed behind the refreshment counter is almost inaccessible, and the Pit and Box w-cs and urinals are in a most offensive and disgraceful condition.
>
> There is space in the area of present Pit-urinal for a w-c and urinals. But the whole must be reconstructed. The trough removed: water laid on (there is none at present) and slate or earthen-ware basins put up [to replace the saturated wood]. The apertures in wall for ventilation must be enlarged. . . .
>
> Again, below the stage, for the use of performers and servants of the theater, there is a w-c in the worst possible condition[;] being directly under the stage it sends up into the Pro-Scenium and House a constant current of foul air.[38]

Whereas the suburbanite could escape this at home, the theaters made contact unavoidable. Retreating to the comfort and privacy of box seats did not ensure freedom from contagion, for it was believed that disease was contracted by inhalation of noxious vapors. The vapors were thought to emanate as much from social factors as engineering defects, and the stench of contagion (synonymous with the masses and lower classes) produced much anxiety. Providing some portions of the building, such as the dressing rooms and pit, with water closets and urinals seemed, paradoxically, to make theaters more productive of disease-carrying miasmas for it allowed human waste to be expelled inside the building, whence it must be removed by water or other means and, in the interim, ventilated. The lack of water at Marylebone Theatre suggests that urine must have collected until after the performance — at least — to be hauled manually out of doors. The galleryites, by and large, relieved themselves outside the theater building, whereas the under- or unventilated, badly trapped, and underpressurized water closets or "dry" closets of the more prosperous classes propelled the vapors back to their producers and into the auditorium, in this case first wafting over the bar of the refreshment counter.

Where facilities were provided directly off the back of the auditorium and windows or vents were impossible, the problem was most acute. There was no pretending that only the abject wallowed in their filthy mire.

The extent to which proximity to contagion is and is not a matter of socio-economic privilege is noteworthy. In cholera epidemics, the alcove was inherently suspicious, in which case it is difficult to see why the theater box would escape concern. Indeed, rather than providing a retreat from the great unwashed, it might have been thought to trap and hold the vapors rising from them. This may — and I emphasize that this is a conditional assertion — explain why the number of boxes in certain kinds of new theaters diminished in favor of the dress circle after 1858. (New theaters' purely commercial nature, erected by an impresario or syndicate rather than by the earlier system of subscribers raising a building fund and taking boxes as a privilege, like interest on debenture bonds, may also have been a factor, as might a simple change in taste.)

For the sake of argument, I put forward a case for the miasmatic influence on auditorium reform. Normally, a mixed "mob" was not uniformly putrid, but an economy of the body developed within theaters that reduced all visitors to a common plight, suggesting that something must be done to ensure the patronage of the better-off classes. Changes in theaters' interiors during the London building boom of 1858–70 are typically attributed to shifts in fashion as well as the supposedly inexorable evolution of picture frame aesthetics (oddly credited with both illusionism and greater realism).[39] Certainly, the middle classes were attracted back to a wider range of theatrical entertainments in the 1860s, with the popularity of the Prince of Wales's and light francophile operettas. But whereas purpose-built opera houses catering exclusively to the elite continued to ring each tier with boxes (i.e., Covent Garden of 1858 which also provided water closets and self-acting urinals on every tier, Her Majesty's of 1868, and the projected National Opera House of 1875–81),[40] in ways emblematic of class-exclusive auditoria, dramatic and lighter musical theaters markedly played down the importance of boxes.[41] At the rebuilt Adelphi (1858), a grand and spacious theater hosting a series of wildly popular dramas by Dion Boucicault and Augustin Daly, the fourteen boxes comprised only 6.5 percent of seating. Where class exclusivity was more certain, whether an opera house or a neighborhood theater, a different architectural concept prevailed: the Pavilion, also rebuilt in 1858, had a tier of boxes around the pit, but this was in Whitechapel where there was no pretense of filling them with anything but the local version of the bourgeoisie, and even this conceit was later abandoned.[42] The Holborn Theatre (1867), designed in the year of the last London cholera epidemic and opened the following spring, was a cheaply built amphitheater designed to attract the clientele of the nearby legal community; it was originally ringed with twenty-one boxes at the first circle level, but later, presumably when profits disappointed, they were eliminated.[43] Meanwhile, the Globe, just off the Strand, which attracted a range of the respectable classes to surprisingly risqué opera bouffe in the early 1870s, offered only 4 percent of seating in its boxes. Thereafter, at a point that coincides with medical and governmental acceptance of contagionist theories of disease transmission, the percentages in dramatic or light musical theaters crept upward: 8 percent at the Opera Comique (1870), 11 percent at the Criterion (1874), 13.5 percent at the Lyric (1888), and 14 percent at the new Garrick (1889). The exceptions to the trend were the Shaftesbury, opening in 1888 with Johnston Forbes-Robertson in *As You Like It* and less than 1 percent of seating allocated to the boxes, and D'Oyly Carte's Savoy Theatre, opening for Gilbert and Sullivan operettas in 1881 with 6 percent of the audience accommodated in the eighteen boxes.

What I wish to argue here is that with the very real concerns about disease transmission and the necessity to convince the prosperous patrons that theaters could accommodate them inside safely away from the urban stench, a concern about social segregation became conflated with a health issue up to 1868, and that a resulting element in the West End was the creation of greater class specificity in theaters so that miasmatic contamination from the lower orders was simply not possible. As long as it was popularly believed that epidemic diseases were airborne, theaters with middling class clienteles seemed to downplay the presence of boxes, encouraging segregation by socioeconomic and dress standards enforced by prices rather than by segregating the prosperous by family or social units into boxes. Furthermore, I contend that the crucial decade of 1858–68 demonstrates how, for a brief period when the theater was winning back the middle classes and establishing a range of genres especially for them, a mistake in epidemiology partially dictated an architectural trend of major proportions; the shift back to more box seating in new constructions after 1870 followed a new understanding among medical professionals about the transmission of contagion and helps to demonstrate the economic success of new leisure formulae.[44] It appears from architectural evidence, which is neither corroborated nor contradicted by other data, that during the decade 1858–68, the concern was not about public gathering per se, but interclass contamination.

Concepts of boundaries, usually spatial, were complicated by odor. Whereas formerly the upper classes could wear musk-based perfumes to mask the mingling of scents, the more delicate floral fragrances preferred in the Victorian era permitted the detection of odoriferous intrusions as a sort of early warning system of proximity to contagion. In new theater constructions, the middling classes were shifted from boxes (where at one time they thought themselves protected from neighboring vapors) to the stalls and dress circle (where they could exist in a uniformly classed miasma) or into old theaters such as the Prince of Wales's under the Bancrofts, which catered exclusively to them. In extant theaters, public health officials' preoccupation became to separate the elements, shooing the pittites' and galleryites' essences up shafts directly emanating from each section to the outdoors, just as they insisted that different kinds of playgoers depart by separate exits.

It was not just a matter of making theaters clean. Emphasis fell on making the poorest and mixed theaters safe, for notably some of the most prestigious theaters with exclusive clienteles were allowed to be the greatest sanitary offenders. Three examples suffice to demonstrate the point. In 1860 it was observed that in the old Her Majesty's Theatre, "The Water-Closets have been thoroughly repaired: slate floors substituted for wooden floors (which were very old & the cause of much offensive odour); the drains and pipes new trapped. . . . All [they] now require is daily washing down with a solution of Chloride of Lime or Zinc, which the Manager undertakes shall be done."[45] But apparently this promise was not fulfilled, for in 1865 the dressing rooms were described as "filthy — nay — pestilential," and in 1868 the existing facilities for the boxes on the grand tier were called "miserably deficient."[46] At the height of the five-year-old Opera Comique's success with opera bouffe (a largely middle-class entertainment), the smell emanating from the ladies' water closets (at the back of a cloak room leading off from the rear of the lower circle) percolated freely through to the auditorium.[47] In the case of the Haymarket the discomfort in the boxes must be regarded as a condition that the social elite regularly endured, but the more elite the theater was the less likely officials were to press very hard for repairs.[48]

The greatest compulsion to legislate cleanup was exercised on the lowest theaters: at East End houses like the old Garrick, which had absorbed so much filth that it could be inhabited no more, the authorities' gloried in purifying and ventilating it while neglecting the opera houses. Edwin Chadwick argued against the belief, widely assigned by medical officers and magistrates, that intemperance was a cause of fever and mortality; instead, he urged officials to look farther back in the chain of events to discover that "discomfort is found to be the immediate antecedent to the intemperance; and where the external causes of positive discomfort do not prevail in the towns, the workpeople are generally found to have few or no rival pleasures to wean them from habits of intemperance."[49] The remedy, then, was twofold: provide moral amusements for the impoverished classes while also improving the cleanliness of their living conditions. It was imperative, therefore, to keep even the most offensive working-class theaters open. But by 1869 the inspectors noted conspicuous improvement in East End theaters, coinciding with growing consensus among the medical profession that the contagionist theory of disease transmission had won out.[50] However, concern about the return of cholera in 1871–72 heated up the rhetoric:[51]

> With the probability before us that either in the present or next year cholera may revisit London, it is impossible for managers of theatres to be impressed with the duty of using every possible precaution against that disease: and among the most effective precautions is Cleanliness in every portion of a Theatre, as well behind as before the Curtain. It is especially important that Dressing Rooms, in some of which many persons assemble, should have a full share of attention: and that drains and closets be constantly and carefully watched. Untrapped drains and urinals or closets imperfectly supplied with water are among the most certain conveyors of Cholera and kindred diseases, and any accumulation of dust or dirt are in the next degree dangerous in case of cholera, and at any time injurious to health.[52]

Except at the lowest theaters, improvements were lackadaisically enforced and depended entirely on the goodwill of the manager. At Astley's and other theaters with slate urinals, the channels stank from the permeated urine; the Sangers happened to be disposed to improve the situation.[53] In 1871 the Lyceum's urinals could not be kept clean: "They are in fact merely wooden troughs lined with lead, and very offensive. Partitions between each urinal and basins for each should be immediately supplied, as the present ones are neither decent nor capable of being kept in proper order."[54] In five successive annual reports, urinals at this first-class theater were condemned, as were the unventilated water closets. At the Folly Theatre, J. L. Toole's farce emporium accommodating a prosperous clientele of up to six hundred per night, the inspectors in 1878 noted: "It would be an improvement if the urinals behind the dress circle were removed, but if it cannot be dispensed with, double doors should be fixed to prevent the smell from entering the house in the event of the servants not keeping it properly cleaned."[55] It did not seem to occur to anyone at the Folly to compel the servants to keep things properly clean or to question why the large air shaft shown on the plans to run behind the dress circle water closet (and the stalls water closet directly beneath it) was entirely ineffectual. Improvements were made several years later, yet in 1885 complaints resumed about unpleasant smells in the house resulting from defective drains.[56]

Clear statements that the unventilated air of the rear pit (usually under the circle) and gallery were especially poisonous suggest that there was no largess in banishing the Haymarket's pittites to the upper balcony in 1880, only better air for otherwise unprofitable sections, in recognition of the fact that the middle classes would no longer put up with it in a theater of such construction.[57] C. J. Phipps not only eliminated the Haymarket's pit, but also closed off the area under the first balcony, converting it to storage.[58] The early Victorian solution of moving the pittites back from the orchestra to behind the stalls was one way of localizing the miasmatic stench (enclosing it, as it were, on five sides rather than one), but eliminating the pit (as proposed for Her Majesty's as early as July 1879)[59] was the only real remedy if the middle classes were to be fully comfortable and safe in their backed and upholstered seats in the stalls, circles, and private boxes. Significantly, at Her Majesty's Theatre, when the pit was converted to a full floor of commodious stalls, the boxes that ringed the lower level were also converted to stalls-style row seating.

How does this relate to the theater's status as "public" in the era of private enterprise? A box is by definition and nomenclature a "private" box. The hygienic "private" public of a class-exclusive theater such as the Prince of Wales's or Haymarket under the Bancrofts encloses the hygienic bourgeoisie. This differentiation was originally a segregated geography of the building interior, but later — by the 1880s — a theater's clientele was made synonymous with a particular repertoire and management (e.g., operetta under D'Oyly Carte at the Savoy, sentimental comedy under the Bancrofts at the Haymarket, society comedy under Alexander at the St. James's, serious drama under Irving at the Lyceum, or high comedy under Wyndham at the Criterion). A house not only became wedded to a particular subspecialty of repertoire, but the repertoire itself was thus "cleansed" for a particular kind of "public." The historiography equates the clientele with the repertoire, the repertoire with respectability, and respectability with profitability but mistakes the complexity of the whole motive.[60] What had recently been an unsafe boxed alcove became an unnecessary socio-familial delineator, and with the advent of dimmed auditoria in the period it was completely redundant.

A dramatist describing Covent Garden in 1835 explains the problem under the old system:

> If you go to the Pit you are either smoked out of it or trampled to death with orange-women. . . . If you go to the Boxes with parties, the arrangements of the saloon, its outlets, and other things connected with it — such as the continual opening and shutting of the box-doors, &c. &c. — exclude immense numbers of that truly respectable class who would be the strongest supporters of the legitimate Drama; and, perhaps, I do not overrate it when I say one-sixth part of the community, owing to bad management, are thus wholly excluded, whereas, by a different line of conduct, the Patent Theatres would even obtain a monopoly — all parents naturally siding with what will more immediately protect the morals of their children.[61]

When the theaters eliminated the smoking (thought in the Georgian, but not Victorian, era to purge deadly miasmas), the hockers, the box doors, and the bad managements, the respectable classes returned in numbers during the "yuppie" economic upswing of the 1860s. Respectable repertoire existed all along, but it simply had not deployed a respectable ambiance for its consumption.

In the meantime, undesirable repertoire became synonymous with undesirable smells. For example, when the amateur Whittington Club was challenged about its announced performance of *Lady of the Camellias* (a play never licensed) at Arundel Street, Captain Horton Rhys appealed that if he had to substitute another play, he would be "at his wits end and lose money into the bargain." The Examiner of Plays decided that because it was an old play (and had in fact been performed all over the realm, illegally, just never in London) and he hated to see a row in the newspapers so soon after the opposition to Passion Week closures, he would let it go provided that Rhys never repeated it: "he was for having it licensed, but I bad[e] him not to bring it under my nostrils."[62] Clearly, the genteel and middling classes could tolerate stinking closets, whether while using them or while taking refreshment in saloons adjacent to them or while merrily watching entertainments. Their own miasmas were of no concern, and when miasmas proved erroneous as a theory of disease transmission, prosperous patrons continued to attend theaters seemingly oblivious of the stench. There is not a single letter of complaint on these grounds in all of the Lord Chamberlain's nineteenth-century records. Ideas could stink, or aesthetics be offensive, but not the effluvium of an operagoer.

The theory of miasmas, developed in the time of the great plagues, took a cultural turn in the nineteenth century: territorial offenses were categorized based on olfactory assaults, public space was medicalized, and the primacy of the visual gave way to bourgeoisified aesthetic syncretism that sought to unite observed nature (or art) with sound and poetry as well as odor, even to the extent that stage pantomimes were perfumed. Eventually, the entire hushed theater building could be regarded as "pure" and safe even though it was by this time darkened, for the ascribed sources of contagion in the West End were exiled downriver, as it were. Just as the prosperous classes vacated the ancient residential areas of London and Westminster, the solution for theaters—if they were to be elite in clientele and thus repertoire—was to distinguish the leisure pursuits of each socioeconomic stratum so distinctly that West End theater buildings no longer had to cope with the mingled miasmas that ultimately could not be expunged, masked, or satisfactorily vented. And when miasmas gave way to contagionism, pointing the blame at water, not air, the stink remained. Thus, one can conclude that patrons exerted economic pressure for their own theaters, fully stratifying entertainment on class grounds at the midpoint of Victoria's reign, not because the market would bear it but because consumers regarded their very survival to depend on it. While officials documented sanitary breaches under all circumstances, prosperous patrons seemed content provided that they could recreate in the unmingled vapor of their own kind. Even when the fear that may have motivated this subsided, the habit remained.

Appendix: Sanitary Facilities in London Theaters, 1855

Theater/Date Built	Capacity[a]	Clientele	Facilities[b]
Adelphi, 1806	?	[Burlettas, music and dancing with spectacle and pantomime.]	Urinals and water closet (w.c.) and urinal for pit well ventilated and lighted; the same for boxes.
Astley's, 1842	2,050	All classes from every part of the town [circus].	Well-ventilated urinals in lobbies of upper and lower boxes, pit, and gallery.
Bower Saloon, 1837	>1,000	[Recently had trouble with] loose and disorderly juveniles of both sexes.	Neither a w.c. nor a urinal in the house. Audience obliged to go thru the tap of the public house to a ground where there is a privy and urinal with 2 compartments.
Britannia, 1841	1,000	[Melodrama and burletta.]	In a ground outside— 3 closets with common bogholes—no light in them, but a gas lamp in the urinals which had to [suffice]. Also a separate closet for women on the pit floor; lighted common boghole also.
City of London, 1835	>1,550	Persons in the neighborhood, mainly weavers.	2 water closets.
Garrick, 1854	462[c]	Principally the neighborhood, tradespeople, and mechanics.	None in the theater; one in court opposite.

Theater/Date Built	Capacity[a]	Clientele	Facilities[b]
Grecian, 1825	~1,400	Respectable tradesmen, clerks from city, mechanics, the neighborhood.	Opposite in the gardens, 4 w.c.'s with sanitary pans and 11 urinals on excellent principles, well ventilated and lighted.
Haymarket, 1821	?	[Middlebrow drama and comedy.]	10 boxes and pit. None to gallery. The pit urinals and w.c.'s are all in one behind the pit passage; they want ventilation.
Lyceum, 1834	?	[English opera, ballets of action, musical entertainments etc., indicating elite.]	1 w.c. and urinal for pit, lighted and aired; same on dress circle and boxes above, no separate light for w.c.; same on gallery, but no light to this—it is on the roof, and the manager objects to lights there as the boys would smoke them between the acts.
Marylebone, 1842	2,300	Families from Bryanston and Montagu [Squares]. Schools in winter, respectable tradesmen, mechanics, etc., all from the locality.	On pit floor, a urinal well lighted and ventilated. A w.c. on every landing but gallery. Nothing in gallery, but a public urinal outside.
Olympic, 1849	?	[Music, dancing, burlettas, spectacle, pantomime, horsemanship.]	W.c. in pit, 2 w.c.'s and urinals in boxes, all lighted with gas and ventilated. None in

Theater/Date Built	Capacity[a]	Clientele	Facilities[b]
			gallery, but a large public urinal around the back of the theater.
Pavilion, 1828	?	Persons in the neighborhood and many from the docks, many sailors.	2 urinals and 4 w.c.'s leading off from the large passage. They require inspecting again as the place was by no means clean.
Princess's, 1842	?	Fashionable, better class of tradespeople, housekeepers, etc., not confined to the neighborhood.	[No information.]
Queen's, 1772	>1,200	Persons in the neighborhood, often superior chaps to the audience in the City [of London Theatre].	W.c. to boxes, no urinal in the theater, one near the public house nearby.
Standard, 1835	>2,000	Tradesmen, mechanics, their children, silk weavers from Spitalfields, etc.	[No information.]
St. James's, 1835	?	[Burlettas, music and dancing, spectacle, pantomime.]	For pit, a w.c. and urinal in one. No light in the w.c., but the urinal is lighted. There should be a hole in the door of the former which would effect the purpose. In the gallery, a urinal ventilated and lighted.
Sadler's Wells, 1765	2,100	Tradespeople in the neighborhood,	2 w.c.'s for boxes; none for pit, but

Theater/Date Built	Capacity[a]	Clientele	Facilities[b]
		brickmakers, mechanics, watchmakers.	near gallery entrance is a convenient urinal shut off sufficiently large for the theater and properly lighted.
Strand, 1820	?	[Burlettas, music and dancing with spectacle and pantomime.]	Nothing for pit, a w.c. for boxes and urinal for gallery at bottom of stairs, lighted.
Soho, 1840	?	[Burlettas, music and dancing with spectacle and pantomime.]	[No information.]
Surrey, 1805	>3,000	Sometimes nobility and gentry, tradespeople, mechanics. In gallery, 4 women to 1 man in the pit, the husbands and brothers being in gallery to save expense.	W.c.'s; none except in boxes. A large public urinal outside.
Victoria, 1818	2,200[d]	Principally mechanics in the neighborhood.	Only 1 w.c. to whole of theater — this for the boxes. There are excellent public urinals around the theater itself lately erected.

Principal Source: PRO LC7/13.

[a] Based on information compiled by the Lord Chamberlain's Office in 1843 and provided by the theaters' managers in letter form and during interviews on presentation of sureties, PRO LC7/5. Comparisons with Diana Howard, *London Theatres and Music Halls, 1850–1950* (London: Library Association, 1970), suggest that these figures may be very low.

[b] Adapted from the inspection survey of 1855 (PRO LC7/5). No data are available for Covent Garden or Drury Lane, which, as patented rather than licensed theaters, were not at this time subjected to annual inspections.

[c] From Howard, *London Theatres*. The previous structure held more than 1,400.

[d] According to Charles Kemble's testimony to the 1832 Select Committee, this figure should be 4,832. The audience consisted mostly of the working class on Mondays and the better classes in the middle of the week. *Report from the Select Committee Appointed to Inquire into the Laws Affecting Dramatic Literature* (1832; reprint, Shannon: Irish University Press, 1968), pp. 1238–43, 1267, 1270.

Notes

Sincere thanks are due to David Mayer, whose observations first prompted this research and whose ideas materially contributed, and to Ellen Donkin, who ensured due regard for contemporary myopathy.

1. See Sir John Harington's "A Discourse on a Stale Subject, Called the Metamorphosis of Ajax" (1596) describing the valve and cistern latrine installed in his home near Bath. It anticipates the basic engineering of modern (i.e., Victorian) water closets: an all-ceramic or metal casing built on the syphonic principle with flushing cantilivred cistern and a trapping mechanism to prevent the escape of sewer gas. In 1884 Humberson's first forced flush model was patented — the mechanism still in use today — but the first patentee of a water closet was Alexander Cummings. See Roy Palmer, *The Water Closet: A New History* (Newton Abbot: David and Charles, 1973). This dispensed with the pan mechanism, which was neither very savory nor sanitary. See Lucinda Lambton, *Temples of Convenience* (London: Gordon Fraser, 1978).

2. They were probably installed earlier. The reference in the Answer to Bill of Complaint, Court of Exchequer, by the architect James Wyatt, March 1, 1793, reads: "Mahogany seat to ladies w.c. £3.3.0." Public Record Office (PRO) E112/1824 #7586. I am grateful to Robert Hume and Judith Milhous for drawing these records to my attention.

3. As a universal principle, this is contradicted by S. Rolleston: "Our Ladies in England are asham'd of being seen even in going to or returning from the most necessary parts of our houses, as it was in itself shameful to do even in private, what nature absolutely requires at certain seasons to be done: whereas I have known an old woman in Holland set herself on the next hole to a Gentleman, and civilly offer him her mussel shell by way of scraper after she had done with it herself." *A Philosophical Dialogue* (1751), quoted in Lucinda Lambton, *Chambers of Delight* (London: Gordon Fraser, 1983), pp. 6–7.

4. Athenaeus, book xii, cap. 17. For further elaboration, see Captain John G. Bourke, *Scatological Rites of All Nations* (Washington, D.C.: W. H. Lowdermilk, 1891), p. 139.

5. Tyne and Wear Archives, Newcastle, Th/RO/1/1, Newcastle Theatre Royal Subscribers Committee Minutes, March 31, 1837.

6. For the merits and demerits of various models, and advice on installing private and public facilities, see S. Stevens Hellyer, *The Plumber and Sanitary Houses* (London: T. B. Batsford, 1877).

7. Reports by Shirley F. Murphy, Medical Officer of Health, Public Health Department, December 10, 1891, July 12, 1899, Greater London Record Office (GLRO) LCC/MIN/10,926.

8. William Budd, *Malignant Cholera: Its Mode of Propagation, and Its Prevention* (London: John Churchill, 1849); "Outbreak of Fever at the Orphan School in St. John's Wood," *Lancet* (November 15, 1856): 555; "The Propagation of Cholera," *Lancet* (April 15, 1868): 217–19; Anne Hardy, "Parish Pump to Private Pipes: London's Water Supply in the Nineteenth Century," in *Living and Dying in London*, edited by W. F. Bynum and Royal Porter (London: Wellcome Institute, 1991), p. 84; R. J. Morris, *Cholera 1832: The Social Response to an Epidemic* (London: Croom Helm, 1976), pp. 181,

183–84; Margaret Pelling, *Cholera, Fever, and English Medicine, 1825–1865* (Oxford: Oxford University Press, 1978), pp. 203–49.

9. Carlo M. Cipolla, *Miasmas and Disease: Public Health and the Environment in the Pre-Industrial Age* (New Haven: Yale University Press, 1992), p. 5. See also Michael Durey, *The Return of the Plague: British Society and the Cholera, 1831–1832* (Dublin: Gill and Macmillan, 1979), pp. 101–34; Anne Hardy, *The Epidemic Streets: Infectious Disease and the Rise of Preventive Medicine, 1856–1900* (Oxford: Clarendon Press, 1993).

10. John Hollingshead, *My Lifetime*, 2 vols. (London: Sampson Low, Marston, 1895), 1:90.

11. Presumably, what the Lord Chamberlain had in mind when inaugurating inspections was "the safety and convenience of the public," as later written regulations stipulate, within the jurisdiction given by Article viii of the 1843 Act for Regulating Theatres allowing his office to close theaters and patent houses as he deemed fit. But there is no specific charge as to safety. Article ix allows the Lord Chamberlain to establish Rules for Order and Decency, but the tenor is in regard to riots, not sanitation. I interpret the presence of urinals as definitive evidence of provision for men; descriptions of privies or water closets not linked with documentation of urinals are likely to be provided for women's use only, whereas descriptions of "privy and urinal" or "w.c. and urinal" may be solely for men's use.

12. For example, outside Sadler's Wells in 1893–94 (PRO LC1/601), the East London Theatre (Effingham) in 1866 (LC1/167) and 1870 (LC1/232), at Alcester in 1874 (Warwickshire Record Office CR 114A/740), and outside the Grand Theatre and Opera House, Leeds in 1882 (West Yorkshire Archives, Leeds, GT/3/1). See also Jim Davis, " 'Scandals to the Neighbourhood': Cleaning-up the East London Theatres," *New Theatre Quarterly* 6.23 (August 1990): 235–43.

13. Inspection Report, August 8, 1891, and Memo, August 4, 1893, GLRO LCC/MIN/10,782.

14. In 1864 the Lord Chamberlain attempted to codify structural requirements: not only must new theater constructions be detached from other buildings (for ease of access), "There must be at least 3 separate and distinct entrances for the Public; it being presumed that there is one besides set apart for the Performers & Servants. . . . The Box & Stalls entrance it is assumed will always be in the main-front. Two staircases, one for entrance one for discharge of audience to be provided for the Gallery more than —— persons and amphitheatre. In no case can the Boxes, Stalls & Pit be allowed to be discharged through one passage." Draft Regulations for Exterior to Theatres, PRO LC1/141. In 1899 the Medical Officer of Health proposed a ratio of one water closet per twenty artists or male staff, one for every fifteen female staff, and for the audience "not less than 1 water closet to 150 males, 1 water-closet to 100 females, and 1 urinal stall to 40 males." The recommendations were excised from draft copies of revised LCC Regulations, and nothing like these proportions were achieved. GLRO LCC/MIN/10,926.

15. E. O. Sachs and E. Woodrow, *Modern Opera Houses and Theatres*, 3 vols. (1896–98); J. G. Buckle, A.R.I.B.A., *Theatre Construction and Maintenance* (London: "The Stage" Office, 1888); John R. Freeman, *On the Safeguarding of Life in Theaters[:] Being a Study from the Standpoint of an Engineer* (New York City: American Society of Mechanical Engineers, 1906).

16. Covent Garden Ledger, 1822–29, f. 145, payments to Mr. Edwards, chimney sweep and night man. British Library Add MS 23167.

17. Staffordshire County Record Office, D 877/204/3.

18. PRO LC1/469.

19. Draft Regulations, PRO LC1/141.

20. Lime and charcoal, according to Lindsey Blyth's findings reported to the Board of Health, "induce in certain organic compounds a condition of great readiness to become oxidized by the air," rendering the organic infectant into a harmless ozonous state. *Builder* 15.746 (23 May 1857): 292–93.

21. General Remarks for 1865, PRO LC1/153.

22. Letter, September 19, 1865, reproduced in Catharine B. Johnson, ed., *William Bodham Donne and His Friends* (London: Methuen, 1905), p. 268.

23. Edward Pigott to Spencer Ponsonby-Fane, August 22, 1894, PRO LC1/617.

24. PRO LC1/58.

25. February 21, 1876, PRO LC1/313.

26. In 1846 public conveniences were unknown. *Builder* 4 (1846): 231. By the 1890s each new facility was proudly hailed. See, e.g., "A New Underground Convenience," *Surveyor* (January 11, 1894): 23.

27. Durey, *Return of the Plague*, p. 50.

28. Report on the International Sanitary Conference, Constantinople, The British Commissioners to Lord Stanley, October 3, 1866 (no. 38), PRO PC1/2672.

29. The British Cholera Commissioners to the Earl of Clarendon, May 25, 1866 (no. 21), PRO PC1/2672.

30. William Budd, "Fever at the Orphan Clergy Asylum," *Lancet* (1856): ii, 618.

31. This predates the construction of Shaftesbury Avenue, and thus the West End theater district was strung along an axis of the Strand between St. Clement Dane's Church and Charing Cross Station, and the south end of the Haymarket. In the East End, Wellclose Square was a nexus of entertainment, licit and otherwise. Across the river, Westminster Bridge Road and Waterloo Road, bisected by Lower Marsh Street, demarcate the main Lambeth Theatre district.

32. PRO LC1/58.

33. W. B. Donne to Fanny Kemble Butler, in Johnson, *Donne and His Friends*, p. 225. "Typhus fever" refers, in this context, to typhoid though the pathology of the two diseases were not yet distinguished from each other. Typhus is transmitted by body lice and is associated with the crowded conditions that came about in the poorest housing, especially in winter. Typhoid is usually transmitted via food or water and flared during the hottest months.

34. "The Thames and Its Neighbourhood: Deodorizing," *Builder* 17.857 (July 2, 1859): 439.

35. *Builder* 17.863 (August 20, 1859): 545.

36. Ibid.

37. *Builder* 17.867 (September 17, 1859): 612.

38. PRO LC1/70.

39. Consider, for example, Percy Fitzgerald's description of the 1880 Haymarket proscenium, a two-foot-wide gold border on four sides of the opening: "There can be no doubt the sense of illusion is increased, and for the reason given; the actors seem cut

off from the domain of prose; there is no borderland or platform in front; and, stranger still, the whole has the air of a picture projected on a surface." Fitzgerald, *The World Behind the Scenes* (1881; reprint, New York: Benjamin Blom, 1972), pp. 20–21. This is exactly the aesthetic complained of by Bertolt Brecht: "As for the world portrayed there, the world from which slices are cut in order to produce these moods and movements of the emotions, its appearance is such, produced from slight and wretched stuff as a few pieces of cardboard, a little miming, a bit of text, that one has to admire the theatre folk who, with so feeble a reflection of the real world, can move the feelings of their audience so much more strongly than does the world itself." "A Short Organum for the Theatre," *Brecht on Theatre: The Development of an Aesthetic* (New York: Hill and Wang, 1964; London: Methuen, 1964), p. 187.

40. PRO LC7/63, 68.

41. Moody reports, "By 1836, Vestris had abolished the [Olympic's] gallery altogether, replacing it by a second tier of boxes," which further contrasts with the trend later in the century away from boxes for elite theaters producing light fare. Jane Moody, "Aspects of Cultural Politics in the London Minor Theatres of the Early Nineteenth Century" (Ph.D. diss., Oxford University, 1993), p. 48.

42. The *Illustrated London News* (November 6, 1858, pp. 429–30) depicts two tiers of boxes originally encircling the pit; however, the pit of 2,000 seats and the gallery of at least 1,000 did not leave much reliance on patronage of the boxes for this 3,500-seat theater. In the plans for September 1874, these boxes do not appear. Because this is not among the indicated alterations, one can safely presume that the boxes were removed some time in the previous decade and a half (PRO LC7/72).

43. The *Illustrated London News* (June 22, 1867, p. 630) describes the rationale for this as follows: "There are no stage-boxes or proscenium-boxes, as it would have been impossible for persons in the second row in a stage-box to see the stage or to look into the ring of the amphitheatre. The architects have therefore substituted twenty-six [*sic?*] private boxes, which are placed behind one row of balcony-stalls, all round the theatre, having their floor raised considerably above the stalls, so that persons standing in front cannot look into the boxes" (see also the illustration on p. 616 and compare plans in PRO LC7/65).

44. For example, 1877 plans of Sadler's Wells show no boxes, but eight were added in 1878. PRO LC7/76.

45. April 7, 1860, PRO LC1/83.

46. PRO LC1/153, 202.

47. Mr. Fowler (architect of Opera Comique) to Ponsonby-Fane, January 10, 1875: "The question of the smell of the w.c. in Ladies room percolating into the Boxes has been brought before me & although I have nothing really to do with the question I have ordered the abolition of it & putting it in another place and before Mr. Nation opens the House this will be done." PRO LC1/211. Judging by its location, the men's facilities should have been just as offensive. PRO LC7/71.

48. From 1855 to 1865 the Haymarket's pit urinals and water closets were the subject of frequent complaints. PRO LC7/13, LC7/70, LC1/83, LC1/98, LC1/153. From 1861 to 1865 the box urinals and water closets were offensive (LC1/98, LC1/153), and from 1869 to 1871 inspectors called for ventilation to be installed in the wall of the women's dress circle water closet (LC1/221, LC1/223, LC1/247).

49. Edwin Chadwick, *Report on the Sanitary Condition of the Labouring Population of Great Britain* (1842; reprint, Edinburgh: Edinburgh University Press, 1965), p. 203.

50. PRO LC1/221. Whereas the contamination of water was repeatedly proven to be the aetiology of cholera in England, the mass epidemics at the disease's "source" — Lower Bengal — were still being attributed to air currents, meteorological factors, and electrical variations in the atmosphere. "Cholera and Air Currents," *Lancet* (October 24, 1868): 550.

51. This, like all other anticipated outbreaks after 1866, was prevented. See Anne Hardy, "Cholera, Quarantine, and the English Preventive System, 1850–1895," *Medical History* 37 (1993): 250–69.

52. Inspection Report, 1871, PRO LC1/247.

53. Inspection Report, 1871, PRO LC1/233; Inspection Report, 1872, PRO LC1/263.

54. PRO LC1/247 (regarding 1871).

55. PRO LC7/25.

56. PRO LC7/32.

57. For example, Reginald Ward (of Holland Villas Road, Kensington) complained to the Lord Chamberlain on November 3, 1866, about the ventilation in the lower part of the Olympic Theatre. Horace Wigan, the lessee, insisted that with two large ventilators at the back of the pit, two large air shafts to the roof and two more from the stalls onto the stage, and forty shafts in all from the building to the street, this was the best-ventilated theater in London: "the only one where you were sure to escape a headache." Still, Ward insisted that the experience of playgoers at ten o'clock on a Saturday evening would prove this theater as inadequate as others, even if the weather was not "close." PRO LC1/167.

58. By the summer of 1895, Beerbohm Tree was considering reverting to the old plan: dropping the floor of the stalls by five feet and inserting a pit underneath the first circle. This was eventually accomplished. Gerrard James & Wolfe (Tree's solicitors) to Clerk of the London County Council, July 13, 1895, GLRO LCC/MIN/10,827.

59. PRO LC7/63.

60. See Michael R. Booth, *Theatre in the Victorian Age* (Cambridge: Cambridge University Press, 1991), pp. 53–54; Anthony Jenkins, *The Making of Victorian Drama* (Cambridge: Cambridge University Press, 1991), pp. 15–16; George Taylor, *Players and Performances in the Victorian Theatre* (Manchester: Manchester University Press, 1989), p. 106; and George Rowell, *The Victorian Theatre, 1792–1914*, 2d ed. (Cambridge: Cambridge University Press, 1978), p. 84.

61. Mr. Otway, *An Attempt to Deduce from Facts, the Causes of the Present Disgraceful State of Our National Theatres* (London: C. Harris, 1835), p. 5.

62. W. B. Donne to Spencer Ponsonby-Fane, August 4, 1862, PRO LC1/113.

Touching Netherplaces

Invisibility in the Photographs of Hannah Cullwick

CAROL MAVOR

"He took me for his housemaid," she said to herself as she ran.
"How surprised he'll be when he finds out who I am!"
[Alice talking about the White Rabbit]
  Lewis Carroll, Alice's Adventures in Wonderland

On May 11, 1988, I had my first appointment to see the Munby Box at the Wren Library, Trinity College, University of Cambridge (Fig. 1). I was led through the center of the magnificently beautiful space (a small wondrous castle lined with ancient books and crowned by promising windows) to an old lovely library table. I took a seat. A soft crimson cloth was laid before me. Two men then heaved the heavy polished wooden box onto the velvety cloth. The box with its many enigmatic drawers and tiny, graspable handles could have been an excessively large jewelry box or a magnificent scientific box for displaying rare and common butterflies by their Latin classifications. It gave the sense that something beautiful was inside. It invited inspection. They gave me a pair of white gloves.

A Story in a Box

The Munby Box is a creation of the Wren Library to hold the photographs of working-class women that were obsessively collected by Arthur Munby (1828–1910), a Cambridge-educated man who was a second-rate poet, an acquaintance of the Pre-Raphaelites, and a man-about-London-town with plenty of family money and an insignificant career with the Ecclesiastical Commission that did not interest him. What did interest him were working-class women, especially those involved in manual labor (despite the fact that he "had never worked with anything heavier than a pen in his life"), especially those who upset conventions of gender.[1] For example, there were the mining women who wore pants, lifted big heavy rocks, and nearly approached Munby in size. There were harnessed milkwomen with big red hands and broad shoulders. Besides the many manual workers, there were also performers, like the girl acrobats (small and skinny without flesh and without curves) who looked liked boys in their skintight tights. He also wrote about these women in his

Figure 1. The Munby Box, ca. 1970. A creation of the Wren librarians to hold Munby's collection of photographs of working-class women. (Master and Fellows of Trinity College, Cambridge)

diaries and made sketches of them. The Wren Library also holds these, but they are not in the Munby Box.

Hannah Cullwick (1833–1909), a lower servant for all of her life beginning at age eight, met Munby in 1854. The two developed a strange secret courtship that lasted for more than thirty-six years. Their relationship circulated around Munby's voyeuristic interest in her work and her pride in being obsessively hardworking. She began writing her own volumes of diaries at his request; he found her endless accounts of her endless drudgery tantalizing. He also was very interested in having photographs of her taken "in her dirt" and often made arrangements for this. He was intrigued by Hannah Cullwick's special ability to masquerade as a lady (Fig. 2), and there are photographs of this as well. There are also some unusual photographs of her as other, rather shocking, characters: a chimney sweep who looks more like a slave (Fig. 3), a bare-chested Magdalene (Fig. 4), a man with short hair (Fig. 5). Interestingly enough, the character of Magdalene was decided on cooperatively by Hannah Cullwick and a photographer by the name of Mr. Stodart. But it was Cullwick

Figure 2. Howl, Hannah as a lady, 1874.
(Master and Fellows of Trinity College, Cambridge)

who first suggested that Munby cut her hair. And it was Cullwick who once proposed that she go about with Munby dressed as a man so that no one would know her identity. The two were finally married in 1873. (Almost all of the photographs of Hannah are of her as an unmarried woman.) Yet all through their long courtship and all through their marriage, Hannah Cullwick preferred to continue as a lower servant, working mostly as a maid-of-all-work.[2] Her diaries end soon after the marriage. She refused the name "Hannah

Figure 3.
Hannah as a
chimney sweep,
1862. (Master
and Fellows of
Trinity College,
Cambridge)

Figure 4. James Stodart, *Hannah as Magdalene*, 1864.
(Master and Fellows of Trinity College, Cambridge)

Figure 5. Fink, Hannah wearing men's clothes, 1860.
(Master and Fellows of Trinity College, Cambridge)

Munby," preferring to be called simply "Hannah." Hannah wished to remain, in her own words, "his slave," which she saw as being a more honored position than a "wife nor equal to any vulgar man."[3] Of course, even before her marriage (because of her class and her station), Hannah was rarely referred to by her surname. I want to keep this difference intact: for the remainder of this essay I will honor her as simply Hannah.

Despite the volumes of diaries that they both kept and despite the forty-odd photographs of her in the Munby Box, it is hard to get a hold of Hannah.[4] One wonders if her invisibility within this space of excess representation is not tied to her own desire to defy visibility. She made invisibility into an art. She wore her thirteen-and-one-half-inch biceps as proudly as she wore her dirt. Her dirt, her masculine stride, her lack of womanly manners all enabled her to go through the streets of the city freely, without the usual constraints placed on the Victorian lady. As Liz Stanley has pointed out, Hannah "goes out alone to public houses late at night, walks through crowds of drunken men without fear, wanders at night across fields and waste ground, and all without molestation or harassment."[5] Hannah writes in her diary: "That's the best thing o'being drest and rough, and looking 'nobody' — you can go anywhere and not be wonder'd at."[6]

Hannah's job also required that she not be visible to her employers and their guests. The work must look as if it was done invisibly. Hannah's diaries are filled with many passages about her struggles not to be seen and the outrage that her employers bestowed on her when she was covered with signs of her occupation, especially if she was dirty. But for the most part, Hannah was as good at covering up her traces as she was at removing household dirt and grime. This skill, of making one's presence invisible, turned out to be quite useful when she desired to spend the night with Munby. Munby explains it well in a passage from his diary: "She [Hannah] had leave to stay out a few nights during her mistress's absence: and she wished to spend them with me. In her innocence and confiding love she wished it: ought I to refuse? Her coming would compromise neither herself nor me, because it would not be known to any one: *she who washes dishes and makes beds can remove all traces of her own presence.*"[7]

In one curious place, deep inside the mysterious Munby Box, Hannah has been washed away entirely; she is *unpictured*. Tray 12 of the box contains a small gold frame with a note describing a photograph that is not there (Fig. 6). This note moves me more than any of the actual pictures. Its words are simply:

Hannah, going to the Public house for the Kitchenbeer as she does daily. Taken in the street about noon on Friday, the 2nd of February 1872.

NB. The house in Pochester Square against which she stands, is that of an acquaintance of mine.

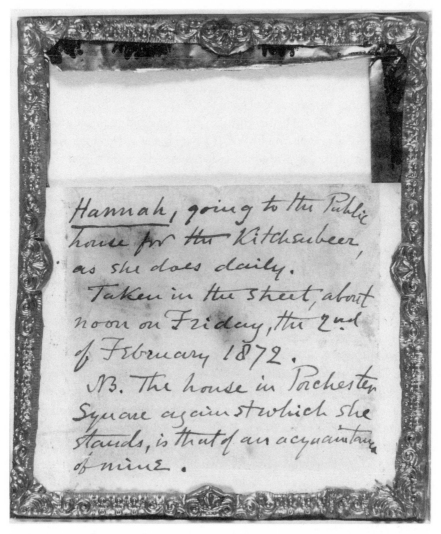

Figure 6. Copper frame with note describing a photograph of Hannah that is missing from the Munby Box, n.d. The note, written in Munby's hand, reads as follows: "Hannah, going to the Public house for the Kitchenbeer as she does daily. Taken in the street about noon on Friday, the 2nd of February 1872. NB. The house in Pochester Square against which she stands is that of an acquaintance of mine." (Master and Fellows of Trinity College, Cambridge)

All that remains is a trace of her remembered presence, written in Munby's hand.[8] I am drawn to this missing picture: it represents Hannah's invisible flesh. I want to touch it. I caress the place of her absence with gloved fingers. I am reminded of the extraordinary words of the French philosopher Emmanuel Levinas: "In a caress what is there is sought as though it were not there, as though the skin were a trace of its own withdrawal, a languor still seeking, like an absence which, however, could not be more there."[9]

Invisible Gloves

May 11, 1988
Very strange to be writing with white gloves on as I search the photographs for meaning behind "dirty" working-class women.
(My first diary entry on the Munby Box)

In two early articles on the photographs of Hannah, photo credit is given on the one hand to Hannah (by Heather Dawkins) and on the other to Arthur Munby (by Lenore Davidoff).[10] Although the photographs were, in fact, taken by several photographers (none of whom were either Munby or Hannah), these two articles express the conflict over who is empowered by these images. I am led to ask, alternately — as though turning a glove inside out again and again — whether the photographs are expressions of Munby's own fantasies about a working-class woman, not unlike a painting of Jane Burden by Dante Gabriel Rossetti. Or are they Hannah's own self-portraits that unexpectedly prefigure the work of current feminist photographers and performance artists like Cindy Sherman and Eleanor Antin? As complex representations over an equally complex space of negotiation (the space of Hannah's body), they are neither and both. Which side of the glove is the right side — the inside or the outside? The leather or the fur? Like Alice's White Rabbit, this essay has dropped its gloves.[11]

In my searching, however, I will not be seeking a singular conclusion about the relationship of power between Munby and Hannah. I choose not to imagine them as simply the subject and object and vice versa — like a loom, stuck in "permanent weaving," moving backward and forward, until the discourse becomes so tight that the other is strangled by its sealed-up world. I will not pattern Hannah.[12] Instead, my essay registers her as invisible, which far from making her disappear, renders her flesh a palpable-palpating specter. Though you may not see her, she will touch you.

My use of the term "invisible" is informed by Maurice Merleau-Ponty's unfinished book, *The Visible and the Invisible*.[13] I am drawn to his efforts to imagine the other (as well as the subject) without sacrificing or closing off the possibilities of his or her identity. Merleau-Ponty uses the inside-out, outside-in structure of the glove (its reversibility) as a model of this double-open space in which subjects perform. In clarifying the metaphor, he points out that we understand the reversibility of a glove (what he would call its chiasm) without the need for a spectator on each side:

It suffices that from one side I see the wrong side of the glove that is applied to the right side, that I touch the one *through* the other (double "representation" of a point or plane of the field) the chiasm is that reversibility —

It is through it alone that there is passage from the "For itself" to the For the Other — In reality there is neither me nor the other as positive, positive subjectivities. There are two caverns, two opennesses, two stages where something will take place — and which both belong to the same world, to the stage of Being.[14]

In this passage, not only are both parties invisible (erasing subject/object asymmetry) — like "two caverns, two opennesses, two stages where something will take place" — they are understood through sight's relationship to touch and touch's relationship to sight. Like the visual understanding of a layered collage, one knows just what is on top, what is buttressed, what is nearly touching but not: by either actually touching the collage or imagining what it would feel like to touch it. As Merleau-Ponty puts it, "The invisible is what is not actually visible, but could be . . . what exists only as tactile or kinesthetically, etc."[15] In other words, the invisible can include the visible (as it does in the word "invisible" itself); yet the invisible goes beyond the visible and is not limited to the visible. However, in a culture that privileges the seen over the unseen, invisible caresses, invisible sounds, and invisible smells are often elided (overlooked).

Jacques Lacan uses *The Visible and the Invisible* (in *The Four Fundamental Concepts of Psycho-Analysis*) to provide his audience with an unfamiliar and expanded notion of the gaze that will be of further use to this essay. Lacan develops Merleau-Ponty's theory with a stronger emphasis on how we see, more precisely how we do not see. For Lacan, all that is not visible is part and parcel of the gaze as well. Lacan maintains that the gaze is everywhere and all-encompassing — that when we look at someone, we are also being looked at by someone else, who is also being seen by an-other, and so on. (Sometimes, we get unseen glimpses of this: for example, when we hear a sound that suggests another's presence or when we smell someone whom we cannot see.) The gaze, for Lacan, is not what we see (that is vision), but the fact that we are always being *gazed* at on all sides from all directions. According to Lacan's gaze, one is in a space of "radiated reticulation."[16]

By analyzing Merleau-Ponty, Lacan suggests the possibility of what I will call a *gaze of the invisible*: a sensate gaze from inside the body. This interiorization forces us to confront our own subjectivity. After all, we can feel ourselves touching ourselves, we can even smell ourselves smell ourselves, but we can never see ourselves seeing ourselves. "There is no coinciding of the seer with the visible," except in a mirror, which itself is only representation, a copy of ourselves on a cool icy surface: Lacan's "Mirror Stage" par excellence. Thus the seeing of ourselves seeing is purely constructed, suggesting the falsehood of our visual perception of self (the mendacity of our subjectivity), which is part and parcel of our mythical visions of the other. Traditional seeingness, as Lacan explains, is focused on the exteriorization of looking. In his words, "the phenomenologists have succeeded in articulating with precision, and in the most disconcerting way, that it is quite clear that I see *outside*, that perception is not in me, that it is on the objects that it apprehends."[17]

Lacan then continues to tell us that we (also) try to imagine that we can see ourself seeing (that we can see *inside*), in order to defeat the fact that vision is always outside of us and that we could never know how the other perceives us. This unproblematized (and mythical) approach to looking is sustained in order to carry the all-seeingness of the vision we desire—so that we can see what we want to see: "And, yet I apprehend the world in a perception that seems to me to concern the immanence of the *I see myself seeing myself*. The privilege of the subject seems to be established here from the bipolar reflexive relation by which, as soon as I perceive, my representations belong to me."[18]

In such a scheme we entertain vision *falsely* as outside and inside at the same time, in order to hold onto representations of the other that are subject to our own constructions—in order to ensure that representation belongs to us—in order to colonize seeing. Differently, my emphasis on the *gaze of the invisible* seeks to truly entertain a sensate gaze from both inside and outside of a reticulated body, which must come at the cost of shattering the *visualized* construction of the subject-object dichotomy.

However, my enthusiasm for Merleau-Ponty's invisible is continually gloved and lined by Luce Irigaray's critique and reconceptualization of the invisible in her essay, "The Invisible of the Flesh: A Reading of Merleau-Ponty, *The Visible and the Invisible*, 'The Intertwining—The Chiasm.'" Although Irigaray understands Merleau-Ponty's invisible as a fecund place for representing the other, she also sees his conceptualization of it as problematic. But rather than abandoning his text completely, she reconceptualizes the invisible in (feminist) terms that are also particularly useful to this essay.

According to Irigaray, Merleau-Ponty is unable to acknowledge the other's difference from his own subjectivity and thereby he actually (despite his intentions) does *not* make a space for the other. As a result, his invisible remains otherless: barren. Fueling this problem is the basic fact that he refuses to let go of his overall privileging of the visual; Irigaray describes it as his love for painting: "His [Merleau-Ponty's] analysis of vision becomes even more detailed, more beautiful, as it accords him the privilege over the other senses, as it takes back a great deal of the phenomenology of the tactile, but by giving it the privilege of closing up the aesthesiological body. . . . His phenomenology of vision almost mistakes itself for a phenomenology of painting or of the art of painting . . . he speaks of it with the lyricism of one who loves art rather than with the rigor of a philosopher, as if one must give oneself over to its weight and measures."[19]

This, in turn, sets off a theoretical bartering that simply exchanges "seer and visible, touching and tangible, 'subject' and 'things' in an alternation, a fluctuation that would take place in a milieu that makes possible their passage from one or the other 'side.' "[20] This easy slipping and sliding from one side to the other is a nonstick exchange system that works (mythically), with *apparently* nothing left over, because the categories are, in fact, (perplexedly) un-differentiated by Merleau-Ponty.

Nevertheless, Irigaray (moved by Merleau-Ponty's conceptualization of the invisible) recasts his theory so as to emphasize that reversibility always leaves something "remaining." According to her, all of the other cannot be caught: "it is impossible to have relations of reversibility without remainder." The remainder, which cannot be seen, is, for Irigaray, the invisible: a body full of holes that moves spatially without clear form, an aesthesiological body, a flesh that has been sublimated, a specter, a body that moves beyond visualization. Irigaray's focus on the rich possibilities of "remainder" are in keeping with Michel de Certeau's notion of alterity, in which the other, even while under the fingertips of citation in the ethnographic text, "keeps nothing of its own, it remains capable, as in a dream, of bringing forth something uncanny: the surreptitious and altering power of the repressed." De Certeau's dream body flows into Irigaray's *invisible* aesthesiological body, which together suggest Hannah's body, which is "not there," yet it is "not, not there."[21]

My approach here, then, draws specifically from a braid of invisibility, one that twists through and around the work of these three, very different but related, authors: Merleau-Ponty, Lacan, and Irigaray. In addition to this braid (this *gaze of the invisible*), I will also draw on my encounter with the miraculous box in Cambridge.

Sexuating Hannah[22]

Swept the passage & took the things out of the hole under the stairs — Mary uses it for her dustpans and brushes. It is a dark hole & about 2 yards long & very low. I crawl'd in on my hands & knees & lay curl'd up in the dirt for a minute or so & then I got the handbrush & swept the walls down. The cobwebs & dust fell all over me & I had to poke my nose out o' the door to get breath, like a dog's out of a kennel.

(Diaries of Hannah Cullwick)

Valentine's day was while I was there & i slipp'd out in my dirt to get one for Massa. It took me a few minutes to select one. I found one — a dog with a chain round his neck & thought it fit for me . . .

(Diaries of Hannah Cullwick)[23]

There have been a number of studies of Hannah, but not one has granted her sexuality, flesh, desire. I find this surprising because, for me, the photographs and the diaries are overflowing with sexuality, flesh, desire. Those texts that have broached the subject of sexuality find it only in Munby's world — at least that has been their focus (Derek Hudson, Peter Stallybrass, and Allon White). Those authors who have centered on Hannah have dealt with other issues of her representation: Davidoff has depicted her very real oppression as a female servant, Stanley has celebrated her tenacity and virtue, Dawkins has read her deconstructively as a textual effect. Their texts, then, register Hannah in four ways: as simply invisible (Hudson, Stallybrass, and White — and I am using this description *not* in Merleau-Ponty's sense of the term), as victim (Davidoff), as heroine (Stanley), as text (Dawkins). Though all of these works have contributed to my understanding of Hannah, they are unsatisfactory because she is *all* of these things plus more. One of the most important aspects of this space of "more" is that Hannah too, like Munby, was a person who acted on and acted out desire.[24]

So, although Hannah left "thousands of closely written quarto-size pages," "penned at a breathless pace," and although there are many photographs of her in the Munby Box, her own sexuality has, curiously, been written out of the stories of her life.[25] Represented as if without her own sexuality, without her own desire, and certainly without her own perversion, she has been imagined as extremely desirable, but not desiring. Falling into what Michel Foucault has named the repressive hypothesis, apparently, "We, Other Victorians" have continued to dream Hannah as Fair Woman.[26]

Not surprisingly, Munby, in contrast to Hannah, has been granted various spaces of sexuality, albeit limited in how he has been imagined: the repressed homosexual (Hudson), the sexual exploiter of cross-class relationships with manly women and blackened women (Davidoff), the actor of an unnamed, but nevertheless present and very erotic form of sexuality (Dawkins), or the neurotic, analogous to Freud's "Rat Man" or his "Wolf Man" or even Freud himself, because he shares their confused (and highly sexualized) fantasies of an elision between "pure" mothers and "dirty" nursemaids (Stallybrass and White).[27]

Liz Stanley's introduction to *The Diaries of Hannah Cullwick: Victorian Maidservant*, remarks on the absence of Hannah's point of view in Hudson's *Munby: Man of Two Worlds*:

The publication of Derek Hudson's biography of Munby in 1972 has led to a resurgence of interest in Munby himself as a "man of two worlds," as the biography is sub-titled. Much of this interest seems to derive from Munby's life-long obsession with lower-class women — and women who were truly *working* women, whether in the coal pits of Wigan or digging the roads of London. A further and related interest comes from theorising about Munby's possible sexual proclivities. Whether he was sexually interested in and aroused by lower-class women only, whether he was impotent, or whether, in displaying little interest in women of his own class sexually or otherwise, he could be considered a repressed homosexual, are the kinds of questions explored. However, little of this interest has focused on Hannah, even though a large proportion of Munby's writings are about her and indeed a significant amount of the Munby collection at Trinity College, Cambridge, is by *her*. And so, although Hudson writes that Munby's biography "is her book as much as his," nevertheless he writes it from Munby's point of view only and states that her diaries and letters "can be sampled only briefly."[28]

I am in agreement with Stanley's efforts to shift attention away from the question of Munby's sexuality to Hannah; however and quite surprisingly, this new emphasis is undermined by Stanley's insistence on Hannah's ordinariness. Stanley states this thoroughly unconvincing perspective on the second page of her introduction: "For me, it is precisely her 'ordinariness' that makes Hannah so 'extraordinary.' She is an ordinary lower-class woman of the Victorian period; but her life, and her working life, is fully documented. The result is not only that she is 'The most thoroughly documented housemaid of the Victorian age,' but also the most thoroughly documented, thoroughly ordinary working-class woman of a period about which we still know all too little."[29]

Hannah is not ordinary. Her sexuality is extraordinary. As if, in an effort to keep her as clean as the floors that she scrubbed, Hannah has been denied sexuality.[30] Like a number of other scholars who are working on subjects of feminized fetishes (Emily Apter, Mary Kelly, Elizabeth Grosz, Mandy Merck), I want to, at the very least, grant Hannah some "perversions" of her own.[31] By considering Hannah's own autoerotic tendencies and her love for such things as touching the hands of a bourgeois woman, or pushing her naked body up an ash-ridden chimney, we will confront her sexuality. However, I am not interested in finding a name or a category for her sexuality: her performances of invisibility defeat such categorization. I want to find a language that sexuates her persistent invisibility. Her flesh represents more than hard work.

Hands

My face was dirty (I'd been cleaning the dirty scullery out) & my arms black'd & my *hands* look'd swell'd & red, & begrimed with dirt — *grener'd* as we say in Shropshire. That is, the cracks in our hands ingrain'd with black lead & that, so that even scrubbing will not fetch it out, & in cold frosty weather one dare not brush them.[32] I had not worn gloves for years then, not even to see ladies in, so I was without gloves to the lady at Mr. Clark's that day. I saw Mrs Green & her daughter look *hard* at my red hands.

(Diaries of Hannah Cullwick)[33]

There are many enigmatic photographs in the Munby Box, but probably the one of only Hannah's hands (Fig. 7) is the most enigmatic. This picture of her large calloused hands represents Hannah's *different* sexuality synecdochically, perhaps not unlike the familiar trope of the uterus for female sexual difference in the nineteenth century.[34] As Thomas Laqueur writes of this pervasive figure: "The silent workings of a tiny organ weighing on the average seven grams in humans, some two to four centimeters long, and the swelling and subsequent rupture of the follicles within it, came to represent synecdochically what it was to be a woman."[35] When the uterus was in place, it represented an idealized maternal nature; when it wandered, it represented her hysteria. Hannah's swollen and ruptured hands, rough, strong, and big, represented her class and her servitude. Her hands were out of control and stood in opposition to the tiny, smooth hands of a lady. Rather than hiding them, Hannah flaunted them, paraded them. They represented her sexuality, not only as signs of masochism, but also as (tantalizing) signs of her remarkable difference. Her hands fingered between categories: though a woman, her hands marked her as masculine. In the Munby Box, which is filled with conventionally proportioned full-length, half-body, and three-quarter body portraits, the photograph of Hannah's hands is nothing less than startling: they appear gigantic among a brigade of miniature women.

Recalling that Susan Stewart describes the miniature as a space of order and containment — "a diminutive, and thereby manipulatable, version of experience, a version which is domesticated and protected from contamination" — the box functions as a miniature museum for housing Munby's collection of mostly white, mostly British, lower-class working women with a few exotic specimens thrown in for good measure (from France, Zurich, Constantinople, Venice, and Africa).[36] The specimens often registered by height and other physical characteristics and by small stories of (anthropological-like) contact with the "other." Munby has inscribed the vital statistics of his specimens and the tales of his encounters with them, rather haphazardly in pen, on the back

Figure 7. Fink, Hannah's hands, n.d.
(Master and Fellows of Trinity College, Cambridge)

of the photographs. Most of the photographs are *cartes de visite* and are therefore quite small in scale. The Munby Box is a small, albeit dense, box, with little pictures of what were *actually* rather gigantic hard-working and hard-bodied women.

The workings of the miniature (whose very essence is that of containment and control) even managed to conquer the overwhelming scale of a truly gigantic woman from Nova Scotia (Fig. 8). Miniaturized by the camera that shot her, she looks (in the context of the box) to be, roughly, the same size as the other women *pictured*. Munby's words on the back of the *carte* (written below her autograph) affirm his ease with this young woman, whose place in the collection he must have envisioned from the initial moments of their encounter. Though a novelty, she will always fit the part, the drawer, the box.

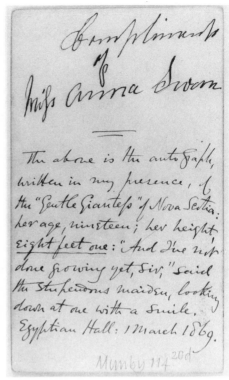

Figure 8. The "Gentle Giantess" of Nova Scotia, 1869.
(Master and Fellows of Trinity College, Cambridge)

Figure 9. The back of the *carte de visite* featuring the "Gentle Giantess" of Nova
Scotia, 1869. Below her autograph, Munby has written the following: "The above is
the autograph, written in my presence, of the 'Gentle Giantess' of Nova Scotia: her
age, nineteen; her height, *eight feet one*: 'And I've not done growing yet, sir' said the
stupendous maiden, looking down at me with a smile. Egyptian Hall: March 1869."
(Master and Fellows of Trinity College, Cambridge)

Munby wrote, with clear amusement on the back of the *carte*, below her
signature: "The above is the autograph, written in my presence, of the 'Gentle
Giantess' of Nova Scotia: her age, nineteen; her height, *eight feet one*: 'and I've
not done growing yet, sir,' said the stupendous maiden, looking down at me
with a smile. Egyptian Hall: March, 1869" (Fig. 9).

In contrast to the Liliputionized "Gentle Giantess," Hannah's hands refuse
containment and pop out of their small drawer as a grotesquerie from the
borders of Brobdingnag. Interestingly enough, I find that Hannah's big disconnected hands mirror my own as I fondle the tiny pictures of hard-working

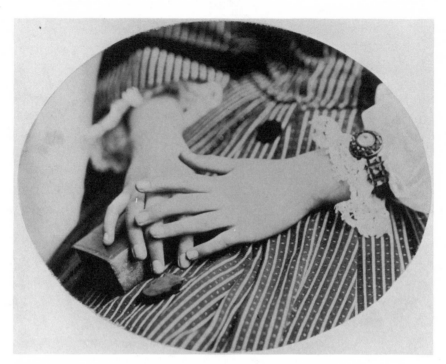

Figure 10. O. G. Rejlander, *Hands*, ca. 1860. (Gernsheim Collection, Harry Ransom Humanities Center, University of Texas at Austin)

women who have been fetishistically frozen in a lovely miniature museum (inside a) box: a team effort by inspector Munby and the librarians of the Wren Library.

The unladylike nature of Hannah's massive hands readily comes through when one compares Mr. Fink's portrait of Hannah's hands to O. G. Rejlander's *Hands* (ca. 1860, Fig. 10).[37] We know that the hands in the Rejlander picture are those of a (young) lady's because all of the signs are there. She appears to be wearing a proper lady's daytime dress. She is holding a small but thickset book. Her fingers are long and slender and show no signs of labor. Her fingernails are highly manicured, extremely white and are as finely crafted as the white lace that finishes off her sleeves. (Her cuticles have been carefully and artfully pushed back.) She wears a decorative bracelet that could be a locket for holding a treasured snip of fine hair. Her lily-white hands, soft as down, are demurely closed away from the viewer. Her hands, which modestly cover her sex, may have been subjected to recipes for whitening and softening that were popular with the ladies of the period.[38]

The lady's hands are connected to her body, Hannah's are not: her body appears invisible, with only a trace of it to be seen, blurred and faded in the far right background of the picture. As a result, her hands take on the status of portraiture, as though they were a face, as though they, not her face, said it all.

We know that Hannah's hands are those of a *different* kind of woman, a working-class woman and a special one at that. Her fingers are blackened with dirt. Whereas the lady may have taken pleasure in soaking her hands in honey, yellow wax, rose water, and myrrh, Hannah took pleasure in blackening hers with grime. And, because simple grime was never enough, Hannah used patches of black lead (that she would spit on) literally to draw on her skin. In order to build up the coarseness and texture of her hands, she would clean grates without gloves.

Hannah's hands gesture together in a remarkable performance. Her right hand appears aggressive and proud as it parades its remarkable callouses. The left hand, a partner in crime, points at the right hand with four of its thick knuckles. The brush in Hannah's left hand is a stage prop that stands in remarkable opposition to the lady's small book. The book, which could hold recipes for femininity, mirrors the lady's hands as the brush (which could hold grime of all sorts) mirrors Hannah's hands: porcelain hands versus Hannah's hands. The slave strap on Hannah's right hand (that she wore as a sign of her servitude to Munby, along with the small steel chain and padlock that went around her neck, to which only Munby had the key) is an unsettling costume that stands in remarkable contrast to the lady's jeweled bracelet.[39]

The photograph of Hannah's hands is entirely tactile. The Rejlander image is a picture of a different kind of touch: polished smoothness punctuated by fastidious bumps. For, even the raised elements of this picture (the facets of the bracelet, the book's tooled leather cover, the neat pleats of her dress, the soft lace at her sleeve) gently play into the picture's delicate surface. Even the photograph's oval format, without sharp edges, emphasizes smoothness. Because the overall image so closely mirrors the photographic paper's smooth surface, the hand of our eye glides across the picture's surface. The photograph feels as impenetrable as the lady it signifies. Differently, the *portrait* of Hannah invites overall fingering. Feel her callouses. Feel the silky brocade fabric with its raised floral design. Feel the leather wrist strap; imagine what it feels like to wear one. Feel the brush in her hand, in yours. Feel her muscular arms. As Hannah once said about her own hands (to Munby), "They are quite *hard* again — feel — . . ."[40]

I am always rather shocked at myself for seeing sexuality in this strange picture of hands. Why are Hannah's hands so sexual to me? Certainly, the diaries are partly responsible for this unexpected reading. Both Hannah and Munby wrote about hands as a sexual space that they enjoyed. Hannah often described the literal pain that she went through in order to gain admiration from Munby. For example, on one occasion she wrote: "It's to make my hands harder inside why I rub the brass with them whenever I can. It's anything but a pleasant feeling except that it's to make them more fit for M. to admire, for he likes a working woman's hands to be big & hard."⁴¹

And indeed, Munby does like a working woman's hands to be big and hard, as is exemplified in this passage from his diary:

> . . . I passed a tallish young woman, evidently a servant, who was noticeable for the size of her *gloveless hands*. She seemed to be alone in the crowd, and (*with a view to her hands*) I asked if she meant to dance at all—only liked to look on: for which she was not sorry. So after a little chat we walked away, and I (still with a view to my hobby) proposed to rest on the bank near, under the trees. *She gave me her hand to help her up—and, oh ye ballroom partners, what a breadth of massive flesh it was to grasp!* She sat down by me, ready to talk, after the blunt fashion of such maidens, but not forward. . . . She was a maid of all work at Chelsea, it seemed. . . . I looked at her hands, and spoke my opinion of them. "How can you like them she says," like Margaret in the garden; "*they are so large and red, I'm ashamed of them.*" "They are just the hands for a servant," say I: "They show you are hard-working, and you ought to be proud of them. You wouldn't like them to be like a lady's?" "Yes I should!" said she, bitterly: "and I should like to be a lady, and I wish my hands were like yours!" And she looked enviously at my hand, which was quite white and small by the side of hers. . . . Her right hand lay, a large red lump, upon her light-coloured frock: it was very broad and square and thick—as large and strong & coarse as the hand of a sixfoot bricklayer . . . *the skin was rough to the touch, hard and leathery in the palm: there was nothing feminine about it in form or texture* . . . and yet she was only nineteen.⁴²

Munby's record of his encounter with a maid-of-all-work from Chelsea is a textbook case of Freud's description of the fetish. Early on in Munby's story of yet another discovery, sexual intrigue is promoted by the fact that he spotted her hands secretly and voyeuristically, unaware that she was exposing herself, oblivious to the fact that she was "gloveless" (pantless). Munby is fixated on hands and seems to have fetishized them to stand in for the "castrated penis" (so the Freudian story goes). Even a Freudian skeptic would have to acknowledge that Munby's description of the young woman's hands (red, large, and hard) sounds very much like a description of an aroused male. Like Freud, Munby reads her sexual difference in relation to his own (she may not have a penis, but she has hands that mirror male genitals). Yet, in a surprising turn-around, she reads his hands to be more like a lady's. This passage is a wondrous description of difference at play: it is arousing, comical, and definitely sexual.

Hannah describes a similar play of difference around marked and unmarked hands. Her story is one of sexualized play, not between a masculinized woman and a feminized man, but between two (different) women. She writes: "I've been busy cleaning windows & glasses this month, for the flies & the dust makes so much dirt. My hands are very coarse & hardish, but no more so than usual. Mrs. J. has very white hands & she often comes & lays her hands lightly on mine for me to feel how cold they are — *we* say it's to show the difference more than anything else."[43] I love this passage and the repeated image of two women touching their hands upon each other: one rough, hardened, reddened, large, maybe warm — the other soft, frail, white, and always cold. In this play of hands is a suggestion of an unexpected reciprocity. In Hannah's rough/delicate grasp is the possibility that her desire is not simply played out for Munby only.

Painting with Soot

On April 26, 1865, Hannah described an emphatically haptic and autoerotic moment in which the reader senses *her* desire: a desire that has been consistently overlooked by Cullwickian scholars. Hannah is all alone; Munby is not there, but his presence is felt nevertheless. She is undressed and has "got on a stool and up the chimney out o sight":

> The soot was thick all around, and soft and warm and i lay in it and fetch'd a shower or two down wi my arms, and it trickl'd over like a bath — i stopped in the chimney and thought about Massa and how he'd enjoy seein me when i got down and all that, and wonder'd what he was doing and then i come down — it seem'd quite cold out o the chimney and i got into the water [in a bath] and wash'd me — it took me a good while to get clean and the water i made thick and black. i just put on my shift and petticoat and bundled my other clothes up and run into bed — Massa wrote after and said at the very time i was in the chimney he was at a ball, and among ladies with white necks and arms and all so grand, and how he look'd at them and thought of me the while, and he could well imagine the contrast as he'd seen me so often.[44]

In this passage, Hannah's sensate body is emphasized through touch: the touch of the soot "soft and warm" that she trickles over herself like a bath, the touch of the "cold" air that she feels once she is outside of the chimney, the touch of the blackened water that feels "thick," the touch of light clothes (like shifts and petticoats) on her recently bathed body that has just jumped into bed.

For me, and I imagine for Hannah too, the fluidity between things is what makes this kind of play erotic: the flow between clean and dirty, between blackened then whitened skin, between the ladies at the ball and Hannah in her grimy tub, between Hannah's sexual play alone (onanistic, in that she touches herself with black soot, water, and white petticoats) and that with the others named (but not seen) in the scene. Desire and sexuality are markedly insistent and deviant, charged by the unsaid — in short, erotic.

While reading Hannah's words, my body is taken away (erotically) with the flow, "for my body does not have the same ideas I do."[45] We, Hannah and I, give ourselves away. In this fragment of Hannah's writing and elsewhere in her body of work (the photographs and the diaries), and in my own writing, eroticism becomes a meaningful tool for the ways in which it breaks down categories (often spinning on the taboo), opens up dark (invisible) passages, compels my body to feel what the other has left behind.

What is left over from the story of the chimney crawl is all the black soot that touched her body and was shed like skin: a thick, black mucous that stayed in the tub. This rich "remainder," that gloved and lined her body, that communicated with the interior and the exterior of her body, calls into question any reversibility between black and white. No one is simply black, nor simply white — instead they are metaphors for the body that are distinctly related to issues of class. Hannah painted herself as both black and white. When she was a lady, she painted herself white: whitening her dark reddened hands with smart white gloves and, most certainly, dusting her face, not with soot, but with the "Ophelia powders," so popular then.[46]

As in Hannah's bathtub story, residues of blackness can also be found floating around many of the soap advertisements of the period: most notably an illustration for Pears' Soap (Fig. 11) that also features a bathing scene.[47] The point of the Pears picture is that the wonderful soap, so powerful and pure, can wash a Negro white. The before and after pictures, with "PEARS' SOAP" blazoned in black and white between the two images, tells the consumer that blackness can be washed off in the bathtub: just like Hannah washed off her soot.

Yet, certainly unbeknownst to the advertisement's creator, the picture also suggests an indeterminable reciprocity between the races of the two children. In the top picture, one is somewhat surprised to see that it is a little white boy who stands in service to the little black boy in the tub. The white boy's servitude is reinforced by his work apron. Save for their hair and the color of their skin, the two boys are quite similar in stature and shape — their facial features are different, but not remarkably so. Perhaps the most surprising aspect of this picture is that the soap in the white boy's hand is black, which suggests blacking up as much as scrubbing yourself white. Similarly, not only is race unfixed, but so is class. Conventionally, it would be the white boy who has wealth and who is served; yet drawing from the picture itself, one would have to surmise that the owner of the lovely little slippers that have been carefully stepped out of, at the base of the tub, belong to the black boy — not the white boy who

208 **Carol Mavor**

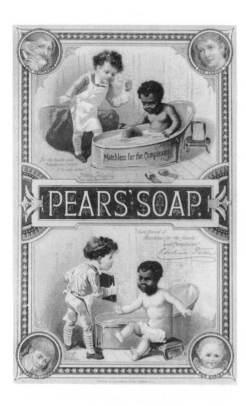

Figure 11.
Pears' Soap advertisement, ca. 1892. One of a number of soap advertisements from the later part of the Victorian period (ca. 1885– 1901) that used the image of the black child or adult being washed with the product. (John Johnson Collection, Bodleian Library, Oxford University)

serves him. Likewise, the little aristocratic mirror and the elegant footstool on which it stands also suggest refinement, ornament, leisure time. Even the bathtub looks splendid: elegant, like Madame Récamier's "fainting couch" in Jacques-Louis David's famous portrait (1800). To whom do these lovely things belong? Race and class and the relationship between the two have been rendered undecidable.

By the time we get to the "after" picture, the joke is that the little blackened boy forgot to wash his face. Dumbfounded, he peers at himself in the mirror (held by his little white boy), with his arms outstretched, his right foot caught in a kick. Race (as manifested by the body of this half white and half black boy) has been visualized as even more uncertain. Could he (the once black and now racially mixed boy) be the same race as the boy who holds the looking glass?[48] And what if he had washed his face? What race would he be then? Is he a "pickaninny" or not? The race of this child is invisible and is as unfixed as black oil floating on water.

The image of the half-washed (half-breed) in the Pears' Soap advertisement reminds me of a passage from Munby's diary, in which we find a description of parts of Hannah's skin as figuratively painted extra white, while wearing her mistress's fancy dress (on the sly). Munby writes that in the "ball dress of black gauze and lace . . . her neck and bosom, and even her shoulders, were bare. Dazzling white, they seemed, by contrast with her hardworking arms, which of course were also bare."[49] Whiteness here is a metaphor for the bourgeoisie (white mistress) against Hannah's darkened arms, which are a metaphor for the proletariat (black slave). By veiling Hannah's body with the materials of another class, her arms suddenly become "not white" as they perform in contrast to her suddenly "dazzling white" neck, bosom, and shoulders: Munby's passage unveils Hannah's whiteness and her darkness as culturally determined. As Peggy Phelan reminds us, "The same physical features of a person's body may be read as 'black' in England, 'white' in Haiti, 'colored' in South Africa, and 'mulatto' in Brazil. More than indicating that racial markings are read differently cross-culturally, these variations underline the psychic, political, and philosophical impoverishment of linking the color of the physical body with the ideology of race."[50] Similarly, in the Pears' Soap advertisement, the ideology of blackness is linked with dirtiness and ignorance: blacks could be white if they just washed, or blacks do not even know enough to wash their own faces; blacks need the white man to instruct them on how to be clean, civilized, and cultured; and so forth. As another Pears advertisement boasts, Bishop Q. of Wangaloo, in Unpacific Seas, was better able to lead his "native flock" after he changed his "nigger face" to white with the help of a cake or two of pure Pears' Transparent Soap.[51]

In a reversal of the Pears' Soap advertisements, Hannah seems to have spent much of her energy painting herself black, not only through soot and dirt, but also with the black lead that she used to clean the grates that framed fireplaces (like the one that she crawled up). She literally used the black lead, like makeup, as is indicated in the following passage from her diary, in which she describes a visit to Mr. Stodart's to have her likeness taken:

> So I went one morning [to Mr. Stodart's] just as I was, but he was busy & the second time I went he let me in. I had slipp'd out without asking leave afore the lodgers' breakfast, & I was partly black wi' cleaning boots & grates & that. I had a dirty lilac frock on & old boots, & a coarse white apron on & my face & arms grimed, but I put a good *patch o' black lead* on my left arm to do 'em more with.

> No one noticed me much in the streets, I think, & I got to Mr Stodart's & he took me up to his room smiling & said, "Well, you *are* dirty." But I said, "Oh no, sir, this is only what I am every day, but I want to be done thoroughly black like I am sometimes at work." *And I show'd him what the patch of black lead was for, me spitting on it & then daubing it on my arms & after all drawing them across my mouth and nose.*[52]

The racist ideology connecting Hannah's painting of herself with black lead and being black is even more specifically addressed in yet another advertisement of the late Victorian period. This particular advertisement, for black lead itself, appeared in 1894 and is a continuation of the relentless relationship between servants, cleanliness, black bodies, white bodies, progress, colonialism, and the like. The drawing shows a muscular "minstrel" leading a footrace, complete with white challengers in the background (Fig. 12). "No Dust!" is stamped across the chest of this champion as he runs through a space of racial puns. Below his picture it is written that the *race* is "Black Led," a play on the James' Dome Black Lead that it is advertising. The figure's exaggerated lips, bright white teeth, and protruding eyes figure him as racial stereotype, as minstrel. It is as if he too, like Hannah, has drawn on himself with black lead. What color then is this man? Could he be white like the women minstrels that Munby drew in his journal? (Munby was fascinated by the fact that these "selfmade negresses" washed their black off every night.)[53]

Or more complicated yet, is the "No Dust" champion a black man who has painted himself as minstrel? After all, not all painted minstrels were white underneath. As Douglas A. Lorimer has written in his book *Colour, Class, and the Victorians*:

> For the mid-Victorians the Negro remained an exotic and novel being, and they were prepared to accept even the exaggerated and farcical antics of the black minstrels as authentic. In 1866 [one year after Hannah's diary entry] Samuel Hague, an English entertainer and promoter, attempted to cash in on sympathy for the recently emancipated slaves and the popularity of the minstrel shows. He bought 26 ex-slaves from Georgia to Liverpool and staged a "genuine Negro" entertainment. Hague's audiences did not take to his attempt at realism, and soon the promoter had the ex-slaves like the white entertainers in the company of burnt cork. English audiences were thereby satisfied that they had seen the genuine article, the real black minstrel.[54]

In Hague's performance, African slaves (from America) must masquerade as minstrels in order to be seen as "genuine Negroes." Race here is assumed (as it is culturally determined) and worn as a mask. Similarly, as Joan Riviere demonstrated in her famous article from 1929, females often masquerade womanliness: through dress, through coquettish ways, through an embracement of maternality, and so forth. Women masquerade as feminine in order to be seen as "genuine women." Irigaray understands this masquerade of femininity as a "loss" to women. For, " 'femininity' is a role, and image, a value, imposed upon women by male systems of representation. In this masquerade

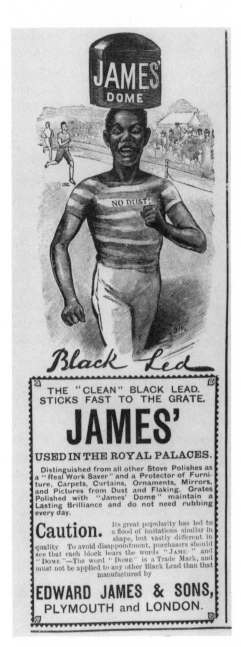

Figure 12.
James' Dome Black Lead
advertisement, *Illustrated Sporting
and Dramatic News*, 1894.
(Newspaper Library, The British
Library)

woman loses herself, and loses herself by playing on her femininity. The fact
remains that this masquerade requires an *effort* on her part for which she is not
compensated. Unless her pleasure comes simply from being chosen as an
object of consumption or of desire by masculine 'subjects.' " This unfruitful
kind of masquerade, in which the woman plays into masculine desire (without

subversion), sounds very much like the concept of "passing": blacks passing as white, gays and lesbians who pass as straights, even the poor who pass as middle class.[55] As Phelan writes, "Passing performances *in general* seek to use one form of invisibility to highlight a usually privileged form of visibility."[56] Hannah seems to have broken this rule by refusing to privilege any form of visibility, so that it becomes impossible to determine what she is passing as: rather than highlighting any race, class, or even gender, she highlights invisibility.

Hannah, the champion of the *gaze of the invisible*, was able to paint on both the skin of a *whitened* lady and the skin of a *blackened* slave, as is represented in the other set of "before and after" pictures: Hannah as a lady (ready to sit for Gainsborough, 1874) and Hannah as a chimney sweep/slave (ca. 1862).[57] Munby kept them side by side in a leather traveling mount that he probably took with him on his travels around Britain and abroad.

Starting with Hannah's hat and her slave scarf, we can begin to see many fits of unfixing standardized social roles. The pretty hat, appropriate for the times, might have been worn for an informal walk or for a game of archery with other ladies. The tail of the hat is tasteful and flirtatious: long ribbons that trimmed the backs of hats were known to contemporaries as "Follow me Lads."[58] The slave scarf, bright against her darkened skin, plays into the Orientalist "taste" of the period and it too has sexual connotations. It recalls the dark women found in paintings by the Frenchman Jean-Léon Gérôme, like the scarved black slave who bathes a white woman in his *The Bath* (1880–85, Fig. 13).[59]

Yet together, the two pieces of millinery strangely echo one another, as if the scarf on the lady's head and the scarf on the slave's head were the same bit of silk. Both the lady and the slave are represented synecdochically by a similar (if not the same) object of female fetishization: a piece of clothing, a scarf, an object of tactile stimulation. (Freud was reluctant to grant women any perversions of their own, but he did admit that "all women . . . are clothing fetishists." Lacan's teacher, Gaëtan Gatian de Clérambault, hypothesized that women fetishists required the tactile stimulation of pieces of cloth.)[60] Difference and sameness, like in the Pears' Soap advertisement, are entangled. Who is the opposite of whom? What is being painted on? class or race? Who is other to whom? Are both women slaves?[61] Hannah, as slave, as newlywed to a bourgeois man, and as a maid-of-all-work, made her class truly invisible. Munby saw her intriguing invisibility from the beginning. On March 12, 1860, in the midst of calling her his Juno, while at the same time speaking of her lowly ways, Munby writes: "And so we get back to class distinctions: I love her, then, because she is *not* like her own class after all, but like mine!"[62]

Looking further at the pictures, we can see that Hannah's lady's dress is too tight; undoubtedly, it is being pulled by the girth of her biceps, which Munby measured at various times as "thirteen, fourteen, and once even eighteen

Figure 13. Jean-Léon Gérôme, *The Bath*, 1880–85. (Mildred Anna Williams Collection, Fine Arts Museums of San Francisco)

inches round."[63] This is just one example of Hannah as a *misfit*. Consider also the image of her wearing a man's suit: now her clothes are too big. Her jacket is overly roomy, with sleeves large enough for two of her giant hands (Fig. 5).

Three days after their wedding on January 18, 1873, Munby discloses that no matter what Hannah wears, the guise does not fit: "We had good fare and warmth at the White Horse, & Hannah played her part [of the lady] very fairly, by dint of natural sweetness. But now that she was drest in black silk, her shapely hands looked somewhat large and laborious, and her dear complexion somewhat coarse; whereas her face looks ladylike and her hands delicate, when she is in her own servant's dress. C'est sélon."[64]

What is particularly delightful about Hannah's guises is that the characters never quite fit the woman: there is a fascinating tension between convincing and not convincing. The photographs seem to confirm and almost take pride in the fact that Hannah had no looking glass.[65] They, the images, perform in the box as a seemingly endless series of almost right theatrics that call identity into question. Rather than fixing her sexuality, her race, her class, or her gender, they unfix it: they render her (some-body called Hannah) as invisible. Like Cindy Sherman's recent takeoffs on master paintings, the excitement lies not in the author's masterful deception, but rather in her masterful presentations of incongruities.

Hannah Not Only Painted Herself Black, She Also Painted Herself Celestial Rosyred

Investment in the look is not as privileged in women as in men. More than the other senses, the eye objectifies and masters. It sets at a distance, and maintains a distance. In our culture the predominance of the look over smell, taste, touch and hearing has brought about an impoverishment of bodily relations. The moment the look dominates, the body loses its materiality.
    (Luce Irigaray)[66]

"No gloves, no flowers! Massa, shall I do?"
She cries; "I have no looking glass, you know!"
    (Arthur Munby, from a sonnet that describes their wedding day)[67]

Though Hannah had no looking glass, there are moments when she sees herself looking at herself in a mirror. At other times she knows that people (most often Munby) are looking at her. And at still other times, she looks at herself in photographs. Clearly, the visualizing of the self was a significant part of her life. But I am arguing that when Hannah looked, and/or experienced herself being looked at, she experienced the gaze as an expanded constellation of the senses that included sight but was not limited by it. Hannah's performative life can be imagined as a fecund response to Irigaray's assessment of the problem of the "predominance of the look."

Hannah, on a ride with identities, managed *not* to "impoverish bodily relations" and not to "lose the materiality" of her body. Brushing up against her, through the diaries and the photographs, signifies a "Hannah" that is transmitted differently: invisible to the petrifying eye, but rich in an invisibility that is comprised of crisscross spectral movement through color, gender, and class — through unsaid erotics — through haptic autoeroticism. Though not consciously fighting the gaze (that we have so thoroughly fetishized in critical theory), Hannah's imagination of a different self (her invisible self) requires a scrambling of the senses, which allows touch to feel sight and sight to feel touch: as in a blush, when your burning neck can feel yourself being looked at, or when you see someone else blushing and can see their hot cheeks feeling your look. Hannah always seems to feel her body feeling.

Irigaray cites (and sites) touch, admittedly essentially, all over the female body.[68] Though this is not the place to debate the intricacies, usefulness, and liabilities of Irigaray's essentialist tactics, her emphasis on the tactile female body is noteworthy as a road to liberating Hannah's invisibility. Irigaray (rather shockingly and famously) situates the female body in a state of auto-eroticism, always *in touch* with itself: "As for woman, she touches herself in and of herself without any need for mediation, and before there is any way to distinguish activity from passivity. Woman 'touches herself' all the time, and moreover no one can forbid her to do so, for her genitals are formed of two lips in continuous contact. Thus, within herself, she is already two — but not divisible into one(s) — that caress each other."[69] This stuff makes me blush, but I am attracted to the notion of a self-caress. It is a useful entryway into the less morphological uses of touch that Irigaray finds in the female body, specifically women's use of language, cast by touch:

> "She" is indefinitely other in herself. This is doubtless why she is said to be whimsical, incomprehensible, agitated, capricious . . . not to mention her language, in which "she" sets off in all directions leaving "him" unable to discern the coherence of any meaning. Hers are contradictory words, somewhat mad from the standpoint of reason, inaudible for whoever listens to them with ready-made grids, with a fully elaborated code in hand. For in what she says, too, at least when she dares, *woman is constantly touching herself*. She steps ever so slightly aside from herself with a murmur, an exclamation, a whisper, a sentence left unfinished. . . . What she says is never identical with anything, moreover; rather, it is contiguous. *It touches (upon)*.[70]

This is classic Irigaray, with her emphasis on the fact that women often speak differently than men, and when they do their language is often fragmented, contradictory, spoken from many lips.[71] Such voices have been oppressed and repressed by being categorized as hysterical, but Irigaray and other French feminists (especially Hélène Cixous) have celebrated it as a language of fecund feminine difference.

The Victorian era, the Golden Age of (female) Hysteria, twists on the fact that the Victorian period was also the Golden Age of Women's Writing.[72] Hannah's performative roles reflect some of the hysterical multiplicity that was a part of seemingly all women's lives in that time: ranging from those who were labeled "hysterical" for merely speaking their mind to those who were clinically ill.[73] The latter performed hysteria under especially debilitating and serious constraints in unexceptional spaces: as a way of fulfilling the masculine ideal of femininity as the fainting, weak, frail woman; to escape the caged life assigned to them; or to become stars in the clinic.[74] Hugh Welch Diamond, the pioneer of psychiatric photography in England, even photographed his patients as Ophelia types (with shawls draped over their shoulders and in one instance a crown of wild weeds on the head) or in staged settings reminiscent of the Victorian "art" photography of Julia Margaret Cameron or Henry Peach Robinson.[75] The complicated relationship between acting and hysteria was culturally acknowledged: that is why the Victorian actress Ellen Terry visited a London asylum to prepare herself to be mad on stage.[76] So, while George Eliot and Mrs. Gaskel were publishing their novels as never before, women were both culturally inscribed as hysterical and were writing their own bodies as hysterical: woman's body was a contested site, a tabula rasa. Changing from costume to costume, Hannah "steps so slightly aside from herself with a murmur [in a man's suit], an exclamation [as a blackened slave], a whisper [in a lady's dress], a sentence left unfinished [in a man's suit]." She "*touches (upon)*" many identities, but her relationship to them is never more than "contiguous." Hannah *looks* different.

In the following passage from Munby's diary, we find a representation of Hannah's own body-rich gazing that took place when "Massa" paid her a visit. Because the diary entry is not Hannah's, but Munby's, it feels further from the actuality of what we might perceive to be her real experience. For, despite the fact that Hannah's diaries were written so that Munby could read them, one is inclined to see her as a more reliable narrator of her own life than Munby: after all, her words came from her own hand; they are contiguous with her. This entry from Munby's diary is additionally suspect because it was written some forty years after the actual event. (Munby wrote the entry on Saturday, January 11, 1890, but Michael Hiley has reasoned that the incident took place in the late 1850s.)[77] However, as should already be clear, my intention is not to get at a single kernel of truth. I am more interested in Munby's text as part of a complex representation that registers their bizarre charades (with Munby as the straight man) as part of a reciprocal endeavor. As in the earlier quotation in which Munby lost it over a young woman's gloveless hand (". . . oh ye ballroom partners, what a breadth of massive flesh it was to grasp!"), Munby is again hilariously melodramatic, every bit as much of an actor as his cohort. And Hannah is playfully erotic as she looks different(ly) in her mistress's mirror:

She was then a general servant in a tradesman's well to do family at Kilburn; and one day, I went to see her, at her own suggestion, in her master's house, for the family were all absent, and she wished to show me her work, and the places where she worked. She showed me the kitchen she had to scour; the big kitchen grate that she blacked, the chimney that she swept, the scullery where she cleaned the sink, the hole in which she cleaned the boots and knives; and the scenes of many other sordid but necessary tasks. And she took me upstairs and showed me her attic, a little bare room, with a blue-check quilt on the bed, and one chair, and a common washing stand in the corner, with jug and basin; "what I never use," said she, "for you know I always wash me at the sink." *There was no looking glass in the room; she seldom used one.* Then as we came downstairs, she opened, by way of contrast, the door of her mistress's luxurious bedroom. On the bed lay a ball dress, of black gauze and lace, with crimson garniture; and this made me wish to see for once how Hannah would look in a lady's condition. I told her to put on the ball dress. She hesitated to profane the Missis's things by touching them, much more, by wearing them; but to please me, she consented. She took off her own servant's dress and put on that of her mistress. It was too short and too narrow for her, and it would not meet her healthy rustic waist; still, she was able to wear it; and, seeing a rose in the room, I brushed out her bright hair in a lady's fashion, and placed the rose within it. Thus she stood before me to be looked at; smiling and slightly blushing; feeling awkward and strange, in that unknown garb, but not looking awkward at all, but most graceful. I gazed on her in a kind of rapture: so lovely a figure she was, so ladylike, so sweet, that I longed "to take her away from her slavery," and make her a lady indeed. "And now, dear," at last I said, "turn round, and look at yourself." She wondered what I meant; for she had forgotten, that behind her stood a large cheval glass, capable of showing her from top to toe. But she turned round, and saw herself reflected at full length in the mirror. The effect of this revelation was startling. It was not her beauty, that struck; nor yet the sight of herself in a garb she had never worn before: but now for the first time she noticed that her neck and bosom, and even her shoulders, were bare. Dazzling white, they seemed, by contrast with her hardworking arms, which of course were also bare: but *in an instant, they were suffused, like her face, with one universal blush — celestial rosyred. Love's proper hue.* She shut her eyes, turned sharply from the glass, and suddenly flung herself into my arms — "that I might rather feel than see the beating of her heart." "Oh Massa," she whispered, "I am naked!"

Never before had I felt so strongly the need of self control in her presence: never, before or since, have I been filled with a more passionate ardour of love and reverence for that pure and innocent soul, who had trusted herself so utterly to me. I soothed and comforted and at length released her.[78]

Part of the sexual charge of this melodramatic performance rests on touch: it was taboo for Hannah to try on her mistress's black and crimson dress because her lower-class body would debase the same fabric that would later rub up against an upper-class body: Hannah "hesitated to profane the Missis's things by touching them." There were cultural laws against such touching. The breaking of this prohibition was erotic.

It was also erotic for Munby to brush out her "bright hair," which, of course, entails touching it in a most agreeable way. As Elisabeth G. Gitter writes in "The Power of Women's Hair in the Victorian Imagination," "the combing and displaying of hair, as suggested by the legends of alluring mermaids who sit on rocks singing and combing their beautiful hair [a popular theme in Victorian painting], thus constitutes a sexual exhibition. And the more abundant the hair, the more potent the sexual invitation implied by its display, for folk, literary, and psychoanalytic traditions agree that the luxuriance of the hair is an index of vigorous sexuality, even of wantonness." As Gitter points out, the brushing of a woman's hair has long been a sign of sexual exchange (with the hair signifying a range of complex meanings from "the exclusively female power to weave the female web," to "a glittering symbolic fusion of the sexual lust and the lust for power that she embodies" — but for the Victorians, who saw to it that a woman restrained the sexuality of her hair through chignons and other elaborate (pinned-up) styles of the period, the brushing out of a woman's hair meant letting her sexuality out.[79]

Lewis Carroll, Munby's contemporary who was driven not by working-class women but by bourgeois little girls, played out sexual desires through bowers of girl-hair. The comparison between Carroll and Munby is apt: Hudson wrote a biography on both and draws comparisons between the two. In his book on Munby, Hudson writes: "Munby's compassionate feeling for working women was comparable to his contemporary Lewis Carroll's intense concern for little girls; Munby's inner compulsion culminated in his secret marriage no less surely than Carroll's crystallized in the *Alice* books." However, unlike Munby's, Carroll's diaries rarely contain anything that even suggests erotic inclinations.[80] Thus, much has been made of his explicitly erotic statement (a rarity among his own volumes of books, diaries, and letters): "I can imagine no more delightful occupation than brushing Ellen Terry's hair."[81] A similar charge comes through Carroll's lovely portrait of Irene MacDonald, who, caught by the camera wearing a delicate nightdress, flaunts hair that looks wild, slept in, and untamed (Fig. 14). (Lucky for Carroll, all little girls, because of their presumed innocence, wore their enticing hair down all of the time. In

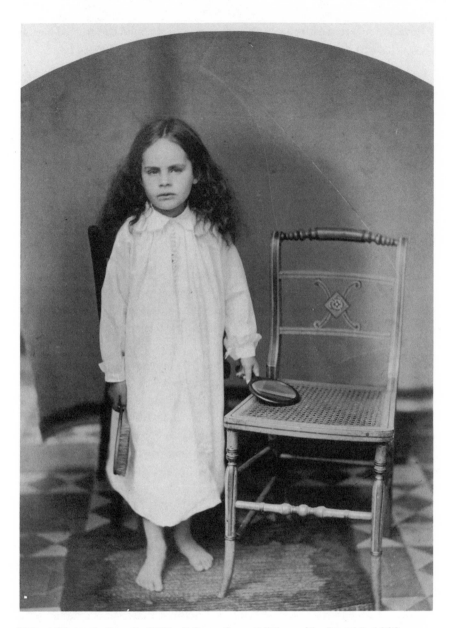

Figure 14. Lewis Carroll, "It Won't Come Smooth" (Irene MacDonald), 1863. (Gernsheim Collection, Harry Ransom Humanities Research Center, University of Texas at Austin)

fact, when they reached an age that required them to pile all of their hair on top of their heads, he quickly broke off his relationships with them.) Taming such a mane appears to be an impossible job for the cumbersome hairbrush that is oversized in her girl-hand. Miss MacDonald's pouting face has the picture's title written all over it: "It Won't Come Smooth" (1863). The staging of this little girl suggests that she is pleading for help with all of her lovely hair. Like Munby in Hannah's hair (though with a different end in mind), it is not difficult to imagine Carroll fiddling with Irene's hair in preparation for the closing of the (camera's) shutter. Like Carroll and the other "Other Victorians," Hannah and Munby were familiar with the codes of hair brushing: the two were partners in this eroticism. In a moment of haptic foreplay, leading up to the consummation of their looking, Hannah's came smooth.

But the most erotic touch of all comes near the end of the performance, with Hannah closing her eyes, shutting out sight itself, like a long erotic kiss, in order to *feel*: "She shut her eyes, turned sharply from the glass, and suddenly flung herself into my arms — 'that I might rather feel than see the beating of her heart.'" This passage is charged with looking, especially the kind of looking that produces shame that you can see: a blush. How are we to read Hannah's blushing?

Webster's first definition of blush reads as follows: "to become red in the face especially from shame." For the Victorians, as indicated by a host of authors of the period, from Charles Darwin to Charles Dickens, it was usually the woman who blushed. As Darwin informed them, "the relaxation of the muscular coats of the small arteries, by which the capillaries become filled with blood" was a feminine thing.[82]

Young women were a particularly shame-prone segment of this already shame-prone culture: they were its hot spot.[83] While on the threshold of womanhood, the Victorian girl was introduced to the elaborate rules of the blushing system. Rules that, like the laws of Wonderland, were impossible to obey. The general code of behavior went as follows: when faced with a possible shame-inducing situation (which was, of course, for a young Victorian lady nearly every moment of every waking and sleeping hour), a woman must blush and not blush at the same time. For when confronted with something like sexual innuendo, a blush would indicate a woman's knowledge of sexual practice, yet a nonblush might indicate her familiarity, ease, and nonembarrassment with the topic. Despite the highly visualized nature of the blush, there was no clear way of demarcating guilt from innocence. No wonder the Victorian era boasted of so many "fallen angels!"[84]

Ruth Bernard Yeazell has demonstrated the hysteria surrounding the Victorian girl's doomed blushing meter through Dickens's *Our Mutual Friend*. In Dickens's famous satire, which speaks to the period's obsessive devotion to the innocence of the girl, "the cheek of a young person" is shown as a fetishized testing site for the aforementioned (impossible) sexual contradictions. And because Georgina Podsnap (the owner of the cheek in question) is in the habit of blushing whether it is appropriate or not (what choice had she?), all tests are fallacious. This frustrates her father to no end, because "[Mr] Podsnap's idea of his young person is that of a creature who cannot exist."[85]

Likewise, one could argue that the period's idea of the ideal woman, the angel in the house, is that of a creature who cannot exist. No wonder Hannah said when considering the possibility of marriage, "For I never feel as if I *could* make up my mind to that — it is too much like being a *woman*.[86]

Not surprisingly, Hannah, far from an angel in the house, blushed differently. Unlike Georgina Podsnap, she did not speak with her cheeks out of social ineptness. Nor did she, I think, blush out of shame.

For, though the looking glass blush seems to suggest shame, it also seems to defeat shame through its performance. The shameful and shameless blush mirrors Hannah's other *becoming* identities (woman, slave, black, white lady, etc.) that read simultaneously as both real and false personages. So that when she *makes* (not fakes) blushes, one senses that she is neither ashamed nor not ashamed. In "Shame and Gender: Contribution to a Phenomenology of Oppression," Sandra Lee Bartky demonstrates how women are especially prone to "*rituals* of self-shaming undertaken in order to bear more easily [an anticipated] shame."[87] Embedded in "ritual" are descriptive words like "prescribed," "system," "custom," "ceremonial act": all of which play the "ritual of self-shame" as performance. Hannah, in a sense, saw shame coming and grabbed it before it was inflicted on her: that way, she could take pleasure in performing it on herself.

In a series of acts that were almost always based on shame, Hannah (who eventually learned to speak French, who read philosophy, who read Anne Thackeray's "Village on the Cliff," who planned to read Samuel Richardson's *Clarissa*, and who recited Shakespeare while cleaning the floor) must have been at least imperfectly conscious of her role as performer.[88] She must have known (at least subconsciously) that the black and crimson ball dress would not fit, that it would enhance (rather than diminish) her fantastic biceps, that it would make a strange spectacle of her, that it would unfix the categories of lady and servant. And she (I think) must have known that a good blush (all the way into her arms!?) would induce plenty of passion in herself and in Munby. Just thinking about such a moment of anticipated shame must have made her turn "rosyred."

Hannah herself writes provocatively about blushing when she describes the circumstances around the taking of the Magdalene picture (see Fig. 4):

And then the young man [the photographer by the name of Mr. Stodart] said he would like to take me again in other ways [he had just taken her, blackened—"cleaning a pair o' boots in one & another like blacking the grate"] & that he wasn't so busy now if I could come—one to be done as Magdalene, & I shd want nothing to wear but a white skirt. Massa said the Mr Fink (the one as took me for him in London once) wanted me to be done as *Una*—what that is I hardly know. Well, I went again & was done. I had to strip off my servant's things—to my shift, what I hardly liked, but still I knew there was no harm in that, & Mr S. was a serious sort o' man & we neither of us laugh'd or smil'd over it. He took me in a kneeling position as if praying, with my hair down my back & looking up. The side face was good for it, but the *hands* was too big & coarse he said, so it wouldn't do as a picture. And so it's best for me to be done as a drudge what I am, for my hands & arms are tho' chief to *me*, to get my living with, & I don't care about my face if Massa likes it.

But Mr S. gave me one or two of the Magdalenes on cards . . .

When I was stripp'd for the Magdalene I was little confused, having my steel chain & padlock round my neck, for Mr. S. said, "Is it lock'd[?]" *I blush'd a bit* as I said, "Yes, & I've not got the key." "Ah, there's some mystery about that," he said. And so it was done wi' the chain on, but as I said the hands was too big, & the position too stiff to look well. But I kep' the cards he gave me, & he also gave me a likeness of himself in colours, & he's exceedingly good-looking I think, & I've put him in my album. I paid Mr S a good bit for the picture, having 3 or 4 different ones . . .[89]

In this text, rather than suffusing her face and arms in "celestial rosyred" (as she did in Munby's story), she blushes just "a bit." Her tiny coloring comes out when Mr. S. learns that she has not got the key to the locked steel chain and padlock round her neck. (We know, along with Hannah, that only Munby had the key. We may blush too.) This blush, as before, feels playfully deliberate and for show. She punctuates the story (seemingly without shame) when she almost eagerly adds, "& I've not got the key." She wore the chain with pride; after all, one imagines that she could have arranged to have the chain taken off (as the Magdalene picture was planned before she arrived at the studio). But like her hands and arms, the chain is a big and clunky part of her own complex self-representation of invisibility. Both her hands and her chain undo the religiosity of Magdalene. Both fight against Magdalene's supposed helplessness. Both besmirch the purity of her white gown. Both play into her exposed breasts, which are not feminine at all, but as firm and as startlingly masculine as the thick chain and her thick hands.

The picture of Hannah as Magdalene is indicative of the Victorian interest in representing the other Mary: the unchaste Mary Magdalene. Hannah's portrait of 1864 is one instance in the plethora of representations of Magdalen, a topos well established in narrative form by the 1850s.[90] Julia Margaret Cameron, a prominent Victorian art photographer with a great interest in representing the popular literature of the period, took many, many pictures of her maid, Mary Hillier, as a Magdalene type. Naturally, they all emphasize the infamous hair.[91] My personal favorite is one that, despite its title, *The Angel at the Tomb* (1869, Fig. 15), is read as a Magdalene picture because of its sensational display of hair. But even when modeling for pictures, which through their titles and attributes are specifically of the Virgin Mary, Hillier almost always conjures up the unchaste Mary through sensual displays of skin and (especially) hair. Mike Weaver describes Hillier's incredible hair as "tousled and tangled as never before in the history of art."[92] Differently, Hannah's greasy hair sticks close to her head, with tired strands catching themselves on her shoulders and neck, while others fall uninterestingly down her back.

I think that the picture of Hannah as Magdalene is extremely erotic, but not in the conventional sense of Cameron's beautiful pictures of Mary Hillier as Mary Magdalene. Like Spenser's Una from his *Faerie Queen*, Hannah is sexually charged through a display of black and white.[93] Her hair serves as a black veil over exposed, very white, sexually ambiguous breasts. The whiteness of her breasts brings color to my face. The image is further eroticized, because, unlike the hair of Mary Hillier, Hannah's hair looks like it really did take part in Mary Magdalene's sensual performance of anointing the feet of Jesus with the musky smelling spikenard, only to wipe his feet dry with her own lovely hair. One is reminded of the fact that Hannah performed similar acts of eroticism through her habit of washing Munby's feet, a ritual that she appears to have taken great pleasure in. Furthermore, Hannah's hands, large with featherlike fingers, take on the character of strange, displaced angel wings: they are both heavenly, manly, grotesque, and beautiful — they must have looked very erotic to Munby. And her eyes are not cast up to God but hold their look, without shame, on the other person in the room: Mr. S.

Interestingly enough, "Mary" was itself an invisible name for female servants during the Victorian era. So it is not surprising that Hannah was also referred to as the ubiquitous "Mary."[94] (The fact that Cameron's own maid was actually named Mary and posed as both the Virgin Mary and Mary Magdalene is an intriguing part of this extension of the invisibility of "Mary.") One of the most humorous uses of "Mary" to signify the commonly undifferentiated maids of the period occurs in *Alice in Wonderland*, when Alice finds herself shrunken to the size of a rabbit and then mistaken by the White Rabbit as his housemaid: "Very soon the Rabbit noticed Alice as she went hunting

Figure 15. Julia Margaret Cameron, *The Angel at the Tomb*, 1869. Albumen, 13⁹⁄₁₆ × 9¹⁵⁄₁₆ inches. (Collection of the J. Paul Getty Museum, Malibu, California)

about, and called out to her in an angry tone, 'Why, *Mary* Ann, what *are* you doing out here? Run home this moment, and fetch me a pair of gloves and a fan! Quick, now!' " Alice shared with Hannah (even if for only a brief period) the invisibility of being a servant named "Mary." And like Alice, Hannah's adventures took place in a netherland.[95]

Smarting My Eyes

> . . . in a certain way nothing is as sensitive, especially to touch, as my sight.
> (Luce Irigaray)[96]

Hannah's pictures annihilate us by refusing categorization, which then undoes our own subjectivity. Her pictures are in our eyes, but they are not controlled by us: they do not accept us, even as we suck them in with our own eyes. As Lacan has remarked, "The picture is in my eye. But I am not in the picture."[97] Of course, all pictures do this, but I think that Hannah's photographs exaggerate this annihilated relationship; for though her pictures can be framed in various ways, they never seem to contain Hannah, not even in a mythic sense. She remains invisible.

Lacan's two-line statement of annihilation ("The picture is in my eye. But I am not in the picture") was sparked by his recollection of being out at sea with some fishermen. While staring at a bit of flotsam that had floated by — a sardine can — one of the fishermen exclaims (to Lacan): *"You see that can? Do you see it? Well it doesn't see you!"* The fisherman's statement, riddled with irony, is poking fun at Lacan. The fisherman is illustrating how Lacan is "rather out of place in the picture," out on a fishing boat in the middle of the sea. For amongst "those fellows who were earning their livings with great difficulty," Lacan "looked like *nothing* on earth" — not unlike the flotsam floating on the surface of the waves. The "joke" disturbed Lacan. For seeing himself as the fishermen saw him, as a bit of garbage, as nothing, was annihilating.[98]

It is in this double way that even an inanimate object, like the picture of Hannah's hands or the Munby Box itself, actually does gaze back at us, but in such a way as to *over look* the viewer. It is annihilating. As a result, our gaze within its constructed socialization (as primary, as the only true sense) always falls short. We cannot see Hannah, but she gazes back at us.

The gaze that Hannah gives the viewer is her expanded gaze, her *gaze of the invisible*, which is "forever organized or disorganized, around an impossibility of seeing [*un impossible à voir*]. Insurmountable other of the visible, not reducible to its invisible other side. It is a question of another world [a nether world], another landscape, a *topos* or a locus of the irreversible."[99] That is why in the empty frame with the accompanying note that tells us that Hannah has gone to get kitchen beer, we can take pleasure in the fact that she is not there. For she is also "not, not there." Invisible to the naked eye, she can be touched in the netherplaces of another landscape that destabilizes the reversibility of black and white, upper class and lower class, man and woman.

I close the box and take off my white gloves that are covered with a black soot that is impossible to see. Knowing that the box never *really* contained her, knowing that her ashes will never rest, knowing that I can never wash her off, I know that I love her and that she can never be mine. I take pleasure in this annihilation. I blush an invisible blush.

Notes

Moira Roth introduced me to Hannah and I am very grateful for that. I also owe thanks to Jane Blocker, Joy Kasson, Helene Moglen, and Della Pollock, who have offered provocative criticism.

1. Lenore Davidoff, "Class and Gender in Victorian England: The Diaries of Arthur J. Munby and Hannah Cullwick," in *The Double Vision: Sex and Class in Women's History*, edited by J. Newton, M. P. Ryan, and J. Walkowitz (London: Routledge and Kegan Paul, 1983), p. 57.

2. A maid-of-all-work did everything, including the lowliest of jobs. Hannah took pride in the fact that she could do everything, doing her jobs with her own peculiar strength and enthusiasm, which included "boot cleaning, knife cleaning, cleaning the silver and plate covers of serving dishes, cleaning and trimming oil lamps; emptying 'slops' and cleaning toilets, drawing and carrying water; dressing, washing and looking after infants and children of employers, their relatives and friends; gutting and plucking game birds and other fowl, gutting and skinning hare; keeping and balancing household account books, estimating what provisions were required when these were daily released from lock stores by 'the Missis,' ordering from tradesmen and tradeswomen; answering the bell to visitors, carrying boxes and hampers to and from railway stations, carrying visitors' luggage up and down stairs, escorting ladies of the family to and from social functions to protect them; laying and waiting at table, cooking elaborate as well as plain food, preserving fruit in season, making marmalade; making cushions from plucked feathers, sewing clothes for employers' charities, replacing the linen covers of their religious tracts and attending their charitable balls." Liz Stanley, Introduction to *The Diaries of Hannah Cullwick: Victorian Maidservant*, edited by Stanley (London: Virago, 1984), p. 5.

3. Cullwick, *Diaries*, p. 17. It seems that Hannah was always ambivalent about the institution of marriage. She rarely wore the wedding ring that Munby gave her. After he presented the marriage license to her, she wrote: "I car'd very *very* little for the license of being married either. Indeed, I've a certain dislike to either, they seem to have so little to do with our *love* & our union . . . I like the life I lead." Once married, Hannah became ill and was forced to move back to the country to "rusticate" herself.

4. By Munby's request, the diaries and photographs "were locked up until 1950 by which time, as he had foreseen, the shock and degradation of such a story would have died away." Davidoff, "Class and Gender in Victorian England," p. 31.

5. Stanley, Introduction to *Diaries*, p. 4.

6. Cullwick, *Diaries*, p. 274.

7. Arthur Munby, as cited by Derek Hudson in his *Munby: A Man of Two Worlds: The Life and Diaries of Arthur J. Munby, 1828–1910* (London: Gambit, 1972), p. 134.

8. However, it appears that Hannah briefly describes the circumstances of the photograph in her diaries. See Cullwick, *Diaries*, p. 91.

9. Emmanuel Levinas, *Otherwise Than Being or Beyond Existence*, translated by Alphonso Lingis (The Hague: Martinus Nijhoff, 1981), p. 90.

10. Heather Dawkins, "Politics of Visibility, Domestic Labour, and Representation: The Diaries and Photographs (1853–74) of Hannah Cullwick," *Parallelogramme* 10.4 (April–May 1985): 47–50 (this is an early article by Dawkins; later she wrote a much more substantial and very useful article — "The Diaries and Photographs of Hannah Cullwick," *Art History* 10.2 [June 1987] — in which the error was rectified); Davidoff, "Class and Gender in Victorian England."

11. After completing this essay, I received a copy of Griselda Pollock's article on the photographs and drawings of women coal miners that are contained in the Munby archives at Trinity College. Pollock's orientation is from a very different perspective. Whereas my writing, as the reader will soon see, focuses on Hannah (her desire and her sexuality and my erotic relationship to it), Pollock's focuses on Munby and other male artists and writers (of the same period) who were fascinated with "the complex of dirt, bodies, sex, and labor as it seemed to be presented to the bourgeois tourist by the mining industry and its communities"; "The Dangers of Proximity: The Spaces of Sexuality and Surveillance in Word and Image," *Discourse* 16.2 (Winter 1993): 19. But, like me, Pollock also gives a brief personal narrative that focuses on her experience of entering the wondrous Wren Library and being presented with the box ("a large chest"). She too indulges in the oddness of wearing white gloves, in order to inspect the dirty women represented. It was a pleasure to read about her similar experiences. And it was through her article that I better understood why I first began telling the story of my white gloves and the box: it gives me authority; it proves that I was there. For early on, when I first presented a version of this essay to Chicago art historians, my respondent was surprised to learn that I had actually spent a lot of time with the box. I was shocked that this was not clear to him, and I was possibly even more shocked at the fact that my voice (for him) was not credible unless I had worn the archivist's gloves and leafed through the "real" material. So, by the time that I got to the University of North Carolina at Chapel Hill later that year (1990) and delivered my story of Hannah again, you can bet that my tale of the gloves, the box, and the men who brought it all to me was there. I performed it with all of the authority I could muster. (The title of the lecture was "A Utopic 'Play' of Difference: Hannah Cullwick, Victorian Maid-of-All-Work, Monster of Inexhaustible Beauty." It was also delivered that same year at SUNY— Binghamton and at Lower Links, Chicago.)

12. Luce Irigaray, "The Invisible of the Flesh: A Reading of Merleau-Ponty, *The Visible and the Invisible*, 'The Intertwining—The Chiasm,' " in *An Ethics of Sexual Difference*, translated by Carolyn Burke and Gillian C. Gill (Ithaca: Cornell University Press, 1993), p. 182. Originally published as *Ethique de la différence sexuelle* (Paris: Les Éditions du Minuit, 1984).

13. Maurice Merleau-Ponty, *The Visible and the Invisible, Followed by Working Notes*, edited by Claude Lefort, translated by Alphonso Lingis (Evanston: Northwestern Uni-

versity Press, 1968). Originally published as *Le Visible et l'invisible* (Paris: Éditions Gallimard, 1964).

14. Merleau-Ponty, *The Visible and the Invisible*, p. 263.

15. Ibid., p. 257.

16. Jacques Lacan, *The Four Fundamental Concepts of Psycho-Analysis*, edited by Jacques-Alain Miller, translated by Alan Sheridan (New York and London: W. W. Norton, 1977), p. 84 (quotation). Originally published as *Le Seminaire de Jacques Lacan, Livre XI, "Les quatre concepts fondamentaux de la psychanalyse"* (Paris: Éditions du Seuil, 1973).

17. Merleau-Ponty, *The Visible and the Invisible*, p. 261; Lacan, "The Mirror Stage as Formative of the Function of the I as Revealed in Psychoanalytic Experience," in *Écrits: A Selection*, translated by Alan Sheridan (New York: Norton, 1977), originally published as *Écrits* (Paris: Éditions du Seuil, 1966); *The Four Fundamental Concepts*, p. 80.

18. Lacan, *The Four Fundamental Concepts*, pp. 80–81.

19. Irigaray, "The Invisible of the Flesh," p. 175.

20. Ibid., p. 159.

21. Ibid., p. 184; Michel de Certeau, *The Writing of History*, translated by Tom Conley (New York: Columbia University Press, 1988), p. 251. See also de Certeau's specific response to Merleau-Ponty, "The Madness of Vision," *Enclitic* 7.1 (Spring 1983): 24–31.

22. "Sexuate" is Irigaray's descriptive term for a language that points toward a sex that is beyond reversibility, that bathes in the remainder of reversibility. See "The Invisible of the Flesh," p. 184. She also uses the term, less poetically, to define laws ("sexuate rights") that she imagines for future societies. These laws do not seek to give women equality with men; instead, they are interested in keeping differences intact and respecting the rights that those differences entail, through law. (The new laws that Irigaray lists address rights to virginity, rights to motherhood, rights to human dignity, rights to media coverage directed at women, etc. — an extremely varied and at times, seemingly outrageous, list indeed.) The bottom line is that Irigaray does not believe in the reversibility that lies underneath the concept of "equal rights." However, despite differences in tone (between sexuating language and sexuating law), the concept still remains the same: men's language (including judicial law) cannot simply be reversed and applied to women. See "The Necessity for Sexuate Rights" and "How to Define Sexuate Rights," *The Irigaray Reader*, edited by Margaret Whitford, translated by David Macey (Oxford: Basil Blackwell, 1991). "The Necessity for Sexuate Rights" was originally published in Irigaray, *Je, Tu, Nous* (Paris: Grasset, 1990). "How to Define Sexuate Rights" was originally published in Irigaray, *L'Oubli de l'air chez Martin Heidegger* (Paris: Les Éditions du Minuit, 1983).

23. Cullwick, *Diaries*, pp. 119, 57.

24. Hannah and Munby are well-known figures in Victorian studies, and a number of works have addressed this odd couple. I have already cited several texts: the article by Davidoff; the two articles by Dawkins; the biography on Munby by Hudson; and Hannah's diaries as edited by Stanley. Peter Stallybrass and Allon White address Cullwick in "Below Stairs: The Maid and the Family Romance," *The Politics and Poetics of Transgression* (Ithaca: Cornell University Press, 1986), pp. 149–70. Michael Hiley has compiled a very useful collection of writings and photographs that extensively picture

Victorian working women (with less theorization than the aforementioned accounts): *Victorian Working Women: Portraits From Life* (London: Gordon Fraser, 1979). Interestingly enough, Hiley actually grants Hannah the most sexuality of her own—not through his own writing, but simply by virtue of including two erotic passages from the diaries that the major critical texts have left out. See nn. 44 and 78 below. Also of interest is Liz Stanley's "Biography as Microscope or Kaleidoscope?: The Case of 'Power' in Hannah Cullwick's Relationship with Arthur Munby," *Women's Studies International Forum* 10.1 (1987): 19–31.

25. Stanley, *Diaries*, pp. 306, 26.

26. "We, Other Victorians" is the title of Michel Foucault's introduction to *The History of Sexuality*, vol. 1, translated by Robert Hurley (Pantheon: New York, 1978). The book was first published as *Historie de la Sexualité*, vol. 1, *La Volonté de savoir* (Paris: Gallimard, 1976). The title of Foucault's introduction is derived from Steven Marcus's book on the "other Victorians": the prostitute, the hysteric, the pimp, etc. See Marcus, *The Other Victorians: A Study of Sexuality and Pornography in Mid-Nineteenth-Century England* (New York: Basic Books, 1964). Foucault (*The History of Sexuality*, p. 4) is interested in the ways in which "those 'other Victorians' . . . seem to have surreptitiously transferred the pleasures that are unspoken into the order of things that are counted. Words and gestures, quietly authorized, could be exchanged there at the going rate. Only in those places would untrammeled sex have a right to (safely insularized) forms of reality, and only to clandestine, circumscribed, and coded types of discourse. Everywhere else, modern puritanism imposed its triple edict of taboo, nonexistence, and silence." Similarly, Foucault imagines our current discourse to be in a similar "insularized" space; our insistent discussion of sex (supposedly out in the open) is just as much a "repressed" language as the discourse that we have *imagined* that the Victorians spoke.

27. Much has been made about the fact that Munby's own nursemaid was also named Hannah (Carter). She took care of the Munby family for twenty-eight years.

28. Stanley, Introduction to *Diaries*, p. 7.

29. Ibid., p. 2.

30. Lewis Carroll, who took pictures of little girls as obsessively as Munby collected pictures of working-class women, has been read similarly. Whereas historians are quick to read Carroll's sexuality, the little girls are always represented as without any sexuality at all, as if caught in some Edenic moment before the onslaught of desire. Furthermore, Carroll's sexuality has also been narrowly and simplistically read as that of a repressed homosexual. Not surprisingly, Derek Hudson has also written a biography of Carroll: *Lewis Carroll* (London: Constable, 1954). For more on the sexuality of the girl-children in Carroll's life, see my "Dream Rushes: Lewis Carroll's Photographs of Girl-Children," in *The Girl's Own: A Social History of the Victorian Girl*, edited by Claudia Nelson and Lynne Vallone (Athens: University of Georgia Press, 1994).

31. It is interesting to consider why Hannah's own sexual orientation has not been examined, whereas Munby's has been the site of explicit *perversions*, including homosexuality. *Mere* silence on Hannah as a sexual subject has registered her as a heterosexual, whereas Munby can be easily envisioned as a repressed homosexual. What kind of heterosexual is she? And does she fit that space any better than she fits the space of homosexual? Why have her own complex performances not led the theorists and

historians to regard her as "queer"? Could she not be a queer man gloved in a woman's body? For more on an expanded understanding of queerness, see Eve Kosofsky Sedgwick's extremely useful texts on the subject, especially *Epistemology of the Closet* (Berkeley: University of California Press, 1990) and *Tendencies* (Durham, N.C.: Duke University Press, 1993).

32. Black lead was used by maids and housekeepers to clean the grates around stoves, fireplaces, passageways, etc.

33. Cullwick, *Diaries*, p. 61.

34. In the Munby Box, the hands are paired with a photograph of Hannah as an elderly woman, and together they are accompanied by a note in Hannah's hand. The note reads: "Dearest Massa / I have been a hardworking servant forty two or three years & I have been yours thirty year or more, and I am still your faithful wife & loving servant. / Hannah, 1884–."

35. Thomas Laqueur, "Orgasm, Generation, and the Politics of Reproductive Biology," *Representations* 14 (Spring 1986): 28.

36. Susan Stewart, *On Longing: Narratives of the Miniature, the Gigantic, the Souvenir, the Collection* (Baltimore: Johns Hopkins University Press, 1984), p. 69.

37. Rejlander was a famous Victorian photographer. Not only was he an "art" photographer (treating the recently invented technology of photography as art), he also "may have been the first photographer to specialize in details of the human form, taken for the use of figure painters." Edgar Yoxall Jones, *Father of Art Photography: O. G. Rejlander, 1813–1875* (Greenwich: New York Graphic Society, 1973), p. 74. Interestingly enough, Rejlander had a maid, "Frizzlewig," who sometimes served as his model. Though Fink's photograph of Hannah's hands is undated, it appears to be contemporary with Rejlander's portrait of the lady's hands. Coincidentally, Hannah had visited Rejlander's studio, and several of the portraits in the Munby Box are by him. I thank Ann Paterra for guiding me to Rejlander's *Hands*.

38. The conservation of fine aristocratic hands was a major preoccupation for many bourgeois women of the period. Etiquette books supplied recipes for the whitening and the softening of hands. One book, *Rules of Etiquette and Home Culture*, written in 1889, gives the following recipe: "Melt together, in a dish over boiling water, four ounces of honey, two ounces of yellow wax and six ounces of rose water. Add one ounce of myrrh while hot. Before going to bed, rub this thickly over the skin. . . . A good way to keep the hands white is to wear at night large cloth mittens filled with wet bran or oat meal, tied closely at the wrists." I am indebted to Kelly Baum for presenting me with this and other useful insights on the maintenance of the bourgeois Victorian woman's hands.

39. Hannah originally wore the leather wristband to help a problematic wrist, but it was later transformed into a sign of her servitude to Munby. The wristband horrified one of her employers, but Hannah, who always insisted on her personal freedoms, refused to take it off and was soon terminated. As she once wrote, "I was *born* to serve, & *not* to order"; Cullwick, *Diaries*, p. 85. Her insistence on wearing the slave band stands in interesting contrast to the fact that, once she was married, she rarely wore her wedding ring.

40. Hannah, as quoted by Munby in his diary, cited in Hudson, *Munby*, p. 71.

41. Cullwick, *Diaries*, p. 66

42. Munby, as cited in Hudson, *Munby*, p. 71; emphasis mine.

43. Cullwick, *Diaries*, p. 111.

44. Hiley, *Victorian Working Women*, p. 32. Because this is an intriguing story whose eroticism centers on Hannah's own experience and imagination, it is interesting that this passage is not addressed by either Dawkins or Davidoff.

45. Roland Barthes, *Pleasure of the Text*, translated by Richard Miller, with a note on the text by Miller (New York: Farrar, Straus and Giroux, 1975), p. 17; originally published as *Le Plasir du texte* (Paris: Éditions du Seuil, 1973). The full sentence reads, "The pleasure of the text is that moment when my body pursues its own ideas — for my body does not have the same ideas I do." The quotation is symptomatic of an erotics of reading that is carried by *Pleasure of the Text* in which Barthes gives himself away to the reader.

46. One of the most well known was "Lily Powder," which was made by Queen Victoria's own *perruquier*: Mr. Willie Clarkton. See Neville Williams, *Powder and Paint* (London: Longmans, Green, 1957), p. 105. I am indebted to Anna Snoderly for this reference.

47. Though the actual evidence of intimate physical contact between Hannah and Munby is limited, they did bathe each other and there are diary entries that discuss pleasurable kissing.

48. The philosopher and performance artist Adrian Piper (who *looks* "white" and claims her black identity) has suffered and theorized the issue of just who is black and who is white in a series of works going back to the late 1960s. In her article, "Passing for White, Passing for Black," *Transition* 58 (1992): 4–32, she reveals the great efforts that whites have gone to to keep racial purity intact. In the end, it becomes clear that all of us are either passing for white or passing for black, and the whiteness and blackness are a social condition.

49. Hiley, *Victorian Working Women*, pp. 28–29. I will discuss this particular diary entry in full later in this essay.

50. Peggy Phelan, *Unmarked: Politics of Performance* (New York: Routledge, 1992), p. 8.

51. See Jean and John Comaroff, "Medicine, Colonialism, and the Black Body," *Ethnography and the Historical Imagination* (Boulder, Colo.: Westview Press, 1992), esp. pp. 224–25, and *Illustrated London News*, May 14, 1887, p. 557. There are endless examples of such racial ideology in the advertisements put out by Pears. One of the most famous and clearest (in terms of cleaning up the other) features a drawing of Sudan natives looking at a huge rock that has been inscribed with giant white letters that spell out "Pears Soap is the Best." The top of the advertisement reads: "The Formula of British Conquest." See *Illustrated London News*, August 27, 1887, p. 249. A most disturbing aspect of these advertisements is the fact that they are printed right next to "real" news stories of British colonialism and racial conquest.

52. Cullwick, *Diaries*, p. 75; emphasis mine.

53. The following passage from Munby's diary, 1883 (Hudson, *Munby*, pp. 157–59), speaks to this fascination:

> Passing through Scotland Yard about noon, I saw a large crowd, in the street, & heard the banjos of some Ethiopian Serenaders. But there were surely female voices as well as male: and going up, I was astonished to see that two of the five "niggers"

were young women. Yes: there were two young women, drest in fantastic ballet costume, and with shining black faces & necks & hands. Their heads were bare; their hair decked with network and rolls of scarlet cloth: they wore pink calico jackets, petticoats of spangled blue, ending a little below the knee: and red stockings and red boots. One of them came up to me, when the singing was over, with her tambourine; and earned a sixpence for her courage in blackening her face.

. . . They wash their black off every night.

I remarked to her that this was the first time that I had ever seen female niggers (except one, & that long ago) singing in the open street. "Yes Sir," she said "it's a new thing; but we mean to stick to it." I watched these two selfmade negresses going through the crowd by turns, collecting money after the performance. They did it very quietly and simply; appealing in silence — with not even a smile, for the lamp-black varnish disguised whatever good looks they had, so smiles would have been useless . . .

54. Douglas A. Lorimer, *Colour, Class, and the Victorians: English Attitudes to the Negro in the Mid-nineteenth Century* (Leicester: Leicester University Press, 1978), p. 88.

55. Joan Riviere, "Womanliness as Masquerade," *International Journal of Psychoanalysis* 10 (1929): 303–13; Irigaray, *This Sex Which Is Not One*, translated by Catherine Porter with Carolyn Burke (Ithaca: Cornell University Press, 1985), p. 84, originally published as *Ce Sexe qui n'en est pas un* (Paris: Les Éditions du Minuet, 1977). Irigaray assigns the term "mimicry" to the masquerade of femininity that is performed consciously as a subversive act in order to uncover the masculinist standards that exploit her sex. One of the best (recent) examples of this is the California news reporter who managed to mimic femininity all the way up to the winning of the Miss California Beauty Pageant; after being crowned, she announced her other identity.

56. Phelan, *Unmarked*, p. 96; emphasis mine.

57. As Dawkins ("The Diaries and Photographs of Hannah Cullwick," p. 182) has pointed out, there are two copies of Hannah as slave/chimney sweep; the original has been captioned as "Hannah as a slave." Another traveling mount features her as a wholesome working girl (with a pretty bonnet, a lovely shawl, a beautiful big basket, a bright white apron) *and* as a fashionable young lady (with beautifully exposed shoulders, flowers in her hair, ribbons on her wrists).

58. Madeleine Ginsburg, *Victorian Dress in Photographs* (New York: Holmes and Meier, 1983), p. 58.

59. For an excellent discussion of Gérôme and Orientalism, see Linda Nochlin's "The Imaginary Orient," *The Politics of Vision: Essays on Nineteenth-Century Art and Society* (New York: Harper and Row, 1989), pp. 33–59.

60. Sigmund Freud, Minutes from the Vienna Psychoanalytic Society, 1909, published as "Freud and Fetishism: Previously Unpublished Minutes of the Vienna Psychoanalytic Society," edited and translated by Louis Rose, *Psychoanalytic Quarterly* 57 (1988): 159. For more on women, clothing, and haptic fetishes, see Emily Apter, "Splitting Hairs," in her *Feminizing the Fetish: Psychoanalysis and Narrative Obsession in Turn-of-the-Century France* (Ithaca: Cornell University Press, 1991), pp. 99–123. See also Yolande Papetti, Françoise Valier, Bernard de Fréminville, and Serge Tisseron, *La*

passion des étoffes chez un neuro-psychiatre, G. G. de Clérambault, 1872–1934 (Éditions Solin, 1987).

61. See Monique Wittig's useful and lucid insights on the relationship between race and gender and slavery in "The Category of Sex," *Feminist Issues* 2.2 (Fall 1982): 63–68.

62. Munby, as cited in Hudson, *Munby*, p. 54. The question of Hannah's class is indeed complicated. Despite the fact that she was a working-class woman her entire life — doing unbelievably difficult labor at incredibly low wages — I still have trouble registering her as *simply* lower class. After all, her lower-class life was shaken by such things as a trip to France or the wearing of fine clothes. And though she did not receive money from Munby except as a paid maid, there is a difference in the fact that he was (since the beginning of their relationship) always looming in the background as a possible crutch. So although Hannah was certainly lower class and led a very hard life, her class situation was substantially different from that of other maids-of-all-work who were in more class-isolated situations. One could argue that she "passed" as lower class and she "passed" as upper class. This is a touchy issue: no one would ever want to underestimate Hannah's life struggles, yet it is curious that other scholars have not seen the rough edges around the issue of her class.

63. Davidoff, "Class and Gender in Victorian England," p. 48.

64. Munby, as cited in Hudson, *Munby*, p. 320.

65. Both of their diaries appear to almost flaunt this fact.

66. Irigaray, interview in *Les Femmes, la pornographie et l'érotisme*, edited by M.-F. Hans and G. Lapouge, as quoted in Griselda Pollock, *Vision and Difference* (London: Routledge, 1988), p. 50.

67. Hudson, *Munby*, p. 318. This is one of at least thirty-six sonnets that Munby had written to Hannah and placed in an envelope some thirty years after their marriage. Interestingly enough, most of them were copied in Hannah's handwriting.

68. Discussions of Irigaray's essentialism are abundant. The following is a short list of texts that I have found useful on the topic: Diana Fuss, *Essentially Speaking: Feminism, Nature, and Difference* (New York: Routledge, 1989); Eléanor Kuykendall, "Toward an Ethic of Nurturance: Luce Irigaray on Mothering and Power," *Mothering: Essays in Feminist Theory*, edited by Joyce Trebilcot (Totowa, N.J.: Rowman and Allanheld, 1984); and Carolyn Burke, "Irigaray through the Looking Glass," *Feminist Studies* 7.2 (Summer 1981): 288–306. Burke provides a relatively early (American) entry into Irigaray that manages to feel its way past the usual pronouncement of essentialism. Burke insists on distinguishing "analogy" from "morphology," stressing that Irigaray promoted the latter. Accordingly then, the "lips" of "When our lips speak together" should not be reduced to an anatomical specification; rather, their figure should be used to suggest another mode (not another model). In this morphological space, Irigaray's lips imply plurality and a mode of being "in touch" that differs from the phallic mode of discourse. The lips that speak together play on the vaginal lips and the lips that encircle our mouths — and the lips that speak between women — and they also suggest a language that sounds different, as when you hum with your lips together. Irigaray, "When Our Lips Speak Together," in *This Sex Which Is Not One*.

69. Irigaray, *This Sex Which Is Not One*, p. 24.

70. Ibid., pp. 28–29; emphasis mine.

71. In her first book, *Le Langage des déments* (The Hague: Mouton, 1973), Irigaray (a

trained psychoanalyst with doctorates in linguistics and philosophy) discovered that male schizophrenics were better able to articulate their condition through traditional language, whereas female schizophrenics tended to speak their condition through the body.

72. Elaine Showalter, *Female Malady: Women, Madness, and English Culture, 1830–1980* (New York: Pantheon, 1985). See esp. chaps. 2 and 3, "The Rise of the Victorian Madwoman" and "Managing Women's Minds," pp. 51–98.

73. As Showalter (*Female Malady*, p. 5) writes, "It is certainly possible to see hysteria within the specific historical framework of the nineteenth century as an unconscious form of feminist protest, the counterpart of the attack on patriarchal values carried out by the women's movement." Yet, as Showalter goes on to explain, one should not romanticize it nor essentialize an "equation between femininity and insanity." Rather, one must investigate how, in a particular context, notions of gender influence the definition and, consequently, the treatment of mental disorder.

74. The documented cases of women who were suspected of performing their roles for notoriety mostly come out of the French clinic, Salpêtrière, run by Jean-Martin Charcot: the much-photographed Augustine is the most famous. "Because the behavior of Charcot's hysterical stars was so theatrical, and because it was rarely observed outside of the Parisian clinical setting, many of his contemporaries, as well as subsequent medical historians, have suspected that the women's performances were the result of suggestion, imitation, or even fraud. In Charcot's own lifetime, one of his assistants admitted that some of the women had been coached in order to produce attacks that would please the *maître*. Furthermore, there was a dramatic increase in the incidence of hysteria during Charcot's tenure." Ibid., pp. 150–51.

75. Ibid., p. 87.

76. However, Ellen Terry "found the madwomen much 'too theatrical' to teach her anything." Ibid., p. 92. For more on the relationship between madness, Ophelia, and Ellen Terry, see Nina Auerbach, *Ellen Terry: Player in Her Time* (New York: Norton, 1987), esp. pp. 238–41.

77. It is difficult to tell when the incident actually occurred. "Munby mentions it in his diary entry for Monday 2 February 1863, saying it happened 'once, long ago.'" Hiley, *Victorian Working Women*, p. 135, n. 14.

78. Munby, as quoted in ibid., pp. 28–29; emphasis mine. This account, like the chimney story, is not addressed in the major critical writings on Hannah.

79. Elisabeth Gitter, "The Power of Women's Hair in the Victorian Imagination," *Publication of the Modern Language Association of America* 99.5 (October 1985): 938, 936, 943. It is difficult to imagine what Munby meant by brushing her hair out in a lady's fashion; possibly after brushing it, he pulled it back in some "fashion," though it is difficult to believe that it truly would have been a lady's fashion.

80. Hudson, *Munby*, p. 3. But much has been made of the missing diaries, which many feel contain evidence of Carroll's love for Alice Liddell, the "real" Alice of Wonderland fame.

81. Carroll, as cited in Morton N. Cohen, "The Actress and the Don," in *Lewis Carroll: A Celebration: Essays on the Occasion of the 150th Anniversary of the Birth of Charles Lutwidge Dodgson*, edited by Edward Guiliano (New York: Clarkson N. Potter, Inc., 1982), p. 2. (Charles Lutwidge Dodgson is the birth name of Lewis Carroll, the latter

being his pen name.) Carroll's quotation comes from one of a number of the diaries that are now mysteriously missing. By 1930 four of his thirteen volumes of diaries had disappeared. Whether they were lost or intentionally destroyed by members of his family (to cover up any dark shadows in his life) is a matter of debate. In any case, Langford Reed, who published a biography on Carroll in 1932, managed to get a hold of the missing diaries before their disappearance; Reed's text is Cohen's source for the Ellen Terry quotation. See Langford Reed, *The Life of Lewis Carroll* (London: W. and G. Foyle, 1932), p. 90.

82. Charles Darwin, *Expression of the Emotions in Man and Animals* (London: John Murray, Albemarle Street, 1890), p. 328. The first edition was published in 1872. Interestingly enough, the volumes contain photographs by Rejlander (some even of Rejlander), demonstrating a range of expressions including from grief to joy.

83. After all, Darwin (in *Expression of the Emotions in Man and Animals*) uses shame as a way of distinguishing man (cultured and civilized) from the primate that he grew out of. Shame becomes a mark of intelligence and sophistication. Such thinking prompted Darwin to investigate whether "Negroes" and the mentally ill were shame prone. He was able to cite a few instances of blushing in these categories (using albino Negroes in order to register a true blush in the former category!). Darwin's text demonstrates as much racism and sexism as anyone might want to find.

84. Here I am referencing the prevailing model of the ideal woman of the period: the "Angel in the House." The common usage of the phrase is indebted to Coventry Patmore's verse sequence, *The Angel in the House*. The first part of the book was published in 1854, with subsequent parts appearing in 1856, 1860, and 1863. In its entirety, *The Angel in the House* (London: George Bell and Sons, 1892) is a long (and very dull) narrative of the courtship and marriage of Honoria, "whose unselfish grace, gentleness, simplicity and nobility reveal that she is not only a pattern Victorian lady but almost literally an angel on earth." Sandra M. Gilbert and Susan Gubar, *The Madwoman in the Attic: The Woman Writer and the Nineteenth-Century Imagination* (New Haven: Yale University Press, 1979), p. 22. Honoria, selfless and dedicated to the male gender, reinforces Patmore's (*The Angel in the House*, p. 73) sentiments that "Man must be pleased; but him to please / Is woman's pleasure." In an age of religious doubt, the period's embracement of the "angel in the house" enabled characters like Honoria to become objects of worship and "patterns" for Victorian ladies at home. And indeed, Honoria is like a (displaced) Virgin in her purity and "vestal grace," even after marriage (p. 205). For, even after having been "won" by her husband, Honoria is still so pure that she does not really belong to him: she belongs to the heavens. As Honoria's husband confesses, ". . . this Temple keeps its shrine / Sacred to Heaven; because, in short, / She's not and never can be mine" (p. 206). Nina Auerbach has suggested that for many Victorian women life as angel was just too difficult; rather than finding themselves engaged in the power of flight, they found themselves in never-ending fall. Auerbach uses Alice's fall at the start of *Wonderland* ("Down, down, down. Would the fall *never* come to an end?") as a Victorian mirroring of the fall of mankind through Eve; for the biblical story was the governing principle behind the various assessments of the Victorian woman as temptress, as weak, as evil, as fallen or subject to falling. Auerbach, *Women and the Demon: The Life of a Victorian Myth* (Cambridge: Harvard University Press, 1982), p. 167.

85. Ruth Bernard Yeazell, "Podsnappery, Sexuality, and the English Novel," *Critical Inquiry* 9 (December 1982): 343.

86. Cullwick, *Diaries*, p. 170; emphasis mine.

87. Sandra Lee Bartky, "Shame and Gender: Contribution to a Phenomenology of Oppression," *Center for Twentieth-Century Studies Working Papers*, Working Paper no. 7 (Fall–Winter 1989–90): 8; emphasis mine.

88. Probably the most shocking act of shame was the fact that Hannah licked Munby's boots clean.

89. Cullwick, *Diaries*, p. 77; emphasis mine.

90. Dawkins, "The Diaries and Photographs of Hannah Cullwick," p. 180.

91. As is written in John 12:3, "Mary [Magdalene] therefore took a pound of right spikenard [a costly ointment with a musky odor valued as a perfume in ancient times], of great price, and anointed the feet of Jesus, and wiped his feet with her hair; and the house was filled with the odor of the ointment."

92. Mike Weaver, *Whisper of the Muse: The Overstone Album and Other Photographs*, exhibition catalog for the J. Paul Getty Museum, Malibu, 1986, p. 39.

93. Mr. Fink and Mr. Stodart were both seeing the play of oppositions in Hannah when they suggested the she model as Una and Magdalene, respectively. Stodart's suggestion that she wear only her white "shift," which was then coupled with her head of black hair, indicates not only the metaphorical symbols embodied in Mary Magdalene, but also a character like Spenser's Una. Una with her white lamb, her white ass that she rides, and her physical whiteness is self-contradicted by her black stole, her veiled face, and her sadness. In fact, "her sadness (. . . identifies her fleetingly with Mary Magdalene) . . . [as it signifies] the Fall of Man with its consequent veiling of truth." A. C. Hamilton, General Editor, *The Spenser Encyclopedia* (London: Routledge, 1990), p. 705.

94. Stanley, Introduction to *Diaries*, p. 32.

95. Carroll, *Alice's Adventures in Wonderland*, pp. 55–56; emphasis mine. For an interesting analysis of Alice and class, especially her anxiety about the lower class, see Nancy Armstrong's very useful article, "The Occidental Alice," *Differences* 2.2 (1990): 3–40.

96. Irigaray, "The Invisible of the Flesh," p. 174.

97. Lacan, *The Four Fundamental Concepts*, p. 96.

98. Ibid., pp. 95–96. What is always overlooked in Lacan's sardine story is the double annihilation that class difference performs. Even if Lacan could somehow (magically) escape the all-discriminating annihilation of vision itself, he would still never be part of the fisherman's netherworld. Lacan's eyes and his class keep him perpetually *out*: out of the space of the frame, out of the sardine can, out of the working class.

99. Irigaray, "The Invisible of the Flesh," p. 153.

The Politics of Seduction

Theater, Sexuality, and National Virtue

in the Novels of Hannah Foster

JEFFREY H. RICHARDS

The novels of Hannah Webster Foster (1759–1840) show a thematic richness and a complexity of text that have only recently begun to claim the scholarly attention they deserve. Like many novels of the early republic, Foster's *The Coquette* (1797) and *The Boarding School* (1798) explore the problems faced by women caught in the trap of sexual seduction, a narrative situation usually explained by the influence on American writers of Samuel Richardson's famous books, *Pamela* and *Clarissa*. But as Jay Fliegelman has shown, seduction as a theme has a power and a resonance in early republican society that goes beyond what earlier critics have explained as a desire to imitate a master or titillate a leisured class or even enforce traditional moral categories.[1] Foster, a writer with a greater grasp of irony than many of her American contemporaries, includes in her novels a number of concerns that play against a reading of the seduction plot as a one-dimensional illustration of the mistakes of a fallen woman. Instead, by linking the private trials of women in finding their way to personal independence with a variety of public concerns connected to both American and female identification, Foster suggests that the lives of women serve as registers for the political and social problems of post-Revolutionary American society.

The image of a woman as, in Fliegelman's phrase, "an all-too-seducible daughter," is tied in Foster's work to another theme, the woman on public display.[2] Both *The Coquette* and *The Boarding School* depict situations in which women enter the social arena for their own personal reasons, only to find themselves judged for their performances by a larger and more demanding audience than the individual is often willing to admit.[3] In the terms of 1790s sentimentalism, a female character finds herself approved or reproved by a society that values virtue on the one hand, but throws temptation in the way on the other, as for instance by admitting such formerly banned and potentially subversive forms as the novel and the theater to be acceptable amusements. Forced to contend with the allure of media that expose women to public view, yet told through social admonition that she must portray herself with modesty and restraint, the American woman as figured in sentimental novels seems trapped in a world where all life is performance. The problem she faces is to determine where playacting stops and acting in earnest begins.

In addition, female characters who appear before the public in period novels or plays do so in the larger cultural context of the post-Revolutionary concern about virtue and corruption.[4] This context includes a republican political rhetoric that calls on one sex, the female, to provide the education in virtue needed to sustain an independent nation — indeed, uses the body of a woman pictographically to represent America and Liberty — yet denies to that same sex the political liberties it extends to the male. In other words, the apparently private decisions of individual women in stories of seduction are linked in the minds of commenting observers to public images of women as teachers of virtue and as icons of the republic. In her novels, Foster encourages readers to see that the role of women in a republic cannot be disconnected from either that republic's own political self-definition, its iconographic representation, or the relationship of American women to a social culture for which theater and theatrically derived codes of behavior turn personal decisions into public displays. The real story of both *The Coquette* and *The Boarding School* is that social pressures constrict the space in which women may test out roles without suffering adverse, even dire, consequences.

In the context of a new and somewhat tentative republic of letters, Foster's *The Coquette* (1797) has received some small attention from historians of the early American novel as the best of an otherwise tedious batch of didactic fictions that form the "sentimental" tradition in the new United States.[5] More recently, however, several critics, including feminist historians and literary scholars, have demanded a reassessment of the book. Linda K. Kerber, Cathy N. Davidson, Carroll Smith-Rosenberg, and Kristie Hamilton, among others, have attempted to liberate Foster's once best-selling novel from the charge that it simply valorizes a conservative sexual ethic. Instead, they argue, if the point of the book were simply to identify her submitting to a seduction as morally reprehensible, the character Eliza Wharton (based on the historical Elizabeth Whitman, a relative of Foster's husband) comes across as a far more appealing figure than any fallen woman has a right to. Though the historical legitimacy of the "feminist critique" has been challenged by Klaus P. Hansen, the fact remains that as a result of feminist approaches to Foster's work, current and future readers will be unlikely to read *The Coquette* with the same derisive dismissal that has often characterized American critical response to the sentimental novel.[6]

With this in mind, I wish to consider both *The Coquette* and *The Boarding School* as products of a culture that sees the separate motifs of seduction and female social performance conjoined through the issue of national self-representation. In pursuing the argument, I will first discuss the general cultural understanding of seduction in the last quarter of the eighteenth century; and second, look at the seduction situations in Foster's novels, the limitations those situations place on women's ability to perform themselves in a social setting, and by extension the ways in which those performances mirror political ideals of behavior in a republic.

What does seduction mean for American readers in the 1790s? As Hamilton remarks, the seduction theme in *The Coquette* has complexities that are not accounted for when one views Foster's novel as only a narrative about male predation and female folly. Following Kerber and Davidson, Hamilton points out that Eliza Wharton's plight, that of a woman who tests the limits of republican freedom and finds herself seriously compromised by reigning notions of gender identity and class structure, serves to question the idea of a clearly defined code of behavior in the new political order. In other words, Hamilton cautions, the viability of a normative virtue for women, one represented, for example, by Eliza's correspondent Lucy Freeman (the future Mrs. Sumner), cannot be maintained so simply for those who, like Eliza, lack the financial and social resources of the eighteenth-century upper-middle class. The political freedom of the time would seem to call for personal freedom as well; but for a woman, and especially an educated, ambitious, and culturally sophisticated woman with only modest means, nearly every behavior with public repercussions brings with it comment and debate.

If in the seduction of the coquette, readers see warnings to the "American fair" about what is possible for a woman, they may also see admonitions to the nation as a whole (*The Coquette*, p. 159). Indeed, the theme of seduction, the presence of a female protagonist who, while praised for her education and intelligence, seems almost deliberately naive, and the topicality of the narrative (in its time, the novel was read as a roman à clef) all serve as warnings to a republic figuratively rendered as woman.[7] As represented in the visual arts, the theater, and the literature of the postwar period, a figural woman often embodies a political entity; the threatened seduction of a woman mirrors the vulnerability of a new nation, independent yet virginal, as she tries to find ways to behave in a society of other, older nations.[8] While European countries (figured as predatory males) put Columbia under their gaze, waiting their chance to seduce her, she, in turn, seeks ways to protect her virtue as unsullied country and looks for opportunities to assert herself truly in the perfidious arena of state. Foster's novels, foregrounding as they do the issues of female behavior in a republic, serve as seeming, if imperfect, allegories of national behavior generally.

In other words, rather than measure Eliza's character simply as one of liberated heroine versus fallen woman, I would argue that a reading of Eliza's actions requires an awareness of allegorical possibilities that, even though they do not blossom as allegory per se, show Foster simultaneously affirming and denying American culture as found. That is, Foster provides both a valorizing of women's centeredness in the figuration of the republic and a critique of that position, measured through the character and misfortunes of a single woman. The spirited Eliza, in this scheme, represents a desire on the part of women to liberate themselves from oppressive social constraints *and* a desire on the part of the country as a whole to expand the range of its culture beyond stoically limited notions of social performance. At the same time, Eliza's story reflects the dangers for both woman and nation when liberty is read as license and being is read as acting. That is to say, the woman who *acts* as if she is free knows all the while that one false step — one, in fact, true to her desire — will deny her even the constricted world given to women of "virtue." She will be less likely to come to harm, however, than the fully honest woman who speaks and behaves freely in the belief that her innocent essence matters more than her virtuous performance. For a nation that is itself ostensibly free, the sense of being under constant observation undermines the liberty it professes, just as surely as if it were being judged by the society of nations as a woman whose virtue were always under siege.

Behind this reading are cultural phenomena other than sentimental novels themselves. One is the frequent pictorial representation of America or Columbia as a woman exposed to brutality or to insidious temptation. Paul Revere's print *The Able Doctor; or, America Swallowing the Bitter Draught* (1774) provides a pornographic reading of British-American politics in the immediate prewar period; in this case, the Indianized female America, pinned to the ground by well-dressed British gentlemen, peered at, and poured into, is pure victim, a figure whose sexuality is reduced to vulnerability.[9] In other topical pictures, America-Columbia is pictured as a suppliant, a grieving daughter, or a nearly naked woman exposed to war or one of its metaphors, such as a thunderstorm.[10] Some artists pose Britannia and America together; in Revere's print, the mother, Britannia, turns away helplessly as her daughter is abused. In a British wartime print, maternal Britannia suffers when her coy daughter, Miss America North, dallies with male figures representing France and Spain.[11] These pictorial representations lie behind and condition readers' responses — when sexuality is at issue — to a centrally placed woman in a novel.[12]

Seduction as a motif is part of the postwar debate over corruption or luxury, a struggle fought in the popular press, the prefaces to novels, and on stage.[13] Royall Tyler's prologue to his play *The Contrast* (1790) asserts that "Vice trembles" when the author (in service to "native themes") writes with "candor."[14] In the preface to the first American sentimental novel, *The Power of Sympathy* (1789), William Hill Brown likewise affirms the importance of moral instruction in the novel, particularly for "the fair Reader," and dismisses "novels which *expose* no particular Vice, and which *recommend* no particular Virtue" as "not beneficial" at best.[15]

As Tyler's successful play makes clear, urban Americans are unsure where to draw the line between rural American virtue and naiveté on the one hand, and proper foreign influence and corruption on the other. In *The Contrast*, the virtuous Maria's laments demonstrate the impossibility of free choice for women in postwar society. Flirt, and you lose your reputation; conform to parental authority, and you may be given in marriage to a despicable rake. Thus, as Fliegelman notes, the parent bound by a patriarchal code of enforcement drives the child into debauchery by overzealous exercise of authority.[16] In the play, Maria's only hope is to expose the Chesterfield-adoring Dimple as a lascivious fraud and engage a man of honor, the Washington-worshipping Manly, to protect her virtue. Yet through the prologue, which announces the play as an American text, and through Manly, who denounces luxury as the "bane of a nation," an audience could not fail to see a connection between Maria's vulnerability and the fate of the republic.[17] Through Charlotte, Tyler admits that fashion, theater, and coquetry have their attractions, but he still asserts that good Americans must continue to affirm homespun, honesty, and earnest love as basic to national identity. Rakes love Europe and themselves, hate America and women; to take up with a rake, whether as friend or lover, is not only self-defeating, but also un-American. However, to recognize a libertine takes a degree of sophistication that Americans might well fear as itself corrupting. In any case, the point of Tyler's play echoes that of the pictorial record: national virtue can be maintained only when female chastity is protected.

Keeping in mind the concurrence of a pictographic convention that figures the nation as female, cultural debates that put national virtue and female behavior in the public light, and, of course, a political rhetoric that emphasizes a newly won freedom from tyranny, one can imagine how the seduction situation in American fiction would inspire more than casual interest in readers of the 1780s and 1790s. This is not to say that seduction as a literal phenomenon is of no importance; on the contrary, premarital intercourse, adultery, rape, and other sexual acts that victimize women appear in the public record from the earliest days of English settlement.[18] Even so, the seduction motif has reverberations for political bodies as well as human ones; the persistence of seduction as a significant plot element in novels of the first decades of the republic has as much to do with feelings about the American polity, figured in terms of class, gender, and stance toward virtue and culture, as it does with ambiguities in the lives of actual women. Although both of Foster's novels, *The Coquette*, and that of the following year, *The Boarding School*, dispense advice and caution to women about their behavior, both also suggest that the condition of women is a register of national health as a whole.[19] The often-quoted admonitions in *The Coquette* to the "American fair" — that is, the young women of the republic — could as well be lessons to fair America; even though both female and American independence can be sustained only through rigorous protection of virtue, the liberty to act, even to maintain one's reputation, can rarely be exercised without threat of loss. Thus the ambiguity embedded in *The Coquette* and embodied by Eliza Wharton in her free seeking of pleasure and self-determination against the implied norm of what Kerber calls the "Republican Mother" reflects political issues for the new nation as a whole.[20] In the American taxonomy of gender, as long as women are not enfranchised by the state, woman *is* the state.[21]

Seduction, however, is only part of the story. In the social arena, a woman's enacting virtue or submitting to vice is frequently judged as a moral absolute. In the theater, another arena where the dramas of virtue and vice are performed, moral issues intertwine with the relativity of role playing. Inevitably, the moral ambiguity of stage plays infiltrates a society unused to drawing distinctions between performance and reality. Antitheatrical moralists think that the stage encourages the vices it portrays and that actors are persons of doubtful reputation, a stance that prompts early thespians to shape their performances as exhibitions of moral uplift. In the 1790s, the demand for theater as a cultural activity in an emerging nation overwhelms arguments for its suppression — but the memory of prewar moralizing persists. If the conduct of women comes to stand for national behavior as a whole, then the attitudes that female characters take toward the theater show both the difficulty of choice for women and the implied threats that theater represents to the country overall.

In *The Coquette* and *The Boarding School*, Hannah Foster imagines a social world whose attractions women must resist, yet on whose stage women must know how to perform if they are to live in the world at all — a world that both is and is not a playhouse. Entering a society where theatricality governs much of what passes as interpersonal relations, and where going to the theater represents the most fashionable of amusements, Eliza Wharton and the other women in Foster's novels confront a dangerous loss of self-definition as they tread the uncertain space between republican mother and ruined coquette.

The problem for the protagonist of *The Coquette* is learning to understand the kind of acting that is required to make the right impression among virtuous people. From her first letters, however, Eliza Wharton writes against expectation. Though polite society assumes that she will mourn the loss of her betrothed, the minister Haly, she instead celebrates liberation from her "paternal roof" and chooses the path of honesty; for the late Haly she has felt the "sincerest friendship," but only obedience to parents could have led her to an engagement with a man so opposite her personality (pp. 5–6). This overt rejection of patriarchal authority would seem to be well inside the new Revolutionary American tradition. But by the internal conventions of sentimentalized virtue, Eliza would have to mask her own lack of heartfelt enthusiasm — something she has a hard time doing. For Eliza, other forces regulate her actions; she is, she tells Lucy Freeman, "naturally cheerful, volatile, and unreflecting"; and though she is excited to be reentering the "gay world" of visits and parties, she promises, "I shall never again assume those airs, which you term *coquettish*, but which I think deserve a softer appellation; as they proceed from an innocent heart, and are the effusions of a youthful, and cheerful mind" (p. 7). Youthful, cheerful, volatile, unreflecting, honest, sincere, and, above all, innocent, Eliza defines herself in ways that affirm bourgeois convention even as they deny the authority of social expectations to limit the freedom of her conduct.

Innocence by itself, then, cannot sustain a spotless character; thus, Eliza's innocent freedom makes her vulnerable, even in a republic of virtue, to corruption. Her female friends advise suspicion and modesty, even as they encourage her to avoid remaining long in melancholy — but Eliza by and large rejects such advice. When her friend, the wealthy and well-married Mrs. Richman, expresses concern that Eliza be "suitably and agreeably connected," the latter retorts with a statement of principles that, as it turns out, proves fatal in a world where appearances matter: "Let me then enjoy that freedom which I so highly prize." "But beware, Eliza!" Mrs. Richman responds; "The round of fashionable dissipation is dangerous" (*The Coquette*, p. 13). Yet as many recent critics have observed, Eliza finds the rules of determining the difference between freedom and dissipation to be unclear at best. From Mrs. Richman, she receives a more pointed warning later, about the roué, Major Sanford. He has earned "censure," Eliza's friend says, "by being a professed libertine; by having too successfully practised the arts of seduction; by triumphing in the destruction of innocence and the peace of families!" "Must I then become an avowed prude?" asks Eliza. "By no means" is Mrs. Richman's response; one can be polite, yet "forbidding" — that is, give the seducer entrance into the house of virtue but there resist his "arts" (p. 20).

What *The Coquette* suggests, *The Boarding School* — a book that has received little comment and less praise — makes overt: the arts of seduction must be fought by other arts, those of virtue.[22] Mrs. Williams, the schoolmistress of Harmony Grove, recognizes that young women even from the best homes may lack full education in the ways of the world; they require a complete course of instruction in self-defense, as it were, a school of martial as well as marital arts that teaches women how to walk confidently into areas hostile to virtue, repel all threats, and emerge with reputation intact. Unfortunately for Eliza, the haphazard schooling she gets from letters and conversations with her female friends does not fully prepare her for those who calculate and deceive — though perhaps had she had a woman with the method and character of Mrs. Williams to teach her first, those admonitory epistles from the sorority of the virtuous might have had greater effect. As it is, the other women in Eliza's life all play by different rules from those of "natural vivacity." Lucy Freeman urges the choice of Rev. Boyer for Eliza's suitor, for all the obvious reasons of virtue, honor, and stability, and repudiates Eliza's alleged desire "to shine in the gay circle of fashionable amusements" (*The Coquette*, p. 27). Mrs. Richman later draws the analogy between Richardson's characters Clarissa and Lovelace and her acquaintances Eliza and Sanford: "beware, my friend, of his arts. Your own heart is too sincere to suspect treachery and dissimulation in another." Yet she urges Eliza to be governed by "sincerity and virtue," telling her that one of the qualities that makes her vulnerable must also be used in her own defense (p. 38).

In the social world that Eliza inhabits, one of parties and visits and cultural events, the sincere woman plays against a person who is seemingly all show but is undone when she cannot wear another face to meet the faces of fashion. For virtue to thrive, those who would be virtuous must know the rules of social behavior — a kind of theatricality where performers are also spectators — but resist the distractions of costume for entertainment's sake. Eliza, as the daughter of a virtuous but ineffective mother, and as a woman of small material resources, "confined to the rigid rules of prudence and economy," is, among the professionally wealthy — those like Sanford whose whole mode of being is dedicated to "show" and "equipage" — an amateur (*The Coquette*, pp. 61, 115). She can, for instance, put on a socially correct front. In one scene, as she anticipates the arrival of her righteous suitor, Boyer, she says, "I must begin to fix my phiz . . . and try if I can to make up one that will look *madamish*" (p. 61). But Eliza suffers from her sincerity as well. In the climactic scene, Boyer comes to press her for an answer to his marriage suit. Meanwhile, fearful of losing the object of his intrigues, the unsavory Sanford appears in the garden to make one last appeal before Eliza chooses the minister as her spouse. During his speech, "a consciousness of the impropriety of this clandestine interview" causes Eliza to blush; Boyer enters, catches the two in an agitated tableau — "mute as statues" — and, finding a woman whose sincerity exposes her consciousness of the impropriety of being alone with Sanford, storms off to tell Eliza's mother that he renounces the attachment to her daughter (pp. 91–92). Eliza has made him, he accuses, "the dupe of coquetting artifice," while she, with "no inclination to self defence," takes his accusations, all her "natural vivacity" departed (pp. 92–93).

The natural is not so base here as foolish. Although many modern critics, including Davidson, Hamilton, and Smith-Rosenberg, denounce Boyer for his priggishness, the fact remains that by the rules of conduct that Foster upholds, he must react to the *appearance* of impropriety; and though modern readers may find his haughty epistolary rebuff to Eliza a smug and arrogant gesture, his abandoning Eliza is the mechanical consequence of her failure to perform appropriately, to look sufficiently "*madamish*" when Sanford has been present. Mrs. Williams, the doyenne of Harmony Grove, attacks both the "language of seduction" and the "insidious and deluding wiles of the coquette," urging instead "the dignity and decision of insulted virtue," a pose that comes directly from a "rational and discreet plan of thinking and acting" in securing from a suitor his "affection" (*The Boarding School*, pp. 103, 98–99).

Though virtue is touted in both of her books, Foster nowhere makes social action a completely moral issue. Rather, she asserts that all social relations are governed by plans, schemes, wiles — motives may differ, but no one can afford innocence where it is tied to naiveté. Eliza has only *appeared* to be "coquettish," as the intensity of her remorse and her abject letter to Boyer show; but in a world of calculation, even among the virtuous, all appearance is judged as if it is reality — a reality that includes some measure of expected artifice. To outfox the seducer, one must adopt the stance most repellent to him: a posture of virtue so assertively put forward that the "charms" of the seducer have no audience. What prevents Sanford from chasing after the "alluring" Julia Granby, for instance, as opposed to her friend Eliza, is "the dignity" of Julia's "manners" and "the very expression of her eye [that] blasts in the bud, every thought, derogatory to her honor" (*The Coquette*, p. 140).

Unlike Eliza, Julia acts with all the certainty of a right-thinking female education, as if she has been tutored by someone of Mrs. Williams's character. In *The Boarding School*, the young women whom Mrs. Williams has been preparing for the world go forth and correspond with each other about the life they meet, their goals, follies, and fears, and their remembrance of their teacher's advice. Following the opening section — Mrs. Williams's lectures — the first letter, by Harriot Henly, notes that at her home in Boston, the streets are full of loud "Bachanalians" and her home full of persons who care nothing for such polite and uplifting entertainments as reading or singing hymns (p. 114). Well might she note the disjunction between a closed, harmonious society where performance is limited to one woman's reading aloud while the others work with needles and the more open, threatening society of the city, filled as it is with theatrical performances of all kinds: plays, professional singing and dancing, exhibitions. Mrs. Williams has told Harriot and the others that they need to be accomplished in such performing arts as music and dancing, but that those arts "sometimes allure their fond votaries from that purity and rectitude which are the chief embellishments of the female character" (p. 42).

She illustrates her point with the story of Levitia, the daughter of parents who, while "not affluent," encourage her to develop her talents. The woman, however, becomes obsessed with performing. Glutting herself on flattery, she accepts a smooth-talking foreigner as guardian, who prepares her for a professional career. Ruin follows swiftly: "She made her appearance on the stage. She sung and danced, for which she was caressed, flattered, and paid. A licentious mode of life, quadrating with the levity of her heart, soon left her a prey to seduction. Her gaiety and beauty gained her many votaries, and she became a complete courtezan" (*The Boarding School*, p. 44). Further disasters succeed. Mother dies, lover flees, father grows ill; and though she returns to her father, she cannot recover her lost reputation: "She is now despised and avoided by all her former acquaintance, and must inevitably spend the remainder of her days in wretchedness" (p. 45).

Theater threatens not entirely by its form. Indeed, the well-educated woman knows many of the same arts as those of the stage. Rather, it is as if knowing how to perform, albeit modestly, enables a woman to determine the rules and artifice of performance generally. Nevertheless, to escape censure, a woman must learn to reconcile knowledge of potential corruption with an appearance of innocence and behave with a restraint that cannot be scorned as prudish. In fact, the social circle that surrounds the stage has greater potency as a corrupting force than the entertainments themselves: "At the play, the ball, the card-table," young women expose themselves as "dupes of adulation, and the votaries of coquetry," falling in love with men who are "all show" (*The Boarding School*, pp. 89–91). A woman must learn further to discriminate between virtuously informed criticism of plays and uninitiated abandonment to brilliant social surface.

But beyond what to Mrs. Williams is a kind of willful stupidity among women who choose not to distinguish between modest approbation and insidious flattery, Foster suggests a general rule of female behavior: apply to amusements the same standards of action allowable in the home. Thus, what Mrs. Williams proscribes: "Loose and immoral books; a company, whose manners are licentious, however gay and fashionable; conversation, which is ever tinctured with profaneness or obscenity; plays, in which the representation is immodest, and offensive to the ear of chastity; indeed, pastimes of every description, from which no advantage can be derived, should not be countenanced; much less, applauded" (*The Boarding School*, p. 78). Far from being the moralizing tract many readers assume it to be, *The Boarding School* skirts issues of morality. Immodest entertainments are condemned not because they are bad per se, but because, as in Benjamin Franklin's scheme for acquiring virtue, they offer "no advantage." One's behavior at the play also registers on a scale of decorum that has little to do with weighing the relative merits of politeness and those of virtue and vice. As Mrs. Williams asks, "Why should those things afford apparent satisfaction in a crowd, which would call forth the blush of indignation in more private circles? This question is worthy of the serious attention of those ladies, who, at the theatre, can hardly restrain their approbation of expressions and actions, which, at their houses, would be intolerably rude and indecent, in their most familiar friends!" (p. 78). The point is that freedom of expression can never be embraced either at home or in the theater without risk of causing "indignation."

By extension, then, if a libertine or profane person were admitted to the home, one would, were he or she a person of manners, either withhold approval or find some other way to denounce behavior unbecoming the virtuous. Yet as with the theater, so for domestic performance: every action of a woman has an audience as surely as the actor's every gesture. Does she stare at potential seducers with sufficient "dignity" to "blast" their intentions — return the male gaze with a very different one of her own? Or does her look invite further familiarities? And does her applause at a witty jest strike observers, both male and female, as too enthusiastic for modesty's sake? Ideally, virtue will reign with such power as to render a woman's rejection of the immodest natural-seeming; but Mrs. Williams is not such a fool as to think that nature can do it without rigorous education.

There is a further implication to her strictures: an overindulgence of theater is unpatriotic. Levitia, we recall, is seduced by a foreigner. Another of Mrs. Williams's examples, Flavia, is left by her Tory father when he flees during the Revolution. A wealthy farmer, however, takes her in and raises her in happy obscurity. At war's end, the father returns to claim his estate — and urge his daughter to share his taste for urban fashions. Her "lively fancy" engaged, Flavia goes with him to the city where, in her naiveté, she is "dazzled" by wealth and "every species of dissipating amusement" (*The Boarding School*, p. 81). From "balls, plays, cards, and parties," it is but a short distance to debt, acquaintance with a libertine from whom she borrows money, and "the sacrifice of her honor" (pp. 82–83). Though the outcome follows the usual pattern, Foster suggests by Flavia's fall that neither complete rural retreat nor full urban indulgence can save a woman's need to be independent. The father, a man with political allegiance to Britain and cultural loyalty to the playhouse and the ballroom — not the more private, domestic space of the parlor — virtually sells the daughter into corruption. Innocent, yet dangerously uneducated, she sacrifices independence and "honor" all at once, without ever consciously assuming "the insidious and deluding wiles of the coquette" (p. 98). No American woman — and no America, whose national deportment is figured in feminine terms — can afford to give herself to a father or lover whose first principle is show, nor assume that she can be protected by a virtuous father-substitute, without an intermediary education in theatricality of, by, and for women.

The Boarding School helps us read *The Coquette* by seeing in the title of the latter a false lead. Like Flavia, Eliza falls from the pedestal of virtue without ever actively assuming the reality of a coquette. To be sure, she is not entirely naive; Eliza receives far more direction from women in what Mrs. Williams calls the "path of rectitude" than Flavia (*The Boarding School*, p. 48). Neither is Eliza entirely unsophisticated about plays and theater or even politics; nor is she beholden to a father of any sort, honorable or not. Nevertheless, without a will for self-defense, Eliza leaves herself every bit as exposed to loss of virtue and independence as Levitia, Flavia, or any other antiheroine in one of Mrs. Williams's cautionary tales.[23]

If what we have been discussing is essentially the theater of social life, where one ideally plays at virtue until one actually acquires it — or one mistakenly falls in love with the brilliant surfaces that make virtue look dull by comparison — there are, in essence, two more theaters in *The Coquette* to which Eliza must pay heed: the theater itself and its texts, and the metaphoric world stage on which people imagine their lives to be roles in a larger drama. For someone like Mrs. Williams, the well-educated, well-defended republican woman should be able to distinguish carefully among all three, recognize each for what it is, yet know when any theater absorbs too much of one's being for safety's sake. The problem with the world Foster creates, however, is that there is no space in which one can *be* without subjection to exacting standards of what constitutes an acceptable performance. Eliza knows her theaters, but she cannot always draw curtains between them or fully appreciate the dangers inherent in overindulgence. Despite the warnings she receives — sometimes couched in contradictory terms — Eliza acts as if it were possible for essence to supersede appearance.

Still, Foster makes it clear that Eliza's sentiments often conform to the Harmony Grove model. Boyer's friend Selby recounts a social gathering involving Eliza, Sanford, Mrs. Richman, and others in which the women divide into groups: one, involving most of the women, surrounds Sanford, who, with a play in his hand, makes "sage remarks" that the women seem witlessly to affirm; and another, engaging Selby, Eliza, and Mrs. Richman, debates the role of women in a republic. When the groups unite, Eliza stands with Mrs. Richman as the latter delivers a lecture to the other women: "We shall not be called to the senate or the field to assert its [the country's] privileges and defend its rights, but we shall feel for the honor and safety of our friends and connections who are thus employed. . . . Why, then, should the love of our country be a masculine passion only?" (*The Coquette*, pp. 91–92). With the crowd finally assenting that Mrs. Richman's speech is "truly Roman, and, what was more, they said, truly republican," Foster — despite the tacit acceptance of female disenfranchisement — asks us to see in the implied competition between play talk and political rhetoric an affirmation of the latter as the right arena for the new American woman (p. 92).

Even so, Eliza finds that the world of plays has its own allure. While Boyer still pursues his marriage plans, Eliza puts him off by demanding the free use of her own time. This includes attending what she calls later "a favorite amusement of mine," the theater (*The Coquette*, p. 100). Boyer will have no part of it; but at the theater, Eliza writes to her mother, she sees "Major Sanford in the very next box" (p. 74). As Boyer later tells Eliza, no good can come from seeking "the adulation of coxcombs . . . nor could the fashionable amusements of brilliant assemblies, and crouded theatres furnish the mind with 'That which nothing earthly gives, or can destroy / The soul's calm sunshine, and the heart felt joy'" (p. 76). But after Boyer leaves her for good, Eliza asks the virtuous Lucy Sumner to tell her about the theater in Boston and to send her plays to get her out of her depression — requests to which her friend readily accedes.

Letter 52, in which Lucy describes the Boston theater, shows how carefully Foster discriminates among acceptable and unacceptable theatrical activities for a woman of sensibility. "Come and see whether they [performers] can afford you any entertainment," she urges Eliza, implying that the theater per se is an appropriate balm for a depressed republican woman (*The Coquette*, p. 112). But once in the theater, what can one see without harm? Lucy herself has just seen *Romeo and Juliet*: "Distressing enough to sensibility this! Are there not real woes (if not in our own families, at least among our own friends, and neighbors) sufficient to exercise our sympathy and pity, without introducing fictitious ones into our very diversions? How can that be a diversion, which racks the soul with grief, even though that grief be imaginary. The introduction of a funeral solemnity, upon the stage, is shocking indeed!" (pp. 112–13). If one cannot "play" death, then surely lighter fare such as the circus would be acceptable. Yet this too gets attacked, largely on gender grounds. Lucy particularly belittles female equestrians: "To see a woman depart so far from the female character, as to assume the masculine habit and attitudes; and appear entirely indifferent, even to the externals of modesty, is truly disgusting, and ought not to be countenanced by our attendance, much less by our approbation." With tragedy and circuses (and cross-dressing/acting) ruled out, there remains one "rational and refined amusement" — museums (p. 113).

But Eliza has already made it clear that she cannot be confined by such dull fare. She has kept Boyer at a distance, using the argument that their "dispositions" are different; yet she has concurred with Mrs. Richman that women ought to take an active role in the affairs of the republic. She defines her freedom as that of choosing her own companions and attending amusements of her choice, recognizing that what held for her mother — stoic acceptance of life's trials — cannot hold for her. As with the country as a whole, Eliza feels the need for the new, yet everywhere she is cautioned about leaving the old.

Foster implicitly argues for a greater role for women in national affairs but, at the same time, uses the voices of several characters to explain the need for clearly delineated, gender-defined limits to allowable behaviors in that role. At once recognizing the desire of women for autonomy and yet urging women to dispose their attentions and favors carefully in order not to lose all, Foster suggests that prudence must govern — but that continual restraint has its costs. Encouraged to read light plays and attend diverting amusements, yet cautioned against frivolity and associating with a man as familiar with the stage as Sanford, Eliza has few outlets for her impulse toward theater. As Lucy Sumner might say, why see *Romeo and Juliet* when one can watch the tragedy of Eliza Wharton firsthand?

Indeed, it appears that Foster has had Eliza on another stage all along, the metaphoric stage of tragic example, for which the novel in America is a new vehicle. Removed from the direct connection to flesh and blood that the theater maintains, the novel uses language that frames the lives of characters in theatrical terms yet seems to adopt a moral stance that questions the utility of the actual stage. Before the postwar reopening of the theaters, a like strategy appears in other texts: sermons, orations, and diaries, for example. And while those same texts continue to use theater metaphors, the novel — often linked in sermons and related tracts to the corrupting stage — both absorbs theatrical conventions and reexpresses experience in ways that convey the intensity of dramatic situation without some of the ambiguities of representation that worry the moralists.[24] Thus Foster, unable to find a place for Eliza at the theater, and unwilling to allow her to act in the theater, exhibits her life on stage anyway — the stage of metaphorical preconceptions that says that every action in a (woman's) life has dramatic, national consequences.

Several characters in *The Coquette* think in terms of scenic or dramatic figures of speech — and no wonder since, as Mrs. Williams tells her charges, adult life is "the stage of action" (*The Boarding School*, p. 48). Noting the differences between them, Eliza tells her mother that although the latter has "passed through this scene of trial, with honor and applause," the daughter must lament her volatility and her lack of "resolution, dignity and prudence" (*The Coquette*, p. 39). When Sanford has routed his rival, Boyer, he gloats to his correspondent Deighton, "The show is over" (p. 94). But of course it is not. Sanford marries another woman to buttress his sagging fortune, then pays Eliza a visit: "A new scene has opened upon us to day," she writes to Mrs. Sumner, concluding her description of her supposedly new relation with Sanford by saying, "I hope the tragic comedy, in which I have acted so conspicuous a part, will come to a happy end" (p. 120).

For Eliza, the comedy, at least, is over; only tragedy remains. Having asserted her freedom to associate as she pleased, all the while remaining connected to the virtuous sisterhood of Lucy Sumner, Mrs. Richman, and Julia Granby, Eliza gives up the one thing an unmarried woman can exhibit without shame — her sexual innocence. Finally seduced by Sanford, she leaves apologetic letters to her mother and Julia Granby, then flees both home and novel, her liberty abandoned and her voice given to others to speak or represent.[25] Her freedom has all along been problematic; in the paradoxical worlds of politics and virtue, liberty turns out to be restraint, innocence masks knowledge, social arts prove often to be base wiles, and the theater deludes, even as it entertains. Led by her independence into believing that her sexuality is her own to give, Eliza learns too late that in fact for the stalwart middle class it is a political commodity, offered or withheld in the public arena. Female sexuality, then, as Shirley Samuels has remarked of its depictions in novels of the early republic, is "political sexuality."[26] Imagining she attends the theater for amusement, Eliza in reality places herself under what seems in the novel to be universal observation. Thus, she shows considerable insight at the end — as does Foster, of the power of the novel as a form — by saying to Sanford, "May my unhappy story serve as a beacon to warn the American fair of the dangerous tendency and destructive consequences of associating with men of your character" (*The Coquette*, p. 159).

In other words, women can serve either as republican mothers or as sexual victims for the greater virtue-teaching of the republic — but nothing much in between. Thus, despite all the talk in the novel about the value of virtue and republican society, the character of Eliza Wharton shows that something essential is missing. Without access to a well-defined play space in which new or even deviant behaviors may be tested — in other words, played at — without fear of real-world reprisal, the republic according to Hannah Foster affords few opportunities for freedom that transcend pre-Revolutionary gender roles.

But it is possible for one woman's story to become the story of the nation as a whole. In a last surge of theatrical language, *The Coquette* effectively apotheosizes the female character its encoded normative rules have all condemned. Julia Granby announces to Lucy Sumner, "The drama is now closed! A tragical one indeed it has proved!" (p. 161). Eliza's death, she remarks, is a "melancholy exit," an echo of Eliza's last letter to Julia, in which she prepares for a possible calling "from this scene of action" (pp. 162, 156). Lucy Sumner herself picks up the rhetoric: "A melancholy tale you have unfolded, my dear Julia; and tragic indeed is the concluding scene!" (p. 166). Yet all women can learn from both the example of Eliza's fall and, as her tombstone expresses it, the "example of calm resignation" that is "exhibited" by her "last painful scene" (p. 169). In the way earlier generations learned to eschew the micro-cosmic stage for the macrocosmic theater of God's judgments, so Foster sustains something of the same rhetoric in a new form. The transmutation of Eliza's story into a drama of example, one played for an audience of "the American fair," shows how Foster hopes to justify her text(s) as something more than frivolous entertainment or bloodless homily (pp. 159, 168). By raising Eliza as a beacon and damning the "Chesterfieldian" Sanford as an "execrable" libertine, one whose "sordid mind must now suffer the depriva-tion of those sensual gratifications, beyond which he is incapable of enjoy-ment," Foster gives the screw a final turn (pp. 111, 163, 167). We are back to a similar political message to that in Tyler's *The Contrast*: the woman embodies patriotic values, the seducer treachery to nation. And indeed, Sanford an-nounces, "I shall fly my country as soon as possible" (*The Coquette*, p. 165). That leaves for readers the elevated remembrances of the penitent Eliza, whose death in her own country through sexual spoliation provides a more powerful image than "virtue alone" can of this political lesson: "To associ-ate [with a seducer], is to approve; to approve, is to be betrayed!" (p. 168). Courted, compromised, and abandoned by a Europeanized rake, Eliza dies physically isolated from, but in memory reabsorbed into, the greater commu-nity of virtuous republican women.

As the strictures in *The Boarding School* make apparent, Foster seems to have understood that women occupy a special place in early republican society. Called upon to feel for their country and those who defend it, women are given the task of figuring the nation, enacting the fate of the republic in the disposition of their sexuality. This they do in a fictional form, the novel, appearing as characters in a kind of macrocosmic, retributive drama and strug-gling to resist the allure of urban theatricality and the actual stage. Theater and theatricality, though not evil in themselves, threaten to seduce woman — and thus perhaps the nation — into a false sense of her own freedom, or so Foster suggests. To combat the pernicious effects of theater, her texts argue that female self-determination is only possible when sexual conduct remains part of the public accounting, where the assertive display of chastity repels a woman's — a nation's — seducers and preserves her liberty to act uncompro-mised by pregnancy, shame, or abandonment.

Yet *The Coquette* also contains within it an element of regret — that for a woman of spirit and essential goodness, as Eliza Wharton represents, an indi-vidual and perhaps a nation too whose forte is brilliance of manner and tenac-ity of independence, there is no approved stage, and no other drama than tragedy, in which to act unconstrained. Free to choose behaviors in a world less bound than before by tyrannical moral presumptions, Foster's Eliza learns too late that health and community standing can be retained—when one lacks the capital for it—only at the cost of rigorous self-madamizing. Seduced, abandoned, dead, Eliza gains liberty through the medium of the example story, whose very telling by other women keeps the subversiveness of her actions alive. But the warning to women and nation is clear: in achieving virtue, Eliza/America has no space for play.

Notes

1. Jay Fliegelman, *Prodigals and Pilgrims: The American Revolution against Patriarchal Authority, 1750–1800* (Cambridge: Cambridge University Press, 1982), pp. 36–38, 96–97.

2. Ibid., p. 96.

3. Hannah Webster Foster, *The Coquette*, edited by Cathy N. Davidson (New York: Oxford University Press, 1986), and *The Boarding School; or, Lessons of a Preceptress to Her Pupils* (Boston: Thomas and Andrews, 1798). Hereafter cited within the text.

4. On the problem for women writers of appearing before the public without compromising their ostensibly retiring lives at home—"literary domesticity"—see Mary Kelley, *Private Woman, Public Stage: Literary Domesticity in Nineteenth-Century America* (New York: Oxford University Press, 1984).

5. Lillie Loshe and Herbert Brown consider *The Coquette* in the context of other American novels influenced by Samuel Richardson's *Pamela* and *Clarissa*; Henri Petter is somewhat blunter in seeing *The Coquette* as the best of a bad lot. See Lillie Deming Loshe, *The Early American Novel* (New York: Columbia University Press, 1907), pp. 13–14; Herbert Ross Brown, *The Sentimental Novel in America, 1789–1860* (Durham, N.C.: Duke University Press, 1940), pp. 14–15, 39, 45–46, 131–32; and Henri Petter, *The Early American Novel* (Columbus: Ohio State University Press, 1971), pp. 258–64. For a more judicious assessment of Foster's contemporary importance among literati, see Robert L. Shurter, "Mrs. Hannah Webster Foster and the Early American Novel," *American Literature* 4 (1932): 306–8.

6. Kerber's book, *Women of the Republic: Intellect and Ideology in Revolutionary America* (Chapel Hill: University of North Carolina Press, 1980), establishes the intellectual and political background against which women like Foster wrote, particularly the demand that women who engage in politics turn their energies toward making the home a nest of republican virtues; see esp. pp. 248–49. Davidson's work has been especially helpful in restoring *The Coquette* itself to modern scrutiny and helps us see Eliza's plight as a complex one, not easily reducible to moral parables; see her article, "Hannah Webster Foster," in *Dictionary of Literary Biography*, vol. 37, edited by Emory Elliott (Detroit: Gale, 1985), pp. 161–63, and introduction to the Oxford edition, the section in "Flirting With Destiny: Ambivalence and Form in the Early American Sentimental Novel," *Studies in American Fiction* 10 (1982): 17–39 on Sanford and Boyer as hypocrites (pp. 27–34), and her subchapter in *Revolution and the Word: The Rise of the Novel in America* (New York: Oxford University Press, 1986), "Reading *The Coquette*," pp. 140–50. *The Coquette*, Davidson maintains, is "not simply an allegory of seduction. The generic shift from sermon to novel in the Whitman/Wharton narrative entails a con-

comitant transformation of focus and philosophy. Set within a specific context of limiting marriage laws and restrictive social mores, the novel is less a story of the wages of sin than a study of the wages of marriage" (*Revolution*, p. 143).

Smith-Rosenberg, in "Domesticating 'Virtue': Coquettes and Revolutionaries in Young America," in *Literature and the Body: Essays on Populations and Persons*, edited by Elaine Scarry (Baltimore: Johns Hopkins University Press, 1988), pp. 160–84, identifies Eliza's struggle as one of freedom and independence in the context of middle-class gender roles. She highlights the contradiction when men demand that "elite women" embody class virtue through sexual propriety yet remain essentially "elegant and non-productive" (pp. 165–66). Noting the specific disparities between the protagonist's modest economic circumstances and the more affluent ones of her social circle, Hamilton sees Eliza's becoming a "coquette" as part of "the competing appeals of the republican expectation of marrying within one's own socioeconomic class and the opportunities for upward mobility in late eighteenth-century, urban America"; "An Assault on the Will: Republican Virtue and the City in Hannah Foster's *The Coquette*," *Early American Literature* 24 (1989): 135–36.

While I am, in fact, focusing on the "allegory of seduction," I do so in the context of these feminist assessments of Foster and the sentimental novel. By contrast, Hansen rejects the feminist claim that *The Coquette* represents a major shift in female representation from reigning middle-class values; and though his cautions against reading into the text a modern feminism that could not have existed for Foster are well taken, his own reading of the novel oversimplifies the "message" by claiming that Foster affirms that woman's education is "best supervised by a country parson"; "The Sentimental Novel and Its Feminist Critique," *Early American Literature* 26 (1991): 45. The figure of Mrs. Williams in *The Boarding School* clearly shows that Foster believes in the efficacy of women to maintain their own virtue. For a somewhat different view of the public that Foster addresses, one that examines her "economy of vision," see David Waldstreicher, " 'Fallen Under My Observation': Vision and Virtue in *The Coquette*," *Early American Literature* 27 (1992): 204–18.

7. On the relationship between Foster's novel and the real-life story of Elizabeth Whitman, see Davidson, Introduction to *The Coquette*, by Hannah Webster Foster (New York: Oxford University Press, 1986), pp. vii–x, and Jane E. Locke, Preface to *The Coquette; or, The History of Eliza Wharton*, by Hannah Webster Foster, new ed. (Boston: Fetridge, 1855), pp. 3–20. The latter identifies a son of Jonathan Edwards as the seducer. James Woodress, *A Yankee's Odyssey: The Life of James Barlow* (Philadelphia: Lippincott, 1958), also provides helpful background, as one of Whitman's suitors was Joel Barlow, but he also notes that despite the lack of a regular theater in Hartford (one of Whitman/Wharton's chief venues) until 1794, "strolling players and performers visited the city in the previous decade" (pp. 73–74).

8. Lester C. Olson, *Emblems of American Community in the Revolutionary Era: A Study in Rhetorical Iconology* (Washington, D.C.: Smithsonian Institution Press, 1991), p. 15; Ruth H. Bloch, "Untangling the Roots of Modern Sex Roles: A Survey of Four Centuries of Change," *Signs* 4 (1978): 249–52.

9. Kerber, *Women of the Republic*, p. 40. Olson (*Emblems of American Community*, pp. 84–85, 112) discusses the history of this print. It first appears in England in 1774.

Revere makes a few changes a few months later for the first American version; then other, often cruder versions follow. In other words, the image of shameless ravishment of a helpless female strikes many chords for its contemporary audience.

10. Kerber, *Women of the Republic*, pp. 116–17; Olson, *Emblems of American Community*, illustration 46, opposite p. 234.

11. Kerber, *Women of the Republic*, p. 156.

12. For the whole matter of filial imagery in the Revolutionary era, see Fliegelman, *Prodigals and Pilgrims*. Olson (*Emblems of American Community*, pp. 125–99) discusses the depiction of America as a child, usually female. Olson's book is one of the first attempts to categorize emblems for the Revolutionary period, but he does not deal with the specific issues of representing the country as woman except to note the frequency of female icons. A more focused discussion of woman as emblem is that of John Higham, "Indian Princess and Roman Goddess: The First Female Symbols of America," *Proceedings of the American Antiquarian Society* 100, part I (1990): 45–79.

13. A useful collection of contemporary documents on the luxury theme can be found in *The Rising Glory of America, 1760–1820*, edited by Gordon S. Wood (New York: Braziller, 1971). All through the 1780s and into the 1790s, many communities argue among themselves about the propriety of opening or reopening theaters, for example. Even supporters of the stage, including Philip Freneau, claim a need for limitations on what is appropriate fare for republican audiences; see Freneau, *The Prose*, edited by Philip M. Marsh (New Brunswick, N.J.: Scarecrow, 1955), p. 295. In addition to other cited sources, including Kerber, Davidson, and Fliegelman, my discussion of late-eighteenth-century American culture is indebted to Kenneth Silverman, *A Cultural History of the American Revolution: Painting, Music, Literature, and the Theatre in the Colonies and the United States from the Treaty of Paris to the Inauguration of George Washington, 1763–1789* (1976; reprint, New York: Columbia University Press, 1987), who in his history notes the prevalence of theater and the theatrical mode in the arts during the Revolutionary and post-Revolutionary periods.

14. Royall Tyler, *The Contrast*, in *Anthology of American Literature*, vol. 1, edited by George McMichael, 4th ed. (New York: Macmillan, 1989), pp. 467, 466.

15. *The Power of Sympathy*, edited by William S. Kable (Columbus: Ohio State University Press, 1969), p. 5.

16. Fliegelman, *Prodigals and Pilgrims*, p. 262.

17. Tyler, *The Contrast*, p. 490.

18. See Kerber, *Women of the Republic*, pp. 245–46, and Laurel Thatcher Ulrich, *Good Wives: Image and Reality in the Lives of Women in Northern New England, 1650–1750* (New York: Knopf, 1982), pp. 89–105. Cathy Davidson's reconstruction of the eighteenth-century female reading audience in *Revolution and the Word* has made it clear how powerfully sentimental fictions engage women of the time.

19. Walter P. Wenska Jr., "The Coquette and the Dream of Freedom," *Early American Literature* 12 (1977–78): 243–55, identifies the context for Foster's *The Coquette* as the social instability in America during the 1780s and 1790s. Thus metaphors of "confinement and contraction" contend with Eliza's desire to break away, leaving Lucy Freeman as the model of " 'modest freedom' . . . that is at the heart of Winthrop's definition of civil liberty" (pp. 246, 253).

20. Kerber, *Women of the Republic*, p. 12.

21. One might speculate here on the gender shift for the American icon. In the late eighteenth and early nineteenth centuries, America-Columbia-Liberty is almost universally female, especially before and after the war. During the Revolution, however, the Indian icon, a standard emblem for America, is represented more as male than before the war. As Olson (*Emblems of American Community*, p. 15) notes, this may reflect the connection of aggression and masculinity that wartime elicits. In the late nineteenth and early twentieth centuries, the female emblem coexists with Uncle Sam. By the mid-twentieth-century, it appears that Uncle Sam has won the day. Is it a victory for patriarchy? Or is it that the vulnerability expressed through the often weeping or ravished or exposed woman grows increasingly discomforting to a nation that identifies itself in more aggressive, imperial ways in geopolitics?

22. Even Cathy Davidson ("Hannah Webster Foster," p. 162) remarks that *The Boarding School* "is didactic and prosaic, lacking in art and ingenuity." I would argue that though the book is indeed didactic, it is far more subtle than Davidson and less sympathetic readers have suggested. For a recent reevaluation of *The Boarding School* that puts Foster's novel in the context of friendship among women, see Claire C. Pettingill, "Sisterhood in a Separate Sphere: Female Friendship in Hannah Webster Foster's *The Coquette* and *The Boarding School*," *Early American Literature* 27 (1992): 185–203.

23. Frank Shuffelton, "Mrs. Foster's *Coquette* and the Decline of the Brotherly Watch," *Studies in Eighteenth-Century Literature* 16 (1986): 211–24, sees Foster's novels as expressing the problem of a culture that has decriminalized sin and left the virtuous exposed without the protection of the "brotherly watch." For women, that is replaced, as in *The Boarding School*, with a "sorority of affection and care" (p. 222).

24. For a discussion of *theatrum mundi* metaphors in early American writing, see Jeffrey H. Richards, *Theater Enough: American Culture and the Metaphor of the World Stage, 1607–1789* (Durham, N.C.: Duke University Press, 1991).

25. On Eliza's anguish over her mother's pain — not anger — see Fliegelman, *Prodigals and Pilgrims*, pp. 262–63. However, there is no warrant for claiming, as Fliegelman does, that Eliza commits suicide (p. 263). The historical Whitman died of puerperal fever (Davidson, Introduction to *The Coquette*, p. viii).

26. Shirley Samuels, "The Family, the State, and the Novel in the Early Republic," *American Quarterly* 38 (1986): 384. For an expanded version of this essay, see Samuels, *Romances of the Republic: Women, the Family, and Violence in the Literature of the Early American Nation* (New York: Oxford University Press, 1996), pp. 3–22.

The Museum in/as Performance

Raids and Reifications

Performance at Hull-House

Museum, Microfiche, and Historiography

SHANNON JACKSON

Indeed, we shall find little in this room to declare to us the general object of the museum, which is to throw the light of history and of art upon modern industries. The historical object it has in common with all museums; the artistic object it possesses in common with all arts and crafts workshops; but the combination of the two ideals, and the concrete expression of them in the midst of a foreign population largely wrenched away from its hereditary occupations, is peculiar to Hull-House.
Marion Foster Washburne on the Hull-House Labor Museum, 1904

Who hung this up? Does anyone know what this is doing here?
Hull-House Museum tour guide encountering a new display, 1993

History, writes Michel de Certeau, "is the *product* of a *place*." In *The Writing of History*, de Certeau challenges historians to interrogate the institutionalized places, unquestioned practices, and constrained modes of writing that constitute what he calls "the historiographical operation." His critique incorporates contemporary understandings about the nature of representation that have dismantled the intellectual foundations on which many academic disciplines — anthropology, sociology, literary studies, and so forth — formulated their objects of knowledge and assumed their legitimacy. These ideas echo and extend those of metahistorians such as Michel Foucault, Michael Taussig, Hayden White, Joan Scott, and Dominick LaCapra who encourage more self-reflexivity in the historian's craft, questioning periodizations, narratives, categorizations, and acts of contextualization.[1] Many have also argued for a performative understanding of historical documents — how letters, autobiographies, speeches, legal documents, and essays are situated speech acts reflecting the contingencies of certain contexts and employing familiar tropes to reach specific audiences. By exploring history as an institution, however — from archival operations to collegial networks to the mundane materiality of so-called evidence — de Certeau pushes metahistorical interrogations.

This essay is largely my attempt to come to terms with the "placeness" of two history-telling venues — one, the turn-of-the-century Hull-House Labor Museum, and two, the set of archives, museums, and writing practices in which contemporary Hull-House researchers such as myself currently partici-pate. The first venue (which presented the history of labor) is thus a phenome-non of the past, its extant remains located in the second venue (which presents the history of Hull-House). Each incorporates a variety of written texts, im-ages, human beings, and objects in very different ways, demonstrating how particular media can change the meanings and rhetorical force of the histories they present. The double meaning (and double pronunciation) of the word "present" can be extended here to suggest that presentations of the past are simultaneously the exertions of a particular present, that is, of a particular place that preserves (keeps present), uses available material (what is present), and interprets (makes understandable, palatable and useful in the present). At the same time, these remaining representations assume a referent, that is, they presume to document an absent "presence." To make explicit the partiality of these presential mechanisms, this essay continually vacillates between my in-terpretations of lost performances and my encounters with their extant histor-ical signifiers. Throughout I try to understand the implications of de Certeau and other critics for theorizing past historiographical operations and for writ-ing with an awareness of the place from which I construct them.

But First, Some "History": Originary Fieldsite Number One

The Labor Museum described by Marion Foster Washburne in my epi-graph was one of hundreds of performance-based reform activities—includ-ing social clubs, pageants, citizenship classes, festivals, storytelling, theater—practiced at the Hull-House Settlement of Chicago, a symptom, reaction, haven, and self-styled antidote to what many have called one of the most vola-tile periods in American history. During what is now named the Progressive Era—the period spanning the end of the nineteenth century to the early twen-tieth century—immigration, industrialization, urbanization, and the chang-ing role of women placed the United States in a liminal zone aptly fitting Antonio Gramsci's description of transitional states: "The old is dying and the new cannot be born; in this interregnum there arises a great diversity of morbid symptoms." It was during this tumultuous period and in what they thought were the most "morbid" locations that white, upper-middle class, predominantly Anglo-Saxon settlement workers (or "residents" as they called themselves) set up house, seeking to ameliorate the social conditions of dis-placed immigrants, the exploited working class, and other "unfortunates." For young, educated women (and later men) who felt stifled by the traditional activities and privileges of a bourgeois existence, the settlement also offered a socially sanctioned outlet for their energies and, as its founder and Nobel Peace prize winner Jane Addams wrote, a way to fulfill their own urges "to learn of life from life itself." For many of these reformers—and for the liberal bourgeoisie who visited — the settlement was an education in morbidity, whether it was an exposure to the disease and garbage of the "slums," an introduction to the dehumanization of the factory system, or an encounter with immigrant cultural difference — a dense and unfamiliar diversity of language, habitual behavior, hygiene, and work pattern fueling the nationalist anxieties of hereditary Americans concerned with the racial purity of the United States.[2]

The Labor Museum was a particular response to these conditions. Confounded by the older members of her immigrant neighborhood who did not speak English, whose styles of dress and whose "primitive" forms of labor "are considered uncouth and un-American," Jane Addams wanted to find a way for them to communicate with reformers and with "the children and more ambitious young people [who] look down upon them and are too often ashamed of their parents." At the same time, she also condemned the monotonous, repetitive labor of factory workers who "are brought in contact with existing machinery quite as abruptly as if the present set of industrial implements had been newly created." Her solution to both of these dilemmas was to gather older immigrants of the neighborhood in one place to perform and to teach the skills in craftsmanship indigenous to their respective countries including metallurgy, woodworking, pottery, and textile manufacture. Using the display of these crafts, the museum would also teach the history of labor — from its primitive origins to industrialized machinery — to give factory workers a sense of their advanced place in a narrative of technological progress. Hull-House would provide tools and supplies, schedule classes and history lectures on the weekends, and employ older immigrants in the community as teacher-laborers. The initial outline of the program stated three goals:

1. Industrial processes themselves will be made more picturesque and be given content and charm.
2. People who are forced to remain in shops and factories . . . will have some idea of the material which they are handling, and it is hoped in time a consciousness of the social value of the work which they are performing.
3. The older people who are now at such a disadvantage because they lack certain superficial qualities which are too highly prized, will more easily attain the position in the community to which their previous life and training entitles them.[3]

Allowing Chicago's Nineteenth Ward neighbors to see their labor in its "historical continuity," to see themselves "in connection and co-operation with the 'whole'" would, it was hoped, both connect alienated workers to the industrial materials they encountered daily and place the crafts of older immigrants in a context that highlighted their significance. It would also form cross-class and cross-cultural links between these neighbors and the bourgeois reformers and Hull-House visitors who might too easily dismiss the contributions of immigrant others as well as the important function of working-class laborers.

Motivated also by the innovative educational theory of John Dewey, Addams demonstrated an interest in adapting performance forms for pedagogical use. She felt that the form of the museum — "the word is purposely used in preference to the word 'school' " — could retain some of the "fascinations of the 'show,' " that interest could be created around the unacknowledged practices of everyday life if they were framed appropriately. Furthermore, Addams maintained that the structures of the traditional classroom and the dullness of book learning could not always accommodate the interests and priorities of Hull-House neighbors: "the residents of a settlement should be able to utilize many facts and forces lying quite outside the range of books, should be able to seize affections and memories which are not available in schools for children or immature youth." By giving its curriculum the "charm of human form," the Labor Museum thus employed a pedagogy of embodied performance in lieu of written text. Young apprentices "learned by doing" from actual laboring performers whose lessons contained "affections and memories" as well as a list of how-tos. The Labor Museum thus channeled the human aspect of this exhibit, one that was capable of giving "concrete expression" to the history of labor, of "making the teaching dramatic," and of charismatically eliciting a visceral connection in participating students.[4] Later, Addams would note how, in the textile exhibit, "the whirl of the wheels recalls many a reminiscence and story of the old country, the telling of which makes a rural interlude in the busy town of life," illustrating the emotional force of the unplanned, less tangible aspects of this pedagogical space.[5]

Several other material factors were in place at Hull-House to motivate and to make possible what would become a well-publicized reform inspiration. In 1897 Hull-House had organized a large exhibition of neighborhood handicrafts, an event that led to the founding of the Chicago Arts and Crafts Society (CACS), whose first president, George Twose, was a Hull-House resident. By this time Twose was already teaching a class in woodworking. Additionally, the Field Museum of Chicago had recently donated a collection of lithographs depicting varieties of women's textile manufacture as well as samples of these textiles. Two factories in the neighborhood had also donated pieces of "obsolete" machinery to the settlement. These donations — objects available in the present for which Hull-House found a use — would become the material basis for the story the Labor Museum presented, a montage that would be arranged to pass as historical narrative. Before elaborating, however, I want to highlight the creation of a different kind of historical montage.

Second: Originary Fieldsite Number Two

The University of Illinois at Chicago is where I go these days to "make history."[6] One hundred years ago, the Hull-House settlement stood at the corner of Halsted and Polk, a site that now marks the University of Illinois parking lot and an entrance to the Dan Ryan Expressway. On the southwestern corner stand two restored buildings from the thirteen-building complex — the "original" Hull-House mansion and the Residents' Dining Hall — that contain the Jane Addams Hull-House Museum. The special collections room is one block away in the university library, the place to which the above cursory narrative is extremely indebted. It is in this room that remnants of Hull-House's past have been helpfully preserved, indexed, and microfiched — that is, made into the documents that historians call evidence:

> In history everything begins with the gesture of setting aside, of putting together, of transforming certain classified objects into "documents." This new cultural distribution is the first task. In reality it consists in producing such documents by dint of copying, transcribing, or photographing these objects, simultaneously changing their locus and their status. This gesture consists in "isolating" a body — as in physics — and "denaturing" things in order to turn them into parts which will fill the lacunae inside an a priori totality. It forms the "collection" of documents.[7]

Two points raised by this passage are especially significant for me. First is the circumspect materiality of historical documents — the grossly "natural" existence of yellowing paper, torn laundry lists, broken combs, and ripped clothing that, if it were not for the denaturing exertions of a larger historiographical apparatus, would seem wholly unremarkable. A second point concerns the construction of the "a priori totality" that presumably redeems these preserved objects, the comprehensive collection that requires a legitimating historical narrative. It is in the temptation to create order from chaos where a circular process of preservation and interpretation instantiates historial periods and discursive categories. Whether telling the story of labor technology or the story of Hull-House, it is here that beginnings, middles, and ends are made. Deciding to observe my own process of historiography — the dubious nature of historical objects and the suspect practices by which I systematize them — has made my historiographical operations feel somewhat tenuous. I find myself a little more hesitant, more than a little nervous, as I try to come to terms with the uncanniness of my enterprise. And, as Michael Taussig says in theorizing a larger social Nervous System (NS) and its effects on scholarly research, it can be "somewhat unsettling to be centered on something so fragile, so determinedly other, so nervous": "And whenever I try to resolve this nervousness through a little ritual or a little science I realize this can make the

NS even more nervous. Might not the whole point of the NS be its always being a jump ahead, tempting us through its very nervousness towards the tranquil pleasures of its fictive harmony, the glories of its system, thereby all the more securely energizing its nervousness? . . . Hence the sardonic wisdom of the Nervous System's scrawling incompleteness, its constant need for a fix."[8] For the historian, it is the fragile nature of the so-called past that paradoxically frustrates social analysis even as it offers itself up for contemplation. The dubious status of this absent presence simultaneously invites and defers the systematic solidity of a referential statement. As I contemplate the contingencies of the historical Nervous System, I begin to wonder whether the nervous gap between historical signifiers and their signifieds, one occasionally and cautiously filled by my researcher's desire for a "fictive harmony," will withstand a metahistorical critique.

Twinges of this nervousness arise when I use the archival index to the *Jane Addams Memorial Collection*. There, the Labor Museum — along with hundreds of clubs and organizations — receives its own entry. By requesting the appropriate microfiche reel, I had access to much of the quoted passages on the goals and significance of the Labor Museum, prose that I attributed to Jane Addams. In truth, the author is circumspect. The original 1900 outline of the Labor Museum was an unsigned, typed, error-ridden document, its sentences lifted and corrected to appear in a 1901 publication called "The Labor Museum: First Report," which did list "Miss Addams" as author. However, the same prose appeared in quotation marks again in a 1904 article on the Labor Museum, this time printed as direct discourse attributed to "Miss Luther" — another Hull-House resident who volunteered as the museum's curator at the time. My quandary about the originator of these oft-reproduced words exemplifies a larger problematic as I try to write the Labor Museum's history and routinely catch myself searching for origins. When did the Labor Museum begin? I find myself asking. In her classic book, *Twenty Years at Hull-House*, Jane Addams suggests that it began on a walk down Polk Street in an Italian neighborhood where "I saw an old Italian woman, her distaff against her homesick face, patiently spinning a thread by the simple stick spindle so reminiscent of all southern Europe," whereupon the idea for the Labor Museum seized her.[9] But investigation of the documents of the Arts and Crafts Society (a different entry) suggests that this organization must have inspired the founding of the Labor Museum, an influence that leaks through the category separation of this archival collection. Meanwhile, the Hull-House inventories (a different reel) records the philanthropic donations that were waiting to be used months before their "locus and status" were changed into the component parts of the Labor Museum's "a priori totality," the "historical continuity" and vision of "the whole" central to its pedagogy. Together, a heterogenous account of precedents, needs, random material objects, and individual inspiration illustrate the fallaciousness of my impulse to find the beginning of the Labor Museum's story, the origin narrative that gives my historian's Nervous System a welcome fix. Meanwhile, the ease with which I earlier turned to the figure of Jane Addams to create a satisfying narrative replicates another impulse often practiced in Hull-House historiography — one exemplified in the museum's guided tours and by the names given to the Jane Addams Hull-House Museum and the Jane Addams Memorial Collection: the tendency to attribute to a single famous individual the efforts of hundreds of Hull-House reformers. This is encouraged especially when historiographical sites present origin-al source material as if their modes of presentation did not entail human intervention. Whether filling a celebratory history of Jane Addams or incarnating the history of textile manufacture, archivists and curators preserve material to tell the stories that in turn influence how and what material will be preserved. Together they fuel a kind of interpretive inertia.

This interpretive inertia can be tempting to a researcher trying to place Hull-House in context, for the a priori totality embedded in the indexes and origin narratives of Hull-House historiography would seem to have completed much of her work. It is when I acknowledge the contingencies of my present-ation of the Labor Museum, however, that I am reminded of the uneasy politics so easily reproduced in these acts of contextualization. Taussig helpfully amplifies the means by which social analysts surround objects of inquiry with information that encourages certain interpretations and discourages others: "[F]or a long time now the notion of contextualization has been mystified, turned into some sort of talisman such that by 'contextualizing' social relationships and history, as the common appeal would have it, significant mastery over society and history is guaranteed — as if our understandings of social relations and history, understandings which constitute the fabric of such context, were not themselves fragile intellectual constructs posing as robust realities obvious to our contextualizing gaze." Instead, he maintains "that first and foremost the procedure of contextualizing should be one that very consciously admits of our presence, our scrutinizing gaze, our social relationships and our enormously confused understandings of history and what is meant by history."[10] In addition to acknowledging the unremarkable materials from which I glean historical evidence and the metaphors of causality to which I succumb to make sense of them, this means admitting to my own presence. As a performance historian, my research also entails the carcinogenic smell of ink toxin and the waning endurance of fingertips as they grip number-two pencils, while stunned eyes remain propped open before the blue light of a projector and hunger pangs tempt me to stop research for another day. While the head archivist dismisses the "irrelevant" things I xerox, I find myself alternately bewildered, frustrated, and amused as I try to "restore behavior"—to theorize relationships and communities, to model embodied performances—from inside a fluorescent-lit, linoleum-floored room, filled with files, indexes, and microfiche reels.[11] These remnants of the past feel more like fetish objects facilitating a scholar's ritual conversation with the dead: I use newspaper clippings instead of hair cuttings, xeroxed diaries instead of totems. My sense that the stuff from which historical data are gleaned has an absurdly mystical function rather than a solidly empirical one in turn provokes an uncomfortable feeling that the historiographical operation is less like fact accumulation and more like ghost-busting. Periodically, I retreat to decompress at the nearby Hull-House Museum, to indulge a nostalgic romance with the settlement's past, for there, as I will discuss later in this essay, the gaps between historical signifiers and their signifieds feel less wide. At other times I simply return to my Evanston apartment, where hunger pains are (happily) more easily satiated. Laying bare mechanisms of contextualization means being aware of interpretive predispositions, motivated as they are by nerves and emotion as well as by contemporary intellectual constructs. It also means subjecting oneself and one's work to what Michael Taussig calls "montage—the juxtaposition of dissimilars such that old habits of mind can be jolted into new perceptions of the obvious." As Taussig argues, "in fact we have been surreptitiously practising montage all along in our historical and anthropological practices, but so deeply immersed have we been in tying one link in a chain to the next, creating as with rosary beads a religion of cause and effect bound to narrative ordering of reality, that we never saw what we were doing, so spellbound were we by our narrativizing."[12]

More Categories and Contexts

Because Hull-House's reform endeavors attempted to facilitate cross-cultural awareness and communication, its museum historiography—whether in the Labor Museum or in the contemporary Hull-House Museum—always mediates issues of cultural diversity. Thus, the histories depicted in the Labor Museum and the Hull-House Museum simultaneously construct and contextualize the ethnic heterogeneity of the Nineteenth Ward. Whether in the former's representation of past labor practices or in the latter's representation of past communities, these curatorial acts demonstrate the collusion of ethnographic and historical frameworks. Barbara Kirshenblatt-Gimblett extends Taussig's insights about the politics of contextualization to the specifics of museum exhibition: "In-context approaches exert strong cognitive control over the objects, asserting the power of classification and arrangement to order large numbers of artifacts from diverse cultural and historical settings and to position them in relation to one another."[13] In this case, the classificatory schemas created around the turn of the century at Hull-House impinge in contradictory ways on those presented at the Hull-House Museum of the late twentieth century. Both deploy acts of montage that pass as historical and ethnographic knowledge.

Several ideological factors were in place to motivate and legitimate the inspiration of the Labor Museum, an account of which yields a social analysis — or a montage — whose juxtapositions offer new angles and revelations about the Labor Museum's cultural politics. The "place" of the Labor Museum's history telling incorporated the nationalist, industrial, and evolutionist ideologies circulating in the "present" of progressive reformers. Furthermore, although the formal apparatus of the Labor Museum distanced it from the classroom environment, it also imported a problematic legacy of exhibition and curatorial operation that offered a structural container for these ambivalent ideologies. The Labor Museum's displays gave importance and status to everyday labor practices. It sought to create an arena of more equitable and democratic social interaction, but Hull-House's bourgeois residents were still the curators who created and contextualized this arena of public communication.[14] And acts of contextualization — whether in the montage effects of museum exhibition or historical writing — are inseparably linked to questions of politics and partiality. Specifically, the Labor Museum's idealization of primitive labor practice and respect for cultural difference found legitimation in the arts and crafts movement. Its espoused beliefs were channeled to respond neatly to Hull-House's more inclusive cultural mission and to fit the interpretive requirements of museum exhibition. In the United States, middle-class followers of William Morris and John Ruskin used theories of the Craftsman's Ideal to distance themselves from the ravages of industrialization. Whether to motivate a different ideal of employment or to inspire new home decoration ideas, the image of the preindustrial artisan and his idealized relationship with nature was nostalgically invoked to unalienate the factory laborer and, more often, to reconnect the bored bourgeoisie to "life itself." Eileen Boris summarizes the movement's unique brand of "imperialist nostalgia": "The idealistic, uplifting, optimistic yet paternalistic spirit of the movement reflects the class that turned to arts and crafts as solution to and escape from the industrial world it did so much to forge. Functional and romantic, modern and traditional, individualistic and communal, nationalist and universal — the arts and crafts movement contained contradictory tendencies."[15]

But it was precisely these contradictory tendencies that made the Craftsman's Ideal so useful in containing and narrating Progressive ambivalence. It provided a way for many to address industrialization while ignoring a larger political economy, to mourn its ravages while still relying on its financial benefits. Linking the figure of the craftsman to the "preindustrial" parts of the world from which many American immigrants came, the museum could thus create an unthreatening evolutionary link between the lives of Progressive hereditary Americans and their cultural others. Understanding difference was synonymous with understanding one's past, one's connection to the natural world, and one's origins in the human race. Thus, in an unself-conscious combination of historical and ethnographic frameworks, extant "peasant crafts" were interpreted as "early" episodes of a long human tradition. Certainly, Hull-House's own historical and ethnographic representations distinguished it from other, less inclusive definitional arenas, such as the cultural performances of the Mount Vernon Ladies Association or of Henry Ford's "Melting Pot" which acted as pep rallies for immigrant restriction or homogenization. Nevertheless, the rhetoric of both arts and crafts philosophies and of Hull-House's tolerance for diversity still set extremely ambivalent terms, interpretations that maintained the supremacy of a certain class while simultaneously integrating cultural others into its community. Moreover, the Progressive discourse of immigrant contributions emphasized the benefits of only some "native traditions" and celebrated certain "immigrant gifts" in a way that dictated the terms of their inclusion. Unlike foreign languages, non-Christian religions, or unhygenic domestic practices, arts and crafts were safe national contributions that spiced the American way of life without dangerously threatening the idealized dream of a clean, ordered, yet diverse America, a dream that Progressives felt they needed to fuel if immigrants were to be integrated.

If a cautiously inclusive definition of American identity undergirded the cultural representations of the Labor Museum, Hull-House curators needed to create the vision of that diversity, to categorize a heterogeneous population and specify the contribution of each culture in its own version of a pluralist wheel.[16] In the act of preserving certain practices, therefore, they simultaneously constructed them along unproblematized divisions of ethnicity. From a confused array of donated art and equipment, from the population of a neighborhood roughly divided by cultural groups that did not always reflect distinct national identities, Hull-House gleaned cultural representatives. The practices of individual agents were interpreted as metonymic embodiments of larger national cultures. Thus, the spinning of a neighborhood woman named Mrs. Brosnahan came to stand for "Irish spinning." Mrs. Molinari's labor stood for "Italian spinning" despite the fact that, at this time, so-called Italians identified with their respective provinces more than with the nation of Italy. In the desire to frame these activities within a grand image of a "gallery of nations," any sense of individual creativity was erased under the larger narrative of national typicality. The inscriptions represented how "[i]n the Western understanding of things, a work originating outside of the Great Traditions must have been produced by an unnamed figure who represents his community and whose craftsmanship respects the dictates of its age-old traditions" even if that meant constructing these works as "age-old" and as part of a "tradition."[17] Furthermore, the divisions between ethnicities drew from earlier labels created by Hull-House reformers in their 1895 collection of articles, maps, and statistics entitled *Hull-House Maps and Papers*. There, they distinguished "groups forming different elements in social and industrial life without confusing the mind by a separate recognition of the people of every country."[18] By this time the American industrial order had created its own discriminations, and it was this system of ethnic categorization that Hull-House replicated. In the process, originary national communities were invented. Not only did a Neapolitan woman's labor come to stand for "Italian," but the image of a spinning Polish girl named Hilda Satt Polacheck—whose family emigrated to the United States to escape Russian invasions—ironically was titled "Russian Spinning." Cultural divisions, like history, are the products of a place.

The selection and values implicit in the construction of the Labor Museum's contextualizations exerted even greater cognitive control when Hull-House's unique gallery of nations also underwent a hierarchical organization. Propelled by the pervasive impact of Darwinist theories of evolution, the latent prejudices embedded in reform ethnography became most explicit when Hull-House curators used the categories of their collection to create an evolutionary history of labor.[19] In the textile room, the museum charted the "evolution" of spinning, one that drew, despite well-intentioned critiques of industrialism, on culturally situated interpretations of history, progress, and technology. Craft techniques from geographically disparate cultures were assembled in one space and positioned along a single time line. Each marked a different point along a linear narrative of progress, a narrative that culminated in the machines developed and utilized in American industry. "Some of the old women still use the primitive form of the distaff," wrote Addams in her initial outline of the Labor Museum. "It will be possible to illustrate the history of textile manufacture, to reveal the long human effort which it represents, to put into sequence and historic order the skill which the Italian colony contains, but which is now lost or despised." Addams welcomed the fact that some women "still" used certain "primitive" methods, for it would allow the Labor Museum to give an embodied representation of a "historic order," that fictive totality created from within the Progressive Era's social Nervous System. Thus, practitioners of extant craft techniques drawn from a geographically diverse pool found themselves unified by the temporal framework of Progressive ideology, the objects of a well-intentioned chronopolitics.[20]

A description of the demonstrations and lectures that accompanied the history of spinning illustrates how enthusiastically Hull-House residents worked to interpret labor practices using an evolutionary model. In this performance, recounted in the Labor Museum's "First Report," a lecturer offered a historical perspective while members of different cultural groups — Navajo, Syrian, Russian, Irish, and so forth — were presented as examples of different time periods: "Even the casual visitor was able to see that there is no break in the orderly evolution from spinning of the Navajo woman with her one disc stick, trailing on the ground like a top, to the most complicated machine, and the lecturer on industrial history needed scarcely to state that history looked at from the industrial standpoint at once becomes cosmopolitan, and the differences of race and nationality inevitably fall away."[21] Thus, the craftsmanship of the Navajo woman was placed at the origin of an evolutionary model; her work in the present was emblematic of the American worker's past. Even more significant is the appeal the writer made to performance as a means of communicating the lesson. In saying that the lecturer "need scarcely to state" the history of spinning because the embodied representation of it was so clear, the writer indicated that performance grounded the lecture; it "real-ized" the history. In placing each woman and her craft in sequence, the incontestable reality of the enactment re-presented a curatorial idea. The moment demonstrates how the immediacy of performance can be co-opted to realize a constructed, ideologically situated historical frame. The impression of unmediated encounter reified a narrative performance mediated by ethnocentric interpretations of history and progress, reinscribing the superiority of the practice that concluded the story.[22] Although positing various labor practices as anticipating "modern" machinery gave those practices a significance they did not often enjoy, it still offered a somewhat prejudiced representation of the quotidian, a historical montage in which the Progressive American present repeatedly positioned itself as another culture's future.

It is, of course, from my location in yet another future — from my presence in the late twentieth century — that I have derived the preceding social analysis-*cum*-montage. My own temporal distance from the Progressive Era presumes to yield perspective on past ideological preoccupations — arts and crafts, immigration, Darwinist evolution — even as late-twentieth-century preoccupations bear on my historical accounting. Similarly, the Hull-House Museum of 1993 faces and defers a set of ideological and pragmatic contingencies in its reconciliation of past and present. The reworked legacy of the Labor Museum's ethnic constructions makes an appearance inside the restored Residents' Dining Hall in an exhibit called "Hull-House and the Neighborhood: Settlement, Investigation, Invention, and Advocacy." The installation attempts to represent in a single room the social and spatial complexity of an immigrant, urban milieu. The museum's representation of the neighborhood's diverse cultural identities draws, as did the Labor Museum, from *The Hull-House Maps and Papers*. An enlargement of the 1895 Hull-

House neighborhood map, a color-coded document, shows the ethnicity of the occupants of each neighborhood building — green for Irish, red for Russian, blue for Italian, yellow for Bohemian. As reformers ran out of colors, they resorted to striped patterns to represent smaller neighborhood national populations such as the Swiss, the French-Canadians, and the Dutch. Hereditary Americans were represented by the color white — a signifier used to denote the absence of ethnicity, the cultureless normalcy of the American. The color white also included all first-generation Americans and immigrant youths who spoke English and attended public school. It did not encompass black Americans born in the United States, however. Instead, they would find themselves cartographically marked in black for "Colored," simultaneously reflecting the internal instability of the white color category and the ambivalent citizenship status of African Americans in the late nineteenth century.

These tenuous boundaries on the Hull-House maps, in turn, threaten to unsettle their curatorial representation in the late twentieth century. The side walls of this contemporary museum are color coded to spatialize the map into three dimensions; newspaper excerpts, photos, and didactics representing selected ethnic experiences hang on green, red, yellow, and blue walls. There is no black wall, however. The near absurdity of the idea amplifies the significance of its absence, for, though there is no French-Canadian wall either, the inclusion of a black wall to match the proportionately large African American population in both past and present-day Chicago would only accentuate the volatile ambivalence of black racial identity, implicating rather than celebrating Hull-House's contribution to that history. Though the contemporary discourse of multiculturalism informs the rhetoric of the exhibit in green, red, yellow, and blue, though plenty of extant material dramatizes Hull-House's Greek festivals, German dances, and Italian parades, little comparable archival data exist to create a parallel story of cross-cultural harmony with African Americans in the last decade of the 1800s. Once again, ethnic and historical representations are simultaneously acts of invention, constrained and enabled by available ideological and material factors. In this case, a less-than-harmonious past cannot accommodate the more inclusive multiculturalist imaginings of the mid-1990s. And so, functioning as discourses of arts and crafts, American immigration, and evolution once did, past cultural identities emerge and disappear within the blind spots of shaky pluralisms and nervous imaginings.

What the Visitor Cannot See

It is probably somewhat misguided — perhaps reflecting my resilient desire for origins — to have used the word "legacy" above to describe the relationship between a past and present Hull-House Museum. Nevertheless, my personal reading of the latter is influenced by my investigation of the former. My so-called knowledge of the past acts as an enabling juxtaposition to my experience of the present, creating a productive montage effect that prompts me to ask different questions of an index or a contemporary exhibit, de-familiarizing historical pedagogies by foregrounding their construction. This dialogic relationship between past and present not only troubles the assumed distinction between them, but also suggests that their interaction is transverse rather than unidirectional. That is, whereas the selective filter of the present represents the past, the (no less selective) filter of the past mediates my understanding of the present. While I sort through the heterogeneous aspects of my visits to the museum, for instance, I am reminded of another traveler-researcher-ethnographer-historian who visited this "same" corner at Halsted and Polk nearly one hundred years ago. Marion Foster Washburne, whose words appeared in my epigraph, toured the Labor Museum and published an account of his experience, an article that was "set aside" to become available to me through the microfiche machine. Often the details and affections documented in his writing seem to surface, pentimentolike, in my tours through Hull-House's contemporary historiographical sites. Because the ghosts and legacies I have invented with his document have proved to be enabling fictions in my research, I want to explore this particular mediation between past and present.

Marion Foster Washburne was a journalist for *The Craftsman*, the publication of the U.S. arts and crafts movement with the widest circulation. Other articles on the Labor Museum had appeared earlier, but Washburne's 1904 essay is particularly significant for the way he self-consciously places his feelings, his thoughts, his own predispositions directly in the text. As a chronicle of his own experience and the experiences he witnessed, this article is thus a fascinatingly "partial" representation of settlement reform methods as well as of Progressive Era politics, goals, and anxieties.[23] Additionally, his use of language and narrative techniques can be excavated for "the content in their form."[24] For example, his extensive use of the first person plural to dramatize how "we came upon" the Labor Museum and how "we feel" about it re-creates the experience for an engaged reader, a gesture that is at once inclusive and coercive. His opening paragraph describes the scene for this reader before entering Hull-House:

> Steadfast amidst the clash of industrial warfare, true to the English tongue and the English better genius in the midst of a modern Babel, clean and wholesome on the edge of the Ghetto, serene among sweat-shops and saloons, in the very center of toiling Chicago, stands Hull-House. (p. 570)

Washburne's dramatization likens the settlement to a lone diamond in a pile of rubble, reproducing the image of the philanthropic institution as the single representative of civilization in a barbarous, urban world. Tropes of the Progressive Era's ethnographic imagination recur. Washburne likens the polyglossia of the immigrant neighborhood to the most feared mythological tale of linguistic anarchy. He will use battle, animal, and mechanical metaphors to describe urban life throughout this text. Smarter, cleaner, English-speaking reformers and journalists must make bold, adventurous journeys, braving the cityscape that Upton Sinclair made famous—a domestic version of an unknown dark continent. As he continues "through a long tunnel-like passage . . . filled with dynamos and the steam heating apparatus," Washburne is momentarily soothed by the presence of "two lithographs in cheerful gilt frames"—a sign of civilization. Before entering the museum, he notes "the light windows of the labor museum" and offers another description of an urban scene:

> [T]here a half-dozen street urchins were looking in. Swearing, twisting, pushing each other, using each other's backs and shoulders to obtain vantage-ground, clad in nondescript clothes, rough in manner, and of many nations, they looked in longingly from the cold alley where they lived upon these glorified workshops which promised pleasantness and peace. (p. 570)

Before Washburne takes his reader into the museum, he depicts the dramatic effect this social experiment seemed to be having on the denizens of the neighborhood. He describes the behavior, dress, ethnicity, and environment of this group of boys in a way that signals their "incorrigibility" to a reading audience of reformers. At the same time, he attributes to them a "longing" desire for "pleasantness and peace" to suggest their attraction to the signs of civilization and thus their latent potential to change—to be reformed.[25]

Of course, these boys might have been looking at something else—perhaps teasing a friend for going in rather than hoping for tranquility and solace from their depraved environment. But Washburne has placed the behavior of these boys on display within an interpretive frame that prevents alternative readings. Not surprisingly, his ideological frame determines what he observes, notes, and describes. Washburne's journalist eye contextualizes and situates based on his own understanding of what is unique and unfamiliar; an ethnographic gaze makes a "show" of the subject on which it lands, exemplifying Barbara Kirshenblatt-Gimblett's theory of how people and things are made into ethnographic objects: "The vitrine, as a way of looking, is brought to the site. A neighborhood, village, or region becomes for all intents and purposes a living museum in situ. The museum effect, rendering the quotidian spectacular, becomes ubiquitous."[26] Even after he enters the museum, Washburne continues to gaze in this way. As he describes a metal shop, "for a shop this room is in appearance, much more than a museum," he notes the "grim picturesqueness" and "general tone of brown." His description of battered, bent, and heavy machinery "spitting blue and yellow flames" anthropomorphizes unfamiliar technologies, creating a picture of a sentient industrial factory in miniature. When he exclaims once again that he "still [does] not see what it is that makes this a Museum. What is it more than a series of manual training shops?," he concludes that the spectatorial structure is all that indicates its status. "True," he writes, "the groups of onlookers mark a characteristic difference" (p. 572).

Washburne and my critique of his point of view remind me of my own excursions into Chicago, even to the urban campus of the University of Illinois. To leave my residence in Evanston for the near west side of Chicago is to substitute a suburban vista with an urban one, to exchange lawn-framed sidewalks for grass-cracked cement, to leave smooth asphalt streets arched by fifty-year-old elms to traverse pothole-ridden intersections with yellowed seedlings marking the efforts of a city beautification committee. To move from Northwestern University to the University of Illinois is to leave an enclaved private institution for a visibly public one, to encounter fingerprint-covered walls instead of spotless ones, to ride small elevators with peeling linoleum and broken bulbs in lieu of spacious elevators with vacuumed carpet and recessed lighting. Of course, the fact that I decide to notice and attribute meaning to the characteristics of my new study environment reflects the degree to which I have internalized another aesthetic, the extent to which my view of the world is filtered by a suburban semiotic. Paralleling Washburne's ambivalent attributions, my impulse to read "dingy" into an institution that another might see as "privileged" tells you more about my point of view than it does about the thing described. Because spectatorial structures and predispositions affect what an "onlooker" is able to perceive, a student habituated to the sights, sounds, and schedules of the University of Illinois — a participating insider rather than a detached outsider — would offer a different account.

Washburne begins to demonstrate a self-conscious awareness of the limitations of his point of view, however. As he walks through the museum, he happens upon a group of boys who are learning to make sleds. Washburne is at first critical of their skills and decides that the product of their labor, if it is finished, will be marginal at best. But he recognizes something else:

> The direct object of such training may not be obvious to the casual observer, for it is plain that the boys have not time in these few hours of work a week to master even the beginnings of good carpentry. What does take place is what the visitor cannot see, although he may afterwards experience it himself. It is a change of mental attitude. (p. 571)

Here Washburne acknowledges that his role as observer-visitor may not be fully capable of tracking and representing the experience of the Labor Museum for the people of the neighborhood. Because approaching the Labor

Museum as an embodied laborer or apprentice characterized the experience intended for its students, perhaps it was the boys' role as "participant" that gave them full access to its pedagogy. Since the Labor Museum's effect was to be visceral, intellectual, and emotional, channeling all levels of experience to ground education, perhaps Washburne's role as the casual "observer" distanced him from that knowledge. On the other hand, though spectatorial predispositions constrained his initial encounter, they did not fully neutralize his capacity to sense that the "object" of the Labor Museum may not be "visible," that its affective power lay in "what the visitor cannot see." As the article continues, Washburne's text precariously figures an authorial subjectivity trying to move beyond the superficial encounter of "the casual observer" so that he himself (as well as the reader) "may afterwards experience" the elusive effects of the Labor Museum.

As Washburne's outsider status prompted him to note the clothing, nationality, and manners of the boys outside the window, so this status still affects his perception of the laborers inside. Concentrating on what he can observe, indeed on what he was trained to observe, he focuses, at first, on degrees of cleanliness and physical deformity:

> Standing at the table is a clean old German kneading clay, his squat, bowed legs far apart, his body leaning forward, his long and powerful arms beating upon the clay like piston rods . . . one sees that he is bent and twisted by his trade, conformed to his wheel. Upon this he slaps his clay. (p. 574)

To Washburne, the German potter is an emblem of the physical laborer whose work and body are one, the joints and limbs of his body likened to the machinery around him. This individual is received as a kind of living ethnographic object precisely because his audience member — one of the "group of onlookers" — seems disposed to turn him into one. However, the movements of Washburne's description are more complicated. As he continues, he seems intent on defining the human being beyond these observable characteristics, or more accurately, of sensing the invisible through the visible:

> His hands open, his thumbs work in; one almost sees him think through his skillful thumbs and forefingers. Like some mystery of organic nature, the clay rises, bends, becomes a vase. . . . The old potter rises, lifts the vase in his mitten-like hands, and, bending, straddling sideways, his face unmoved, carries it tenderly to its place. (p. 574)

To Washburne's eye, this worker seems so intent on his manual craft that his intelligence has a corporeal residence, epitomizing the bourgeois projection of the Craftsman's Ideal and its nearly extinct unalienated laborer. At the same time, Washburne tries to "see" his thoughts, to locate an elusive sense of agency nearly imperceptible in a "face unmoved." The intense curiosity with which he notes the potter's expressionless face and "tender" comportment illustrates Washburne's only barely fulfilled hope to learn more of this German potter's subjectivity, his desires, his experiences, and his dispositions.

Meanwhile, as I scrutinize this text through the machine that has become the ubiquitous tool of the historian in the age of mechanical reproduction, I find myself identifying with Washburne's search. As a performance historian, I have been trained to question the logocentrism of extant evidence and to "see" beyond the surface of these representations. Attempting to negotiate the apparently non-negotiable spectatorial structures of print and of the microfiche machine, I then feel dependent on texts like Washburne's for what of the invisible or ephemeral nature of the Labor Museum — its elusive agents, its structures of affect, its unplanned performances — they can make accessible to me. Mine is perhaps the frustration of a performer/ethnographer accustomed to engaging in the experiential medium of a fieldsite or of live performance. Unfortunately, participant-observation — the "intense, intersubjective encounter" that many ethnographers use to ground their scholarship — is simply not an option for the historian.[27] However, mine is also the frustration of a researcher more firmly rooted in a metaphysics of presence than she would like to admit. I feel the strangeness of historical writing when reminded of the obvious and confounding fact that the Hull-House people, places, and practices about which I am writing are undeniably . . . not here. The "direct object" of my inquiry is quite simply not present. This phenomenological reminder is always at least a little unsettling. On the other hand, the conundrum of my absent fieldsite will only persist as long as I continue to imagine it in some nebulous past. For, as my earlier subtitle indicated, I do have a field, one that does not exist beyond the archives, but *is* the archives, its documents, its museumography, and its employees. Of course, caught as I am in the operation of a kind of historiographical "differance," these representations always seem inadequate. In fact, my longing to experience the past might well be an epiphenomenon of my encounters with these Hull-House mediators and thus another trick of a historical Nervous System. Negotiating past/present as absence/presence, historical representations posit an unmediated (now lost) presence. Thus, they carry with them "the destiny of their own non-satisfaction," an always-deferred promise of referentiality.[28] But Washburne's dilemma with the German potter forces an extra degree of humility and an important corrective to my perceptions of lack. For even if these once-living Hull-House residents and neighbors were still here, how could I be sure that they would tell me their secrets? And even if they were somehow "present," why do I think that they would have any secrets to tell?

Washburne responds to his own conundrum by beginning a new paragraph, one that redirects its curious gaze from an external to an internal focus on the author. For the first time, he uses the first-person singular and shares an internal monologue. In doing so, the text suggests that the Labor Museum's display of unfamiliar objects and humans was also a space in which visitors could begin a self-investigation:

> Looking at him, I wonder. My heart aches. My flower-pots at home made by such as he, gain a new significance. They are no longer mere receptacles for holding earth and guarding the roots of my plants. The rough, red surface of them is written all over with the records of human patience, human cooperation with nature, human hopes and fears. (p. 574)

Washburne's reaction seems to illustrate that the goals of the Labor Museum are being fulfilled. He comes to interpret the objects occupying his own life differently for having been introduced to the people and processes that created them. Not only have workers been reconnected with their own labor processes, but also a member of the bourgeoisie is "un-alienated" from his own material life. Other moments use a romanticized anti-industrialist rhetoric as Washburne invokes Ruskin and Morris who "recognize that the commercial custom of rating a laborer at what you can buy or rent him for is as low, as inadequate a measure of a human being as could well be devised." The shift in writing style and increasing degree of self-consciousness dramatizes what Kirshenblatt-Gimblett calls "the museum effect": "Bleeding into the ubiquity of the common-sense world, the museum effect brings distinctions between the exotic and the familiar closer to home. Calibrations of difference become finer. The objects differentiated draw nearer. One becomes increasingly exotic to oneself, as one imagines how others might view that which we consider normal."[29] The Labor Museum had seized Washburne's affections, evoking memories of his own life whose normalcy was de-familiarized by the museum effect. The image of the German potter juxtaposed with his own ceramic pots created a personal montage, forcing him to see the latter anew. Illustrating the transverse relationship between self and other, the text shows how the museum momentarily re-contextualized Washburne's personal life even as it simultaneously contextualized the exhibit for his reader.

Authenticity and a Historian's Nostalgia

Washburne's ceramic pots and my microfiche reels share a similarly ambivalent status, one that has a frustratingly confused effect on both of us. Each, we are disposed to believe, contains traces of a past context of production; the "surface of them is written all over with the records of human patience, human cooperation with nature, human hopes and fears." As researchers, both Washburne and I hope for the ability to discern this elusive record so as to touch somehow the lost past to which these objects refer. In both cases, the recognition and subsequent decoding of the record is simultaneously exhilarating and lacking, for the connection with the past they seem to offer is always thwarted by their failure to do so. The potter is not his fingerprints; Jane Addams is not her letter. These metonymic signifiers offer and withdraw the promise of connection, of communication. They encourage the desire to possess lost performances, the ephemeral, affective, and embodied aspects of the past that leave only partial traces of having been. It is this longing for what is lost that periodically takes me away from the library to visit and re-visit the Hull-House Museum, for there the material reality of museum exhibits suggests a closer connection to a represented past. There I can touch it, walk through it, sit down on its chair. Or so I like to imagine before I am reminded otherwise. Susan Stewart amplifies: "Nostalgia is a sadness without an object, a sadness which creates a longing that of necessity is inauthentic because it does not partake in lived experience. Rather, it remains behind and before that experience. Nostalgia, like any form of narrative, is always ideological: the past it seeks has never existed except as narrative, and hence, always absent, that past continually threatens to reproduce itself as a felt lack."[30] The act of preservation—whether in a museum or historical writing, whether by Washburne or by myself—is intimately bound up with anxieties about authenticity and temporality. It is always about loss in spite of possession.

Washburne continues through the Labor Museum, each room offering a new exhibit. The text vacillates between their description and the reaction each induces in "the visitor." As a space that represents an idealized past (whether of the craftsman's labor, of American society, or of the human race), Washburne's response is mixed with more than a small dose of nostalgia. Here he describes the cooking room, where Hull-House neighbors were taught nutritional science surrounded by the images, texts, and objects narrating the history of cooking:

> A low window seat to the right, and a big table before it, covered with a blue and white homespun cloth, make one wish that one could go back at once to the old colonial days, and make apple dowdy and mulled cider in this picture-booky place. (p. 575)

As the efficacy of nostalgia's narrative lies in what it erases from memory as much as in what it retains, the idealized and selective vision of "apple dowdy and mulled cider" substitutes for the "the colonial days," representing only that which induces longing in the visitor. Here, the charm attributed to the past by means of temporal distance paradoxically makes one long to partake of it, to see the gap between past and present collapse. But the charm may be partly induced by the presential consciousness elicited by this brand of exhibit.

Tangible items such as the "blue and white homespun cloth" suggest that the past is somehow accessible. This cloth *is* what it signifies. History is still here.

In the next moment, however, the materialized reality of this "picture-booky place" will be disrupted for Washburne as the gap between past and present, between referent and representation, reasserts itself:

> A dear little painted dresser stands next to the window seat, set out with old blue and white china; but an abrupt modern note is struck by the case of laboratory samples which hangs beside it. (p. 575)

Washburne's rhapsodies about the charms of the "old blue and white china" — a signal of the arts and crafts aesthetic — are stalled by the abrupt reminder of modernity, the place from which this history is produced. His next encounter with the arts and crafts dishware is even more disturbing:

> Here is a fine old carved side-board with more blue and white china on it — modern blue and white, alas! and not half so pretty as the old kind. (p. 575)

An object signifying the past but created in the present is a poor antidote for this peculiar form of historical anxiety. The effectiveness of these representations is proportionate with the degree that they hide the act of preservation and mask the fact of reproduction.

Washburne's nostalgic perception is triggered not only by the charm of objects such as the cloth and china, but also by the people of the Labor Museum who double as historical signifiers. As earlier discussed in relation to the Labor Museum's contextualizations, his spectatorship marks the intersection of ethnographic and historical methods of interpretation, exemplified as Washburne continues into other rooms and categorizes unwitting exhibits:

> Addams hopes sometime to have the living workers in the Museum dressed in their national and historic costume as they go about their work. This Italian woman, with big gold ear-rings swinging against her dark and scrawny neck, unconsciously carries out the idea. But the sweet-faced Irish woman near her, . . . her white Irish hands deftly twisting the thread, is altogether too respectable and modern to look her part. (p. 576)

To Hull-House students, "this Italian woman" was Mrs. Molinari; to Washburne, she was an anonymous representative of Italian culture whose outward appearance read "authentic." Washburne drew on a travelers' semiotics to judge the degrees to which these human exhibitions fit the categories to which they were assigned, the degree to which they "looked their part" in an impromptu pageant. His text also signals the rupture inherent in his own semiotics and in representational practices more generally when he refers to the Irish woman's "part" as national signifier. National identity is here somewhat ironically characterized as an assembly of external props, costumes, and facial expressions. Significantly, however, respectable and modern were adjectives used to describe the woman whose "white Irish hands" looked less ethnic, whose outer appearance did not adequately signify an "un-American" cultural background. The presumption that one is less civilized if one evokes the past makes his description somewhat ambivalent; a "dark and scrawny neck" mingles a degree of cultural anxiety into this idealized space. His reference to modernity reflects the ideology used to contextualize these women and their labor. Being labeled "modern" in this timeline meant the loss of ethnically identifiable characteristics, the "national and historic costume" that signified cultural and temporal difference to this ethnographer-historian. The Irish woman and the modern blue and white china are thus ambivalent figures — the attribution of their "modern" status simultaneously makes their authenticity questionable. Meanwhile, the Italian woman's status as authentic is secured through her imputed primitivity.

Next to the restored building housing the 1993 ethnic neighborhood exhibit stands the Hull-House mansion — a site simultaneously billed as original and restored; its interior is filled with pictures, props, and furniture of another era. Frayed children's books and preserved immigrant newspapers are strewn on an upholstered divan and coffee table as if spontaneously left by their readers. The effect of this sepia-toned vision of lived space is disrupted, however, by "the abrupt modern note" of stark white pieces of paper whose typed black lettering contextualizes these remnants of the past: "Russian Newspaper, circa 1909." "Children met here for Jenny Dowd's Kindergarten class, 1893–1903." Across the hall, a writing desk holds a pen poised over a pile of papers inscribed in Jane Addams's indecipherable penmanship, a hand familiar to me after hours of squinting at microfiched copies of her letters. I respond to the documents on the desk with fetishistic fascination — Did she touch these? I ask myself. The incontestable reality of this materialized exhibit lends a feeling of authenticity to the history it narrates. For a moment I imagine that I have come upon a piece of the past, a piece of Jane Addams, before realizing that — alas! — the papers are themselves microfiche copies. The fickle promise of authenticity extends and retracts itself continually as I pass a fireplace, a bulletin board, a photograph. The same strange feeling occurs when I try to forget the slide show that depicted how extensively the original mansion was torn down before it was "restored," when I try to ignore the cash register and items for sale at the foot of the staircase, or when I try to pretend that I am not standing on the linoleum floor of an addition created to accommodate the administrative and lavatory needs of museum exhibition.

In the middle of his tour, Washburne's confrontation with the paradoxes of museum representation undergoes a new twist when he finds an object whose relation to a historical referent is not simply questionable, but nonexistent:

> Lacking in both bones and wood is this awkward, monstrous creature, made of brown basketry. . . . We are relieved to learn that it is here because a Scandanavian friend of the House made it as a masquerade costume for his son. At any rate, the figure crouches beside the window, an anomaly humped and hideous, a plain warning against things which are merely curious and ingenious. (p. 577)

Had this been contextualized with misleading didactics and donated pictures, perhaps Washburne would have seen a significance anyway. By letting him in on the joke, the Labor Museum's workers saved him from mistaking a "curious" object for a historiographically meaningful one, from being duped into creating an outsider's interpretation of what was actually an inside joke. The moment reminds me of another one I overheard nearly one hundred years later while a museum employee was initiating a new tour guide in the practice of contextualization, an encounter that ironically reframes my anxieties about authenticity and historical narration. The two stood before an array of uncontextualized objects awaiting de-mystification. It was the material culture display. Objects such as a spinning wheel and a sewing machine were familiar to me. And I quietly took pride in being able to recognize a cigar maker. The ensemble of wood and metal that looked like an unfinished oversized umbrella or a ("humped and hideous") deformed ostrich stumped me, however, much as the unfamiliar machinery confounded Washburne:

"This is a drying rack," said the touring guide who helpfully extrapolated. "They would do other people's laundry at home and then hang it out to dry on these spindles."

Nearby was an enormous washtub with a mechanized apparatus of some sort in the center. "And this?" asked the initiate. "This is nice."

"Oh. They wouldn't have had it in their homes at this time, though."

"Really?"

"Yeah, that's a washtub of a later period and would have been too expensive," she laughed, "We saw it and got it for a good deal."

The initiate nodded and pondered the anomalous purchase in a confused silence, perhaps wondering what she was going to be able to say about it on future tours. Whether or not future bright-eyed museum visitors receive the washtub as an accurate material signifier of the past will depend on whether the initiate ignores or incorporates this piece of unfortunate information. Whether she decides to create the satisfying (if "inaccurate") narrative this dubious washtub invites, or whether she (like the Labor Museum guides before her) decides to reveal the masquerade to her visitors, "history" precariously rides on the whims and imagination of a tour guide. Her acts of contextualization may or may not redeem an object that (like an earlier monstrous creature) serves as "a warning" to museum curators against things that are "merely curious and ingenious." At the Labor Museum and at the Hull-House Museum, unremarkable objects such as these tubs, racks, and brown basketry can be made remarkable. The denaturing process of historical narrative tenuously invents or erases historiographical significance.

The ensuing awkward silence in the Hull-House Museum was broken when an assistant curator joined the tour guide and the initiate. As they searched for ways to contextualize more objects, the three continued to tread along the fragile cordons of a historical Nervous System. They came to a pair of boots:

"So, here is a pair of boots," said the assistant curator. Slight pause. "Hmmm, Cathy, what do you usually say about this pair of boots?"

"Well," the other cautiously responded, "I usually say something about how boots from back then are really similar to boots now."

"Mmmm, yes," the other two nodded in unison.

Performative Disruptions: Accidents and Interludes

Washburne's "monstrous creature" and the tour guide's washtub also testify to the impromptu aspects of these spaces, a performative flexibility within the museum frame that laborers, curators, students, guides, and friends can appropriate for their own use, innovation, and "masquerade." Washburne inadvertently documents more performative dislocations enacted at the Labor Museum when he recounts his conversations with two Irish women. Although his quotations and descriptions of the two women are suspect in terms of their historical "authenticity" and suggest a great deal about his use of them to figure his own authorial subjectivity, it is useful to try to theorize the encounter through its problematic representation. In the absence of "the voices of the women themselves," such a document might be excavated for what it suggests about the agency of these "humans-turned-exhibit" as mediated through Washburne's own self-representation. He quotes the first woman, Mrs. Sweeney, who was actually the museum's cleaning lady, replicating the phrases and lilts of an Irish speech pattern:

> Mrs. Sweeney, a neighborhood woman, employed in keeping the museum clean, rolls her bare arms in her little red shoulder shawl and examines the pictures with me. "This is an Irish lady spinnin, anyhow," she explains, pointing with a soaked forefinger. "Shure, I'd know her, big or little, in all the world." Perhaps she overlooks a little the Kentucky spinners, whose picture hangs next, and disregards their blue and white quilt, which makes a

background for the pictures; but, at least, she has seen the work of her own people under a new aspect: that is, with some historical perspective. (p. 577)

Once again, Washburne's ambivalent tracking system determines what he textually highlights; an eye conditioned in bourgeois propriety receives Mrs. Sweeney's "bare," "soaked" flesh as unusual and noteworthy. On the other hand, it shows Mrs. Sweeney deciding to conduct her own efforts at contextualization. The Labor Museum is not a social space where she feels silenced by her role as domestic servant and relegated to an unseen backstage. Unlike Washburne, she probably is not examining the pictures for the first time but is taking the opportunity to highlight what she feels is significant about the Labor Museum's pedagogy. Her selection is motivated by the cultural familiarity of the "Irish lady spinnin." Using the image as an object of identification, Mrs. Sweeney asserts her own place in a national community, one whose members share a cultural history and experience. Of all the other lithographs on the wall, it seems that Mrs. Sweeney underscores only this one. Washburne notices explicitly that she bypasses the American image of the Kentucky spinners but recuperates Mrs. Sweeney by suggesting that she has been influenced by the museum's efforts at contextualization — at least she has seen her people "with some historical perspective." But did she really? It seems, instead, that Mrs. Sweeney decided to ignore the historical perspective she was offered, one that placed the labor practices of the Kentucky spinner after her own in an evolutionary narrative. By "overlooking" some pictures, by "disregarding" certain material objects, Mrs. Sweeney conducted something like a resistant — or at least selective — reading of the Labor Museum's textual and imagistic didactics. As a cultural receiver, her interest in this educational performance may have had little to do with its interpretation of "the whole." The moment suggests that, although dominant pedagogies are prevalent, its signifiers are not necessarily stable. An individual agent can disrupt claims of temporal inevitability to offer a new context in which to interpret the representations of her ethnicity.

Washburne does not name the second woman with whom he speaks. But, having researched other inventories and memoirs, I suspect that it is probably Mrs. Brosnahan. For several years, she functioned as one of the spinner-demonstrators and thus also as the display's object. By speaking, however, and participating in her own self-contextualization, she is also the subject of display. After using free-indirect discourse to report that "she herself" knows the entire process of linen making from sowing flax seed to dyeing the fabric, he quotes her directly. The decision to include such a long direct quotation suggests the impact of this encounter on him, one the text attempts to reproduce for the reader by displacing Washburne's own authorial voice:

"But, shure, dear," she exclaims, "it is not your chemical dyeing at all, but the home-dyeing, that I know. We made the dyes ourselves from log-wood, and barks, and stuff we took out of the bogs of old Ireland. But one thing I will say for it: it never faded as your high-toned dyes do." (p. 579)

Mrs. Brosnahan vacillates between the first and second person pronoun to represent her labor processes, a discursive practice that delineates her own boundaries between self and other, or between an Irish "we" and an American "you." Not unlike Mrs. Sweeney, Mrs. Brosnahan places herself within a circle of cultural affiliation to underscore the significance of past practices. In the process, the quotidian realities of daily life are held up as emblems of a delineated national culture.

Furthermore, the fact that Washburne's text began directly quoting here might suggest something of a shift in how her personal narrative was performed. After articulating the various stages in the process of linen making, did she particularly emphasize this statement? If she had been intently focused on her spinning, did she stop so that her eyes could meet Washburne's at this point in her discourse? Was it meant to be an interpretive aside that recontextualized all that had come before? Jane Addams's writings on the Labor Museum suggest that she counted on women's oral narratives in this performance space. As earlier quoted, she was glad that "the whirl of the wheels" spurred "many a reminiscence and story of the old country." Here Mrs. Brosnahan deployed the mode of personal narrative — "the rural interlude in the busy town life" that charmed Jane Addams — to distinguish her history. Although a Progressive hereditary American such as Washburne might nostalgically reinterpret her statement as the loss of the Craftsman's Ideal, it also provided a space for a certain kind of self-definitional performance — one that was to become increasingly pointed and politicized:

Presently she tells her story:
"Yes, we all spun and wove in the old country . . ."
"And how did you happen to come here?" I asked.
Her serene face darkens. "Never will I forgive them that misled us to it!" she exclaims. "There in the old country we had our comforts, our own bit of land, my man making a dollar and a quarter the day, Irish money; a blissid union of ten children and never a shoe wanting to the foot of one of them. O, wirra the day that we left! I landed here with a baby in my arms — crippled — "
"Crippled? how?" I cried.
She passed the question. "Yes, crippled. She is a hump-back, dear, eleven by now, and none higher than my waist. The next to the baby had the spinal meningeetis soon after we landed and his reason fled." (p. 579)

Mrs. Brosnahan's story was far from the uncritical tale of a benevolent United States welcoming "the poor," "the tired," and "the hungry." In a move that was itself simultaneously nostalgic and resistant, she elegized lost national origins while defining herself against the idealizations of a Progressive American ideology. As she continued, she told also of how her husband "took to the drink" in response to the sorry situation they faced. This story exceeded the conventions of the "rural interlude" Addams described picturesquely circulating around the Labor Museum. Instead, the narrative heightened the political and economic realities of an immigrant American, circumstances the museum often displaced by a romanticized emphasis on cultural production. Mrs. Brosnahan thus told a different history from the one forwarded in the lithographs, glass casements, and textiles that surrounded her, using her capacity as performative signifier to push those narratives into the background. At the same time, she negotiated this new role on her own terms, evading the questions of a journalist now fascinated anew by her extra self-disclosure. Washburne would leave the museum troubled not to have known the cause of the crippled child's "mysterious" injury, another of the Labor Museum's invisible secrets. As her encounter with Washburne concludes, this Irish woman hints of the difference between her life experiences and her Labor Museum persona. It is to the latter that she eventually returns:

"And what did you do?" I asked.
"I begged on the streets, dear. Oh, I can smile and laugh with the best when I am at work here, but there's something else in my heart." She turned to a young lady pupil, whom she was teaching to spin, unreeled the broken thread, mended, and set it right with a skillful touch or two. "No I ain't discouraged," she told the young lady, in her soft, smooth voice, "for discouraging won't do for a pupil. You'll spin, dear, but it'll take a deal o'practice." A minute more and she and Mrs. Sweeney are speaking the Gaelic together, and laughing like two children. She dances a quiet shuffle under her decent skirts. "And can I dance?" she asks. "It is a good old Irish breakdown dancer I was in my young days. You should see me do a reel and a jig." Her hidden feet nimbly shuffle and whisper on the wooden floor. (p. 579)

In this passage, Mrs. Brosnahan's movements, focus, and action change rapidly. At the moment that she comes closest to sharing her deepest emotions—the "something else in my heart," she quickly turns away to her pupil instead, suggesting that her role as teacher of labor practices (combined with the presence of a stranger) discouraged too lengthy an indulgence in this sort of personal narrative. The next spoken words Washburne reports have the quality of double entendre: "No I ain't discouraged." Are they said to Washburne about life in America or to her student about her spinning prospects? "A minute more" and Mrs. Brosnahan has engaged a third interlocutor, Mrs. Sweeney, in "the Gaelic." Washburne seems charmed as "they laugh like two children," interpreting their conversation as another idyllically ethnic practice. Though he safely interprets them within a harmonizing ideological frame — as unthreatening "immigrant gifts" that spiced the American way of life and delighted the adventurer-journalist, his text also suggests the improvised creation of an oppositional linguistic space from which he is excluded. Their code switching masked their conversation and so, ultimately, the secret joke they shared. The laughter seems to have been fleeting, however. If non-English speaking had become too extensive and stories about the trials of immigrant life too long, the Labor Museum's idealized portrait might have been threatened. But fortunately, Mrs. Brosnahan concluded the visit by readdressing Washburne and offering an Irish jig — another "native tradition" that, like arts and crafts, could be celebrated as an unthreatening immigrant "contribution." Whether this dance too had a "hidden transcript" beneath its display on Hull-House's Progressive public stage, whether Mrs. Brosnahan used an open admission of self-display to parody the ideology of cultural harmony she was supposed to signify, also remains hidden from Washburne (and from his historian).[31] Meanwhile, I also keep wondering at what — or at whom — the two women were laughing. Perhaps they were laughing at Washburne. Sometimes — when again I catch myself searching for "elusive subjectivities" in a microfiched article — I suspect it is me.

For obviously, the wanderings and wonderings of the previous paragraph are as much an index of my authorial subjectivity — its affections, its hermeneutic gaze, its perceptions of loss — as they are an analysis of the Labor Museum's performers. More than simply a description, my narrative is partly an attempt to come to terms with my own invented involvement in this text. As Washburne searches to move beyond the vision of a casual observer, I am attempting to see beyond the distanced perspective of a historian, a move that nostalgically posits a "beyond," the lost performance of a woman whose name may not be Mrs. Brosnahan after all. She, Washburne, and myself share a similar situation, however, in that we are all spectators in the midst of the histories we construct. Like Washburne, my position as spectator to history also makes me its producer, a double status that impinges on my narrative performance in this text. Like Mrs. Brosnahan who recounts a particular history of Ireland and immigration, both Washburne and I construct our narrative performances in light of our own historical and cultural situation, inflected as well by the longings and identifications induced by particular tales of the past. Additionally, our historical narratives have themselves been placed on display — Mrs. Brosnahan's for Washburne, Washburne's for me, and mine for you. In all of these cases, the "places" and people from which historical narratives emanate have been explicitly incorporated as part of the historical performance itself. Rather than masking or erasing this human intervention, we have acknowledged our "human hopes and fears" as we interpret our own historical inventions, as we perform that which is available to us, that which moves us, and that which amuses us. In my own case, I often find myself most amused when I encounter the nervous gaps in the historiographical operation and realize that, despite tremendous efforts to disguise it, history has never been narrated any other way. I close with a final episode from the Hull-House Museum.

The initiate's tour continued throughout the museum and ended as she, the assistant curator, and the tour guide regarded a large framed piece of paper:

"Now this is from the Tarsitano Family Reunion," said the assistant curator, holding the frame. "Mr. Tarsitano used to come to Hull-House, and now I think his family owns a grocery store. Here are the names of some of the family." The three regarded the frame for a few moments. Slyly the assistant curator looked up and met the eyes of the other tour guide, who smiled slowly. Suddenly, they both burst out laughing.

"You know, neither of us really knows why this is here," said one.

"Yeah," said the other, "actually . . . having you here will be a good way to pin down exactly what we should say about this."

She continued chuckling to herself as she turned to another wall.

"Now over here is a picture of . . . wait, it used to hang right here."

"What?"

"Well, there used to be . . . well, I guess it doesn't matter, now. It's not here," she laughed again, even louder this time. The other woman joined in once more.

"You have to be careful what you say," she said. "Things are always coming up and down without you knowing, and you'll find yourself pointing to something that isn't even there."

Laughing, they moved along on the tour while another nerve snapped.

Conclusion

Although the story of Washburne's encounters as well as my own have been adjusted in both our re-creations, the movements of these texts suggest something about their contradictory, affective impact on us. After hearing about Mrs. Brosnahan's Irish linen, her crippled child, and drunken husband, for instance, after seeing her "eyes gleam," her hands spin, and her feet dance a jig, Washburne seems profoundly moved:

> We feel that this living woman — this worker and victim and survivor — is the most precious thing that the Museum has shown us. Indeed, we suspect the founders of deliberate intention in placing her there, where she is not

measured by petty, momentary standards, but by the laws which underlie human evolution. We catch a glimpse of the importance of her function in a historic industrial order; and while our minds leap to the new truth, our hearts thrill with a new sympathy. (p. 580)

Within the safety of the first-person plural, Washburne has turned his eyes inward, placing himself under examination only to grow more humble. He claims to be relieved of the "petty, momentary standards" by which Hull-House immigrants are judged. His heart is able to "thrill with a new sympathy" because the Labor Museum has provided him with a way to understand Mrs. Brosnahan and her experience. In concluding the visit (and after attending a lecture where "these thoughts become more definite and these emotions strengthened to resolution"), Washburne feels the "museum effect" to such a degree, feels a closeness and connection to Hull-House to such an extent, that he finds a new subject position for himself as he exits Hull-House into the "riotous city":

> We, too, wistful children of a half-civilized state, look back through these windows into a warmed and light world of happy industry; and even while we shove and push for the best places, wish in our hearts that we were working within. The light and heat, even the joy of doing good work under right conditions, may be artificial and evanescent, but without, around us, all is struggle and clamor. (p. 580)

Washburne has become one of those boys whom he earlier observed outside the Labor Museum window. He struggles for the best seat as the boys earlier pushed "to obtain the best vantage ground." He wishes he was working within, the same "longing" Washburne earlier attributed to the boys. However, this connection he feels—a new sympathy turned to empathy as his bourgeois superiority is redeemed by an encounter with simple primitives—is still one that retains his ideological filter. He still sees civilization in stark contrast to the city, still characterizes the urban landscape as "riotous," "struggle," and "clamor," and still presumes the "evanescence" of Hull-House. Finally, Washburne's sympathetic transformation illustrates one of the most problematic aspects of an uncritically "humanist" ideology advanced in many a museum. As Sally Price writes, such an exhibit "allows *our* self-recognition and personal rediscovery and permits a renewed contact with *our* deeper instincts; the result is that *we* increase *our* understanding of *ourselves* and *our* relationship to art."[32] Thus, "becoming exotic to oneself" can still maintain the category of the "exotic," resulting in selfish acts of appropriation rather than encouraging a more radical personal transformation. It is this component and its effect that make such contextualizations so engaging; the affective power of the harmonious, cross-cultural links they seem to forge is precisely what masks their insidiousness.

For my part, this narrative is the performative record of the particular "effects" that Hull-House and its historiographical sites have had on me. Visiting Jane Addams's Hull-House Museum is a complicated experience for someone who happens to be doing research on the settlement. While there, I do not always engage in moments of ethnographic eavesdropping or meta-historical musing on my own self-(mis)guided tours. Sometimes I cower in scholarly humility as I read a didactic that quotes a source I do not recognize or refers to a neighborhood church I did not know existed in Chicago's Nineteenth Ward. The reaction is a symptom of larger research anxieties as I adjust with intimidation and confusion to the practice of fact accumulation which seems to be so much a part of the historiographical operation. Internalizing a kind of hyper-empiricism, I scribble reminders to myself — "Find poem: 'Ode to Maxwell Street.' . . . Get date of photo of Greek boys' wrestling club." These are the moments when I forget Derrida's critique of presence and succumb to the presential temptations of performance historiography. Caught in a historian's double repression, I assume the presence of the document's referent and disavow the representational nature of the document itself. Though I can often maintain this functional ontology for hours at a time, inevitably the problem of absence returns. For usually these visits end with me leaving the museum to linger in bewilderment at the intersection of Halsted and Polk Streets, a place that was at one time walked by the inhabitants of an immigrant neighborhood and that is now traversed by college students in jeans, sweatshirts, and backpacks. It is then that de Certeau's questions in *The Writing of History* resurface in my mind. "What do historians really fabricate when they 'make history'? What are they 'working on'? . . . *What in God's name is this business?*"[33]

Notes

The opening quote comes from Marion Foster Washburne, "A Labor Museum," *The Craftsman* 6.6 (September 1904): 570–80 — hereafter cited in the text.

1. Michel de Certeau, *The Writing of History*, translated by Tom Conley (New York: Columbia University Press, 1988), p. 64. See also Michel Foucault, *Archaeology of Knowledge*, translated by Alan Sheridan (New York: Pantheon, 1972); Joan Scott, *Gender and the Politics of History* (New York: Columbia University Press, 1988); Hayden White, *The Content of the Form: Narrative Discourse and Historical Representation* (Baltimore: Johns Hopkins University Press, 1987) and *Tropics of Discourse* (Baltimore: Johns Hopkins University Press, 1978); Dominick La Capra, *History and Criticism* (Ithaca: Cornell University Press, 1985); and Michael Taussig, *The Nervous System* (New York: Routledge, 1992).

2. Antonio Gramsci, *Selections from the Prison Notebooks of Antonio Gramsci*, edited and translated by Quintin Hoard and Geoffrey Nowell Smith (London: Lawrence and Wishart, 1971), p. 276; Jane Addams, *Twenty Years at Hull-House* (1910; reprint, New York: Penguin, 1981), p. 72. For a history of the settlement movement, see Allen Davis, *Spearheads for Reform* (New Brunswick, N.J.: Rutgers University Press, 1967); for a critical analysis of Hull-House, see Rivka Shpak Lissak, *Pluralism and Progressives: Hull-House and the New Immigrant* (Chicago: University of Chicago Press, 1989); for a historical excavation of museum exhibition during the same period, see Donna Haraway, "Teddy Bear Patriarchy: Taxidermy in the Garden of Eden, New York City, 1908–36," *Primate Visions: Gender, Race, and Nature in the World of Modern Sciences* (New York: Routledge, 1989), pp. 26–58. Words such as "unfortunates" and "slums" were frequently used in reform literature of the period.

3. All previous quotations are from Jane Addams, "First Outline of Labor Museum at Hull-House" (1900), reel 51, *Jane Addams Memorial Collection*.

4. Ibid.

5. Addams, *Twenty Years at Hull-House*, p. 260.

6. Of course, "these days" refers to a time in 1993 when this essay was originally written. Thus my use of the present tense throughout actually implies a "present" that is now past.

7. De Certeau, *The Writing of History*, p. 73.

8. Taussig, *The Nervous System*, pp. 2–3.

9. Addams, *Twenty Years at Hull-House*, p. 172.

10. Taussig, *The Nervous System*, pp. 44–45.

11. Richard Schechner's theory of performance, articulated in *Between Theater and Anthropology* (Philadelphia: University of Pennsylvania Press, 1985).

12. Taussig, *The Nervous System*, p. 45.

13. Barbara Kirshenblatt-Gimblett, "Objects of Ethnography," in *Exhibiting Cultures: The Poetics and Politics of Museum Display*, edited by Ivan Karp and Steven D. Lavine (Washington, D.C.: Smithsonian Institution Press, 1991), p. 390.

14. For essays on the concept of public history, see Susan Porter Benson, Stephen Brier, and Roy Rosenzweig, eds., *Presenting the Past: Essays on History and the Public* (Philadelphia: Temple University Press, 1986).

15. Renato Rosaldo, *Culture and Truth: Social Analysis: The Remaking of Social Analysis* (Boston: Beacon, 1989), p. 68; Eileen Boris, *Art and Labor: Ruskin, Morris, and the Craftsman Ideal in America* (Philadelphia: Temple University Press, 1986), p. xiv.

16. See Benedict Anderson, *Imagined Communities* (London: Verso, 1983). For a general discussion of pluralism in relation to American nationalism, see e.g., R. M. Smith, "The 'American Creed' and American Identity: The Limits of Liberal Citizenship in the United States," *Western Political Quarterly* 41.225 (1988); Hans Kohn, *American Nationalism: An Interpretive Essay* (New York: Macmillan, 1957); and V. Shapiro, "Women, Citizenship, and Nationality: Immigration and Naturalization Policies in the United States," *Politics and Society* 13.1 (1984). For a discussion about whether settlements (in particular Hull-House) anticipated Horace Kallen's more specific definitions of "cultural pluralism," see Lissak, *Pluralism and Progressives*. For references to conservative cultural performances, see Michael Wallace, "Visiting the Past: History Mu-

seums in the United States," in Benson, Brier, and Rosenzweig, *Presenting the Past*, pp. 165–202.

17. The term "gallery of nations" frequently titled the pageants and immigrant performances of the Progressive Era. Sally Price, *Primitive Art in Civilized Places* (Chicago: University of Chicago Press, 1989), p. 56.

18. Quoted in Residents of Hull-House, *Hull-House Maps and Papers* (New York: Arno, 1970), p. 15. For analysis of the relationship between industrialized labor and the construction of ethnicity, see Eric Wolf, *Europe and the People without History* (Berkeley: University of California Press, 1982).

19. George Stocking, *Race, Culture, and Evolution: Essays in the History of Anthropology* (Chicago: University of Chicago Press, 1982).

20. Johannes Fabian, *Time and the Other: How Anthropology Makes Its Object* (New York: Columbia University Press, 1983), p. 23.

21. Jane Addams, "First Report: The Labor Museum at Hull-House" (1902), reel 51, frame 7, *Jane Addams Memorial Collection.*

22. Stocking, *Race, Culture, and Evolution*, p. 112.

23. My analysis is inspired by recent critiques of ethnographic writing. See, e.g., James Clifford and George Marcus, *Writing Culture: The Poetics and Politics of Ethnography* (Berkeley: University of California Press, 1985), and Clifford, *The Predicament of Culture: Twentieth-Century Ethnography, Literature, and Art* (Cambridge: Harvard University Press, 1988).

24. See White, *The Content of the Form.*

25. On youth and moral reform, see Jane Addams, *The Spirit of Youth in the City Streets* (New York: Macmillan, 1909), and Paul Boyer, *Urban Masses and Moral Order in America, 1820–1920* (Cambridge: Harvard University Press, 1978).

26. Kirshenblatt-Gimblett, "Objects of Ethnography," p. 413.

27. Clifford, "On Ethnographic Authority," in Clifford, *The Predicament of Culture*, pp. 21–54.

28. Jacques Derrida, *Of Grammatology*, translated by Gayatri Chakravorty Spivak (Baltimore: Johns Hopkins University Press, 1976), p. 143.

29. Kirshenblatt-Gimblett, "Objects of Ethnography," p. 410.

30. Susan Stewart, *On Longing: Narratives of the Miniature, the Gigantic, the Souvenir, the Collection* (Durham, N.C.: Duke University Press, 1993), p. 23.

31. See James Scott, *Domination and the Arts of Resistance: The Hidden Transcript* (New Haven: Yale University Press, 1989).

32. Price, *Primitive Art in Civilized Places*, p. 34.

33. De Certeau, *The Writing of History*, p. 56.

Museum Author-ity and Performance

The Musée Gustave Moreau

ELIZABETH GRAY BUCK

In January 1895 the Sar Péladan wrote an open letter to Gustave Moreau in the literary and artistic journal *L'Ermitage* sardonically encouraging his premature death. The author of the Symbolist manifesto and creator of the *Salon de la Rose + Croix*, Péladan revered Gustave Moreau as the greatest living French painter and his work as the best example of Symbolist ideals. Moreau, however, had frustrated Péladan's attempts to exhibit his paintings. According to Péladan, Moreau had allowed him to visit his studio on one occasion ten years earlier but would only show him the paintings already hanging on the walls. Moreau apparently assured Péladan that he was indeed capable of understanding his art but that "he was more jealous of the two hundred canvases hidden in his home than a caliph of his wives, and that he would only finally allow them to be seen when he himself no longer cared for them."[1] Moreau went on to tell Péladan: "Year after year, I add augmentative details, when the Idea comes to me, to my two hundred posthumous works since I want my art to appear to the public all at once, and in its entirety, at a moment after my death."[2] Péladan approached Moreau again after Moreau's appointment to the École des Beaux-Arts, claiming that as he was now a public instructor, he had renounced his right to work in isolation. Moreau refused, claiming that it would only expose him to the persecution of his colleagues. Péladan found his refusal irrational and so publicly and audaciously asked Moreau to "die soon, die quickly, for the greater good of art, for your own glory."[3]

Péladan's wish was fulfilled in 1898, when Moreau died after a battle with stomach cancer and left his "house situated at 14, rue de la Rochefoucauld, with all that it contains: pictures, drawings, cartoons, etc. the work of fifty years" to the state with the express purpose of presenting its contents to the public in a museum format (Figs. 1 and 2).[4] But the story does not end with Moreau's will. Péladan's remarks allude to a performance on which the foundation of the future Musée Gustave Moreau depends: a carefully planned future death. Before any public exposure of his paintings, the artist wanted to die. That is, in order to exhibit the body of his work, the body of the private artist needed to disappear. Moreau's performance, reported by Péladan and recorded by Moreau himself in the museum archives, indicates a tension be-

294

tween the role written for his paintings and his own presence, between the public nature of images and the empirical existence of their maker. His plans comprise a performance of an absent artist and a present art object that bears his name—a performance that at once literally demands the "death-of-the-artist" and yet also assures the absolute survival of his name—staged in his private home.

This essay will examine the script that Moreau wrote for himself, his work, and the future visitors to his studio. It will focus on the performance of the Musée Gustave Moreau in the context of the national museum in late-nineteenth-century France, whose paradigms we have inherited, and will suggest ways in which the visitor to Moreau's museum was—and is—asked to perform beyond his/her traditional museological role. I will argue, above all, that this script plays against the well-rehearsed exhibitions of the national collections. In other words, this essay is a preliminary attempt to write about the difficult and complex relationship between state-sanctioned representation located in the national museum and the presumptive authority of the Musée Gustave Moreau.

According to the conservators of the museum, this intensely private man conceived the idea of preserving his own work and research material as early as 1862—that is, two years prior to his first, and arguably his only, critical success at the age of thirty-eight and well before his appointment to the École des Beaux-Arts in 1891. He wrote in his notebook: "On this evening, the 24th December, 1862, I think of my death and of the fate of all those works and compositions I have taken such trouble to collect. Separately they will perish, but taken as a whole they give an idea of what kind of artist I was and in what kind of surroundings I chose to live my dreams."[5] The desire to preserve the entirety of his work intact and untouched, located specifically in a space that would somehow clarify or illuminate its meanings, seems therefore evident from an extremely early moment in his artistic career. To retain an unaltered collection, Moreau sold only a few paintings, and many of the larger projects that he produced from this time were museum-scale (that is, very large), apparently intended for a public audience. During the 1880s Moreau appears to have planned the presentation of his oeuvre as a posthumous exhibition and sale, the provisions for which were articulated in his mother's will in 1884.[6] Sometime after 1890, however, following the death of his longtime companion, Alexandrine Dureux, Moreau began to envisage a more permanent exhibition. In 1895 he started the alterations to enlarge his home, enclosing the small garden out front, to create a museum space devoted to his work.

In 1880 J. K. Huysmans referred to Moreau as "a mystic locked up in the middle of Paris in a cell into which even the noise of everyday life that nevertheless beats furiously at the doors of the cloister does not penetrate."[7] This

Figures 1, 2. Inside the Musée Gustave Moreau. (Photos by author)

image of hermetic confinement and extreme privacy is maintained in Moreau's own notes pertaining to the founding of his museum. Among these are numerous references to the destruction of private correspondence, especially that relating to Mlle. Dureux.[8] According to his wishes, Henri Rupp, Moreau's student and friend who was instrumental to the opening of the museum, maintained an almost absolute silence on the subject of Moreau's personal life.[9] Except for his famous maternal attachment to which even Péladan refers, little personal information regarding the artist was made available until the 1960s by a scholar closely connected to the museum.[10] Apparently, Moreau even forbade any publication of his own image as if, as Pierre-Louis Mathieu writes, "he wanted to make disappear any trace of his physical existence."[11]

The ironic distinction between Moreau's chosen profession and his life was evident to Péladan: "the man does not resemble the work: little, anxious, nervous."[12] Because he was an instructor at the École des Beaux-Arts during the last years of his life, Péladan expected Moreau to behave accordingly; to conduct himself "as a publicly decorated painter, patented, official, a national professor supported by the State, and show your work."[13] Moreau only exhibited occasionally during his lifetime — six times at Salons and twice at the Exposition Universelle de Paris — and the reviews were often mixed. He never won the coveted Prix-de-Rome, a distinction given to promising students that ensured them a measure of professional acceptance. Few of his works were purchased by the state, and only one — *Orpheus* (1865) — remained on display to the public at the Luxembourg gallery. Even at the end of his career, when he had earned a reputation as an instructor at the École des Beaux-Arts, Moreau resisted publicly exhibiting his work. And so Péladan's claim that Moreau's work was "official" and "patented" was tenuous. In fact, it would appear that the paintings that were exhibited were seen as something of a curiosity rather than an accepted contribution to the *patrimoine*.[14] As Péladan recognized, it seemed improbable that a man who described himself as belonging to "the very interesting family of timid people who are unable to say one word in public without provoking disastrous emotions" would choose a legacy with an emphasis on public display.[15]

It is hardly surprising, then, that Moreau's bequest posed a problem for the state. Although Moreau died on April 18, 1898, the Minister of Public Instruction and the Fine Arts was not authorized to accept the terms of his will in the name of the state until February 28, 1902, four years later.[16] Like the Caillebotte collection accepted by the state a year before Moreau's death, Moreau's legacy also provoked considerable debate, resolved only when Henri Rupp agreed to fund the venture by renouncing his own inheritance.[17] At the time, the attitude of the French government toward contemporary art was ambivalent at best: approximately only one out of four official acquisitions of contemporary art was exhibited at the Luxembourg, the gallery reserved for the work of "living" artists. Furthermore, although this was a period noted for museum making, other personal museums founded in France prior to the Musée Gustave Moreau, such as the Musée Victor Hugo and the Musée Ingres, were established either by the French government itself, as in the case of the former, or by a local arts organization, as in the latter — not by the artists themselves.[18] These artists had also long been recognized by the state as contributors to the nation's cultural heritage, whereas Moreau's standing in that regard was problematic. Moreover, the work collected and displayed by the state in national collections such as the Musée du Louvre was almost without exception *finished* — that is, both complete and also exhibiting the "finish" or the polished surface of the traditional museum piece. Moreau's museum, however, was filled with only partially completed canvases, drawings, watercolors, and a few pieces of sculpture.

Given these more obvious difficulties raised by the unprecedented nature of Moreau's bequest, I will examine the museum in light of recent scholarly work in cultural and performance studies. Specifically, I want to see the Musée Gustave Moreau as a disruptive performance. Although I do not intend to suggest that Moreau throws off all of the conventions of French art and display that embraced most of his peers, I do see his museum as highly suggestive of the possibility for a museum to do so. Moreau's plans for the survival of his work defied the established museological paradigm and resisted the traditional staging of art objects. Whereas the national collection obscures the paradoxical relationship between the dead artist, his/her name, and state co-option, the Musée Gustave Moreau displays the problematic nature of the connection. Therefore, rather than allowing the ideological machine of the state to co-opt his work into an extant paradigm that privileged the "national" artifact over the subjective or anonymous one, Moreau claimed the right/write to represent himself, to inscribe his own name, not that of the state or of the people. In reserving control over the exhibition of his work — even to the extent of rarely showing it for fifty years — he resisted the customary deferral of the "signature" to the state. Moreau thus destabilized the ways in which the museum could be used by the French government: if anyone (with sufficient rank and privilege) can establish a museum, the state's authority to police the roles of reception and display becomes limited and the investment of power is revealed as assailable. Though Moreau's resistance to state-sanctioned museum logic was bourgeois, the museum that bears his name nevertheless opens up the museological representation to new, and perhaps more democratic, viewer interpretations.

In the few pages of this essay, I will define performance as an appropriation of authority within the cultural text. Although this is an admittedly narrow approach to performance, it is nevertheless a useful way to emphasize the feasibility of viewer participation within the representation of culture. Derived largely from studies in popular culture, it claims for the spectator a power ignored in most museum literature. The writings of Michel de Certeau and James Scott in particular examine the creative and complex relationships between the governors and the governed, the elite and the populace, and are particularly suggestive of a more complex and creative relationship between the museum and its viewers, between the practices of the institution and those of its inhabitants. In *The Practice of Everyday Life*, de Certeau focuses on the ways in which the "users" of culture and its signs operate within the dominant power structure. In order to make the repressive system habitable, de Certeau claims, the cultural practices of the populace enact a tactical mode of resistance that both saps and deflects the power of the elite, a process he calls "making do." This process takes place in the gap between the production of a cultural representation and the use to which an-"other," a person who is not its maker, puts that representation.[19]

In *Domination and the Arts of Resistance*, Scott also recognizes a user's manipulation of elite culture. He characterizes the relationship between those "subject to elaborate and systematic forms of social subordination: the worker to the boss, the tenant or sharecropper to the landlord, the serf to the lord, the slave to the master, the untouchable to the Brahmin, the member of a subject race to one of a dominant race" as a performance.[20] He defines the libretto of the relationship as the "public transcript," whereas what he calls the "hidden transcript" describes the "discourse that takes place 'offstage,' beyond direct observation by powerholders."[21] Scott's goals are to excavate the "hidden transcript" from the self-representative texts of the powerful, to investigate the disruptive role or roles of the governed on the controlled public stage, and to examine both the spoken and unspoken performances of agents that violate the public record. Although the "arts of political disguise" may mute their disruptive intent, they nevertheless threaten the ways in which the powerful (re)present themselves.

Following Scott and de Certeau, the relationship between the spectator and the museum spectacle is more problematic than a "public transcript" of their transactions might suggest. This essay articulates the potentially disruptive dynamic "written into" that relationship by the Musée Gustave Moreau. In the process, I will briefly consider the national collections of the Louvre and the École Française d'Extrême Orient as places whose roles were to authorize the state through representation and to display that authority. In contrast, the Musée Moreau's personal autograph interrupts the hierarchy of power manifested in the national collections. Unlike the paradigm established by the national museum that defers its own authority along a chain of signifiers meaning "nation," I will claim instead that the inscription of a signature and its personal appropriation of power makes the Musée Gustave Moreau disruptive in a specifically performative sense.

By the time that Moreau's museum was established, the French government had long recognized the value of the art object in the service of the state. One of the French Revolution's greatest inventions, used to buttress its own power, was the modern museum. While concurrently engaged in the destruction of all royal artifacts, the revolutionary government founded the Louvre on August 10, 1793. The original project was begun for the Crown in the early eighteenth century under the direction of the Count d'Angiviller and was based on the model of the national museum in Vienna. The plan foundered when the monarchy collapsed. The palace of the Louvre itself was declared public property the day that Louis XVI was taken prisoner, on August 10, 1792.[22]

The doors opened to the public one year later during the festival of National Unity. According to the rhetoric employed to describe the first national museum and to justify the collection, the Musée du Louvre would "liberate the products of human genius and return them to their rightful owners — the people." It would serve as a training ground for a new kind of art that, according to Gabriel Bouquier, a member of the influential Committee of Public Instruction, showed a "vigorous and manly style that must . . . capture the energy of the people who, in breaking the chains that bound them, has voted for the liberty of humankind."[23] The displays of Greek and Roman statuary, works by the Old Masters, French history paintings, and the captured spoils of war literally embodied the new social order, exhibiting transcendental, eternal values that placed them *outside* history (as opposed to the now removed decadent objects commissioned by the Old Regime) and *inside* a rewritten history as the triumph of the new order over the old (the revolutionary council was able to complete d'Angiviller's project in only a year). The national collection of the Louvre also rendered the values of citizenship transparent: in a space open to the "people," the citizen-spectator could now view the sacred objects formerly held hostage by the royal family and aristocracy.[24]

The deeply symbolic, even overdetermined, nature of the French national museum therefore attempted a staging of the past through representation. The precession of art objects from the earliest moment of high Western civilization — note that the antique remains of Gallic Stone Age culture were not included in the narrative of history presented in the national collection — to French history paintings suggested a natural evolution of the artistic product to present-day France. The visitor to the Musée du Louvre was clearly positioned as a spectator of an ideal past from which he/she would want to be descended and the beneficiary of Western cultural wealth. Though the original intent of the national museum may have been "revolutionary," it instead articulated a very conservative viewer/object relationship. The protocol of museum visiting that it posited was decidedly theatrical: the audience was firmly situated before the objects in prescribed positions determined to present both the unfolding of the history of art and the inherent superiority of the national artifact.

The creation of such a monolithic and totalizing national survey museum has received considerable scholarly attention in past years.[25] In general, this attention has focused on the ways in which the ideologies located in the national collection operate on the visitor — for instance, how the planned circuit of the space precludes visitor digression. Some more recent texts dedicated to subjects as divergent as the historiography of art history, the reopening of the Guggenheim Museum, and the role of the ethnographic museum in a postcolonial age have also used metaphors of the theater to describe the museological space and its function in culture.[26] Donald Preziosi, in particular, has exploited theatrical terms to explain the museum's relationship to the discipline of art history. In his view, the museum functions as a stage on which the ideal past of the "revolutionaries," present, and future are clearly displayed. Preziosi represents the conventional presentation of artistic objects as a display designed to demonstrate the art historical principles of "time, place, personality, mentality, and the artisanry or the genius of individuals, groups, races and nations."[27] It also projects transcendental values of human creativity and a transcultural artistic impulse. As he argues, the museum aims "at the dissolution of troubling ambiguities about the past by fixing meaning, locating its source in the artist, the historical moment, the mentality or morality of an age, place, people, race, gender or class, and by arranging or formatting the past into a rationalized genealogy."[28] As we have seen in the Musée du Louvre, it thus resolves and obscures problematic aspects of the past and of history for a totalizing and complete narrative through theatrical representation.

The École Française d'Extrême Orient, concurrently established with the Musée Gustave Moreau, represents this kind of "ideal" museum. The authority of the French government operating within the museum and represented by its enclosed objects was exported to the colony of French Indochina. The nature of the collection and the methods of classification narrated a fiction of Indochina in which the objects of Vietnam, Cambodia, and Laos were displayed together, as if belonging to a single nation united under enlightened French rule. The specimens were separated into classes of objects, labeled according to Western categories of art objects (incipient, height, degenerate), and organized according to periods of Chinese domination. Labeling all the objects conceived of as anonymous, local, or artifactual (in Western terms) as "primitive" established the Western intellectual as the cultural authority, the one authorized to inscribe cultural meaning. While the museum thereby established the French as the guardians of Indochinese culture on an implicit level, the text — or, to use Scott's phrase, the "public transcript" — cast the curators as the promoters of Indochinese education and liberation. The inhabitants of Laos, Cambodia, and Vietnam were not actually learning about their own culture when they visited "their" public museum, but rather about the West. The museum firmly established the paternity of the French state through representation in the name of the "people."[29]

According to this paradigm, the museum operates as a monolith. It is a *place* rather than a *space* — the locus from which discourse originates and is maintained rather than through which it is *practiced* and changed.[30] As described by Preziosi's work, art objects in the national collections are selected and displayed to activate certain decisive and prescribed meanings — such as the concepts of nation, period, artistic creativity, and the attendant associations of patriotism, evolution, and genius — and to ensure a closed circuit of signs. From Preziosi's point of view, the museum is a stable text, one in which the instabilities and contradictions of social relations, artistic productions and reception, and ideologies are erased.

And, in fact, the state expended vast amounts of effort at the end of the nineteenth century to ensure a "correct" reading of the museological script as described by Preziosi. The Musée Gustave Moreau was established at a time of enormous museum activity in France: 173 museums were created between 1860 and 1900, and 82 between 1900 and 1920.[31] Following the devastating effects of the Franco-Prussian War during 1870–71, the fine arts were especially called upon to play an active role in the recovery process. The editor of the *Gazette des Beaux Arts*, Charles Blanc, in 1871 wrote: "Today called by our common duty to revive France's fortunes, we will devote more attention to the role of art in the nation's economy, politics and education. We will continue to back the cause of beauty so closely aligned with the causes of truth and good. And we will struggle for the triumph of those teachings which will help the art rebuild the economic, intellectual, moral grandeur of France."[32] The rebuilding of the country was synonymous with an intensified program in the arts and the establishment of museums to house the work. The museum therefore articulated not only an unproblematic and heroic past but also a comparable future. The state expanded its boundaries to include its own representations and claimed the territory of the nationally correct artifact. These artifacts sometimes included unknown names: paintings purchased by the state at the Salon by young artists depicting traditional historical and mythological subjects. These objects were then distributed through a network, established by Napoleon, to provincial museums.[33] Moreau's work, however, was never colonized in this way. During his lifetime the state bought only one of his paintings, *Orpheus* (1865), and his use of untraditional and esoteric subjects made his images particularly unsuited for the role of ambassador.

During the second half of the nineteenth century, the state also began seriously to regulate and to police both the reception and the display of art objects. Newly published guidebooks and museum regulations articulated a protocol for museum visiting and of museum displays. The museum spectator was expected to be quiet and orderly and to adhere to certain standards of "bonne tenue" that prohibited those who were not "decent." Those accompanied by dogs, picnic baskets, and even children were forbidden.[34] The new rules presumed that the new visitor did not know how to behave within museum walls and therefore needed to be closely regulated, policed, and reprimanded. Those caught laughing or behaving "indecently" (as were two young women in Marseilles) were removed from the premises.[35] Moreover, the exhibits in the museum itself were subjected to new regulations. Following the war, the government made the first systematic attempt to identify the holdings of rural museums. The newly appointed curators and directors applied a scientific rigor to the collections. For the first time, they identified each work with plaques that included the artist's name, title, and date, and each piece was maintained in a regulated inventory. According to Daniel Sherman, the correct scientific and educative structure was deemed important to elevate the public's taste by making it proud of its own heritage.[36] The once unlabeled and unnamed artifact was thereby subjected to intense scrutiny as the curators and museum directors actually created both the museological object and the appropriate setting in which to display it.

Within this theoretical framework, the Musée Moreau presents a very different conception of the museum space and its function. Although he was supported financially by the state during his tenure at the École des Beaux-Arts, unlike either Victor Hugo or J-A. D. Ingres, Gustave Moreau was himself hardly a publicly recognized master, neither canonized nor celebrated by the state. According to Paul Flat, who published the first guidebook to the newly opened Musée Gustave Moreau, he was at once "illustrious and unknown; since his name, which signified for *délicats* the most complex, varied and modern art of our time, awakens no echo in the public."[37] For Péladan, Moreau was the ultimate practitioner of Symbolism, yet his work could not claim widespread support or recognition — especially as it had remained hidden for the last twenty years of his life. His artistic signature was hence not easily recognizable. Furthermore, rather than conforming to a recognizable style, such as Realist, Impressionist, Academic, and so forth, Moreau's paintings were generally characterized as "bizarre" or "unique." In 1876 George Lafenestre wrote a commentary typical of Moreau's reviews: "he astonishes the crowd, many connoisseurs must shrug their shoulders, he horrifies serious people and enchants a small group of *délicats*. He is a strange artist, he is a unique artist since he will kill off his imitators."[38] Not only did he paint alone and in solitude, cut off from any contact with contemporary Parisian life, as described by Huysmans, but his work was often represented as unconnected to the artistic world as well, better suited to a tomb than the crowded halls of the Salon. And though he was a popular instructor at the École des Beaux-Arts, none of his students copied his style.

Unlike the Musée Moreau, the names inscribed on the other small museums founded at the end of the century, such as the Musée Victor Hugo and the Musée Ingres, were widely revered. Their presentation of art objects and artifacts complied with the paradigm of the museum and museum visiting. That is, the objects displayed within their walls were seen both as representative of a superior nation and as contributions to the continuing evolution of the nation's artistic product. These museums produced a disciplined and passive reader/viewer who came to their homes to pay homage to the great men of France. The artistic products housed therein referenced those that had already entered the cultural text: either as published books or public images hanging in the national collection — as, for instance, Hugo's notes for *Les Misérables* or Ingres's *Roger and Angelica*, a larger version of which belonged to the collections of the Louvre. The unfinished product in these places persisted in buttressing the public sphere rather than in acknowledging an individual's claim to author-ity.

In this context, it would seem therefore that Moreau's life, work, and museum were, and are, enigmatic. None of the traditional vantage points as described by Preziosi aid a contextual understanding of his legacy. Instead of the heroic artistic genius whose products deserve state-supported conservation, we are offered the image of a small, anxious man, protective of his private life to the point of *pudeur* (as described by Robert de Montesquiou).[39] Furthermore, Moreau's great oeuvre of fifty years not only remains unfinished but also resists inclusion in (traditional) art history's evolutionary narrative of modernism in which the art objects "progress" toward the pure, painterly surface. And his museum eludes the prescribed, state-sanctioned model for these structures. Against the general text of the museum constructed by the French following the Revolution, the Musée Gustave Moreau thus emerges as a disruptive performance. The very conception of a museum founded by an artist whose credentials were only marginally established and whose signature was unrecognized by the state prior to his bequest interrupts the museological paradigm that demanded the paternal co-option and canonization of the work. In fact, one review of the museum after it opened in 1902 took offense at Moreau's presumption: "(e)ven though it offends our taste, we will not further elaborate on the singular vanity that this member of the Institut expresses in erecting himself the monument to his own glory."[40] Moreover, Moreau's performance references representability: it calls attention to the inscription of power, the instability of the constructed viewer, and the mimetic nature of self-presentation through representation. It challenges the power invested in the museological structure by the state and proposes alternative spectator roles.

Because the script for the museum visitor that Moreau provides is so sketchy, so unfinished, so partial, it is difficult for him/her to understand the text of the museum and its meaning — and, more importantly, to recognize his/her role as visitor. For an audience to assume quietly the roles assigned by an exhibit, the display must be legible within the contexts that Preziosi offers. By contrast, the meaning(s) activated by the Musée cannot be located in the artist's biography (he refused publication of his private life), artistic genius (as Ary Renan phrased it, he was considered "obscurely famous" in his own lifetime and celebrated only in the twentieth century as the instructor of two modernist "masters"), or the historical moment (he was considered often more atypical than representative of the period and its styles).[41] Therefore, the spectator/viewer must somehow read this space differently. Whether Moreau is ultimately read as a premier Symbolist, as Péladan and Huysmans did, or as an idiosyncrasy of French modernism, the space of his museum must be appreciated for prompting alternative considerations of museum ideologies and spectatorship.

In her short book on the French Revolution, *Rehearsing the Revolution*, Marie-Hélène Huet examines the complexities of spectatorship during the turmoil. She states, in fact, that the genius of the Revolution was its engagement with the theater. Although she initially describes the spectator's role during the Revolution as traditionally that of a passive receiver/viewer — following Diderot — unlike Preziosi, she also claims that the spectator *is* capable of moving beyond this role, to exceed the prescribed text, to actively challenge, alter, rearrange, and rehearse the script offered to him/her. She states: "first) what interests the spectator is the spectacle per se. His position as a receiver is established, constituted, made use of independently of the significance of the message received . . . a public is formed the moment there is a spectacle. Second) Spectator-receiver's raison-d'être lies in the possibility of a transmutation from the role of *receiver* to that of *actor*. To *retell is to act* and thereby claim the pleasure which is deferred in the time of the performance" (emphasis added).[42] For Huet, an instability inhabits the role of the spectator. Whereas the author of the spectacle may assume he/she has some definitive control of the text, the receiver-viewers always violate that control. The viewer only watches the spectacle, only agrees to maintain the prescribed distance or alienation from it, in order to become an actor at a later moment. The belief and acceptance of the message in the script are *"tied to the possibility of a reversal of roles."*[43] One only watches or listens in order to replay the part later.

In Huet's model, the social relation between the empowered and the oppressed is theatrical. It is dependent on the presentation of the message of power and requires the complicity of the oppressed. Yet the presentation is never quite complete, even though it may appear to be — the message is always retold, altered, and recrafted by the viewers. The performance of power, the public transcript, is not stable because the script is consistently subject to revision and the actors are constantly changing. The desire to overturn the power relation in the social field may therefore exist as what might be called the "ghost in the political machine." This political instability corresponds to the theater's dynamic of deferred desire — to "the reversibility of the spectator into an actor, to the spectator's ever-present and always deferred desire to speak" — and to the actor's own deferred speech. As Huet states, the actor is always "a 'spokesman' who expresses himself as another . . . one never speaks in his own name."[44] As described by the historian François Furet, the vacuum of power that appeared after the death of Louis XVI was filled by those who spoke for a generalized "other" who was not present — the "public" or the "people" — in whose name they meant to signify the "nation."[45] The possibility for infinite representation, introduced by the theater and maintained in the political sphere, attests to the unstable nature of power itself. Huet claims that the "very specificity of the theater lies in the way it maintains violence and alienation in a forever unresolved tension: the deferred desire of the spectator, the conferred authority of the actor — the spectacle is a borrowing, hence always a debt to be settled."[46] For Huet, then, the spectator who does not perpetuate the dynamic of deferment, the one who actually speaks in his/her own name, threatens the representative paradigm of social power.

This model suggests that representation is the dominant force in social relations. It implies that the "real" continues to exist only insofar as it can be retold. Though representation may privilege the *idea* of a preexisting reality, it is actually devoted to the *representability* of historical fact, the endless mimetic retelling of factual information, and to the reproduction of that text as "truth." It further indicates the investment of the state located in the national collection of art objects and artifacts and suggests that the collected objects (re)present the state itself. Yet also implicit in the text written by the collection resides the latent power with which the spectator is armed. As both Huet and Scott claim, this power requires a constant surveillance to ensure compliance with the rules, especially since the passive spectator desires above all to become the one to rewrite the script, to assume the role of the actor who also thereby may become an author, one who perhaps speaks in his/her own name.

Moreau himself can be seen as Huet's spectator. He was at once an avid visitor to the Musée du Louvre and he taught many of his classes there.[47] It is therefore not difficult to represent his transition from the role of a passive recipient of museological meaning to that of an actor. In this model, his plan for the presentation of his own work is his own long-awaited performance — silently and anonymously waiting for his own death in order to act out the role that he could not play during his lifetime. And yet Moreau is more than a spectator-become-actor. In the careful deliberation of the museum's contents and the constant reworking of large-scale images designed to adorn its walls, Moreau is the *author* of his museum's script. He does not merely re-present the contents of the national collection but rather his own work. He rewrites the totalizing transcript of the Louvre in a way that forces it not only to recognize his paintings — to place his work within the pantheon of its artistic products, especially once the Musée Gustave Moreau became part of the Réunion des Musées Nationaux post–1945 — but also to acknowledge its own investment in the products that it chooses to exhibit. In either case, his script alters the terms of the libretto itself. His bequest assumes for itself an author-ity that previously the state had reserved for representations of itself.

As Michel Foucault wrote, the author does not die in the text but rather returns to haunt his/her production, sometimes in problematic ways. For Foucault, the author is an ideological construction in culture, one whose role extends beyond the boundaries of the "real" person and whose name both marks and contains a given text. Foucault claims that we need what he calls the author-function in order to curtail the "proliferation of meaning," to bind the irregularities and the fragments of representation, to "neutralize the contradictions" of the text: "the author provides the basis for explaining not only the presence of certain events in the work, but also their transformations, distortions, and diverse modifications (through his biography, the determination of his individual perspective, the analysis of his social position, and the revelation of his basic design)."[48] For Foucault, the name of the author is a totalizing ideology that stabilizes a text and its meanings. The fragments written before the final finished, closed product are subsumed within the author-function — that is, they cannot, or at least should not, suggest alternate, multiple, various, or conflicting texts. In the social sphere that defines the author-function, therefore, the constructed author is allowed only a small degree of authorized power that is at once contained and bound by the author-function. Foucault thereby suggests that the rights an author can indeed appropriate in culture in fact may *exceed* author-ized roles and can potentially disrupt the author-function.

At the Musée Gustave Moreau the ghost of the painter circulates among the unfinished paintings, and yet here his name refuses to bind the work as the final signified in the way that Foucault suggests. The author-function that Foucault describes is an attempt to curtail the author-ity that Moreau appropriates. Foucault's model suggests a finished product, a whole body of work to which the fragments can refer and to which even the continuing revisions of scholarly analysis, as in the case of Marx or Freud, can return. Moreau's unfinished work together with his unpublished and unknown life offer little to bind his oeuvre. Furthermore, the author-function implies a cultural attempt at immortality, a perpetual postponement of the author's death. Foucault suggests that an actual author does not exist or is at least irrelevant to the author-function. Instead, the sociocultural machine appropriates both a name and a biography to clarify and elucidate the work. Through the continued celebration of and references to the inviolate body of the author, still alive in the body of the work, the author-function negates the specificity of the actual dead human being — a specificity that haunts the Musée Gustave Moreau. Moreau resists and subverts the "immortality-function" indicated by Foucault's model and insists on a "real" author, one who deliberately planned his own death so that, strangely enough, the objects would survive. Unlike other museum places, the visitor is poignantly aware of Moreau's absence and seeks fruitlessly to locate his presence in the partial images he left behind.

As his life and the museum, the paintings that Moreau produced refuse any clear prescribed reading for the visitor. Moreau's last finished project, one of the few in the museum, now hangs on the second floor. This work, entitled *Jupiter and Semele* (1895), was in fact purchased by the collector Leopold Goldschmidt and donated to the museum in 1903. There exist two notes by Moreau purporting to explain the painting's content, one written for the collector and the other written for the artist himself and dated October 10, 1897. These notes identify some of the mysterious figures that crowd the canvas, but neither exhaustively details the iconography, and both ultimately fail to explain or to define the picture. As Julius Kaplan wrote, "his commentary, while clarifying his intentions, also reveals his failure to translate them completely in pictorial terms."[49] The notes seem in fact to function apart from the image, as separate musings on the story of the divine god who revealed himself in all his awesome glory to the powerless Semele.

The central figures — an enormous, frontal, and hieratic Jupiter whose body is literally tattooed with jewels and flowers, the pale, nude, and dying Semele, and Bacchus, her son, who flies away from his horrified mother — are nearly lost in the abundant and excessive details. Each square inch of the canvas is filled with minutiae that compete for the viewer's attention. Aside from the clearly larger figure of Jupiter, it is difficult to know where to begin to read this image or how to interpret the plethora of information that the painting offers. According to Kaplan, after an exhaustive iconographic analysis, the meaning is revealed as Moreau's "definitive philosophical statement, in which confrontation, often of a sexual nature, allows man to achieve his ideal and become divine," a reading that he claims did not necessarily reflect Moreau's intention.[50] Rather, Moreau seemed to expect that the viewer should respond viscerally rather than intellectually, that he or she should "only love, dream a bit and not be satisfied in an imaginative work . . . with a simple, disgusting ba, be, bi, bo, bu."[51] Moreau rejects any straightforward analysis of the image based on what he considered a simplistic and childlike iconographical or pictorial vocabulary. Kaplan goes on to assert, however, that the evidence of the second note in the museum archives suggests that Moreau recognized that the viewer was frequently baffled by the image.

The majority of the work in the museum is even more confusing for the visitor because it is incomplete. Numerous large canvases covered only with underdrawing, color blocking, and underpainting are displayed as representative of fifty years of artistic effort. The largest pieces that Moreau had planned for the space — *The Chimerae* (1884) and *The Suitors* (begun in 1852), to name only two — are clearly only partially complete. The former director of the museum describes the sketchiness of *The Chimerae* as "more drawn than painted," and, in fact, some images incorporate the incomplete and finished areas so skillfully that it is difficult to determine if Moreau actually *intended* to leave portions of the canvas unworked.[52] A *Salome Dancing* (1876), one of the variations on the theme of Salome, has also been called "The Tattooed Salome" in reference to the drawing that covers her body. The tattoos could be read either as the incomplete designs for the jewels that will/could adorn her body or as the finished design. It is difficult to determine which reading is the correct one, and this lack of finish defies the art historical need for the complete(d) picture.

As Mathieu relates: "the museum disappointed the public . . . [and as] a result the museum was visited less and less frequently. It became known for its quietness and became an unobtrusive meeting place for those few followers such as the young André Utter, Suzanne Valadon, André Malraux and his future wife Clara," and the Surrealist André Breton.[53] It conformed to few expectations of museum visiting. Rather than the imposing structures built to house collections throughout the nineteenth century, the visitor to the Musée Gustave Moreau entered a home in a bourgeois neighborhood at a distance from the centrally located Louvre and only blocks from the Place Pigalle, to see works that he or she could not place within the narrative of art historical evolution.[54] Breton, in fact, valued Moreau's museum precisely because it refused a singular reading: "(t)his museum appeared to me as the perfect image of a temple, both the ideal image of what a temple should be . . . and the other image of the 'place of ill repute' which it might also become."[55]

Huet claims that the spectator is an "actor 'in waiting,' an incomplete figure who is preparing for a role he too will play and whose model he looks at with eagerness. Hence 'to attend means to prepare for.' "[56] The reversibility of roles lies just beneath the surface of the actor-spectator relation, liable to erupt at any moment and to settle the debt between them. Moreau's museum can be read as a resolution of this obligation. Just as the Revolutionary spectators occasionally snatched victims from the executioners in order to participate in the spectacle, Moreau retrieved the body of his work from state co-optation. He prevented the French government from pressing his paintings into anonymous ideological service for the greater glory of France and the *patrimoine*.

He furthermore extended his own role as spectator/actor and author to the museum's visitor. The drawings and watercolors that reference the larger unfinished canvases are exhibited in unusual display cases, designed by Moreau, that resemble large sketchbooks. Unlike other museums in the late nineteenth century, the visitor to the Moreau museum sits before cabinets and turns pages, touching the original objects. The spectator cannot adopt a singular, assigned vantage point before the images — a site that valorizes only the spectator's vision — but must instead engage the usually forbidden tactile experience. Touching the objects opens them to multiple senses and allows the body of the spectator to incorporate the museum into itself and to become part of the museum in turn. Unlike the anonymity of the viewer invoked by the national collection, the procession of which is alone important for the state, the specificity of the viewer and his/her sensory response replaces the unknown eye. Finally, the sketchbook displays reference the dead artist: the visitor sorts through the drawings and watercolors as through a dead relative's closet. Unlike the conventional museological display that demands a proper distance from the art object — as if the object were actually held in perpetuity by an institution that is only waiting for his/her return — these remains recall both the uncomfortable specificity of Moreau's mortality and the survival of the art object.

The objects themselves also require an active participating body. According to eighteenth- and nineteenth-century French aesthetic theory, the unfinished work requires the greatest amount of viewer involvement. Academics believed that whereas the finished picture presented only a single elaborated theme, the unfinished sketch allowed the viewer to imagine the final product. According to Diderot, who developed this concept: "Sketches generally possess a warmth that pictures do not. They represent a state of ardor and pure verve on the artist's part, with no admixture of the affected elaboration introduced by thought: through the sketch the painter's very soul is poured forth on the canvas. . . . Thought flies more rapidly to its object and defines it at a stroke; but in art, the vaguer the expression, the more room there is for the play of imagination."[57]

For Diderot, the sketch presents the viewer with an opportunity to collaborate with the painter, to inhabit the artistic imagination. And, though Diderot may not have phrased it quite this way, I would suggest that the spectator is thereby allowed to perform, to take part in the production of the art object by imagining its final appearance. The viewer can furthermore transform the museum itself by entering into its form, by touching as well as by seeing its contents, by initiating and controlling its display through direct contact.

Diderot, however, specifically conceived of the incomplete painting as an indication of the artist's genius, a spontaneous moment eventually suppressed by the carefully considered final version.[58] The unfinished objects displayed in Moreau's museum have almost no completed painting to support this notion. Instead, the sketches and canvases reference each other--provoking an intellectual play of similar images from the earliest sketch to the partially completed paintings, yet rarely yielding a final version. Unlike the polish of the traditional museological object, whose finish keeps the viewer at a distance, the rough marks on the surfaces of the canvases constantly evoke the hand of the dead artist, the creator who will never complete them. And so perhaps it is better to cite Bertolt Brecht in relation to the texts that the Musée Gustave Moreau engages and writes: "the illusion created by the theater must be a partial one, in order that it may always be recognized as an illusion. Reality, however complete, has to be altered by being turned into an art, so that it can be seen to be alterable and be treated as such."[59] The viewer cannot finally *complete* these images; they will always remain only partial, inducing an awareness of the museological illusion.

As the work of James Scott and Marie-Hélène Huet suggests, the representation of power staged in the museum requires the complicity of the visitor. For a viewer to read and gauge the script correctly, he or she must assume the role designated for the ideal spectator by the given text. It is therefore necessary for the "dominant to police the public transcript in order to censure any indication of division or weakness that would appear to improve the odds favoring those ready to stiffen their opposition to domination or risk outright defiance."[60] The relationship between the hidden and public transcripts is constantly renegotiated in order to maintain the paradigm of dominance. This implies that the hidden transcript is always exerting pressure on the public message, like water against a dam.[61] Within the walls of the museum, the presented text cannot always control the uses to which the visitors put the images, it cannot control the hidden transcript of the visit itself — the suppressed giggle, the sneer, the spontaneous art history lecture by the "amateur" viewer, the use of the space as clandestine meeting spot, or a myriad of other defiances. All museum visiting could perhaps be examined in terms of the hidden transcripts at work within its walls, although some museums certainly allow more viewer agency than others. (It is especially difficult, for instance, to write a dissenting script while a museum director lectures through earphones.)

Although the unusual presentation of Moreau's work in his former home does present the possibility of dissent from the dominant museum paradigm, it is itself not *outside* of ideology. The degree to which he attempted to control the text presented is evidence of his desire to "police the transcript." Furthermore, as Moreau's social status suggests, he had access to and upheld certain discourses of social power.[62] Yet the way in which his museum space functions creates the *possibility* for the production of a disruptive transcript. It opens up the museological paradigm to viewer scrutiny and reveals a fissure in the walls of the national museum. And, as for Scott, "(w)hether these possibilities (for dissent) are realized or not, and how they find expression, depends on the constant agency of subordinates in seizing, defending, and enlarging the normative power field."[63]

The Musée Gustave Moreau allows a re-reading of the museum against the museological grain and plays the concept of the "author" against its cultural authority. Unlike the smooth and closed surface of the text enclosed within national collections, the Moreau museum leaves the signifier hanging. These half-completed images refer to that finite name, Moreau, which remains irreducible and yet also implies that the work of representation is never finished. Rather than a totalizing image, the text written by Moreau is partial. It proposes posthumous rewriting — by a woman, a visitor, a late-twentieth-century American art historian whose ideas of nationality and power are very different from those inscribed in other museum *places*. For me, the Musée Gustave Moreau is a space in which hidden transcripts can become scripts and the viewer can become an author.

Notes

Many thanks to Drs. Della Pollock, Mary Sheriff, and Carol Mavor and to Jane Blocker, Katherine Nordenholz, and Joe Lucchesi for their invaluable input, comments, and ideas. The project has grown in both scope and depth because of their suggestions. This essay is inspired by and dedicated to Lee.

1. "[Q]u'il était plus jaloux des deux cents toiles cachées dans son hôtel qu'un khalife de ses femmes, et enfin qu'à les laisser voir il cesserait aussitôt lui-même de s'y plaire." Sar Péladan, "Gustave Moreau," *L'Ermitage* 6.1 (January 1895): 30.

2. "D'année en année, j'ajoute des détails augmentatifs, suivant que l'Idée vient, à mes deux cents oeuvres posthumes, car, je veux que mon art apparaisse tout à coup, et tout entier, un moment après ma mort." Ibid.

3. "[m]ourez tôt, mourez tout de suite, pour le plus grand bien de l'art, pour votre propre gloire." Ibid., p. 34.

4. Pierre-Louis Mathieu, *The Gustave Moreau Museum* (Paris: Musées Nationaux, 1986), p. 31.

5. In *L'Assembleur des Rêves: Écrits complets de Gustave Moreau* (Frontfroide: Bibliothèque Artistique et Littéraire, 1984), p. 284.

6. Geneviève Lacambre, *Maison d'artiste, maison musée: L'exemple de Gustave Moreau* (Paris: Musées Nationaux, 1987), p. 12.

7. "C'est un mystique enfermé, en plein Paris, dans une cellule où ne pénètre même plus le bruit de la vie contemporaine qui bat furieusement pourtant les portes du cloître." J. K. Huysmans, "Le Salon Officiel de 1880," in *L'Art Moderne* (Paris: N.p., 1883), p. 135.

8. See Lacambre, *Maison d'artiste*, app. 6, 11, and pp. 46, 49–50.

9. Normally reticent regarding Moreau's affairs, Rupp did once allude to Mlle. Dureux in A. Brisson, "Promenades et Visites — l'ami du peintre," *Le Temps*, December 2, 1899.

10. Péladan, "Gustave Moreau," p. 30: "il fut le plus admirable des fils, quittant dès neuf heures les causeries le plus animées pour aller faire la partie de sa mère." Pierre-Louis Mathieu was the first to publish Alexandrine Dureux's name and relationship to Moreau in response to an article claiming that Moreau was a homosexual: "Gustave Moreau amoureux," *L'Oeil* 224 (March 1974): 28–33, 73.

11. Mathieu, "Gustave Moreau amoureux," p. 31.

12. Péladan, "Gustave Moreau," p. 30.

13. "[C]onduisez-vous comme doit un peintre public décoré, patenté, officiel, professeur national et garanti par l'État, et montrez votre oeuvre. . . ." Ibid., p. 34.

14. The use of the term *patrimoine* refers to the artistic heritage of France and to its corresponding legislated protection. This concept continues to be important to France's idea of nationhood as both the current campaign to save "endangered" patrimonial objects and the designation of 1980 as the "Year of the *Patrimoine*" testify. For an interesting discussion of the *patrimoine* and the museum, see Bernard Deloche, *Museologica* (Lyon: N.p., 1985). Castagnary refers to the confusion felt by the public before *Oedipus and the Sphinx* in *Salons* 1 (Paris, 1892): 199. See also the cartoon from the 1864 Salon exhibition published by Julius Kaplan, *Gustave Moreau* (Los Angeles: Los Angeles County Museum of Art, 1974), plate 1388.

15. Lacambre, *Maison d'artiste*, p. 33.

16. Ibid., p. 35.

17. Ibid., p. 34. The Caillebotte debate centered around two separate issues. First, the collection was comprised of only Impressionist works, a movement whose validity was still contested. It was felt that to exhibit them in the Musée Luxembourg as a group, as stipulated by the will, would appear to lend state support to the Impressionists. Second, the Luxembourg lacked the space to display the entire collection. The debate ended in a compromise: the state was allowed its choice of the collection. Forty works were selected and finally displayed in 1896. *Les Donateurs du Louvre* (Paris: Éditions de la Réunion des musées nationaux, 1989), pp. 159–60. See also Pierre Vaisse, "Le legs Caillebotte d'après les documents," *Bulletin de la Société de l'Histoire de l'art français*, December 3, 1983, pp. 201–8.

18. Felix Bouisset, *Le Musée Ingres* (Montauban: Édition du Musée, 1926); Raymond Charmet, *The Museums of Paris* (New York: Meredith Press, 1967).

19. Michel de Certeau, *The Practice of Everyday Life*, translated by Steven Rendall (Berkeley: University of California Press, 1984).

20. James Scott, *Domination and the Arts of Resistance* (New Haven: Yale University Press, 1990), p. 2.

21. Ibid., p. 4.

22. Andrew McClellan, "The Musée du Louvre as Revolutionary Metaphor during the Terror," *Art Bulletin* 70 (June 1988): 300–12.

23. Andrew McClellan, "The Responsible Republic," *Apollo* (July 1989): 5–6.

24. I owe this image to Andrew McClellan, ibid., p. 5.

25. Carol Duncan and Alan Wallach, "The Museum of Modern Art as Late Capitalist Ritual: An Iconographic Analysis," *Marxist Perspectives* 4 (Winter 1978): 28–50.

26. Donald Preziosi, "The Question of Art History," *Critical Inquiry* 18.2 (Winter 1992): 363–86, and *Rethinking Art History: Meditations on a Coy Science* (New Haven: Yale University Press, 1989); Adam Gopnik, "The Death of an Audience," *New Yorker*, October 5, 1992, pp. 140–47; Mieke Bal, "Telling, Showing, Showing-Off," *Critical Inquiry* 18.3 (Summer 1992): 556–94; Barbara Kirshenblatt-Gimlett, "Objects of Ethnography," *Exhibiting Cultures* (Washington, D.C.: Smithsonian Institute Press, 1991), pp. 386–443. For a compelling analysis of the politics of exhibitions, see Timothy Luke, *Shows of Force: Power, Politics, and Ideology in Art Exhibitions* (Durham, N.C.: Duke University Press, 1992).

27. Preziosi, "The Question of Art History," p. 381.

28. Ibid., p. 383.

29. For the above-cited information on the École Française I am indebted to Prof. Gwendolyn Wright's "National Culture under Colonial Auspices: The École Française d'Extrême Orient," a paper delivered at the symposium on "Formation of National Collections of Art and Archeology" at the National Gallery of Art, Washington, D.C., October 24–26, 1991.

30. See de Certeau, *The Practice of Everyday Life*, e.g., p. 117.

31. Pierre Pradel, "Les Musées," *L'Histoire et ses méthodes* (Bruges: Bibliothèque de la Pléiade, 1962), p. 1034.

32. Quoted by Paul Tucker in "1874: The First Exhibition," *The New Painting: 1874–1886* (San Francisco: Fine Arts Museums of San Francisco, 1986), p. 101.

33. For an interesting discussion of the envoi system, see Daniel Sherman, *Worthy Monuments: Art Museums and the Politics of Culture in Nineteenth-Century France* (Cambridge: Harvard University Press, 1989).

34. Ibid., p. 219.

35. Ibid., p. 223.

36. Ibid., chap. 6.

37. Paul Flat, *The Musée Gustave Moreau* (Paris: N.p., 1902), p. 5.

38. "Il étonne la foule, il faut hausser les épaules à maint connaisseur, il horrifie les gens graves, il enchante un petit groupe de délicats. C'est un artiste étrange; c'est un artiste unique car il tuerait ses imitateurs." Quoted in Pierre-Louis Mathieu, *Gustave Moreau, sa vie, son oeuvre: Catalog raissonné de l'oeuvre achevé* (Paris: Bibliothèque des Arts, 1976), p. 128.

39. Lacambre, *Maison d'artiste*, p. 17.

40. "Bien qu'il blesse notre goût nous n'insisterons pas davantage sur la vanité

singulière dont fit preuve ce membre de l'Institut en élevant lui-même le monument de sa gloire." Louis Rouart, "Gustave Moreau," *L'Occident* (1902), p. 153.

41. Ary Renan, *Gustave Moreau, 1826–1898* (Paris: N.p., 1900), p. 10.

42. Marie-Hélène Huet, *Rehearsing the Revolution*, translated by Robert Hurley (Berkeley: University of California Press, 1982), p. 33.

43. Ibid., p. 41.

44. Ibid., p. 105.

45. François Furet, *Interpreting the French Revolution*, translated by E. Forster (Cambridge: Cambridge University Press, 1981).

46. Huet, *Rehearsing the Revolution*, p. 107.

47. Georges Rouault, *Souvenirs Intimes* (Paris: N.p., 1927), p. 23. See also Ann Prache, "Souvenirs d'Arthur Guéniot sur Gustave Moreau et sur son Enseignement à l'École des Beaux-Arts," *Gazette des Beaux Arts* (April 1966): 229–40, and Frank Anderson Trapp, "The Atelier Gustave Moreau," *Art Journal* 22.2 (1962): 92–95.

48. Michel Foucault, "What Is an Author?," *The Foucault Reader*, edited by Paul Rabinow (New York: Pantheon Books, 1984), p. 111.

49. Julius Kaplan, *The Art of Gustave Moreau: Theory, Style, and Content* (Ann Arbor, Mich.: UMI Research Press, 1982), p. 85.

50. Ibid., p. 86.

51. Ibid., p. 87.

52. Mathieu, *The Gustave Moreau Museum*, p. 53.

53. Ibid., p. 32.

54. This continues to be the case: during the course of my research at the museum, I was frequently interrupted by French students who asked me (1) what they were "supposed" to be seeing and (2) why they had been sent there by their instructors. See also Trapp, "The Atelier Gustave Moreau."

55. André Breton, "Gustave Moreau," *Surrealism and Painting*, translated by Simon Watson Taylor (New York: Harper and Row, 1972), p. 363.

56. Huet, *Rehearsing the Revolution*, p. 34.

57. Quoted and translated in Albert Boime, *The Academy and French Painting in the Nineteenth Century* (New York: Oxford University Press, 1971), p. 84. From Diderot, *Salons*, vol. 2, edited by Seznac and Adhémar (Oxford: N.p., 1960), pp. 153–54.

58. Boime, *The Academy and French Painting*, p. 85.

59. Bertolt Brecht, "From the Mother Courage Model," *Brecht on Theater*, edited and translated by John Willett (New York: Methuen, 1964), p. 219.

60. Scott, *Domination and the Arts of Resistance*, p. 67.

61. I borrow the image from James Scott, ibid., p. 196.

62. Moreau seems to have believed in the artistic supremacy of men, as his vitriolic remarks concerning the diary of Marie Bashkirtseff reveal, and in the artistic supremacy of France: "L'intrusion sérieuse de la femme dans l'art serait un désastre sans remède … Car (Bashkirtseff) savait tout et avait tout lu dans les originaux. C'est à faire frémir." Quoted in *Assembleur des Rêves*, pp. 207–8. For the relationship between art and empire, see esp. p. 250.

63. Scott, *Domination and the Arts of Resistance*, p. 132.

5

Producing History

That Was My Occupation

Oral Narrative, Performance, and Black Feminist Thought

D. SOYINI MADISON

Oppressed people resist by identifying themselves as subjects, by defining their reality, shaping their new identity, naming their history, telling their story.
bell hooks, Talking Back: Thinking Feminist, Thinking Black

The voices of women fill most of my childhood memories: gossip, songs, testimonies, lyrical praise, and insults. I remember how these women talked, their voices rising and lowering in colorful tones and rhythms. Sometimes they would speak through cautious whispers and at other times through robust declarations. Sitting together in the kitchen, they told stories to entertain and to survive. These stories were sometimes set in laughter and sometimes in tears, but they never stopped. I remember most clearly the stories my mother told me about how to be a woman, when I should be wary of life and when I should not. For most of us who have grown older with these stories, they have become what Gloria Anzaldúa and Cherríe Moraga have called "theories of the flesh" that "bridge the contradictions of our experience" — those root metaphors that keep us centered and sane.[1]

Theories of the flesh mean that the cultural, geopolitical, and economic circumstances of our lives engender particular experiences and epistemologies that provide philosophies or "theories" about reality different from those available to other groups.[2] Particularly for people of color, life lived, whether on the concrete pavement of inner-city streets or the backwoods of a rural southern community, is the root of our beginnings and the root of our understandings. The early quotidian experiences of the people we knew were our "first sight,", and it is through them that we began to name and theorize the world.

Theories of the flesh privilege agency and interrogate notions of the "lethargic masses" or the "voiceless victims." The question, "Where do theories come from?" is answered by honoring the "extraordinary in the ordinary" indigenous analysis, expressions, and meditations of what bell hooks refers to as "homeplace." Speaking specifically of black women, bell hooks describes "homeplace" as the "folks who made this life possible." She states: "Though black women did not self-consciously articulate in written discourse the theoretical principals of decolonization, this does not detract from the importance of their actions. They understood intellectually and intuitively the meaning of homeplace in the midst of an oppressive and dominating social reality, of homeplace as site of resistance and liberation struggle."[3] When we speak from theories of the flesh, we are speaking from homeplace and, in turn, naming the location from which we come to voice.[4]

Theories of the flesh mark black feminists' primary ways of knowing, but the second level of knowledge, what Patricia Hill Collins calls "specialized knowledge" and what hooks calls abstract, critical thought, initiates a balancing act in the effort to engage alternative ways of producing and validating knowledge.[5] I hear these questions from black women consistently across the country: how do my articulations — wrapped in scholarly theory — really represent the collective of black women who speak a different language and to whom I am committed? How do I justify writing about the experiences of black women in academic journals that the majority of my people will never read?

Collins describes the relationship between black feminist thought and theories of the flesh — or theories that reflect the lived realities of the masses of black women: "Black feminist thought articulates and makes accessible the knowledge and collective philosophy of black women, but it also creates new epistemologies and creates new dimensions for describing experiences and for liberation."[6] Collins's claims about black feminist thought are congruent with interventionist and postcolonial criticism that argues for merging the "text with the world."[7] And yet cultural criticism has always been part of black artistic and intellectual tradition. As hooks states: "Cultural criticism has historically functioned in black life as a force promoting critical resistance, one that enabled black folks to cultivate in everyday life a practice of critique and analysis that would disrupt and even deconstruct those cultural productions that were designed to promote and reinforce domination."[8] Black feminists are concerned with issues of historical and cultural significance to the collective of black women and to those with specialized knowledge engaged in interpreting black women's experiences.

The conjoining of theories of the flesh and specialized knowledge may be examined in four points made by Collins. First, she contends that the collective of black women telling their stories has carved out from their particular condition unique spaces in which to interpret and to portray their lives.[9] Second, she identifies two levels of thought. At the first level is the everyday taken-for-granted knowledge that is often unreflexive, the nuances of which are often foreign to others, yet ingrained in the language and experiences of the masses of black women. At the second level is the extended and more specialized knowledge furnished by experts who are part of the group. The two levels, she claims, are interdependent.[10] Third, Collins asserts that theory and abstract knowledge claims are obligated to the concrete experiences of daily life they evaluate and judge.[11] Finally, she argues that traditional techniques and tools of dominance cannot be used unreflexively and unself-consciously to analyze disenfranchised people.[12]

Collins cautions us to honor the tellers' experiences through critical and interpretive frameworks that unite the text with the world. Women, particularly those marginalized by race and social class, create and invent spaces in which they depict and interpret their concrete and imagined experiences. Traditional and popular techniques of analysis must be critically and self-reflexively extended when applied to the distinctive forms of these women's expressions. In examining these forms and spaces, indigenous thought and practice emanating from the tellers' language, history, and traditions must guide, alter, add to, and adjust dominant analyses. In oral narrative analysis two symbol systems (teller and interpreter) are brought together. They each inform the other, but more importantly and typically ignored by the conventional case study approach, the teller's symbolic practice is reflexive. It theorizes itself; it uses its own theories of itself to tell us what it means. Narrative performance is thus not only "doing something in culture." It involves an ongoing self-reflexive analysis and critique of what it is doing.[13]

Specialized knowledge may then enter to articulate — to translate and to unveil — extant philosophical systems to those who (without this knowledge) are unable to find, much less hear them. Although this specialized knowledge depends on indigenous theory to tell us what it is we are observing as well as what it means, we may choose to go beyond the role of translator to the role of critic in order to create new epistemologies and descriptions of experience and liberation. It is at this point that the teller's experience is illuminated, made accessible and available as an advocacy discourse for social change and/or affirmation. In turn, the theory and specialized knowledge of the interpreter is given greater relevance, legitimacy, clarity, and a larger purpose through the guiding force of human experience.

In the following oral narratives from the life history of Mrs. Alma Kapper, a black woman from Mississippi who worked as a sharecropper and a domestic, the indigenous theories that inform her life experiences in the past events of the told (the "said" or narrated event) and the emergent event of the telling (the "saying" or narrative event) most poignantly arise from performance traditions.[14] These performance traditions, and the theories of the flesh they enact, are then articulated primarily through the specialized knowledge, or scholarly discourse, of people of color. As a result, the authority of knowledge, and therefore power, that comes with being a critic is now directed by the formal and informal theories of the cultural subjects themselves. This analytic choice was deliberate, but with no intention to shut out other perspectives or claim that this choice should be the rule. Addressing the marginalization of black scholarship as analysis and critical discourse, particularly regarding issues of culture and difference, hooks states: "It must be remembered that black studies programs have explored issues of race and culture from the moment of their inception," and "it can be disheartening when new programs focusing on similar issues receive a prestige and acclaim denied black studies."[15] My purpose is to make a contribution against the great imbalance of scholarly work that ignores black indigenous and intellectual traditions as critical and theoretical constructs that can guide and determine the analysis of texts and performances.[16]

The Poetic Transcription Approach

Dennis Tedlock writes, "Once the audible text is in hand, there is the question of how to make a visible record of its sounds."[17] With this question in mind, I have recorded the narratives using a poetic form of transcription.[18] Sound, as well as the literal word, creates the experience of the oral narrative, and in many moments sound alone determines meaning. Mikhail Bakhtin refers to sound as intonation "contaminated by rudimentary social evaluations and orientations."[19] Collins describes the significance of sound: "it is nearly impossible to filter out the strictly linguistic-cognitive abstract meaning [the literal word] from the sociocultural psycho-emotive meaning [sound]."[20] The poet Etheridge Knight states: "The sounds themselves evoke feelings; that's the way you are touched."[21]

Black people, lettered and unlettered, have traditionally emphasized the sound and rhythm of black language when writing poetry or when recording speech. Locating and representing the range of sounds more than the literal word was "the signifying difference that made the difference," the distinction between how black folks described the world and how others described it.[22] From the Negritude movement, to the Harlem Renaissance, to the black arts movement of the 1960s, many black artists and scholars did not wholly and consistently embrace European poetry and prose forms but chose to arrange words on a page that reflected the intonation, mood, tone, and rhythm of black speech.[23] This preoccupation with sound was part of a West African inheritance.[24] In West African cultures, concrete expression was inseparably interwoven with meaning and *rhythm*. "Rhythm activated the word; it was its procreative component; Only rhythm gave the word its effective fullness."[25] It is *muntu*, the word that lives in *kuntu*, its mode of existence, that is rhythm.[26] Word and rhythm make sound indispensable in understanding the meanings of speech. Without the sound, which in West African cosmology is the rhythm, the identifying context with its social and historical distinctions becomes opaque and the "signifying difference that makes the difference" loses its profundity.

My choice in using a poetic text is consistent with the black tradition of acknowledging that words are alive with sounds that condition their meanings. By placing words on a page in a way that resembles the rhythm of the human voice and the speaker as a social-historical being who colors each word based on that existential fact, the text comes closer to capturing the depth inherent in the indigenous performance of black speech. In the next section I present poetic transcriptions of four episodes from the oral narrative of Mrs. Alma Kapper and analyze their theories of the flesh using insights of black feminist thought and a performance paradigm.

The Oral Narrative of Mrs. Alma Kapper

Mrs. Alma Kapper was born in a small town in the black belt of Mississippi at the turn of the century. Delivered by a midwife and having no birth records that she could remember, she believed that she was in her mid-eighties.[27] Most of her life was spent working as a sharecropper and a domestic worker. She was a widow, but she demanded that her abusive husband leave the house and never see her again many years before his death. Later, when she began having problems with her eyes, she moved to Chicago to live with her brother and his family. Glaucoma had caused partial blindness in both eyes.

I met Mrs. Kapper while doing fieldwork at a social agency in Chicago; one of the programs was the senior citizen day care center where I spent six months interacting with the elders. Arriving in the morning, I would spend the time singing with them their favorite songs, role playing, and enacting memories and characters from their past. Although there were several extraordinary people that I had met, I was drawn to Mrs. Kapper's flamboyant spirit, her quick wit, and the experiences of her life as a sharecropper.

Mrs. Kapper and I worked together on her oral narrative in the afternoons after all the formal sessions were over. The interviews took place in what we called "our private room," which was located down the hall from the seniors' activity room; it was quiet there and we could be alone and undisturbed. The episodes included in this essay are lifted from various sections of the complete oral narrative. On the days these episodes were recorded, Mrs. Kapper was sitting in a very large old chair next to the open window, like she did just about every day. She said that was her "place" because she could hear the birds, listen to the children playing, and feel the warmth of the spring sun against her face. I could see only a trace of Mrs. Kapper's eyes behind her large, dark glasses. Unlike her hands that worked Mississippi fields and kitchens, her face and body seemed untouched by decades of labor and struggle. Her face was small, smooth, and delicate; her body was thin and quick. She was about 115 pounds and about 5′5″ tall, wore a curly black wig that framed shiny threadlike waves around her caramel-colored complexion.

As she sat in the chair in her cotton skirt and blouse that always appeared freshly ironed with sharp creases at the sleeves and pleats, she was turned slightly toward me with both hands resting on the straps of her handbag. Mrs. Kapper wore her handbag around her neck because she felt that wearing it in this way assured her that her "blessings" would not be disturbed by the "thieving" hands of others.

The WORD Spoke Tuh Me

The previous week Mrs. Kapper and I had talked about her family and her extended family, and how she felt so secure in their love. I asked her if she could tell me about a time or a particular incident in her childhood when she remembered feeling this love, a time she could not forget:[28]

Member one day
it twas ah Sat'day
all the other chil'ren went off tuh play
well
I was on the porch by myse'f
I was jus' sittin' on the porch
Mama was in the bed
I thought 'bout all I did
wokin' in the fiel'
takin' care ah Mama an' all lika that∧∧
an' all the res' ah the chil'ren
goin' off havin' fun on Sat'day
so I say "I caint go/I caint go!!!"
l lJus' talkin' tuh myse'fl l
an'
(sits up in her seat straight and tall)
the WORD spoke tuh me
the WORD say
GO WHEN YO' CAIN AN' WHEN YO' CAINT
MAKE YO'SE'F SATISFIED!!
that was the spirit talkin' tuh/me
(she spoke with great confidence)
MAKE YO'SE'F SATISFIED!!
An' I got pleased right then
an' I never did get worried no mo'
and that next Sunday . . . the folks started comin'
an' lettin' me go.
That's the honest truth!
(she leans into me and turns her head)

See that was the Lawd spoke tuh me
(Points her finger)
he tol' meh that
MAKE YO'SE'F SATISFIED
GO WHEN YO' CAIN
AND WHEN YO' CAINT
MAKE YO'SE'F SATISFIED.
And it fell off ah me
jus' lika that.
(brushes her hands back)
I got pleased an' happy
right then.
(points her finger in my direction)
That nex' Sunday evenin'ʌʌ
our door-neighbor came by an' ass' me
woudn' I like tuh go tuh church that
evenin'
I say "yes Mam if I could?"
she say
I'll sit wit ya' mutha' sos you can go tuh church
I say yes Mam I'll go.
From then on the peoples started
comin' an lettin' me go.
(she speaks very slowly and leans back)
I think that was mightyʌʌʌ fine_____.

As Mrs. Kapper begins speaking, her demeanor is stately and authoritative; her back is tall and straight against the chair; her hands are clasped together on her lap, and it appears as though she is looking directly at me through her dark glasses. Her voice is confident and controlling, yet tender like a mother about to teach an important life lesson to her child. She continues to speak with gentle authority until she says "the WORD spoke tuh me," and at this point her confidence rises into gestures and expressions of joy and excitement. As she speaks of the "Lawd" she leans over toward me, smiling big and bright. She points her finger and waves her hands, her head moving back and forth to the rising pitch and volume of her voice. She is having a good time, and the whole room is full of the joyful presence of Mrs. Kapper. On the last line, "I think that was mightyʌʌʌ fine_____," as she leans back against her seat, her voice and gesture begin to soften and slowly quiet down. Mrs. Kapper has performed a memory, an experience from her past, that brings to light the tradition of black women and the "ethics of caring."[29]

In the narrative of young Alma, homeplace as a site of resistance is manifest in her dedication to her mother. It was her mother who was the guide and teacher for what it meant to be human, to resist, and to love life. For young Alma, the mother and extended-mothers were the carriers of culture and the caretakers, but they were also the examples of lives based on invention. Under the poverty and inequity of a sharecropping system in the black belt of Mississippi, it was the mother as the initial protector, the first source of knowing and the primary architect of identity, who profoundly shaped the inventiveness and creativity required not only to survive but also to construct a personhood and create a community. The young Alma, in the tradition of women as caretakers and as managers of homeplace, assumes her position in domesticity and becomes simultaneously mother and daughter to her own mother. Moreover, as nurturer-creator, she assumes her position within the network of extended-mothers who will come to her aid, allowing her to further conjoin the woman-centered environment of the black church.

The moment on the porch is both a revelation and a transcendence of faith that draws from black gospel tradition and the traditional West African philosophy of *nommo* — *nommo*, meaning the power of the word to create or bring into existence all entities, to set forth the "generative power of the community" and to transcend the physical world.[30] Framing young Alma's experience on the porch as gospel emanating from African and African American traditions is a way of getting at that which is both ordinary and extraordinary about it.

For the young Alma, her revelation was unforgettable. She passed from one life experience into another through a performative act of speech or *nommo* that evoked communitas, celebration, and transformation.[31] It all begins with a young girl alone and in despair sitting on a porch who breaks the silence of the summer night by naming her feelings and giving voice to the dilemma of being a child but having to live as an adult. Her feelings are materialized in the voice, words, and sound of a young girl calling out in the night. The ceremony takes shape and enters African and African American performance tradition when the call, ironically spoken to herself, is met with a response. The act of speaking, motivated by a young girl's need and desire, culminates in breath and voice that is then heard by greater powers, greater than the nature of the problem itself. But for her to know that she had been heard there must be a sign, and the sign came back to her in voice, in words that she in turn heard. Through *nommo*, the call was served by the response. Through the dialogue of faith in the gospel tradition, when word evokes word and question evokes answer, a transformation takes place, and this transformation is always joyous.[32]

In black gospel tradition as in the concept of *nommo*, the divine answer brings transformation that is manifested by an uplifted spirit, a celebration in knowing that the existential call brought forth one of the most human and most desired needs, a response. In addition to transformation and spiritual uplift, gospel performance and *nommo* affect and alter the situation of the real world. When Alma hears "the WORD" it speaks specifically to her, directing her in reconciling her material conditions. The gospel does not transform the spirit without a connection to the reality of the caller. The call is motivated by this reality, and the divine response is believed to affect that reality. When this power beyond all powers instructs, this is the guidance that affects the life world, "an' I never did get worried no mo'."[33]

But in order for there actually to be an impact on existence, the gospel must have another moment — the communal moment. We observe this in Alma's narrative when she says "the folks started comin' an' lettin' me go." When the young Alma set the gospel and *nommo* in motion through her call that night on the porch, it would follow that the community would be the major factor in Alma's transformation by solving her problem of loneliness and confinement, as well as by initiating the direction of her spiritual enlightenment. The community folks came in keeping with African and African American tradition, for there can be no transformation and no healing without their initiatives, guidance, and affirmation. This communal coming forth reflects the West African saying, "I am because we are, and we are because I am."[34]

When the joy came to lighten Mrs. Kapper's burdens, it was simultaneously a moment of community; the "spirit" and the "folks" conjoined as the force that transformed Mrs. Kapper's life and soul: "An' I got pleased right then." However, the gospel performance in Mrs. Kapper's narrative does not conclude with her going out on Saturday nights playing with other children, but with going to church every Sunday. It is going to church that becomes the resolution of this gospel on the porch — the house of the divine spirit, where community is not only brought together but where the very nature of the coming together is a celebration.

As profound as the tradition may be with its sustained impact on black life, can the charge that it has historically impeded empowerment and promoted passivity among the masses of black people be ignored? Social critics are disposed to point out the ways that structures of power operate, are sustained, dismantled, and disguised.[35] Black feminists also interrogate styles and structures that reinscribe oppression.[36] When Alma enacts the gospel motif and the word comes, "MAKE YO'SE'F SATISFIED / GO WHEN YO' CAIN / AND WHEN YO' CAINT / MAKE YO'SE'F SATISFIED," is she revealing Christian complacency? Is she the contented churchgoer passive to social injustice, believing that "God will find a way?" Critics of the tradition have argued that when the oppressed are at the brink of despair or outrage over their condition, this moment has the potential for the greatest consciousness and, as a result, the chance for greatest resistance against exploitative forces. Instead, some argue, it becomes a moment of acceptance, of inaction, and of passivity when the call to a mystical force directs the oppressed to divert their salvation away from the struggle for empowerment and liberation in the material world. When this happens, they strengthen the very forces of their oppression.

History has revealed the gospel tradition to be a complex and contradictory phenomenon in the way it influences the values, beliefs, and experiences of black people. When gospel is simply labeled "counter-revolutionary" or supportive of a form of Christian complacency, how does one account for Fannie Lou Hammer, Ella Baker, or Amy Jacques-Garvey, to name a few? The gospel tradition has contributed both to liberation and to the reinscription of oppression. Therefore, it cannot be adequately examined by theories based on political economy that do not consider the feeling-sensing ambivalence of daily living. Nor can it be examined by a social theology that ignores or undermines these experiences. Cornel West, describing himself as a "non-Marxist socialist," explains the incompatibility of Christian tradition and Marxist theory in the daily lives of black people: "My Christian perspective — mediated by the rich traditions of the Black Church that produced and sustains me — embraces depths of despair, layers of dread, encounters with the sheer absurdity of the human condition, and ungrounded leaps of faith alien to the Marxist tradition."[37] What concerns West is not that the Marxist tradition is Eurocentric, but that it is "silent about the existential meaning of death, suffering, love, and friendship owing to its preoccupation with improving the social circumstances under which people pursue love, revel in friendship, and confront death."[38]

The gospel tradition remains a contradiction simultaneously profound, beautiful, regressive, confusing, and liberating. For Alma Kapper, gospel evoked both peaceful compliance, "MAKE YO'SE'F SATISFIED," as well as the inspired volition to move beyond her mother's house and interact with the larger community. Gospel is consistent only in that it has always been present within African American culture be it on a slave plantation, at a rock concert, or over seventy years ago as the young Alma calls out in the night on her porch in Mississippi.

Few of Them Livin'

The following episode was recorded the same day. Further on in the narrative Mrs. Kapper mentioned the absence of white children from the "colored schools." She then described how the white children went to school every day for longer hours and through most of the year. She talked about the "colored" children only being allowed to attend school for a much shorter time because they had to work in the fields. As she spoke about the white children "knowing

everything," she quickly defined this knowing as "scheming." She was ada-
mant as she described how the parents of these children taught them, at an
early age, the custom of scheming against the sharecroppers. In the excerpt
below Mrs. Kapper describes an encounter with the landowner:

Selling they cotton an' stuff.
| | When they sell ah bail of cotton
(whispering)
ya' nevah would know what they get ah pound fo' it! | |
| | An' when they come back wit the ticketʌʌʌ . . .
they say "well_____ we_____ couldn'_____ get_____ but_____
35 cents_____ fo'_____ it_____ ah_____ pound_____ this_____ time_____ " | |
He got that deed ticket
but ya' would nevah know it
an' if he say
he didn' get no mo' than that fo' the nex' bail he sol'
he would settle wit ya' fo' that 35 cents ah pound
he keep those big tickets an' ya' would nevah know it!
An' ah tol' one ah them that once!
ah sho' did!
he say "Alma who tol' ya' all that"
I say I got sense enough tuh know it myse'f
nobody tol' me nothin'!!
They cheat the peoples
(very cautiously, very quietly)
I don' wont them tuh/do nothin' tuh me now
them that's livin'
(whispering)
| | few of them livin' | |
they souf' people but some of them
livin'
I don' wont them tuh do nothin' tuh meh.
Not jus' in the souf
they was all doin' it
every which-a-way
'cause they didn' have nothin'
the colored people I mean
they didn' have nothin'
they couldn' live off the grass.

In this episode Mrs. Kapper recounts how the landowner cheated the workers by misrepresenting the price of the deed ticket. She presents an interesting

tension and contrast—the two contrasting performance modes in the simultaneous enactments of the telling and the told. She is forthright and bold in confronting the landowner within the told or narrated event. She breaks through what is implied as the accustomed silence of the sharecropper, then she bravely and proudly confronts the fraud: "An' ah tol' one ah them that once! / ah sho' did!" Her eyes widen and they appear stern and piercing with anger; her courage diminishes the aura of the exploitative landowner. This is Mrs. Kapper's performance mode within the told experience of field-worker and landowner; in the telling, or narrative event, she speaks in a cautious whisper as if the landowner were some omnipotent force transcending space and time, hearing her as she spoke to me miles away in a little room in the senior citizen day care center. She whispers cautiously and contemptuously almost every word of this episode. The years of resentment and fear embodied in her voice were present at this performative moment, in whispers that at points I could barely hear. The fear and disdain for the landowner, projected in performance, marked a change in what had been her performance mode up to this point—a shift from strong movement and voice to a contained, tense, almost rigid body and voice.

The performance encompassing the sensibility of the sharecropper talking to the landowner in the told, and the performance encompassing the sensibility of Mrs. Kapper talking to me in the telling, dramatically overlaid one another; they exemplified different realities. We can observe here the importance of neither isolating one performative representation from the other, nor of reducing the representation to one mode or the other. To record only the words of this episode, focusing on the told as representative of Mrs. Kapper's personal experience without including the performance dynamic of her whispers and gesture in the telling, would render a misleading account.

This episode also reflects the function of storytelling as an empowering act. Since in the story-world we are in control of who we are and of what happens to us, in this world of our own design we may be queens, warriors, poets, or unafraid of white folks. Mrs. Kapper's performance in the told conveys her opposition to the landowner; she is implicitly boasting in the told. But we understand that the boasting presented in the told is contradictory to her persona in the telling. Nevertheless, the tensions between Mrs. Kapper's telling and her told suggest a broader performance tradition in African American culture, a tradition in which the contradictions and tensions in performance were a matter of survival: the tradition of the "mask," or presentation of self, constructed for white people.

While literature, history, and contemporary experience demonstrate the roles black people perform for the benefit of whites—ranging from the obsequious Uncle Tom, the happy, harmless Negro, the dignified stoic, the lascivious whore or buck, the refined intellectual, the frightful street hood, and the uncompromising black militant—we see these types have traditionally been played out for a variety of purposes: to achieve certain ends or gains, for protection and security, or because performing them was the only effective or acceptable way to be seen and heard. We may argue that they are more than performances for white people; they are social behaviors, internalized and sometimes unconscious, enacted throughout black life whether whites are present or not. To say they are "genuine" social behaviors, or traditional performances consciously and deliberately constructed for white people, or simply stereotypes is consistent, on all three counts, with the ways these types (and others) are played out in black history and culture.

However we choose to focus on the dynamics of these types, Mrs. Kapper's narrative specifically addresses the complexity involved in the presentation of a "black self" before a hostile and untrustworthy, white, dominating presence. Because this dominating and untrustworthy presence required blacks to perform certain roles in their encounters with whites, these performances were a source of shame. To repress the will and the dignity of personhood in order to perform a role complicitous with oppressive forces was at times an act of cunning and clever guile; however, when performed out of fear and powerlessness it brought feelings of disgust and resentment. In the latter case, it may be understood in the black community as something black folks do from time to time, but the dishonor does not disappear. As a result, stories abound about getting back at, getting over on, and telling off white folks. If one cannot indulge the performance through cunning or by reversing control so the dominating presence becomes the butt or fool of your pretense, then there is another alternative. One can reconstruct the event and try to claim dignity through a story. It is in this metaperformance, the performance of the performance, that one might finally get satisfaction.

Mrs. Kapper's performance in the told presented the brave woman who stood up for herself and others against the oppressive landowner. It was this boast within the told that strained against the years of fear and resentment manifested in the whispered telling. The two performances are evident in Mrs. Kapper's narrative: she tells off the landowner, "sho' did!" and at the same time—after more than sixty years, from a distance of thousands of miles, in the safety of a public day care program and in the privacy of our little room behind closed doors—she still felt she had to whisper.

My Mutha Had ah Time

This excerpt was recorded the next day. Mrs. Kapper had arrived early and was alone in our room sitting next to the open window humming "Amazing Grace." I walked over to her and said hello. She smiled and said she wanted to talk about her mother, and she wanted to share a family story concerning her mother and a black farmer. She is sitting with her hands resting on her purse during this entire section; she only occasionally moves her head:

My mutha had ah time.
May older sista' tol' me
Mama had ah hard time
she say Mama was stayin' wit one colored man
he bring her
5 pounds ah lard each mont
5 pounds ah meal
|what else she say he give her|
I didn' 'member
Mama got so po' till she jus' couldn' hardly walk
she say she an' my olda' brotha' would go out there in the fiel'
an' be so glad when the peach tree start tuh comin'
an' the peaches start tuh fallen
they go out there an' eat them half green peaches
an' they would pick them peas
an' carry them home an' put them in salt an' wata'
an' they was staying wit colored people too
may sister say that man give his chil'ren ah ear ah co'n
that man waz about tuh starve my Mama tuh deaf.
Jus' give his chi'ren ah ear ah co'n.
An' his wife would get up an' fry ham
an'
make coffee an' eat that good ol' ham an'
buscuits an' thangs.
An'____ his____ chil'ren ____done____ gone____ tuh____ the____
fiel's____ an'____ gone____ tuh____ work____
off uh that
hard co'n.
But when she got able an' foun' somewhere.
The chil'ren grows up
she done very well
|fo' the few yeahs she was up|.
then ah was bo'n
then it fell tuh me tuh take care
of Mama.
Ah would tend tuh mah cows an' thangs
but ah would tend tuh her first.

Ah would get up in the mornin'
make the fire in the stove
get the wata' an' wash Mama
I'd fix her breakfas' an' thangs
an' feed her an' then I get through wit cleanin' her
aftah she got through wit eatin' I'd go back tuh the kitchen.

As she narrates this episode of her mother's life, her hands are clasped together, palms down on her purse across her chest. Her mood is pensive, without the graphic gestures or vigorous intensity of the previous episodes. Although she is less animated and theatrical, she is nonetheless dramatic. Her stillness is almost inalterable as it enhances, underscores, and intensifies the strength of her deep, thick, commanding voice. The authority and richness of her voice contrasts with the dramatic stillness of her body that brings sounds, smells, and texture to the scene of the peach tree, cooked ham and biscuits, her mother's frailty, and the children having to work in the field hungry. Without one lean of her body, wave of her hand, or toss of her head, this economy remained one of the most compelling of her performance modes.

As she describes the farmer, her body is almost perfectly still and quiet without any gestures that may indicate anger, resentment, or despondency — she is stoic. Only this time in the entire life history is Mrs. Kapper so "unmoving," as though her body is weighted down not only with her mother's hard times but also with the all-too-familiar-telling of "what one of our own has done to us." Only her intonation reveals the range of meanings and attitudes she holds for her mother and the farmer. When she talks about the farmer, her voice is lower and more intense; there are fewer pauses and her lips are tight as though she is forcing the words. Not until she begins to discuss her mother leaving the clutches of the farmer — "But when she got able an' foun' somewhere / The chil'ren grows up / she done very well" — does her voice soften, and a note of tender affection loosens the harsh tightness of the performance. At this point, she seems to come back to the present moment of the narrative event. She then makes eye contact with me, unlocks the tight grip she had on her purse, and gently places her hands on her lap.

The events in this episode, between her mother and the black farmer, took place before Mrs. Kapper was born. Passed down by her mother, her older sisters, and her brothers, the narrative is a significant episode in their collection of family stories. The memory of her mother's life as a sharecropper is reminiscent of the South African saying: "our struggle is also a struggle of memory against forgetting." This history cannot be forgotten because to forget it means they cannot know their mother's struggles. To know their mother, they must know her past, what she did there and how she lived through it. This history is her life and tells them who she is. She is a woman who fought hunger, poverty, sexual abuse, loneliness, sickness and survived it. The narrative is the record and the proof of who this woman is, and to tell her story is to celebrate her life among them, as well as to celebrate more than eighty years of pride in being her daughter.

Yet it was the perception of Mrs. Kapper's mother as woman and as black woman that influenced the material conditions of her life and the farmer's treatment of her. And although black women of a different social class were redefining a "true womanhood" that was still ultimately based on Victorian notions of good manners and a patriarchal morality, and although precepts regarding any notion of a "true womanhood" are regressive in the light of women's diversity and freedom, for better or worse, these women recognized that being black and being a woman carried with it fallacious and injurious perceptions that led to the abuse and disrespect of black women.[39] Uneducated, unprotected, isolated, ill, and sexually exploited, Mrs. Kapper's mother worked the land and cared for her children. "True womanhood," in the times of which she lived, was antithetical to her experience. Mrs. Kapper's mother was not endowed with social graces and genteel civility, nor was it her preoccupation to maintain a home of beauty, charm, and high-browed morals for her husband and children; she did not work to create an appearance of delicate beauty and feminine fragility, nor was she treated as a woman of purity and chastity—unapproachable for carnal sex. Mrs. Kapper's mother was reminiscent more of the slave woman than the "true woman," and the black farmer more of the master than the mate.

The episode illustrates the very complicated forms of mistreatment that occur when racial difference is not the factor but when racial homogeneity is, and when being of the same race but of a different gender and class results in situations as painfully disempowering and oppressive as racism.[40] This black farmer in the late 1800s is representative of those members of a disenfranchised community who have adopted the oppressor's gaze, an objectification of individuals within their own community. The mother was "less" and therefore not expected to need, desire, or deserve that which sustained the dignity and well-being of those viewed as fully human. Beyond her blackness and poverty, she was even more objectified by her gender. She became less equal and less human by virtue of being female. And living in the shadow of slave traditions by which "slave owners controlled black women's labor and commodified black women's bodies as units of capital," the black farmer, although a member of an oppressed group, functioned as both "target and vehicle" of hegemony and power.[41] While the farmer may have held his wife more in line with "true womanhood," complying with Victorian or southern gentry notions of "wife," the narrative reveals that Mrs. Kapper's mother was positioned in opposition to "true womanhood," that in terms of work, chastity, and civility, she was regarded as nonwoman. Her nonwoman positioning then became part of the justification for her abuse. The irony is that this positioning of her as nonwoman was the impetus for a kind and degree of exploitation that was unequivocally gendered. Her body, labor, and even children were exploited because she was a woman devalued as a nonwoman.

As part of her "struggle of memory against forgetting," Mrs. Kapper embellishes the story and revises her mother's sacrifice in descriptions of her own life. The force of this embellishment and revisioning is made clear in hooks's sense of the "struggle of memory" as a "politicization of memory that distinguishes nostalgia, that longing for something to be as once it was, a kind of useless act, from that remembering that serves to illuminate and transform the present."[42] Mrs. Kapper tells the story of her mother and then adds her own experiences of work and nurturing. She positions herself in the story as the one who must now sacrifice for her mother; she is now mother to her own mother. The historical experience of the subject/mother augmented by the contemporary experience of the teller/daughter presents an added heroine, and "like mother, like daughter," she will overcome hard times and do what needs to be done for her family and then pass the story along, as we see in the final narrative.

That Was My Occupation

This episode follows the preceding one by a few lines:

I'd get my milk an' thangs ready tuh go milk the cows
feed my hogs

that was my occupation
(smiling)
throw ah little stuff out tuh my chickens
I could raise some chickens!
(proudly, waving her hands)
in them times.
Sometimes I'd have as many as 40 fryers at ah time on my yard
at one time!
(pointing her finger)
an' I set my hens in
the early winter an' they would hatch
an' when she would quit the nes' an' I couldn' make
her stay on them long 'nough
tuh hatch∧∧
all them eggs_____

I would get me an ol' somthin'/or/other
an' bring the eggs in them an' put them down front the fire
laka that
(She mimes nurturing the egg)
if it started tuh break∧∧
laka it started tuh hatch an' didn' do it∧∧
I'd get me a rag∧∧
(rubs the egg)
ah little warm wata' an' dampen it all way
'round an' make it sof'
(rubs all around the egg)
so that blood would get sof' an'
I would watch it
an' when I'd go back sometime
that shell be done bust on down laka dat
an' I'd wet it some mo'
when I knowed anythin'
that shell done bust
wide open
an' the little chicken layin' in
there
(points to "chicken")
I'd he'p him
pull loose.
They say I wasn'
nohin'
but ah
granny!
(laughing, waves her hands in the air.)

We are witness to the transformative power of Mrs. Kapper's performance through the inseparable act of *nommo*, "all magic is WORD magic," and *kuntu*, meaning and rhythm.[43] Rhythm is the modality of the word, and because the word and its modality of rhythm and meaning are inextricable, it is in the particular conjunction of rhythm/meaning/word that we find performance. Leopold Sedar Senghor writes: "Rhythm is the architecture of being, the inner dynamic that gives it form, the pure expression of the life force. Rhythm is the vibratory shock, the force which, through our sense, grips us at the root of our being. It is expressed through corporeal and sensual means; through lines, surfaces, colours, and volumes in architecture, sculpture or painting; through accents in poetry and music, through movements in the dance. But, doing this, rhythm turns all these concrete things towards the light of the spirit. In the degree to which rhythm is sensuously embodied, it illuminates the spirit."[44] It was rhythm — the act of performance — that transcended time, illuminated meaning, created form, and embodied the spirit of Mrs. Kapper as nurturer and healer; performance is her "occupation." As she nurtures and heals in bringing life forth in the narrative performance of the told, she nurtures and heals in bringing her self-defined identity forth in the narrative performance of the telling. She scoots to the end of her chair as she begins to enact the hatching of the baby chick. With the "egg" in hand, her facial expressions and gestures focus on this little fragile thing she holds. As the imaginary egg hatches, she brings those long ago years to this present moment in time through performance. It was at this moment that she crossed the threshold and became the woman on the farm, nurturing her very own cows, hogs, and chickens — her true occupation.

We observe the value of what Mrs. Kapper describes in this episode as something more than work; for her, it is an occupation. She has worked and known the labor of her mother and others as something outside their own control, something largely diminishing and without self-fulfillment. Work is a site of repression disassociated with creativity and prideful productivity. It is through her *occupation*, rather, that she is in control, empowered, independent, creative — and able to take pride in ownership. In owning the site of her own labor, she has ownership of herself. Because she is finally master of her own work, her work becomes an act of creation. And because what one does and how one thinks are deeply connected, she is euphoric in this new labor of creativity and self-possession through performance.

It was through the transcendence of performance that she was able to re-live the sense and feelings of being "granny" again. It was the emergent performance of granny — what granny told us and what granny did — that demonstrated that it is the work we do that largely defines our existence and organizes our cultural and self-identity; it is in our work that we are fulfilled only to the extent that we believe we are creating something "through our transforming labor."[45] Mrs. Kapper is thrilled to be granny again. Her head rolls back in laughter as she positions her wig and opens her purse for a handkerchief to wipe the tears under her dark glasses.

Conclusion

The aim of this essay has been to illuminate the oral narrative of Mrs. Alma Kapper through black feminist thought, black vernacular, and black intellectual traditions. Interwoven with a performance-centered perspective on life history, these discourses suggest several points.

First, distinctive interpretations of the world are carved out of the embodied, historical, and material reality of a group's life experiences — theories of the flesh — and they offer different perspectives, cast here as traditions, expressions, and forms different from those of groups outside that particular experience and reality. The collective of black women has used distinctive approaches, although varying and divergent, in interpreting, producing, and validating knowledge from their borderland status. Black women are diversely and complexly positioned inside and outside domains of race, class, and gender oppressions. To argue that black women create distinct theories and interpretations is not to essentialize black women as one monolithic group. Black women's experiences are dialectical; they are interpenetrated by racism, sexism, and classism and cannot be traced to one or another form of domination — as if one "ism" were at all times dominant or as if each affects us all uniformly. Black women's theories of the flesh arise not out of essentialist notions of selfhood but out of the fact that black women live a shared history, race, and sex with certain shared experiences, traditions, and cultural meanings and values — however relative or divergent they may be. This is the contradiction and the paradox of the outsider/insider — of living on the borderlands.

Second, these theories of the flesh, or "repositories of a people's theories of themselves," have been difficult for some critics to locate or to understand as self-theorizing.[46] But thinking about theories of the flesh as essentially performative, as emerging from a paradigm of life performances, focuses their location, as well as their meaning and function, for their creators. Through performance Mrs. Kapper unveiled what Collins refers to as taken-for-granted knowledge or "standpoint" and what hooks refers to as the concrete life experiences of black women. Framing this self-theorizing in and as performance puts into high relief where and how people are giving name to themselves, their experiences, and the meanings embedded in both. Above all, Mrs. Kapper's performed narrative makes accessible what Kristin Langellier describes as the " 'fit' — conjunction or disjunction — of a person and his or her world-as-experienced."[47]

Third, then, I have engaged these theories of the flesh — and the "fit" made manifest in their performance — with specialized knowledge, the knowledge of "experts" who express the group's standpoint.[48] This specialized knowledge is interdependent with theories of the flesh, re-articulating them and moving them beyond the argument that black women can produce independent theory. By infusing elements and themes of black women's culture and traditions with critical interventionist thinking, this specialized knowledge provides black women with new tools of resistance. Specialized knowledge functions as a counter-hegemonic discourse in providing epistemologies, grounded in sociocultural practices, that critically interrupt the cultural reproduction of dominance. Black feminism goes a step further by contending that the practice of re-articulating theories of the flesh for the purposes of providing tools of resistance, as well as critically intervening in hegemonic conceptions of the world, must be followed by discussions and elaborations of black women as subjects. As bell hooks states, "opposition is not enough. In that vacant space after one has resisted there is still the necessity to become — make oneself anew. . . . That space within oneself where resistance is possible remains. It is different then to talk about becoming subjects."[49]

And finally, it is in the combination of these four processes — the process of recognizing "the repositories of a people's theories of themselves" carved out of everyday life; of re-articulating specialized knowledge for resistance; of countering dominance through critical intervention; and of affirming subjectivity — that black feminist thought, black discourse, oral narrative, and performance intersect. In narrating her remembrances, in *performance* — in the culmination and materialization of experience — Mrs. Kapper's life, past, and culture came most forcefully and poignantly into being. Mrs. Kapper's performance made manifest both ideology and experience, bringing to life and location her sense of "fit" with her world-as-experienced in the temporal moment of performance, leading, as Dwight Conquergood suggests, "from performance as Agency to performance as ultimate Scene."[50]

In this essay, I have sought to illuminate this performance of Mrs. Kapper through a critical praxis that re-creates "the bonds between the text and world" and requires a combined engagement of intellectual traditions of black discourse, black feminist thought, and a performance paradigm.[51] Hopefully, this performance paradigm is congruent with and enriches the method and purposes of these companion discourses. As Conquergood states, "The performance paradigm privileges particular, participatory, dynamic, intimate, precarious, embodied experience grounded in historical process, contingency, and ideology."[52]

In seeking to draw the intersection of performance, narrative, black feminist thought, and black intellectual traditions, I remained mindful of the challenge involved in the process of interpreting any text — of naming it and struggling to be self-reflexive in the process of assigning meanings to it. This challenge comes to mind again when I remember the instructions of one elderly black woman in domestic work who said to me: "If you want to write about what I'm telling you, don't put any flowers on my story, just tell the truth straight out!"

Notes

The epigraph is taken from bell hooks, *Talking Back: Thinking Feminist, Thinking Black* (Boston: South End Press, 1989), p. 43.

1. Gloria Anzaldúa and Cherríe Moraga, eds., *This Bridge Called My Back: Writings by Radical Women of Color* (New York: Kitchen Table Press, 1983), p. 23.

2. Patricia Hill Collins, "The Social Construction of Black Feminist Thought," in *Black Women in America*, edited by M. R. Malson, E. Mudimbe-Boyi, J. F. O'Barr, and M. Wyer (Chicago: University of Chicago Press, 1988), p. 300.

3. bell hooks, *Yearning: Race, Gender, and Cultural Politics* (Boston: South End Press, 1990), p. 45.

4. Ibid., p. 146.

5. Collins, "Social Construction," p. 298.

6. Ibid., p. 302.

7. Mary Susan Strine, "Critical Theory and 'Organic' Intellectuals: Reframing the Work of Cultural Critique," *Communication Monographs* 58.2 (1991): 194.

8. hooks, *Yearning*, p. 3.

9. Collins, "Social Construction," p. 322.

10. Ibid., p. 302.

11. Patricia Hill Collins, *Black Feminist Thought: Knowledge, Consciousness, and the Politics of Empowerment* (Boston: Unwin Hyman, 1990), p. 26.

12. Ibid., p. 34.

13. Henry Louis Gates Jr., *The Signifying Monkey: A Theory of Afro-American Literary Criticism* (New York: Oxford University Press, 1988), p. x.

14. The "narrated event" and "narrative event" are drawn from Richard Bauman's discussion in his introduction to *Story, Performance, and Event: Contextual Studies of Oral Narrative* (Cambridge: Cambridge University Press, 1986). Although there are other terms and classifications for the reported or past events *inside* the story and the immediate act of *saying* the story, my own sensibilities draw me toward "telling" and "told" because these two terms have more consonance with orality, in addition to having more cultural familiarity.

15. hooks, *Yearning*, pp. 124–25.

16. Traditions of color are abundant in the many ways they theorize themselves, and black artists and scholars have been asserting this in very emphatic and formal discussions, particularly since the Harlem Renaissance in the 1920s with the classic work by Alain Lock in *The New Negro: An Interpretation*, edited by Lock (New York: Albeit Boni, 1925).

17. Dennis Tedlock, *The Spoken Word and the Work of Interpretation* (Philadelphia: University of Pennsylvania Press, 1983), p. 5.

18. Dwight Conquergood, "Rethinking Ethnography: Towards a Critical Cultural Poetics," *Communication Monographs* 58.2 (1991): 179–94; Elizabeth Fine, *The Folklore Text: From Performance to Print* (Bloomington: Indiana University Press, 1984); Tedlock, *Spoken Word*.

19. Mikhail M. Bakhtin, *The Dialogic Imagination: Four Essays*, edited by Michael Holquist, translated by Caryl Emerson and Holquist (Austin: University of Texas Press, 1981), p. 231.

20. Collins, "Social Construction," p. 319.

21. Etheridge Knight, "On the Oral Nature of Poetry," *Painted Bird Quarterly* 32/38 (1988): 12. Knight goes on to describe the materiality of language: "I believe language is not only physical, it's a living thing, a living organism. It's informed by the physical environment, by how we breathe, and our speech patterns. . . . That's the side of language where nuance and inflection come in; we have to agree what the lifting of a

voice means . . . it is the language of nuance, coloring, tone, not necessarily the literal meaning of the words. Sometimes the major meaning of a word is not even in the literal sense of the word so much as in the rhythms and rhymes" (pp. 13–16).

22. Gates, "Blackness," *The Signifying Monkey*, p. 47.

23. Geneva Smitherman, *Talkin and Testifyin: The Language of Black America* (Boston: Houghton-Mifflin, 1977); LeRoi Jones [Imamu Amiri Baraka], *Blues People* (New York: William Morrow, 1963).

24. Leopold Sedar Senghor, *Chants d'Ombre*, translated by Marjorie Grene (West Germany: Eugene Diederichs Verlag, 1945); Paul Carter Harrison, *The Drama of Nommo* (New York: Grove Press, 1972); Janheinze Jahn, *Muntu: African Culture and the Western World* (New York: Grove Press, 1990).

25. Jahn, *Muntu*, p. 110.

26. Ibid., p. 164.

27. Mrs. Kapper's narrative was recorded in 1988.

28. As John Van Maanen suggests in *Tales of the Field: On Writing Ethnography* (Chicago: University of Chicago Press, 1988), when the researcher does her own transcription—re-remembering and re-listening to the voice—the interpretation is enhanced because one discovers new nuances by revisiting the performance. Although sitting through the tapes can be tedious and time consuming, I think it is imperative with the poetic approach to recapture the performance event that only involved the researcher and the teller—the account will be more honest and the interpretation more studied.

The symbol ____ indicates a dramatic *lowering* of the voice; the symbol ʌʌ indicates that the voice has risen to a *higher pitch*; a slash (/) indicates that two words were *spoken together* as one word with hardly a pause between them. Words written in CAPITAL letters were spoken with great *volume* and *intensity*; the symbol I indicates a *whisper*. The lines were broken according to the pause and rhythm of the voice; if there was a one- or two- second pause, another line was started. If the rhythm was generally slower, the break would come at two or three seconds. If the pause was greater, then it was noted.

29. Collins, "Social Construction," p. 318.

30. Molefi Kete Asante, *The Afrocentric Idea* (Philadelphia: Temple University Press, 1987), p. 48; Harrison, *Drama of Nommo*.

31. Victor Turner, *From Ritual to Theatre: The Human Seriousness of Play* (New York: Performing Arts Journal Publications, 1982).

32. Gayraud S. Wilmore, *Black Religion and Black Radicalism: An Interpretation of the Religious History of Afro-American People* (New York: Orbris Books, 1973); Edna Edit, "One Hundred Years of Black Music," *The Black Scholar* 7.10 (1976): 38–48; Charshee Sharlott Lawrence McIntyre, "The Double Meanings of the Spirituals," *Journal of Black Studies* 17.4 (1987): 379–401.

33. Wilmore (*Black Religion and Black Radicalism*, p. 1) elaborates: "From the beginning the religion of the descendants of the Africans who were brought to the Western world as slaves has been something more than what is generally regarded as Christianity. Under the circumstances, it could not have been otherwise. The religious beliefs and rituals of a people are inevitably and inseparably bound with the material and psychological realities of their daily existence."

34. Asante (*Afrocentric Idea*, pp. 188–89) describes African American spirituality coming out of an African-centered consciousness that knows and acknowledges the "WE are": "We can reach our own transcendence, but never without the help of others. If I run to the sea alone, my solitude finds me searching for new ways to come together with others. I know myself only in relation to others, without whom I am a Piagetian egocentric. We say that we can never truly know ourselves without the knowledge of others; or more precisely, in the productive engagement with the other we truly experience our own harmony."

35. Michele Wallace, "A Black Feminist's Search for Sisterhood," in *But Some of Us Are Brave: All the Women Are White, All the Blacks Are Men*, edited by Gloria T. Hull, Patricia Bell Scott, and Barbara Smith (New York: Feminist Press, 1982), pp. 5–12; Barbara Smith, "Towards a Black Feminist Criticism," in *But Some of Us Are Brave*, pp. 157–75; Valerie Smith, "Black Feminist Theory and the Representation of the 'Other,'" in *Changing Our Own Words*, edited by Cheryl A. Wall (New Brunswick: Rutgers University Press, 1991), pp. 38–57.

36. Joyce Ladner, *Tomorrow's Tomorrow: The Black Woman* (New York: Doubleday, 1971); Barbara Christian, *Black Feminist Criticism* (New York: Pergamon Press, 1985); Angela Davis, *Women, Culture, and Politics* (New York: Random House, 1989).

37. Cornel West, *The Ethical Dimensions of Marxist Thought* (New York: Monthly Review Press, 1991), p. xxvii.

38. Ibid., p. xxvii.

39. For a detailed analysis of black women's contestation of the "Cult of True Womanhood," see Paula Giddings, *When and Where I Enter: The Impact of Black Women on Race and Sex in America* (New York: Bantam Books, 1984).

40. Frantz Fanon, *Black Skin, White Mask* (New York: Grove Press, 1963).

41. bell hooks, *Ain't I a Woman? Black Women and Feminism* (Boston: South End Press, 1981), p. 51; Michel Foucault, *Discipline and Punish: The Birth of the Prison*, translated by Alan Sheridan (New York: Random House, 1979), p. 170.

42. hooks, *Yearning*, p. 147.

43. Asante, *Afrocentric Idea*, p. 49.

44. Senghor, *Chants d'Ombre*, p. 60.

45. Paulo Freire, *Pedagogy of the Oppressed* (New York: Continuum Corporation, 1986), p. 141.

46. Gates, *The Signifying Monkey*, p. x.

47. Kristin M. Langellier, "Personal Narratives: Perspectives in Theory and Research," *Text and Performance Quarterly* 9.4 (1989): 271.

48. Collins, "Social Construction," p. 302.

49. hooks, *Yearning*, p. 15.

50. Conquergood, "Rethinking Ethnography," p. 190.

51. Strine, "Critical Theory," p. 198.

52. Conquergood, "Rethinking Ethnography," 187.

Performing History in the Light of History

KAY ELLEN CAPO

Any act of translation is a risky business because it places native meaning within a foreign context. Apart from the meanings of words, there are complicated structural questions. For example, do narrative forms of organization such as closure, sympathy, and suspense translate from one culture to another? Is a writer justified in using Western plot structure if the events being documented originate in a non-Western milieu? As Victor and Edith Turner have pointed out, perceiving how members of another culture experience one another requires more than cognitive understanding. The dramatic enactment of material from other cultures yields insight into the crucial elements of feeling and will, embedded in narrative, myth, symbol, and ritual.[1] Performance uses "local knowledge" to engage with "otherness." In the interpretive process delineated by Clifford Geertz, new chapters of what he calls the "Social History of Moral Imagination" are revealed.[2]

Geertz and Victor Turner see theater as an interpretive instrument, a way to "experience" otherness, to feel, think, remember, value, and imagine alternative futures. The genres associated with the old academic maps of science, social science, and humanities begin to blur; the very instruments of thought are altered and significant correlations emerge.[3] In what follows, the account of a moment of theater and a subsequent reflection, I want to examine the interpretive problem of construing an "other" perceived as embodying values inimical to one's own.[4]

How to Act during an Interrogation:
Theater and Moral Boundaries, 1987

In October 1983 a group of students and I were given a challenge by Amnesty International that tested our capacity for theatrical translation. Couriers of Amnesty had smuggled transcripts of a dissident trial out of Soviet Lithuania. Our job was to create a play about these dissidents for International Human Rights Day and present it as part of a local Unitarian Church service. We had only six weeks. The research task seemed insurmountable. None of us spoke Russian or Lithuanian, and only one person, a Czech, had direct knowledge of life in Eastern Europe. Our production, though highly successful as

343

pro bono documentary theater, provoked questions in us about the moral focus required to write documentary drama.

From the beginning, there were rhetorical and ideological blind spots.[5] It was easy to identify with the dissidents, who appealed to the Western view of human rights espoused by Amnesty International. Yet these were not Western citizens, nor was it a Western trial. We were hampered by ignorance of Soviet Lithuania and by ideological biases. Was it fair to presume, with Amnesty International, that "human rights" and "dissidence" mean the same thing universally? We had to wonder how words like "freedom" cut across cultural frontiers.

The challenge was to write a legitimate play rather than a piece of conservative Western propaganda. No one wanted to defend the Gulag labor camps or the hostile treatment of intellectuals. But we needed a dramatic insight into Soviet culture that would not bury its mystery under Red-baiting rhetoric. An anti-Russian approach left too many questions unanswered, obscuring Soviet society under the weight of Western political bias. We tried to avoid the conservative Western view, but the content of the defendants' speeches, the agenda of Amnesty International, and our own biases gave the performance an "agit-prop" quality.[6]

Our chosen title, *Thoughts in the Margins*, was the name of an underground book of poems by Gintautas (Gintas Iešmantas), one of the three defendants whose story was told in the trial transcripts. Amnesty had hoped to smuggle his poems out of Lithuania to give him international visibility. Like its author, Iešmantas's book was still in exile, but the transcripts of his trial had emerged. To render Soviet repression of Iešmantas and his two codefendants honestly, we had to perceive the margins of Western discourse, seeing censorship and hegemony as conditions that oppress any society. For it is at the boundaries of poetic discourse that one recognizes the limits of current imagination.[7] Inevitably, our play would not merely reveal Soviet moral boundaries; it would indicate the power and limitations of our own moral vision.

Each of the dissidents whose trial we were dramatizing had pressed the margins of Soviet-Lithuanian culture. Iešmantas, a lyric poet and journalist, was condemned for embodying a decadent, bourgeois view of the self. Professor Vytautas Skuodis, a geologist from the University of Vilnius, had written anti-Soviet tracts, including "Spiritual Genocide in Lithuania," a privately circulated book manuscript that attacked the Soviet suppression of Catholicism. The third defendant, a high school linguistics teacher named Povilas Pečeliunas, had taught classes in Lithuanian when Russian was the sole legal language for conducting school.

In the trial, each dissident displayed the Western vocabulary and rhythm of self-assertion that had precipitated his arrest, arguing that constructive criticism would "upgrade the prestige of the state and . . . strengthen its economic base."[8] Friends and relatives were present in the courtroom, but the implied audience seemed to be the Western human rights movement. Or was this "implied audience" a fiction we imposed on the transcripts to make the trial more accessible? As the smuggling of trial records was a rare feat, the defendants could not have assumed that their words would reach the West. Who were they talking to?

We needed to unravel the "otherness" of Lithuanian experience. As Geertz puts it, we wanted to determine "how the deeply different can be deeply known without becoming any less different, the enormously distant enormously close without becoming any less far away."[9] The written text was not enough. Ideally, we should have had notes from a court ethnographer to see the ritual meaning of this social drama in its Soviet context. But a written record of the words was all we had.[10]

Each dissident held that the Soviet constitution assured rights similar to those granted in Western democracies. According to Professor Skuodis, "The constitution of the USSR gives every citizen the right to present suggestions and to criticize." And Skuodis, in his defense, argued that "the charges against V. Skuodis are based on the assumption that his actions are anti-Soviet in nature. I deny that assumption and point out that his actions fall within freedoms given by the Soviet constitution. They are motivated not by foreign radio broadcasts, but by the desire to live in a free society. Is this not a goal we all share?"

Skuodis, who claimed to be American-born, transcended the legal system that had accused him by appealing to international law. He reasoned that as a signatory nation, the USSR should abide by the Universal Declaration of Human Rights (1944), which asserts: "Everyone has the right to freedom of opinion and expression; this right includes freedom to hold opinions without interference and to seek, receive and impart information and ideas through any media and regardless of frontiers." Skuodis's attitude confirms observations made by the British playwright Tom Stoppard, who on visiting the dissident Czech scene noted the energy, commitment, and sense of liberation among convicted writers who no longer had anything to hide. "These people," said Stoppard, "felt they were not breaking any law, that the state was breaking the law."[11]

Taking a "human rights" perspective allowed us to capture the defendants' sense of their own righteousness. Although that righteousness introduced problems that will be discussed later, this approach did offer advantages. First, it was our group's perspective; second, it was the agenda of our sponsor, Amnesty International; third, our metropolitan New York audiences could relate to human rights. With added ethnographic research, ideally on location in

Lithuania, it might have been possible to construe "human rights" in a more local frame. Yet textual performance, our only cultural entrée, did yield subtle awareness of a complex field.

What this perspective left open were many questions about the boundaries of international dialogue. For example, what was the Soviet motive for this show trial? Was there a hole in our Western perception of the person, a silence symptomatic of the East-West impasse? Perhaps such a gap ironically protected both systems from the compromises necessary to create common discourse. Was the issue of individual rights the blind spot that prevented Westerners from truly seeing the USSR? The transcripts were riddled with opposing conceptions of self, other, and community. The legal machinery that framed this crisis was not set up to resolve individual differences about censorship; it was a ritual affirmation of existing Soviet policy on dissent.[12]

T. Darragh, among others, has pointed out that blanks in narrative are illuminating mistakes that, like Freudian slips, point to hidden truths. A blank reveals language "as both an active and a defective process."[13] In the transcripts, defendants created gaps in the state's official narrative by refusing to answer questions. We reasoned that their refusal to answer questions during interrogation would remind an American audience of "taking the Fifth Amendment" and make a foreign ritual seem more familiar.[14] From the transcripts we knew that the Western strategy of passive resistance had crossed Soviet borders through an unsanctioned Russian tract: "How to Act During an Interrogation."

As actors in an ethical drama, the dissidents were "playing" with notions of justice. From the Soviet vantage, they had betrayed communism. From the perspective of international human rights, they were using discourse heroically to manipulate the relation between a political subject and his context. Contrasted with that of the defendants, the discourse of Soviet officials lacked playfulness; determinism is apparent in one of the Prosecutor's final remarks: "Pečeliunas, like a sandwich, took a two-sided stance." The notion of two sides seemed more than the Prosecutor's logic or imagination could bear, and the line was unintentionally funny. Probing the ethical subtext of the defendants, the Prosecutor had revealed a certain obstinacy in his own perspective.

Putting all this in terms of the postmodern ethical scheme outlined by Julia Kristeva, resistance to orthodoxy made the defendants exemplary ethical figures. Kristeva maintains that contemporary moral life does not arise from coercing persons to repeat a preestablished code. Rather, the new ethics emerges "wherever a code (mores, social contract) must be shattered in order to give way to the free play of negativity, need, desire, pleasure, and jouissance, before being put together again, although temporarily and with full knowledge of what is involved. Fascism and Stalinism stand for the barriers that the new adjustment between a law and its transgression comes against."[15] The trial was an ethical dialogue between a post-Stalinist regime and defendants who wanted to deconstruct the moral code of that regime.

To embody the truth of this foreign situation we had to "deconstruct" Western notions of sympathetic character and suspenseful plot. In the transcripts, the character of the Soviet officials was flat.[16] Neither the Judge nor the Prosecutor said much. If the Soviet Prosecutor and Judge were totally unsympathetic, Western prejudices would be confirmed rather than challenged. From a documentary vantage, it was false to imply that the defendants would prevail; only 1 percent of Soviet trials ended in acquittal. Yet a Western audience, schooled in the psychology of suspense and the jury trial, would naturally hope for the victory of the underdogs. We wondered whether the defendants and audience in a Soviet trial would have felt hopeful or fatalistic. Was suspense a valid organizing principle to reveal the subjectivity of these characters in their situation?

At one point in the trial, sympathetic feeling became a focus for ideological debate. Attacking the "reactionary"-feeling tones of Iešmantas's poetry, the Prosecutor pointed to nostalgic rhythms associated with the bourgeois individual. Expressions of emotion and performance of rituals were strictly governed in Soviet countries.[17] Michael T. Kaufman once noted that in communist Czechoslovakia, where improvisational jazz and blue jeans were still taboo, "there are rules governing the performance of even sanctioned jazz. No performers can appear in jeans, presumably because this would cause semiotic overload in an audience, doubling up Western symbols."[18]

Although it resulted in harsh sentencing, the trial had a "liminal" quality. In Turner's view, it offered "messages of discontent," the "seeds of cultural transformation." The dissenters were experimenting with Soviet discourse in a forum where "new combinatory rules" might be established. The court suspended censorship of the very notions it was designed to punish. While on trial, the defendants were free to air forbidden views and defend them as the "real" message of the Soviet constitution. Such liberality did not extend to the courtroom audience or to friends and family members, who were punished for disrupting the proceedings by symbolic gestures of solidarity with the dissenters. Nevertheless, the trial was a place to "play" with new symbols, constructions, and paradigms that could "feed back into the 'central' economic and political-legal domains . . . supplying them with [new] goals, aspirations, incentives, structural models and raisons d'être."[19]

The challenge of establishing fellow feeling for the Soviet Judge and Prosecutor was partially solved through a casting choice. We had three good female actresses and only one major part—that of Pečeliunas's fiancée, Danutė, a witness at the trial. In photographs of Soviet trials, the regular presence of women officials is in startling contrast to their absence in the average Western courtroom. Soviet women were not merely clerks or secretaries; they played leading roles. Thus it seemed legitimate to cast women as Judge and Prosecutor. We hoped that an American audience would think twice about the margins of its own legal system. Several members of the audience commented that seeing females in authoritative roles provoked sympathy for those who conform rigidly to any regime and an awareness of sexual equality as a value in Soviet life.

As servants of a judicial rite that discouraged personal initiative, the Judge and Prosecutor sometimes seemed about to degenerate into puppets. When Iešmantas argued against Soviet censorship of the press, he aroused an unintentionally comic response from the Prosecutor: "Oh really? Then tell us how you imagine it should be. Should it be that any illiterate can publish?" Later, the tables turned as the Judge's Marxist objection to free information gave a chilling rebuke to Iešmantas's proclamation that "truth" is a matter of personal conscience: "What would be the material foundation [of truth]? For example, under capitalism there are classes. Whoever owns the capital owns the press."

A full study of Soviet censorship and legal traditions would have taken months. But Amnesty International did provide current details about the labor camps and copies of correspondence from the defendants to their relatives. The Lithuanian Organization from Brooklyn sent books, underground literature, and folk music. One night we were instructed by the organist of the Lithuanian American church, who answered questions and taught us songs, including the illegal anthem of independent Lithuania with which we decided to end our play.

The administrator of the Lithuanian Information Center brought slides, photographs, and her own national costume, embroidered in vibrant Baltic designs. We learned that Baltic people resent being identified with the Slavs (they are a different race), that Lithuanian is one of the oldest European languages, and that Lithuania had absorbed the revolutionary fervor of neighboring Poland. Despite all the help they gave us, most Lithuanians we met were bitterly anti-Soviet and could offer no sympathetic insight into the Russian mind and milieu.

In addition to the ideological blocks of resource people, student biases deserve mention. One student who had studied Soviet politics at first drafted monologues for Professor Skuodis from lists of statistics. After workshops, Skuodis's character was infused with sympathetic personal history, as in the following soliloquy: "On December 22, my daughters, Giedre and Daiva, were in attendance. The Judge had just declared a recess when the girls threw flowers from the courtroom down to us defendants. There was an uproar! . . . Eventually Daiva was reprimanded by the administration of the school where she studies art. But for Giedre, it was worse. She was forced to resign her position at the State Bank." Skuodis's sarcastic insults to the state offered another key to his character. When asked why his descriptions of "certain atheist authors" used "such ugly epithets as drunkard and adulterer," Skuodis replied: "As I said — the work is not yet edited. Those are just notes — I happen to know that author personally." But Skuodis staunchly refused to reveal the individual's name. Later, he referred to a new work — *The Concept of Calumny and Lying in Soviet Propaganda and Actuality*; the very title seemed calculated to enrage.

Whereas the student who adapted Skuodis's monologues was at first too cold and didactic, other approaches were too sympathetic. One student's senti-mental notion of character obscured political subtleties. Yet she caught human touches missed by her peers, including a portion of testimony that seemed to implicate one witness as a former lover or very special friend of Iešmantas. The witness seemed especially protective of Iešmantas. This adapter also en-larged the testimony of Iešmantas's son, an enlisted soldier who, by Soviet law, was compelled to testify against his own father.

Our star actress and key defense witness was a Czech émigré who had been trained as a professional actress in Prague. Like Skuodis, her father had been stripped of his professorship, so she was deeply invested in the story. She played the role of defendant Pečeliunas's fiancée, Danutė Keršiūtė, a woman who mirrors the defiant gesture of Skuodis's daughters toward the court. Danutė brings flowers into the courtroom and hands them to the three defendants, creating disruption among supporters in the gallery. For her act of solidarity she is sentenced to seven days in prison. After her testimony, as the Judge orders her to prison, Danutė is forced offstage by guards, protesting: "But these are flowers, not a hydrogen bomb!"

The audience's knowledge of Danutė's character was enhanced not only by the actress' defiant performance during interrogation, but by soliloquies. Dur-ing a freeze in her interrogation, Danutė explains that she could not marry Pečeliunas as scheduled because of his arrest, trial, and deportation to a labor camp. Most of her speech was derived from actual letters we had in our possession:

As soon as I found out where Povilas was, I petitioned the warden at the labor camp to let us be married. The authorities imposed a three month waiting period, even though only one month is required. They wanted to confiscate Povilas's apartment. Since he and I were not yet married, I had no claim to it. In our country losing your apartment is a very serious thing because of the constant housing shortage. The Soviet government simply wanted the chance to strike one more blow against Povilas Pečeliunas.

They wanted to make sure that even when he got out of prison, there would be nowhere for him to come home to.

The soliloquies of Danutė and Skuodis demonstrate a shortcut used to give depth to their characters. There was no time within a forty-five-minute play for realistic exposition of defendants' lives outside the trial, whether at home or in prison. Background was rendered mainly during freezes in the plot. Because the Judge and Prosecutor had no moments of psychological revelation, our bias toward the defendants was obvious. Among the state witnesses only Pečeliunas's fiancée had soliloquies.

From voluminous trial transcripts, the "spine" of each defendant began to form around a single protest issue. For Skuodis, religious freedom arose repeatedly as the central motive for dissent. All defendants argued against censorship, but that theme became the special province of the poet-journalist Iešmantas. Pečeliunas, the linguist who refused to teach his high school classes in Russian, functioned as a spokesman for Lithuanian culture and against Russification. His evasive speech established a warm and comic character:

Judge: Did you receive illegal literature?

Pečeliunas: Sometimes I would find articles in my wood box or my mail box, but I don't know who put them there.

Prosecutor: Do you expect the court to believe this?

Pečeliunas: Yes.

Prosecutor: Why did you keep them?

Pečeliunas: I read them. If one wishes to form a world outlook, one must read everything. The articles were poorly written, so I rewrote them and threw away the originals.

Judge: But you agreed with the ideas expressed . . . ?

Pečeliunas: I said one must read everything; but not necessarily agree with everything one reads. . . .

Prosecutor: What can you say about the manuscript of the article, "We Begin a New Era," written in your own hand? Are you the author?

Pečeliunas: Are you asking if it is my handwriting or if I am the author?

Judge: (Annoyed) This is unimportant. It's just a matter of words.

Establishing the spine of each dissident, we organized the trial into separate interrogations of men who emerged as a kinship group. Turner's view of social drama as a process of regeneration helped us decide how to structure the action. As a reiterative social form, the trial presented a local view of power and justice, making Soviet political theory into fact.[20] It involved (1) a breach of norms (the forbidden expression of censored perspectives), (2) a crisis (the arrest and indictment), (3) an attempted redress (the trial), and (4) a recognition of schism (the harsh sentencing of each dissident to years in the Gulag). According to Turner's scheme, social drama may end in "either reintegration or recognition of schism."[21] In this story, reintegration seemed impossible; schism was a necessary condition of the breach. Geertz has articulated the need to combine Turner's ritual view with rhetorical and other symbolic analyses that are able to preserve the specificity of a given social drama or text; taken alone, the ritual perspective lumps disparate events into the same category.[22] In our case, the actors' task called for keen awareness of verbal nuances and of the rhetorical impact intended by the defendants.

As our play was replacing a regular Sunday service of the Unitarian Church, we were asked to include congregational music in the forty-five-minute format, and we met this condition by closing with the outlawed anthem of pre-Soviet Lithuania. Here and elsewhere, an emerging emphasis on Lithuanian nationalism provided perspective. While human rights may be articulated in an abstract way, the struggle goes on locally, within a changeable social order. A sense of locale came with slogans — "Laisvę Lietuvai!" (Free Lithuania!) and "Kalanta!" — spoken by Iešmantas and by gallery protesters who reacted to the incendiary closing of his defense.[23] "Kalanta" was a password for freedom that commemorated a Lithuanian student who had burned himself in public to protest Soviet rule. Kalanta's story had come up earlier during the interrogation of Pečeliunas, the high school teacher accused of feeling sympathy for a student the regime considered psychotic.

Softly chanted as a final act of defiance by prisoners walking offstage to suffer harsh sentences, the Lithuanian hymn was taken up by class members planted in the audience and finally by the community at large. Technically, the effect was somewhat strained, but it was powerful as community celebration.[24] Because Lithuanians at the performance had never heard their national hymn sung in English, their reaction was unexpectedly forceful. They were deeply touched that a group of American students had cared to learn about their remote country.

After finishing the production, we saw many possibilities for changes in character, plot, style, and rehearsal. For example, some roles could have been expanded and others invented. The defiant daughters of Skuodis never appeared onstage but would have been very lively; the son and lover of Iešmantas could have been given larger roles. Dramatic structure and style might also have differed. Working to render a rigid, bureaucratic scene, we chose a presentational — almost forensic — style. Soliloquies allowed characters a personal dimension and accentuated the apparatus of Soviet censorship that makes personal opinions into dangerous secrets. But a farcical approach like that of Dario Fo would have heightened the absurdity of the trial, the gaps in discourse.[25] Music, voiceovers, films, slides, comic tableaus, even acrobatics or juggling might have parodied official gestures and the contorted "juggling" of both sides in a desperate scene.

Having been a Czech dissident, Vaclav Havel takes the perspective that what Westerners saw as absurdity in his early plays was actually realistic; it reflected the social fractures and gaps that made Soviet communication so bifurcated: "It seems that in Central Europe what is most earnest has a way of blending, in a particularly tense manner, with what is most comic. . . . It is precisely the dimension of distance, of rising above ourselves and making light of ourselves, that lends our concerns just the right shattering seriousness."[26]

On a thematic and scenic level, we might have explored censorship through visual and auditory metaphors, by playing with forbidden modes of replication that Westerners took for granted. Tape recorders, photocopying technology, mimeograph machines, typewriters, even handwritten copies were considered dangerous and were controlled by the state because they produced and distributed discourse. Defendants were condemned for possessing any multiple copies; typewriters required registration with the security police. At one point Pečeliunas defended himself against having multiple copies of illegal literature: "I was learning to type. Danutė let me borrow it [her typewriter] for that purpose. I would not be so stupid as to type illegal articles on a typewriter which was registered with the security police and could thus be so easily traced."

As the script developed, communications technology emerged as a stage-worthy presence, a force that resists government attempts to limit informational access in a global village. At one point in the play Iešmantas protested: "The law and the Soviet Constitution do not forbid anyone to reflect and explore. One cannot be put on trial for one's beliefs! There is no such law! . . . Furthermore, the charge that I 'listened to foreign radio broadcasts' sounds naive. A person my age should not be told what to listen to, what to read!" These comments echo Iešmantas's opening remarks, as adapted from his letters: "In the Soviet Constitution Freedom of Press, of Speech, of Church and Heritage exist — but only on paper. Not here, where conversation is never safe from unseen listeners. Where poetry is a threat to national Security. Where a typewriter is a gun and carbon paper is ammunition."[27]

In rethinking the rehearsals, it seems we might profitably have looked at the Soviet trial transcript alongside the text of an American political trial; Abbie Hoffman and the Chicago Seven, the obscenity trial against Allen Ginsberg's *Howl*, or Daniel Berrigan and the Catonsville Nine come to mind. The international atmosphere and issues surrounding censorship might have found embodiment in acting gestures over time. Another rehearsal or performance option would have been to adapt a composite script, interweaving scenes from American censorship trials with scenes from the Lithuanian trial.

A silent character in this trial was the Western Fourth Estate, the press. It would be exciting to see the entire play through the lens of Western journalism. Journalism is a problematic narrative mode. It combines the attempt to construe "true" human stories with the effort to "sell" those stories to a mass audience. Organized as a play within a play, our drama could have shown the Western news media trying to find an "angle" from which to recount the trial narrative. Mirroring some of our interpretive problems, this technique would highlight elements of Western inscription, such as the tendency to report personal information and focus on individual personality rather than on public issues. In an effort to achieve a measure of "humanity" for the dissidents, we had fallen into the personal and biographical camp ourselves.[28]

In the performance of a Soviet text, the choice of acting style itself has intercultural implications. Several directors from the Eastern Bloc — Konstantin Stanislavsky, Bertolt Brecht, and Jerzy Grotowski among them — have had great influence on Western theater. Could one explore East/West value differences by considering how Eastern and Western directors have dealt with actors and thus with "ethos" — the imaginative formation of character? American acting has been greatly affected by Stanislavsky's stress on emotional and physical memory. The psychology of his individualistic approach differs from the "holy theater" of Grotowski, whose famous beehive experiments engaged nonactors in ascetic training calculated to unleash energy and disarm social fear.

A Soviet psychiatrist who worked with Grotowski reported: "It seems that the individual personality was sublimated, higher aims appeared, and, on the other hand, social bonds were widened and deepened." In contrast, Brecht and his followers consider the liberation of personal impulses to be just a part of theater's task; theater must help remake the historical field — the social order — itself.[29] Considering nineteenth-century dramatic interpretation and public speaking in America as cultural performances, Mary Strine has shown how the performance theory of James Rush did remake the social field, giving citizens access to the fruits of Jacksonian democracy — equality, social progress, and the cultural refinement that the orotund delivery style of "elocution" came to represent.[30] Critical discourse needs to account for the ethical and political values that emerge from performance practices.

Our interpretive problem was first to discern what kind of freedom and ethical vision the defendants were fighting for and then what acting style would best present their vision to a Western audience. They seemed to want both individual liberty and social solidarity. Iešmantas, for example, was accused of writing decadent, individualistic poetry; but he held fast to the ideals of Euro-Communism. Thus it was useful to alternate the techniques of Brecht and Stanislavsky when trying to help the actor who played Iešmantas get inside the double perspective of that subjectivity.

In the struggle for a pluralistic world story, literary adaptation is an important tool. This essay has explored some of the deconstructive problems that arise when one adapts the textual artifacts of a nonnative culture. Because values are hard-won discoveries made within a specific milieu, cross-cultural adaptation offers ethical adventure; scripters must actively constitute the "other" from a complex social and psychological matrix. Writing across cultures requires a certain courage. As Dwight Conquergood points out, "When we have true respect for the Difference of other cultures then we grant them the potential for challenging our own culture."[31]

Perhaps both approaches to performance — the Western concentration on the psyche of the individual and the Marxist delineation of social process — are needed if one wants to discover a postmodern style of performance that will help bridge the expressive gap dividing the Cold War stories of East and West. Adapting and performing Soviet materials may reveal social gestures needed to connect two moral universes. Soviet authors have led the West in reviving the nineteenth-century tradition of stage adaptation;[32] according to Nicholas Rzhevsky, their adaptations of classic Russian fiction allowed Soviet authors to manipulate literary codes and engage in autonomous moral discourse outside the realm of sanctioned propaganda.[33]

If theater is seen as a laboratory for living, the imaginative "discovery" of Soviet characters would constitute new "facts," empirical evidence for history and an antidote to conservative propaganda. Moving an audience toward such a discovery would require presenting neither East nor West nor any character as "right." For if no one "knows" the truth, the audience must engage in its own ethical discovery, acknowledging that the moral world is made and re-made as a never-ending communal task.

Our play might have accomplished such a moral "discovery" if the pro-Soviet characters had been understood in wider terms and if the dissidents had been seen less righteously. In the translated transcript, the bold resistance of Skuodis, for example, sometimes verged on arrogance. We wondered whether his critical disposition might have made Skuodis intolerant of others had he assumed power. Pečeliunas was shifty; he was obviously lying to the court. One student even imagined that Pečeliunas might be a Soviet counteragent. We had been informed that such spies were common in political trials, and Pečeliunas did get off with the lightest sentence. Iešmantas's professions of moral assurance were sometimes handled simplistically in our play. Although the David-and-Goliath theme was theatrically seductive, did it warrant deconstruction?

If performance is to engage plural voices in the articulation of wisdom, it must embrace texts derived from disenfranchised or nonliterate cultures.[34] And the norms that govern discourse, including the peculiar discourse of literary adaptation, need to be scrutinized carefully. As Kristin Langellier sees it, reaching out must be coupled with a rigorous reaching in: "For only by examining our own ethics and politics can we claim a humanism that reveals rather than conceals the relations of power in discourse, that gives voice to resistance and difference, and that puts us in touch with the world."[35]

Fostering a plural world of discourse does not guarantee a simpler moral life. Geertz reminds us that accepting "others" means living on an ethical boundary: "Whatever use the imaginative productions of other peoples — predecessors, ancestors, or distant cousins — can have for our moral lives then, it cannot be to simplify them. The image of the past (or the primitive, or the classic, or the exotic) as a source of remedial wisdom, a prosthetic corrective for a damaged spiritual life — an image that has governed a good deal of humanist thought and education — is mischievous because it leads us to expect that our uncertainties will be reduced by access to thought-worlds constructed along lines alternative to our own, when in fact they will be multiplied."[36]

The moral and psychological growth engendered by cross-cultural encounter "comes only at the expense of . . . inward ease." If our play revealed the instability generated by placing Soviet culture in a Western frame, resolving that instability is quite another question. But performance offers a way to experience the "double perception" needed to constitute moral narratives in a decentered, postmodern age.[37]

Stages of Dissent in Post-Soviet Lithuania, 1993

A Cold War Notebook

Bin gar keine Russin, stamm' aus Litauen, echt deutsch.
[I am not Russian at all. I come from Lithuania. I am a real German.]
    T. S. Eliot, *The Wasteland*[38]

Jim [U.S. Navy; assigned to a nuclear silo on a submarine stationed off Cuba]:
    We're going to win the fuckin' war. I mean, they are really *dumb*.
    They've got liquid fuel in their rockets, they're rusty and they're going
    to sputter, they're going to pop, they're going to land in our
    cornfields. . . . You won't believe this. The Russians don't even have
    electro-intercoms in their ships. They still speak through tubes!
Spalding Gray: Suddenly I had this enormous fondness for the Russian
    Navy. The whole of Mother Russia. The thought of these men
    speaking, like innocent children, through empty toilet paper rolls,
    where you could still hear compassion, doubt, envy, brotherly love,
    ambivalence, all those human tones. . . . "Listen Mr. Spalding [he
    said] . . . you would not be doing that thing you do, writing, talking,

whatever it is you do in the theatre, if it were not for me and the United States Navy stopping the Russians from taking over the world."

Spalding Gray, *Swimming to Cambodia*[39]

A story goes that the president [newly elected in the Republic of Croatia, November 1990] . . . mentioned how we should change our rather primitive manners and suggested a red line in front of every post office or bank counter "so people would learn how to stand in line, not to step on each other's toes . . . and to mind their manners as people in the world do. . . ." As expected, this move was saluted in the newspapers as a great leap forward, toward the already mythical "West."

All of a sudden, private space became important, even fashionable in a country where, for forty-five years . . . it was perfectly normal . . . to peer at each other's documents, accounts, letters and bills quite shamelessly. Considering that privacy was a bad word, such peering was even safe. Asking for the right to privacy meant you had something to hide.

Slavenka Drakulić, *How We Survived Communism and Even Laughed*[40]

Latvians and Estonians may well feel that too much space [in my book] is given to Lithuania. . . . There may be some truth in this. The Lithuanians, with their emotional rhetoric and grand gestures, their greater extremism but also their greater readiness to make sacrifices, have indeed tended to elbow their more stolid neighbors out of the limelight. But what to do? This is the way it has been in the history of the Baltic over the past few years. Many people, East and West, have tried to subdue the Lithuanians. No one has succeeded.

Anatol Lieven, *The Baltic Revolution*[41]

We were taught how to behave with KGB. We were taught how to be brave, to be demanding. At the very beginning [of the trial] we sat in the first row. And after, we were allowed only to go in the room after all people sat. We took the last row. We managed to sit near the [loud]speaker and we can hear every word. . . . It was more clear. Even those words which were talked between the Judge and two people near him. It was so funny. . . . And we wrote every word in this trial. . . . We had so small pieces of paper — which was same size as our hand and pencils we had so short. We covered them with the other hand and we held our hands on knees, not before our eyes. We wrote — how do you say? — blind. We [kept] our eyes on the scene of trial. [She laughs.] It was funny.

Irena Skuodienė, explaining how she and her daughters recorded the trial on which our play, *Thoughts in the Margins: Voices of Soviet Dissent*, was based[42]

Encountering Lithuania:
Memories of December 15, 1993, Manhattan

Today the force of my ten-year encounter with Lithuania imposes itself like a neglected friend demanding exchange. I am trembling as I write because Irena Skuodienė, wife of Professor Vytautas Skuodis, has just told me the news that it was she and her two daughters who recorded the trial transcripts that leaked out of Lithuania to the West like an excess of political courage and somehow reached my hands. Calling her from a cramped phone booth, I scribble her every word on the back of my play manuscript, the only paper at my disposal. Enacting this uncomfortable, rushed performance of writing, my body resonates with the performance Irena Skuodienė now tells me about — how she and her daughters transcribed two copies of their tiny courtroom notes each night at home, using "black paper" (carbons) forbidden by the state. They worked by candlelight to avoid detection and could not speak their memories aloud because their apartment was bugged by the KGB. She says "KGB" quickly, in a staccato that compresses defiance, hatred, contempt, even black humor. They wrote silently, passing notes to each other on toy magic slates: "You write on a [magic] slate and it disappears. And we wrote on this if we had something important to say. You lift and you do not need destroy paper. I took all three originals and then remembered. I had in my head some of it that same day what happened. From all those sources I wrote in one place."

Irena Skuodienė's passionate memories resonate with my own sense of urgency as we talk. In the panicky excitement of note taking, the effort of her struggle becomes more clear. Now her words vibrate along the nerves, as if my body were a violin or drum she is using to play back memories. Storied courage and moral energy are passing into me as I realize what it took for her to perform a gesture I take for granted — writing words on paper — and I feel new resolve to pass them on.

And as I try to remember how to spell her name, I also sense the frustration Irena Skuodienė must feel as she leafs through an English dictionary for words. Who wrote my play? Three dissidents, this woman and her daughters, also smugglers, Amnesty International couriers who took the Lithuanian manuscript like an Olympic torch to its English translator in Chicago, Vita Matušaitis. And when by a series of accidents it reached me, I accepted the challenge to write this story into other versions.

Now I hear from Skuodis's wife that she and her daughters felt angry and sad that only an abbreviated version of their handwritten notes was published in America.[43] They presumed that no copy of the whole text ever made it to the West; their remaining copy was, of course, destroyed to avoid detection. The faith of those who perform identity by writing words on paper sets my heart racing as it occurs to me that I may have the only record of their struggle: "I'm not sure," I say hesitantly, "but I may still have the whole manuscript. I think we were working from a much longer text than the one you saw. The manuscript Amnesty gave us was very long. I don't know for sure, but maybe I still have the whole thing."[44] And I sense excitement as she wonders whether I will please send her my article, and of course I promise to do so. Suddenly things are beginning to make sense. The testimony of three men for whom words were the bread of life was transcribed by a learned Lithuanian woman and rather incidentally preserved by me, an American scholar who values their struggle to tell the truth.

Irena Skuodienė tells me that she has lived in Chicago since she, her husband, and her youngest daughter Daiva (age 34) were forced to emigrate on September 8, 1987, after her husband's release from a Soviet labor camp. Her other daughter (Giedre, 36) chose to remain in Lithuania with her husband and two children. Skuodis is now abroad, completing a two-year work contract in Lithuania and may stay longer if another job materializes.[45] Irena has stayed in Chicago at least in part because she and her daughter do not agree with Skuodis's new, more "liberal" politics: "I don't like what happens in Lithuania. Daiva too. We get enough of KGB. . . . It is very hard, very difficult for me. But now I don't share [my husband's] views. It's very complicated. Very difficult. Daiva too. We have similar views about [former president] Landsbergis and events in Lithuania. Daiva has the views from her experience of this communistic system. I learned this system from the very beginning to now. Because I was ten years when Lithuania was occupied by Russia. I learned about this with my skin." Before our talk, I had been surprised to learn that Skuodis backed Algirdas Brazauskas, a former communist who won the presidency despite opposition from Vytautas Landsbergis (a liberator figure to many members of the intelligentsia, including Skuodis's wife) in February 1993.[46] But I never imagined that his decision might alienate Skuodis from members of his own family. I realize now that I am having trouble finalizing this essay because the history of Eastern Europe and the personal history of these dissidents will not stay still. Nothing wants to close.

And suddenly I understand why I am trembling as I write and why I could not make this phone call earlier. I was afraid. Afraid of intervening in the lives of people who had suffered, of taxing their energy for the sake of an academic project. Theirs was and is a painful project of freedom, of life and death. Indeed, over the phone, I could feel Irena Skuodienė become exhausted from reliving so many details of her life, many of them painful. I became exhausted, in turn, from the pressure to record her story exactly, to negotiate the liberal and anticommunist views that could divide us, to live up to the model of intelligence, dignity, and fairness she put before me. I am awed by the demands this story keeps making of me. It—along with the many other people and stories with which it has put me in contact—insists on a response.

Until now, it was safer to keep my relationship with Lithuania on academic terms. Because if I got reinvested in this complicated story wouldn't I once again be swallowed up by its demands? Hadn't my infant son learned to prefer bottled milk ten years ago while I was doing this play? Frustrated with his mother's late arrivals from rehearsal, he gave up nursing and weaned himself. I cannot help worrying what else will be required of me if I attend to the care and feeding of this story again. Moved to intimacy by our talk and feeling guilty for taking so long to make this personal contact, I tell Irena Skuodienė about the nursing episode and she offers comfort from Chicago: "I understand. I understand."

It is exactly thirteen years ago today that the 1980 trial of Skuodis, Pečeliunas, and Iešmantas began in Vilnius, Lithuania. But this amazing quirk of fate will not occur to me for two more days.

Performing Within and Against Nationality

In 1983 my students and I had enacted the trial of three dissidents who referred to their country as "Soviet-occupied Lithuania." To us, then, such talk seemed dangerously declarative. Weren't they bucking a Soviet federation that had absorbed Lithuania into its identity for almost forty years in a political stalemate known as the Cold War? We imagined an almost childlike innocence in their defiant baiting of the Russian Bear. Yet with such desperate courage ("Be Realistic: Ask the Impossible") and with a native grasp of Soviet vulnerability that startled Western leaders, Lithuanians were able to initiate the events that culminated in their independence. By performing Lithuania's political identity, its insurgent leaders won a spot on the world stage. Like the dissidents of our play, they wrote Lithuania into existence, performing "as if" they were subjects in a Western political script of nonviolent protest, democratic dialogue, and universal human rights. Their behavior during the secession crisis paralleled the creative risk of actors who perform as if a set of imaginary circumstances is real. In this case, an independent Lithuania was their imagined circumstance.[47]

Looking back, I remember how we disbelieved the words of Soviet leaders in the trial transcript because they lacked playfulness; imaginatively unable to sustain the circumstances of Soviet Lithuania through convincing metaphors and social gestures, the Judge and Prosecutor seemed to get smaller as they presided over the shrinking discursive space of Soviet Lithuania itself. Their smug, bipolar speeches embodied Soviet determinism, giving our text an absurd, black comic tone. Even twelve years ago, their assumption that Soviet identity was an inevitable requirement for Lithuanians seemed naive.[48] *Thoughts in the Margins* caught the Judge and Prosecutor in the ambivalent act of composing the image of their own cultural power. Seen in this light, Soviet (occupied) Lithuania presented itself as vulnerable to change.[49] As history would soon prove, Soviet power was crumbling under the weight of such heavy-handed rhetoric.[50]

Glossing "Our System Is Based on Slogans," an article for which Iešmantas was put on trial, Irena Skuodienė explained that "all words were slogans. Not working words but slogans. And *perestroika* and *glasnost* were only catch words." Her preference for "working words" was echoed by her daughter Daiva, who expressed surprise that Westerners believed the rhetorical performances of Mikhail Gorbachev; to her they were just propaganda by the former party chief:[51] "No program, just words. And he was really on a ninth cloud — running around the world. But *perestroika* was a soap bubble. I really feel sad how people here trust everything said by the Russian government."[52] Though the tidy Cold War story on which our play and Western journalism depended has been shattered, it seems naive to expect that one can simply recast old enemies as new friends. Used to framing current history in terms of bipolar, national subjectivities, the Western news media has begun to depend on another story angle: the postmodern fragmentation of identities worldwide, manifest in ongoing civil wars within and outside the former USSR.

We tried to "study the nation through its narrative address," to construct "the field of meanings and symbols associated with national life." I see now that our play, like recent stories of Eastern Europe, tended to read "nations" in a restrictive way: "either, as the ideological apparatus of state power . . . or, in a more utopian inversion, as the incipient or emergent expression of the 'national-popular' sentiment preserved in a radical memory." We had read Soviet Lithuania as a state of being imposed by the Kremlin, as "the ideological apparatus of state power."[53] We conversely presented the visions of three trial defendants and some witnesses whose idyll of a democratic, autonomous Lithuania nonetheless seemed to arise from general memories of Lithuania's brief independence (1918–40) and myths of an ancient past that reverberated in the closing poem of our drama spoken by Iešmantas. Comforted in his feelings of repeated loss by the discovery of "a bit of amber / Beside the Baltic," the poet promises that a revolutionary fire "will flame up" and "Centuries will burn," giving everyone a "spark" of new life.[54] In the context of our play, we read "Centuries" as the colonial occupation of Lithuania by Russia and other empires.[55] In the minds of most Lithuanians, amber is an essentially "Lithuanian" thing.

Each defendant refused counsel. Presenting their life histories to the court, they framed themselves in a kind of political romance: theirs was a country frozen in Cold War time, awaiting renewal, rather like Sleeping Beauty or Snow White. They often cross-examined witnesses with bravado, as when Pečeliunas asked Bronius Dobrovolskis if he (Pečeliunas) had been "drunk or sober" during an alleged discussion of "illegal publications." A moment later, Iešmantas asked the same witness, who seemed to be lying for the state, how he could confuse publications with names as different as *Rūpintojėlis* and *Perspectives*:[56] "And you say this, being a responsible employee with a degree in philology? Can you look me in the eye?"[57]

During our phone conversation, Irena Skuodienė answered questions about Dobrovolskis, a department head in the Ministry of Education, but it was hard for her to perform the painful memory of his testimony: "For me it was so sad, picture about this man. He was so weak. So lost. Not very nice picture of this man I have in my mind. He talked about getting underground literature to read from Iešmantas and — oh — it is picture not very nice. Man was not small and his position was not so small but he looked in trial so weak. Oh, no — it's not nice to remember this man." Speculating that he was a government informer, she said: "I don't know. Maybe he was not KGB agent. But he was afraid of KGB. He talked all they wanted him to talk."

Jousting bravely with a court that Daiva Skuodytė maintained was packed with KGB, not average citizens, the dissidents presented themselves as men of passion and desire.[58] I now see theirs as a kind of love story, based on their lost relationship to a childhood space, the independent Lithuania of their youth. In soliloquies, each man presented stories about his recent struggles. But it is only now that I have the time and resources to inquire about how these subjects, all born by 1930, were constituted in pre-Soviet history and to wonder whether childhood memories informed their dissent.[59] Skuodis was born in Chicago and returned to Lithuania as a young child, whereas Pečeliunas and Iešmantas were born in small Lithuanian villages. Each defendant spent most of his early years in a free Lithuanian Republic. How were their experiences of that life constructed?[60] Did their dissent carry feelings of lost privilege? a lost golden age? the scars of terror? They were still young when Stalin's purges began. Irena Skuodienė explains: "I learned this system from the very beginning to now. Because I was ten years when Lithuania was occupied by Russia. I learned about this with my skin. I saw all things that happened. I saw people who were put in automobiles and brought to the station and after a week they were brought to Siberia. It was deportation of Lithuanian intelligentsia — lawyers, doctors, teachers — they were brought to Siberia."

At the time of their trial in Vilnius on December 15, 1980, forty years had passed since Lithuania was occupied by the USSR, but the defendants presented those years as a period of discontinuity from a lost national past. Performing Lithuanian identity, they carved out a national space defined by their own exile. As in fairy tales or stories of martyrs, the suffering of these oppressed men established the value of Lithuania. Mimicked by the Judge and the celebrated State Prosecutor Bakucionus, the dissidents were harassed, shamed, forced to suffer. Yet their enemies appeared weaker rather than stronger by contrast, as Irena Skuodienė's pained description of the state's witness Dobrovolskis indicates. The irony of the dissidents' exile was that it legitimized and sustained the very Lithuanian borders under contest. In their trial they broke silence, emerging from the underground to enact a six-day rehearsal of agency and free speech.

In court, the accused defied a crowd of KGB, buoyed only by family support and their own courage. According to my phone conversation with Daiva Skuodytė, the family knew nothing of her father's status for an entire year after his arrest; they were not allowed to see him before or during the trial and only one time afterward ("Christmas Eve Day we got to see him one last time"). She explains how she and her sister sneaked flowers into the courtroom: "Then they said trial was over. So then we just jumped out of our seat. Those soldiers were crushing these flowers with their boots as if they would be snakes or something. It was turmoil. The judges rush out of the room. They didn't want to have anything more to do with it." When four soldiers with automatic weapons grabbed her and her sister, relatives of the other defendants helped them release themselves. Daiva laughs: "We did not stand there like sheep. . . . Those police had no right to grab me. And I talked back to them. It was a really funny struggle. [She laughs.] I really did not feel fear. I felt anger against the system—that we felt helpless to fight against the system with the truth we believed in." Then, interpreting the force of the memory she has just performed for me: "Anger was the right word. Because it still stays."

The extent of secrecy required by those who were under state surveillance in Soviet Lithuania is almost unfathomable. I have mentioned that Skuodis's family spoke nothing important at home because their home was bugged by the KGB. Important messages were written on the magic slates one sees in children's toy stores; raise the plastic sheet and the message disappears.[61] They could keep no copies of suspect materials, including the trial transcripts that were once so well hidden that even Irena Skuodienė could not find them. Of the nine people who were her closest associates at work, five were KGB informants. It seems that the trial was very "exciting" to her at least in part because it was a public rehearsal for full citizenship, a laboratory of democracy. In court, dissidents and unruly spectators could perform the unnameable country and reveal its pain.

In our play, harsh sentences imposed at the finale by an unsympathetic jurist resounded like a macabre litany of political repression. Judge Ignotas intoned:

I sentence:
V. Skuodis (He stands) to seven years loss of freedom, to be followed by five years of exile.
G. Iešmantas (He stands) to six years loss of freedom, to be followed by five years of exile.
P. Pečeliunas (He stands) to three years loss of freedom, to be followed by five years of exile.
Sentence effective immediately.

Our play met this judicial language of repression with poetry of protest. Actors planted in the audience quietly chanted, then sang the outlawed national anthem in an English translation while guards led the defendants offstage. Against the soundscape of this hymn, the dissenting energy of three silenced exiles remained fixed on the nation-state — rather like a missile defense system. Only when borders cease to be contested are such defenses unnecessary, witness the 1993 headline: "U.S. Is Considering Aiming Its Missiles Away from Russia," a move problematized the same year by Russian elections that confirmed the rise to power of Vladimir Zhirinovsky and his ultranationalist, anti-American Liberal Democratic Party.[62]

When the Iron Curtain was raised by Gorbachev's *perestroika* and various independence movements, Eastern Europe presented a spectacle of post–World War II chaos: enforced deprivation, unemployment, runaway inflation, housing shortages, black marketeering, and millions of refugees. But the ethnic, religious, and class struggles of Western nations also moved to center stage. Robbed of mythical status as the longed-for land of freedom, "the West" revealed glaring inequalities beneath its so-called pluralism — inequalities of which Communist Party doctrine had warned. Poverty, homelessness, and forced marginalization greeted and shocked East Europeans emerging from Soviet into "Western" rule.[63] It is ironic that East Europeans now curry favor with Western audiences by documenting their progress toward a capitalist identity.[64]

If we performed our play today, I wonder how we might interrogate the Western values emulated by its main characters. If Western citizens expected horrors on the other side of the Iron Curtain, many East Europeans imagined a paradise of capitalist opportunity. Neither view was realistic. Despite long hours at two jobs to make ends meet, however, Daiva Skuodytė prefers what she calls "the American way" of life: "You can't be the person you are in that society. You are molded. It's always [talk of] masses, not human beings. I felt offended by that." Of the KGB "who were always on our case," she says that it is "absolutely unfair that older people have to be afraid of something" as if they were still children. "That's why I appreciated American way. You can be who you are. I feel free now living here."

Performing on a Dark Stage:
Rebellion and Identification after the Cold War

When we first performed our play, the current international scene was unthinkable. On the darkened Soviet stage, former citizens of the dismantled USSR are engaging former allies and enemies in the most complicated remaking of territory and political discourse since World War II. Our play, which was performed to dramatize a continuing crisis, has become a historical artifact. And the spaces — geographic and political — that once contained the USSR and its Baltic territories have been remapped. It is important to note that old spaces do not disappear from the memory of nationalists like Russia's Zhirinovsky — who wants to restore ancient borders. Nevertheless, just twelve years after we produced *Thoughts in the Margins* for Amnesty International, Lithuania has managed to earn its place in the history books as the country that helped bring down Gorbachev and the Soviet system. Playing poker with the popular Soviet leader over their right to secede from the USSR, Lithuanian leaders harnessed Western opinion to their vision of independence — despite the general sense that world peace depended on Soviet stability.

Unraveling of the former communist countries has continued in Eastern Europe. Seen against the tragic background of Yugoslavia, Lithuania may appear almost idyllic. Yet the inflation rate in Lithuania rose as high as 1,100 percent after the Soviet collapse. Like most of Eastern Europe, Lithuania suffers from the excesses of capitalism — black marketeering and organized crime.[65] Such excesses have made citizens there and in other countries (Poland, East Germany) long for yesterday's security and reelect former Communist Party members, hoping for a capitalist economy with the "human face" of socialism.[66] Meanwhile, in some quarters Western companies like K-Mart have trained the grumpy sales clerks in formerly state-run stores how to perform the gestures of Western commerce, as if "capitalist" gestures will reinvent the work climate and public space itself. Such companies must also convince factory managers to produce more than is customary to meet market demands or to lay off workers in places where, as in Russia, the right to work has been engrained.[67]

Framed in a bipolar Cold War story, the dissidents whose lives we enacted appeared to be in the vanguard of mass revolution — political and moral heroes. But the rigid inscription of Soviet power to which they objected did not simply reverse itself in the free market economy. The situation remained complex. Irena Skuodienė's first thought after independence was that "Lithuania will be independent if it can destroy all postal systems" within six months. After six months, she felt it was already "too late" because the KGB was able to establish new connections. (It eventually reemerged as the Lithuanian secret police.) From her perspective as from Drakulić's, post offices had been theaters for the daily enactment of fascist control over information.[68] Though their friends insisted otherwise, Irena Skuodienė and her daughter cited evidence that in 1993 family letters going to and from today's "free" Lithuania were still being opened.[69]

It seems there are few assumptions one can make about life in the former USSR, where the rate of change and the performance of newly gained individual rights create, in turn, daily spectacles of territorial conflict. Lithuania, with a majority of Roman Catholics, has been flooded with "German- and American-financed evangelical" preachers. Pope John Paul II's trip (1993) was partly motivated by his concern that fundamentalists were tilling Roman Catholic soil. One token that the religious revival would not simply mean a Catholic or an Eastern Orthodox revival was that among the cheering crowds in Vilnius, Lithuania, were "shorn-headed Krishna followers, who beat drums and waved as the Pope rode by."[70] The pontiff's choice of Lithuania as his first stop in post-Soviet Europe may signal his sense that Lithuania enjoys "originating" status on the world stage for its role in undermining the Soviet Union. But his visit may also show how Lithuania and other former satellites of the USSR have become Gold Rush frontiers full of opportunities that Western government, business, and religious leaders are eager to exploit.

The dissidents presented in our play were punished for using typewriters or carbon paper; no one but the state could reproduce ideas. By 1993, the performance of free speech in places like Russia had erupted into thousands of publications, among them *Inward Path*, a New Age magazine that preached healing and nonorthodox religion. As "Western" crime expands exponentially, there are changed attitudes toward some minority groups. Gypsies, for example, lost ground in all post-communist countries. Slavenka Drakulić, a Croatian journalist, argues moreover that Western feminists and critical theorists presume that the women of former communist countries can be added to a hegemonic, international study of women presided over by Westerners who do not understand the circumstances that inform everyday performances of gender in Eastern Europe.[71] Indeed, what does the jubilant Western category of "post-Soviet" mean to people whose impoverished lives may be worse off since the changeover?[72] And how does the Western celebration and co-optation of "post-Soviet" markets eclipse and even deny democratic rights to self-definition?

During the well-publicized years of the independence movement (1987–

92), Lithuania became a free country with its own parliament. Among the first members of that parliament led by the nationalist intellectual leader Dr. Vytautas Landsbergis was Gintautas Iešmantas, the dissident poet we cast as a moral hero in our play. Another of our characters, the teacher Povilas Pečeliunas, died in 1990. Released from a labor camp in 1988, he had a chance to participate in the secession movement. As I have said, Vytautas Skuodis, the geologist who emigrated to his Chicago birthplace after being released from prison, found work in Lithuania. The courts ruled that Skuodis lost his university post illegally, as a result of his anti-Soviet views. Ironically enough, Skuodis lost face after supporting President Brazauskas, a former communist who helped achieve Lithuanian independence.

In one decade, a country about which most Westerners knew almost nothing was embroidered into the world narrative in an enduring way as Lithuanians effected shocking political change through symbols and inventive gestures. Some argue that contemporary Lithuania is itself a product of brave rhetoric and theatrical flourishes. In the words of Estonia's chief negotiator with Moscow in April 1990: "We [in Estonia] have in fact done what Lithuania did, but by a long series of such small steps that it was difficult for Moscow to tell when exactly we got really nasty. What Lithuania did was take a big step, as if Moscow didn't exist."[73]

During the summer of 1993, newly independent Lithuania was performing its identity as a sovereign state by insisting on the withdrawal of 2,500 Russian troops, a demand complicated by an act of Congress that obligated the United States "to cut off all non-relief aid to Russia" unless Russian troops left the Baltic states by October 6. Russian troops were in fact evacuated on August 31, 1993, distinguishing Lithuania from its Baltic neighbors, Estonia and Latvia, where Soviet strategic forces, bivouacked without permission of either government, added to an acute housing shortage.[74]

Lithuania's independence movement was highly dramatic from the start. Leaders performed freedom by practicing Western modes of nonviolent protest like those recommended in the well-circulated illegal pamphlet that inspired the title of my original essay (1987), "How to Act During an Interrogation." Communist rule was undermined by the sheer size of the Baltic theater of protest. Most spectacular was "the 'Baltic Way' of 23 August 1989 when two million Balts (two-fifths of the entire native population of the region) formed a continuous 370 mile human chain from Vilnius [capital of Lithuania] through Riga [the Latvian capital] to Tallinn [capital of Estonia] to demand independence." Less than a year later, on March 11, 1990, Lithuanian leaders surprised Gorbachev and the world by declaring independence. By that time, their earlier political performances had helped stimulate East European revolutions that occurred during the fall of 1989. The Lithuanian theater of protest included violence, notably Soviet seizure of the television center and tower in Vilnius (January 13, 1991). Fifteen persons were "shot to death or crushed by tanks." On February 9, 1991, Lithuanians voted overwhelmingly for independence from the USSR.[75]

At the time we wrote our play, I was amazed at the extent to which the resistant people of Lithuania were rendered invisible on the world stage. A local source in greater New York, Irene Žemaitaitis, told me that before the secession crisis and despite the presence of a large, active Lithuanian American community (some 15,000 in Westchester and Fairfield Counties), she could not get Lithuanian news reported in local papers of southern Connecticut. One of her friends, a man of Irish/Lithuanian descent, repeatedly had to correct people who assumed that his background was half "Lutheran."

The review of our second production in Stamford, Connecticut, was a noteworthy exception to news trends. Our play was produced to commemorate the bittersweet memory of Lithuania's Independence Day (February 16, 1918) and the 733-year anniversary of the founding of an ancient Lithuanian state. For this metropolitan New York audience, our performance of Lithuanian identity resisted its invisibility in America; the play offered a rare public image of Lithuania and is accordingly still discussed by community members. In her review of our play, Lisa Marie Petersen noted how the defendants' final appeals to the Judge were supported by audience ovations, and how touched the actors were by this applause. The actor who played Iešmantas said: "The support jumped out from the crowd and helped me to understand as they did."[76]

A similar exception to this rule of Lithuanian obscurity was the New York debut of the State Theatre of Lithuania in June 1991, just two months before the struggling Baltic states were given international recognition by the United Nations (August 20, 1991). Featured at the New York International Festival of the Arts were a fiercely anti-Soviet version of Chekhov's *Uncle Vanya* and *The Square*, part political parable, part Gulag romance. Seeing both Lithuanian plays alongside performances from other countries I felt their urgency; the players did act as if their lives depended on a willful construction of identity.[77] Something leaked out of the aesthetic container onstage, an excess of communal aggression and desire that was exhilarating but also threatening because it carried with it the prospect of "real" violence.

The boldness of Lithuania's leaders during the secession crisis (1990–92) stunned me, but our performance did offer a predictive edge. Whatever my shock and euphoria, I knew that everyday dramas of Lithuanian dissent had created the playing field for this David-and-Goliath battle with the USSR. Tiny, seemingly insignificant Lithuania had effectively challenged the Cold War with a rhetoric of human rights and cultural sovereignty. By 1993 Lithuania was getting coverage in major American newspapers, but the story was different in 1983, when we wrote our play. We relied on samizdat (underground) literature and local interviews with Lithuanian Americans. A search of newspaper indexes shows few reports on Lithuania during the years immediately preceding the 1980 trial that was the subject of our 1983–84 productions. One source told me that before the secession crisis, it was common to see Lithuanians falsely referred to as "Russians" in news reports of the *New York Times*.[78]

In stark contrast to the previous news pattern were the blaring front-page headlines and pictures that reported the struggle for independence. I can remember feeling grateful that news of Lithuania was finally surfacing after years of silence. On February 26, 1990, a large front-page picture showed the grim-faced Moscow police chief and his aide, both dressed in heavy officers' coats and Russian fur hats, watch thousands of demonstrators gather below their rooftop perch in Moscow. A blaring lead headline linked this mass performance of Russian dissent with the example set by the defiant Lithuanian election: "Lithuanians Vote Strongly for Independence Backers; Soviet Crowds Ask Change." The real news was not in the spectacle of a Moscow square thronged with 50,000 people who were performing mass dissent, but in the subtitle that gave Lithuania credit for the "First Multiparty Contest in 70 Years," one in which the pro-independence party (Sąjūdis) defeated the communists, giving "the Lithuanian parliament a strong mandate for independence from the Soviet Union."[79]

Later that winter the *New York Times* reported a parliamentary vote of 124–0 in which elected representatives declared Lithuania's independence (March 11, 1990). The declaration was followed by "an outburst of songs and embraces" by leaders who had "solemnly proclaim[ed] the restoration of . . . sovereign powers of the Lithuanian State which were annulled by an alien power in 1940." This news report captured the political theater and mass spectacle that ensued as hundreds of people converged outside Parliament to celebrate sovereignty, "singing national hymns and chanting independence slogans, as the legislators changed the name of the Lithuanian Soviet Socialist Republic to simply the Lithuanian Republic and ordered the hammer and sickle replaced by the old Lithuanian coat of arms." Meanwhile, as if striking scenery from a political stage usurped by the "alien power," a crowd that was gathered outside Parliament used "screwdrivers to pry the copper Soviet insignia from the front of the building, to a roar of approval."[80]

A year later, such coverage of formerly invisible Lithuania was all the more startling because it competed with news of the Gulf War. On a key day of that war (Sunday, February 10, 1991), a large picture and front-page headline in the *New York Times* showed uniformed Lithuanian guards voting in a plebiscite to protest the brutal Soviet attack on the broadcasting station in Vilnius: "Defying Gorbachev, Lithuanians Vote on Question of Independence."[81]

Rescued by its own resources from obscurity, Lithuania is now a global player in world politics. It receives regular notices in the American press for local performances of identity. But if Lithuania helped set the stage for a post-Soviet world, the complexities of that world make it harder than ever to tell the country's current (1993) tale. Political, geographic, economic, and ethnic categories have imploded, and the vocabulary for representing national, personal, or regional identity is in crisis worldwide. The meaning of such otherwise taken-for-granted terms as "nationalists," "communists," or "democrats" suffer daily sea changes. How does anyone perform national identity in such a world? Just what is this "Lithuania" that its people struggle to define and defend, whether from inside current borders or from the subject position of exiles in a global diaspora? Even at the moment of its re-emergence, Lithuanian identity appears multiple, contested, divided.[82] And in the Western press, stories about Lithuania's most-favored-nation status or its attempt to secure gold reserves confiscated by the USSR in 1940 compete with accusations that Lithuania is "whitewashing" its participation in the Holocaust, a policy that threatens good relations with Israel.

Charting the performed identity of a Lithuanian character from 1983 to 1993 is like tracing a subatomic particle: one cannot document its energy level and (political) location at the same time. The dissident poet Iešmantas, who proclaimed fealty to the principles of "Euro-Communism" during his trial and acknowledged his service as a Communist Party secretary, was elected to Lithuania's new parliament as a member of the pro-independence (Sąjūdis) movement led by the future chairman of Parliament, Vytautas Landsbergis. Iešmantas lost his seat when former communists regained power in February 1993.[83] Accused of writing "bourgeois" verse he refused an early pardon from prison, arguing that since he had done nothing wrong, Soviet authorities should apologize to him.[84] Iešmantas's cause was taken up by the international PEN, whose members, including Allen Ginsberg, Arthur Miller, and Susan Sontag, wrote letters to Gorbachev demanding his release and the return of his confiscated poems.[85] When finally freed from prison, Iešmantas became, as I have said, a founding member of the Lithuanian parliament; he is now married to Dalija Martišiūtė, a journalist whose testimony was featured in our play. It is almost uncanny, but we had "invented" a romance or special friendship between Martišiūtė and Iešmantas in our play. A gentle, protective attitude came through as Martišiūtė craftily dodged the Prosecutor's repeated attempts to incriminate Iešmantas.

Pečeliunas, the funny, feisty teacher and scholar of languages who wanted more school classes taught in Lithuanian, endured a hunger strike in prison and was discharged in time to take part in the secession movement. He died of cancer and other health problems in 1990. So far I have no news of his then-fiancée (now his widow) Danutė Keršiūtė, the romantic heroine of our play. We created a trial scene in which she was punished for tossing flowers to the defendants before her testimony ("But these are flowers, not a hydrogen bomb!"); for this her sentence was seven days in prison. Nor do I have current news of the Soviet Judge Ignotas, Prosecutor Bakučionis, or the state's witness, Bronius Dobrovolskis.

Sent to prison for writing literature promoting secession from the USSR, his wife reported to me that Professor Skuodis benefited from Gorbachev's liberalization campaign. When world pressure convinced Gorbachev to free Andrei Sakharov, Sakharov refused freedom until forty of his fellow scientists were also released. According to his wife, Skuodis was evidently among those counted in the tally, but he was not allowed to stay in Lithuania; after his release on February 5, 1987, he was exiled to the United States, his birth-place.[86] On November 2, 1987, he gratefully addressed the Amnesty International group in White Plains, New York, that had pressed for his liberty. This same group had sponsored our play, but my contact had left the area by 1987; thus I was not informed of Skuodis's visit.[87] Another irony of my research is that when I reached her successor at Amnesty in August 1993, Mary Pentcheff was just about to deactivate the file on Skuodis, Iešmantas, and Pečeliunas.[88]

During his trial Professor Skuodis presented himself as a staunch anticommunist. Claiming never to have been a party member, he avowed his conversion to Roman Catholicism, defiantly claiming authorship of the anti-Soviet tract, "Spiritual Genocide in Lithuania." However, his wife mentioned that he gravitated toward liberal views while in Chicago and was controversial among Lithuanian dissidents abroad because he supported the former communist and now president, Algirdas Brazauskas, in the February 1993 election: "So people are angry with him. . . . [N]ow he is appointed to be director of a group about Lithuanian genocide and he is appointed but not verified by Parliament." Pausing to look up a key word in her dictionary, she explains that "It is a party of exiles" whose current leader is opposed to Skuodis "because they have their [own] candidates . . . and they will resist his appointment only because he was chosen by Šleževičius, who is with [President] Brazauskas and is Prime Minister."[89]

The political contest among Lithuanian dissidents who want to keep performing their marginal subject position and those who, like Skuodis, are willing to cooperate with a mainstream government now composed of ex-communists delineates the relationship between pain and power. As Elaine Scarry has noted, political legitimacy has traditionally been founded in the blood and pain of war victims.[90] One could say that the Republic of Lithuania derives its

legitimacy from the bodily experience of Cold War victims, people like Iešmantas, Pečeliunas, and Skuodis who performed their dissenting role through
serving prison sentences, staging hunger strikes in prison, or enduring exile.
Allowing ex-communist rulers to control their free association or appoint
Skuodis as their leader would compromise independence, destroying the outsider status from which members of the dissident community have performed
Lithuanian identity. However sincere the performance of political friendship
offered by ex-communists now in office, the suffering of dissidents under the
Soviet regime cannot be easily erased. But who is to say that Skuodis is no
longer a patriot? Indeed, from the vantage of America — and Skuodis is a dual
citizen — his cooperation with former enemies could be seen as a necessary and
heroic performance of political peacekeeping, analogous to the famous hand-
shake between leaders of Israel and Palestine in the fall of 1993. He may be
trying to "live fearlessly with and within difference(s)."[91]

The cultural situation in Lithuania today is not simple; nor are the lives of
our surviving heroes and their families, who, in the wake of the Cold War,
must create national subject positions without the old frame of binary opposition. I have noted that as a cultural artifact, our play was "the residue of
transactions between artists and spectators."[92] And to write this essay I returned to those spectators, including leaders of Amnesty International and
Gintė Damušis, the former director of the Lithuanian Information Center in
Brooklyn, who was our chief cultural contact while writing the play. She was
later employed as a counselor at the permanent mission of the Republic of
Lithuania to the United Nations in New York. For years, she and other Lithuanian Americans worked with dissidents to symbolically perform and locate an
ideal space — free Lithuania ("Laisvę Lietuvai!"). Then she worked for the
government that bears the name of that ideal.

The process of writing this essay has renewed my attachment to the ideals
of Amnesty and to members of the Lithuanian American community. And yet
I am keenly aware of my "outsider" status in the international struggle that
defines Lithuanian identity and community. Hence I find myself asking: Can
only Lithuanians speak for Lithuania? If so, what does it mean to have or to be
a political ally? to enact political agency on behalf of others? to engage in
critique of Lithuanian self-constructions? I do not know how to understand
those Lithuanians who have expressed gratitude for my interest in their lives.
As a critic and playwright committed to sharing my encounter with Lithuanian identity, how do I construct my own subject position?

Performing the Lithuanian "Other"

Although a communist country, Yugoslavia was not part of the Soviet bloc,
but the Croatian journalist Slavenka Drakulić speaks with authority about

what it was like for a small country to emerge from decades of communist government and see itself in a Western mirror. Drakulić complains that Westerners have constructed people of former communist countries as a primitive race, the pre–World War II "other," steeped in simple attitudes made possible by poverty. She argues that a certain East European nobility emanates from the self-acknowledged "third eye" of socialism that remains at least temporarily horrified by the homelessness, beggary, and unemployment of the supposedly advanced West.[93] This elite and masterful "communist eye" sees poverty through a lens that confirms its own authority while implicitly discrediting Western, democratic notions of "justice": "Like a third, spiritual eye placed in the middle of one's forehead, this eye scans only a certain type of phenomenon; it is selective for injustice. Even if the socialist states have fallen apart, the ideals of equality and justice haven't. They are still with us, built in like a chip. We remember them from school . . . as well as from the clean, beggarless streets of our cities."[94]

In 1993 the American rush to tour Eastern Europe before it became too Westernized seemed to rely on fantasies of the area's primitive aura and originary status. Western travelers saw the new political and cultural spaces exotically, as havens full of noble savages who continued to exist without the basic amenities of the twentieth century — washing machines, driers, sanitary napkins.[95] Though plagued by environmental pollution, the newly opened East European spaces held artifacts of value; entire cities such as Prague or Krakow had resisted the ugliness of post–World War II progress, and the sheer survival of such cities gave a perverse value to the poverty that had frozen their development.[96] Tourists rushed in at least in part because the supposed "backwardness" of Eastern Europe constituted it as a museum of lost high culture and nineteenth-century bourgeois life, a museum made uniquely and seductively performative by its imminent disappearance, by the pressure of time ironically embodied in both decay and progress.

Marianna Torgovnick has pointed out that the problematic framework of primitivism allowed colonial powers to see the precolonial life of subject peoples as a site of origins to which supposedly civilized Westerners could look back as if to their own lost past. Unless the noncivilized or "primitive" is imagined to be "eternally present," Western "origins" become irretrievable. This accounts for the "anxiety often expressed by anthropologists and adventurers about the speed with which primitive societies vanish."[97] Following Torgovnick's reading, I wonder if Eastern Europe in 1993 functioned as an imaginative site of home for Westerners facing the alienation created by an encroaching cyberspace. If Eastern Europe could be imaginatively contained by the West as a place of origins and underdevelopment, Westerners who performed their identity in Eastern Europe could escape — at least for the moment — a sense of postmodern estrangement. And I come again to the hard question: Did our role as Westerners (among other things) compromise our performance of Lithuanian history? As Westerners, what right did we have to speak for Lithuanian "others"?

Linda Alcoff notes that although speaking for others is especially problematic in colonial or third-world situations, it is sometimes necessary to the achievement of political agency. International terrorism and governmental repression prevent some "others" from speaking for themselves, and in this context I believe that theater like ours can be justified. Although speaking for others can reinscribe unjust hierarchies, some situations require messengers and advocates. Some "practices of speaking for" may be critical to enabling "others" to speak for themselves. Alcoff's yardstick is whether one's speaking will "enable the empowerment of oppressed peoples."[98] I believe that in "speaking for" the Lithuanian dissidents in our play, we did participate in a politics of empowerment through visibility. Iešmantas's letters indicate profound gratitude to those who helped dramatize his plight while he was in prison, among them many famous writers. Our play was intended to generate notoriety for Iešmantas so that PEN would make him an honorary member; that membership was eventually granted.

On the other hand, talking *with* Irena Skuodienė and her daughter rather than simply for them seems a more honest place from which to write this essay. For one thing, I respect Daiva Skuodytė's protest against the exploitative, "talk show" approach of the press in Australia, where she and her mother were invited to attend a Lithuanian Youth Congress. She felt that the press lost interest in their stories when it became clear that these women would not generate sensational news pictures by crying in public. As Irena said to me, "I am against publishing anything personal. Their intention was to make me cry to impress people." Reporters who insist on pressuring life history performers to make emotional disclosures remind me of unethical acting coaches who will colonize their students' inner lives for a desired theatrical effect. Daiva Skuodytė assumed the position of an integrated subject — a subject position that the Australian reporters clearly felt did not make good copy: "I would consider myself a more or less balanced person."

Indeed, I wonder — even in the face of the dispersion of Lithuanian identity across history and my own, deeply personal transformations in conversation with Irena — whether the poststructural insistence that subjects are nonunified (constructed in difference) plays into the hands of a media industry that values emotional breakdown and fragmentation. From a market standpoint, the unified subject is not only boring but threatening. It represents the integrity necessary for concerted action; it tends to model efficacy rather than mere affectivity.

I think our play stands as an artifact of binary, Cold War discourse. We directed it toward a possible future (the liberation of prisoners) that has now become history. The play did not solve problems but it did take risks. We tried to write history without essentializing Lithuania or the subject position of its dissidents. I now believe that, following the popular binarism of the day, we did essentialize the difference between the communist tyrants and the anti-communist underdogs. To that extent, I think we also ignored more complex motivations such as loss of the dissidents' childhood home in pre-Soviet Lithuania. An Israeli American friend has articulated the painful seduction still exercised by images of her childhood space: "I felt like Jerusalem was my lover, that I had an erotic relationship to this city. I feel a sense of loss and my visits don't solve it because it is like seeing your lost love in the street. You can exchange a note but you cannot even say hello. There is this look of recognition that immediately opens up a world of stories but you don't have the contact anymore. It's in your past, in your memories. But it's not alive. You can nod at each other but it's not alive. You can't have an exchange."[99]

For me, my friend's desire for a vanished Jerusalem resonates with the Lithuanian desire for an independent homeland. She is remembering a home lost through immigration, whereas the Lithuanian dissidents I encountered were remembering a home nearly lost through decades of Soviet occupation of even their most intimate experience.[100] Yet in each case, the memories seem infused with fantasy and unrealized desire. In each case, the memory, fantasy, and desire combine in a sense of immediate, almost erotic urgency — a utopic urgency that seems to me now to have been the lifeblood of the independence movement.

Memory, Story, and National Space: Writing Lithuania

Scribbling the words of Irena Skuodienė on the back pages of my playscript in a cramped phone booth gave me an image for the performances of history required by this essay. After a decade, I had located the source of the smuggled trial transcripts. Keeping pace with her excited language gave me a sense of how she and her daughters tried to record "every word," encoding notes from the trial on tiny pieces of paper hidden on their knees in the spy-filled courtroom. Now I try to imitate that gesture, to rehearse with my scholar's body what it would be like not to write openly or freely, and I cannot do it. I lack the dexterity, the terror, the courage born of necessity. Under what conditions, I wonder, would subjects in my own country be desperate enough to un-write their political system — to perform the historically (im)possible?

I am overwhelmed by Irena Skuodienė, who struggles for the precise English words to tell me what may be the central story of her life, words charged with eloquence, danger, pride over her routing of the KGB, even laughter. The energy and physical power in her narrated experience seem to translate directly. I feel an immediate sense of her body one thousand miles away in Chicago, sometimes sighing in exhaustion as she struggles for the exact words and the strength to keep telling her passionate story to a stranger who is not quite a stranger. After all, I have pronounced certain code words like the name of Gintė Damušis, a woman we both trust. I have also represented myself as a professor, a person of learning. Trained in geology, she tells me she was not allowed to finish the doctoral dissertation; each draft was rejected. At first, she did not read the political meaning of such blockades: "I was in love with history of science. I am doing so good — and obstacles, and obstacles. After my husband was arrested I understood what happened."

Talking to Irena Skuodienė, I realize how many cultural performances converged in our conversation: the trial, the transcriptions, the translation, our play, and my earlier essay. I realize that although Iešmantas's identity became the central focus of our play, it is the subject position of Skuodis and his family that must take center stage in this essay, not only because Skuodis's wife and daughter were available to me by telephone or because Skuodis now occupies a problematic subject position in Lithuania, but also because I now realize that it was Irena Skuodienė and her daughters who made the play possible. On the telephone, our stories rush out urgently, as if reaching for each other, full of passionate respect. I find myself making this woman I have never met a promise and am immediately anxious about betraying her: "I will continue to write your story. I have a deadline now but I will continue to tell your story. I will talk to your daughter tonight and I will talk to you again. I promise."

Ringing in my ears are the words of theorists who warn about the danger of speaking for others — even others who seem to want their story told. Am I being sucked into that kind of dangerous talk? Am I poised to patronize or to displace her? Still, I promise her because I can. Because my academic position gives me access to print that even 15,000 well-educated Lithuanians in suburban New York cannot easily manage. And because her words — in all of their difference — are becoming my words. They imprint themselves on my life and words, creating a physical residue of talk that will have lasting influence. Her generous words are writing themselves on my body, aching themselves into what is and will be my "experience." These are, I realize, the "working words" of which she earlier spoke.

Then I realize that the nausea and fear I experienced when producing the partial story of our play ten years ago was a fear of being false to some true or complete story of Lithuania. It is the same nausea I have sometimes felt writing this essay: the fear of partiality, of facing the processual nature of identities and stories and nations that are always in flux, always already a mere snippet of truth, at once endlessly caught in and wrenched from the drift of time.[101]

And yet as I talk to Irena Skuodienė in 1993 I feel the urge to write another play, one based on oral history interviews with her and other Lithuanians in America or abroad, one that speaks to the many kinds of exile experienced in America and against the rising tide of radical socialist conservatives, and one that pursues my initial commitment to map out a Lithuanian public space across the vagaries of time. The story of Lithuanian struggle is far from over.

The words of Irena Skuodienė have floated up to me like a bottled message tossed overboard in a sea of change. Separated from her husband by politics as well as geography, she tells me the story of how it is she who now performs the subject position of exile. It is with her story that I will close these remarks to begin the next part of my own journey:

In some ways I don't like what happens in Lithuania. Daiva too. We get enough of KGB. They work very hard. They organize. . . . [T]he net of informants took message to KGB and Communists — message that people were no longer so afraid as they were. It was true. We lost our — we gave no more to — afraid. Young people were not afraid. My age people began to lose this angst. And they made arrangement to go forward with their power and that's why Sąjūdis was allowed.[102] KGB was so quiet and I thought: "What do they do now? They are so quiet." And now I see they were developing — not exactly Sąjūdis — but were preparing something to do with people who are not afraid. If you know about Solzhenitsyn, he said the system will be down only if we begin to say the truth, because the system is based on lies. . . . Lithuanian people said about my husband: "He is a crystal clear person." It was very nice to be in this trial. I felt very good in this trial. Because of him and because of other people, too. If you are talking about freedom you can't get in any compromises. About compromise — I remember when we were taught words of Lenin. He said: "There are compromises and *compromises*." I am sixty-three years old and now I decided to be more strong with principles because you can get chaos without those principles. You can get anarchy without those principles.

Notes

I would like to thank the following people, without whose support this essay could not have been written: Irena Skuodienė and her daughter Daiva, who offered generous telephone interviews under great time pressure and gave me verbal permission to quote them verbatim for this essay; Mary Pentcheff, of Amnesty International, and Gintė Damušis, formerly of the Lithuanian Mission to the United Nations in New York, who were key resource people; the American Professor Algirdas Landsbergis, Irene Žemaitaitis, and Rūta Virkutis, who answered pertinent questions; Professor Charles Wankel, of St. John's University, a 1997 Fulbright scholar in Kaunas, who noted some manuscript problems; and of course my husband and son — Jim and Jamie — who sustained me throughout the writing of this essay.

Over the past fifteen years, several persons and texts have moved me to consider the moral implications of theatrical performance. I am especially grateful to David Bassuk, who introduced me to the work of Paolo Friere (*Pedagogy of the Oppressed*), Augusto Boal's *Theatre of the Oppressed*, and Walter Benjamin's *Illuminations*. *The Fall of Public Man* by Richard Sennett has been a formative influence, along with Wallace Bacon's dedication to that "Sense of the Other" one can perceive in literary texts.

This essay began as an act of "translation" and it ends with the problem of translation. Several colleagues helped me consider whether to retain East European language markings in the published text. Some assured me that Lithuanians now expect that their native markings will disappear in Western publications, but the omission of such markings seemed to contradict the spirit of my essay. Consequently, accent markings have been retained as a way to show respect for the Lithuanian language and all East European people named in the essay.

1. Victor Turner and Edith Turner, "Performing Ethnography," *Drama Review* 26 (1982): 33.

2. In *Local Knowledge: Further Essays in Interpretive Anthropology* (New York: Basic Books, 1983) Clifford Geertz unpacks some of the reasons why the performance-centered metaphors of "play," "ritual," and "drama" have established new paradigms for social scientific analysis. Chapter 2 is entitled: "Found in Translation: On the Social History of the Moral Imagination."

3. Victor Turner, ed., *Celebration: Studies in Festivity and Ritual* (Washington, D.C.: Smithsonian Institution Press, 1982), p. 17; Geertz, *Local Knowledge*, pp. 8–9.

4. Anthropologists have often faced this problem. Geertz (*Local Knowledge*, p. 40) discusses how a nineteenth-century field-worker in Bali accounted for the custom of widow burning (suttee) by a multileveled account that saw the event as evoking beauty on an *aesthetic* level, horror on the level of life *experience*, and "power when . . . taken as a moral vision."

5. In a paper entitled "Undermining the Romance Plot: Feminists' Dramatizations of *Jane Eyre*," presented at the National Meeting of the Speech Communication Association, Chicago, November 1986, Donna Marie Nudd examines the ideological component of adaptation. Nudd explains that when early feminist adapters of Charlotte Brontë's *Jane Eyre* rejected the romance motif as a way to organize the novel's action onstage, they exposed the feminist core of Brontë's story.

6. Even at the outset, we realized that a radical version of East/West relations would have to deconstruct the Western morality tale more thoroughly than our time limit allowed. Giving up universal claims for explaining life meant placing "universal" human rights in a local frame of Soviet-Lithuanian awareness.

7. See Julia Kristeva, "The Ethics of Linguistics," *Desire in Language: A Semiotic Approach to Literature and Art*, translated and edited by L. S. Roudiez (New York: Columbia University Press, 1980), pp. 24–25. For Kristeva, language is *the* site of reproduction of the social system. Precisely because poets tinker with language structures, disrupting the habitual relationship between sign and meaning that an efficient system demands, they threaten the existing order and are sometimes silenced. Poetry is that place where one sees the "dialectic of the subject" worked out against the backdrop of "social constraint": "Murder, death, and unchanging society represent precisely the

inability to hear and understand the signifier as such—as ciphering, as rhythm, as a presence that precedes the signification of object or emotion. The poet is put to death because he wants to turn rhythm into a dominant element; because he wants to make language perceive what it doesn't want to say, provide it with its matter independently of the sign, and free it from denotation. For it is the *eminently parodic* gesture that changes the system" (p. 31).

8. From an editorial note in the trial transcript used as the basis of our play. See nn. 44 and 57 below. It is instructive that the liberalized attitude toward dissent in the Soviet Union under Mr. Gorbachev (1986–87) not only appealed to the Western rhetoric of human rights; it connected a lack of self-criticism with economic and political stagnation.

9. Geertz, *Local Knowledge*, p. 48.

10. Capturing the Soviet context was made especially difficult because the transcripts had been translated by a Lithuanian American who worked for an anti-Soviet immigrant group in Chicago.

11. Stoppard is quoted by S. Freedman in "Portrait of a Playwright as an Enemy of the State," *New York Times*, March 23, 1986, pp. 1, 36.

12. Victor Turner notes that judicial processes often coexist "with religious and magical procedures for resolving crises." This was an area needing further development in our play. For example, aspects of the trial shared an affinity with nonlegal cultural forms such as Russian icons, whereas the moral absolutism of the narrative evoked the perspective of Lithuanian fairy tales. Could one see the post-Enlightenment Western view of absolute "rights" as a similarly strict morality tale? See *On the Edge of the Bush: Anthropology as Experience* (Tucson: University of Arizona Press, 1985), p. 218.

13. T. Darragh, "Error Message," *Poetics Journal* 5 (1985): 120–22.

14. Geertz (*Local Knowledge*, p. 233) has defended the establishment of such cross-cultural comparisons, arguing that it is only "through comparison, and of incomparables, that whatever heart [of understanding] we can actually get to is to be reached."

15. Kristeva, "The Ethics of Linguistics," p. 23. Richard Sennett, in *The Fall of Public Man: On the Social Psychology of Capitalism* (New York: Random House, 1978), has pointed out that theater expresses changes in social psychology that impact on ethical revolution; theater reformulates social gestures in a constantly shifting context. Like political dissidents, actors probe the limits of expression, discovering or inventing behaviors to induce belief across cultural frontiers. In our drama, three dissidents imagined themselves as international citizens, investing a posture deemed outrageous imagined themselves as international citizens, investing a posture deemed outrageous by the Soviet regime with fully considered passion and belief.

16. It is important to note that "empathy," which has long been a tool of insight in psychology and anthropology, is also a basic tool of the actor's art. For a cautionary note on empathy in anthropology, see Geertz (*Local Knowledge*, p. 59), who worries about construing the experience of foreign "others" within the peculiarly Western view of the "self."

17. For a current discussion of the connections among censorship, literary imagination, and social ethics, see George Steiner, "Language Under Surveillance: The Writer and the State," *New York Times Book Review*, January 12, 1986, pp. 12, 36.

18. Michael T. Kaufman, "The East Bloc Tolerates Jazz but Mutes Its Dissident

Note," *New York Times*, January 4, 1987, pp. 1, 14. The head of Poland's Jazz Society, interviewed in this article, misses the provocative meaning of jazz that once embodied spontaneous expression, freedom, redemption, joy: "For me . . . in my youth, jazz offered escape and stretched my imagination. It was tied to yearnings of oppressed blacks, to spontaneity, even to images of abandon and sexuality, and I think that was the way it was for most of my contemporaries. It still reflects some of these elements, but today it is more likely that the attraction is for jazz as music rather than for a comprehensive metaphor of a free life."

19. Victor Turner, *From Ritual to Theatre: The Human Seriousness of Play* (New York: Performing Arts Journal Publications, 1982), pp. 45, 28.

20. Seeing Turner's enterprise as part of an "ethnography of thought," Geertz (*Local Knowledge*, p. 152) feels that it is based in the faith "that ideation, subtle or otherwise, is a cultural artifact."

21. Turner, *From Ritual to Theatre*, p. 69.

22. Geertz, *Local Knowledge*, pp. 26–30. Turner shows sensitivity to the unique symbolic dimensions of social drama in chapter one of *From Ritual to Theatre*.

23. Because Iešmantas's poems had not reached the West, we used a piece by Father Leonardas Andriekus. Replete with images of fire and change, the poem ends with the passing of a torch:

> Then everyone will share.
> A spark — for each.
> In every window a light will glow,
> My window will be dark,
> My flame
> I give to you.

24. As a technique, the hymn was reminiscent of the finale of another drama, *The Long Journey of Poppie Nongena: The True Story of a Xhosa Woman*, adapted by Elsa Joubert and Sandra Kotze. The New York production at the Cubiculo Theatre (1982) and the award-winning National Public Radio play by Karen Frillmann (1984) that emerged from it ended with the forbidden hymn of a united Africa, sung in Zulu by white (Afrikaans) and black actors; it was a powerful image of potential solidarity.

25. Dario Fo, an Italian playwright and director, has used his updated version of *commedia dell' arte* to engage audiences with the economic contradictions of modern life; *We Won't Pay, We Won't Pay* offers an example of his style.

26. Quoted by Freedman in "Portrait of a Playwright as an Enemy of the State," pp. 1, 36.

27. Steiner ("Language Under Surveillance," p. 36) reminds us that Western liberality does not guarantee creativity. Emerging from his dangerous life under Juan Perón, Jorge Luis Borges realized that "censorship is the mother of metaphor." Steiner feels that "Banishing or hounding serious poets to their deaths . . . is a hideous tribute to their importance" in creating alternative modes of conscience. Even when his work can effect no immediate change, the poet's "personal impotence," which frees him "from mire, from the compromise of actual power," can provoke challenges and point to possible redemption.

28. In a recent article, Richard Sennett updates thoughts he elaborated in *The Fall of*

Public Man, arguing that American journalism continues to present politics in terms of the character of candidates, rather than the issues at stake. See "A Republic of Souls: Puritanism and the American Presidency," *Harper's*, July 1987, pp. 41–46.

29. Tadeusz Burzynski and Zbigniew Osinski, *Grotowski's Laboratory* (Warsaw: Interpress Publishers, 1979), p. 128; Bertolt Brecht, *Brecht on Theatre*, translated by J. Willett (New York: Hill and Wang, 1964), p. 190. Turner (*From Ritual to Theatre*, pp. 117–20) has elucidated the alarming elements of Grotowski's approach, which, in stripping away "false" personae, leaves the self bare, unmediated, prey to the shaping influence of state or other authorities.

30. Mary S. Strine, "Performance Theory as Science: The Formative Impact of Dr. James Rush's *The Philosophy of the Human Voice*," in *Performance of Literature in Historical Perspectives*, edited by David Thompson (Lanham, Md.: University Press of America, 1983), pp. 509–27.

31. Dwight Conquergood, "Performing as a Moral Act: Ethical Dimensions of the Ethnography of Performance," *Literature in Performance* 5 (April 1985): 9.

32. The success of Charles Dickens's *Nicholas Nickleby* and Victor Hugo's *Les Misérables* as theatrical hits in Western capital cities has led to more interest in adapting nondramatic works for the stage.

33. Nicholas Rzhevsky, "Literature in the Soviet Theatre: 1960–1980," *Literature in Performance* 5 (November 1984): 13–19.

34. For a history of performance projects aimed at social change and a theoretical perspective on performance as a human right, see Kay Ellen Capo, "From Academic to Social-Political Uses of Performance," in *Performance of Literature in Historical Perspectives*, pp. 437–57, and "Performance of Literature as Social Dialectic," *Literature in Performance* 4 (1983): 31–36. See also Conquergood, "Performing as a Moral Act," p. 11.

35. Kristin M. Langellier, "From Text to Social Context," *Literature in Performance* 6 (April 1986): 69.

36. Geertz, *Local Knowledge*, pp. 44–45.

37. Ibid., p. 45. Geertz (p. 234) notes the balancing act required when one mediates between a "universal" perspective and the ethnocentric ethic of local culture. As he sees it, conjuring the "other" assumes responsibility for imagining a life informed by principle and by the practical necessities of an everyday world.

38. *The Complete Poems and Plays of T. S. Eliot* (New York: Harcourt Brace and World, 1962), p. 37.

39. Spalding Gray, *Swimming to Cambodia* (New York: Theatre Communications Group, 1985), pp. 25, 27. In the Gray text, the material is in narrative form. I have added the character names of Jim and Spalding Gray to make it feel like a dialogue — the way it feels when he reads it in public.

40. Slavenka Drakulić, *How We Survived Communism and Even Laughed* (New York: Harper Perennial, 1993), pp. 96–97.

41. Anatol Lieven, *The Baltic Revolution: Estonia, Latvia, Lithuania, and the Path to Independence* (New Haven: Yale University Press, 1993), p. xx.

42. All future quotes from Irena Skuodienė, wife of the defendant Skuodis in our play, are taken from her telephone interview with me on December 15, 1993. At that time and in subsequent talks, I received permission to quote Irena Skuodienė in her

own words as a way to show my respect for her struggle to accommodate Lithuanian experience, culture, and history to the demands of oral English expression.

43. I believe she was referring to the English translation of a Lithuanian publication, "The Trial of Docent Vytautas Skuodis, Gintautas Iešmantas, and Povilas Pečeliunas," *Chronicle of the Catholic Church in Lithuania*, no. 46, December 25, 1980: 21–35.

44. The translated materials provided by Amnesty International amounted to 166 . typed pages, including a table of contents, an introduction of 3 pages, trial proceedings of 103 pages, 60 pages of letters from the defendants, their families, and other supporters, and documents of the court secretary. I still do not know how the secretary's documents were obtained. By contrast, a trial narrative published by the *Chronicle of the Catholic Church in Lithuania* (see above) is only 13 pages long.

45. In a telephone interview the next day (December 16, 1993), her daughter Daiva told me that Skuodis had only a one-room apartment that was too small for them all to live in; also, his wife has health problems that could not be treated in Lithuania. See n. 52 below.

46. Skuodis's wife acknowledged that Brazauskas was "not a fascist." Brazauskas showed his nationalist stripes early on by organizing a split between the Lithuanian Communist Party and its Moscow counterpart.

47. For the subtitle of chapter 8 quoted above, see Lieven, *The Baltic Revolution* (p. 230), which describes the independence movements, 1987–92. Homi K. Bhabha, in *Nation and Narrative* (New York: Routledge, 1990), p. 2, argues that modern nations reflect the ambivalent qualities of modern life; the transitional, indeterminate nature of Lithuania emerges when one realizes how many vocabularies of social gesture, ideology, and language are required to keep constructing it. Konstantin Stanislavsky made the phrase "as if" a hallmark of his famous acting method, and it has influenced many other acting teachers. See *An Actor Prepares*, translated by Elizabeth R. Hapgood (New York: Theatre Arts, 1948; New York: Routledge, 1989).

48. Author's note of May 1997: These comments were made in December 1993, when Lithuanians abroad were still shocked about the recent electoral victory of ex-communists in Lithuania; in 1996 this same group of ex-communists was defeated in the parliamentary elections. Of course, it is equally naive to presume the inevitability of Lithuania's current independence. Irena Skuodienė expressed her own historically informed fears about the controversial Russian leader Vladimir Zhirinovsky, who was reported on Chicago television (PBS, December 14, 1993) to have boasted that Russia could reclaim Lithuania in one day's fighting. She explains that "Russian expansion follows Peter the Great—expansion to the [Baltic] Sea. It is systematic expanding to Sea. They want more and more of Sea."

49. Bhabha, *Nation and Narrative*, p. 3.

50. Although many Westerners admired Gorbachev, members of the Russian intelligentsia criticized his language as stilted, in the tradition of the Soviet bureaucracy. Russian writers who resisted Soviet hegemony understood the value of linguistic nuance, for, as Kristeva has reminded us, breaking codes in language or action is a condition of freedom (quoted above, "The Ethics of Linguistics," n. 7).

51. This phrase echoes Toni Morrison's 1993 Nobel Prize address, which insists on "'word work,'" and the "'value of language: not official language or the censoring language of the state or the trick language of journalism,'" but the magic language of

discovery that is known to children. " 'We die,' she said. 'That may be the meaning of life. But we do language. That may be the measure of our lives.' " See John Darnton, "In Sweden, Proof of the Power of Words," *New York Times*, December 8, 1993, pp. C17, 20.

52. This and all subsequent quotations from Daiva Skuodytė are from a telephone interview with the author, December 16, 1993, which I was given verbal permission to cite for this essay.

53. Bhabha, *Nation and Narrative*, p. 3.

54. Tacitus and other Roman writers speak of Baltic amber trading in the first and second centuries A.D. (Lieven, *The Baltic Revolution*, p. 421). As the poems of Iešmantas were confiscated and not published, we cited this entry with permission from its author, Father Leonardas Andriekus (*Amens in Amber*, n.d.).

55. Lieven (*The Baltic Revolution*, p. 19) considers the history of occupation through which Baltic elites were mostly assimilated by foreign rulers; until this century, nearly all Balts were peasants, from whom members of the current intelligentsia derive. However, Lithuania "is the only Baltic State with its own indigenous nobility." For playwrighting purposes, it would have been helpful to know more about the ancestral background of Skuodis, Iešmantas, and Pečeliunas.

56. "*Rūpintojėlis*" translates as "The Man of Sorrows." According to Lieven, who offers illustrations (ibid., pp. 26–27), it is "a traditional Lithuanian figure of pagan origin, but presented as Christ" in postures of suffering. These elaborately carved wood figures of Christ are present in shrines throughout the country.

57. All quotations from the play are credited to the copyrighted, unpublished version of *Thoughts in the Margin: Voices of Soviet Dissent*, by Kay Ellen Capo and Ellie Serena, 1983, based on the English translation by Mrs. Vita Matušaitis for the Lithuanian World Community. The text may not be quoted without written permission. It should be noted that most of the play's dialogue is taken exactly from the trial transcripts, though we sometimes borrowed language and ideas from accompanying letters written by the defendants and their supporters.

58. Her reasoning was that the guards, who were Soviet soldiers with automatic weapons, searched only the families of defendants. Others breezed in as if they had already been screened as friends of the court.

59. According to their transcribed trial testimony, Pečeliunas was born on May 17, 1928; Skuodis was born in Chicago on March 21, 1929; and Iešmantas was born on January 1, 1930.

60. Joan Scott, in "The Evidence of Experience," *Critical Inquiry* (Summer 1991): 797, problematizes the originary authority of "experience," arguing that experience is not simply given. It is constructed in discourse: "What counts as experience is neither self-evident nor straightforward; it is always contested, and always therefore political."

61. In our 1993 telephone conversations, Irena Skuodienė and Daiva Skuodytė insisted that censorship of their family's mail was continuing. Letters took weeks rather than days to arrive and looked as if they had been opened and resealed.

62. Michael R. Gordon, *New York Times*, December 6, 1993, A1, p. 8; Serge Schemann, "Yeltsin's Reformers Show Weakness in Russian Vote; Constitution Is Approved," *New York Times*, December 13, 1993, pp. A1, 10.

63. In "The Homeless and the New Cold War" (*New York Times*, January 9, 1994,

sec. 2, pp. 1, 36), Herbert Muschamp observed: "With the evil empire gone, there's no one around to feel ideologically superior to. Homelessness and violence are signs that all is not well in the land of free enterprise. Though the cold war has passed, it has left in its wake a new cold war, a domestic cold war, where women freeze to death on bus stop benches" and street people represent those "left behind by the massive dispersal of community life into the suburban, electronically equipped realm of the private home. . . . The homeless haunt the streets, parks and subways like the ghosts of an abandoned civic idea."

64. A two-page "ad" in the *New York Times* by Czech businesses boasted of peace, stability, and tourist and investment opportunities; it featured a reassuring interview with the Czech foreign minister. See "The Czech Republic: The Move Toward Democracy and a Free Market Is Almost Complete," January 7, 1994, pp. A12–13,

65. See Andrew Solomon, "Young Russia's Defiant Decadence," *New York Times Magazine*, July 18, 1993, pp. 16–23, 37–39, 41–42, 51. I am grateful for input from a telephone conversation with Irene Žemaitaitis on November 12, 1993, and from *Morning Edition* (National Public Radio, December 6, 1993), which reported that only 10 percent of Russian credit was then coming from private banks. If 90 percent of the money needed to create a market economy had to be squeezed out of the bankrupt national budget, Russia's future looked grim indeed.

66. Lithuania returned former communists to power in February 1993; that September the same swing happened in Poland, a change some analysts blamed on forty years of too much social security, and others on the zeal of new capitalists who ignored basic human needs in their push for a market economy. One thing seems clear: if Soviet collectivization involved violence, the speedy privatization of farms and businesses has brought its own terrors. Thus the political resistance of the left is now aimed toward bringing "a market economy with a 'human face.'" Jane Perlez, "Why Poland Swung to Left," *New York Times*, September 21, 1993, p. A6. See also "Former Communists Return: Frustration over Reform Cited in Polish Election," (New York) *Daily News*, September 21, 1992, p. 8.

67. Jane Perlez, "In East Europe, K-Mart Faces an Attitude Problem," *New York Times*, July 7, 1993, pp. D1–2.

68. See Drakulić's quotation under "A Cold War Notebook" above and chap. 10 ("Our Little Stasi") of *How We Survived Communism*, pp. 93–103.

69. Gintė Damušis, a former counselor for the permanent Lithuanian mission to the United Nations in New York and an informant for our play, was confident that free speech existed in Lithuania in 1993.

70. Alan Cowell, "Pope Starts Lithuania Visit, First to an Ex-Soviet Land," *New York Times*, September 5, 1993, International sec., p. 18, and "On Baltic Tour, Pope Reaches Out to the Eastern Orthodox Church," *New York Times*, September 7, 1993, p. A6.

71. Andrew Solomon, "Young Russia's Defiant Decadence," p. 22 (quotation); Drakulić, *How We Survived Communism*, chap. 13, "A Letter from the United States — The Critical Theory Approach," pp. 123–32.

72. Lieven (*The Baltic Revolution*, p. 214) notes that in the "world of post-Communist politics, few parties or institutions are quite what they seem, and few politicians say quite what they mean. This is not always intentional; one of the most difficult though

fascinating aspects of writing about the Soviet region results from the almost complete lack of conceptual landmarks. Nothing quite like these events has ever occurred before, so there are no analytical models to fall back upon, and few of the usual terms and descriptions really fit. . . . The problem is that local politicians and journalists, wishing to imitate the West—or simply for want of anything better—use these false models to describe themselves and then play them back to us, thus confirming naive Western observers in their own misconceptions."

73. Ibid., p. 242; quoted from an interview, April 15, 1990.

74. Steven Erlanger, "Russia to Complete Troop Pullout in Lithuania," *New York Times*, August 31, 1993, p. A8 (quotation). Lieven notes that native military strength in the Baltics remains small. Their chief strategy would be to demonstrate the national will to resist through a guerrilla campaign; this has sometimes been called "the 'CNN Defence,' emphasizing that the real defence of the Baltic States lies in Western public opinion." Lieven, *The Baltic Revolution*, p. 320.

75. Lieven, *The Baltic Revolution*, pp. 219, 429.

76. Lisa Marie Petersen, "Play Smuggled from Lithuania Depicts Plight of Dissidents," *The Advocate*, February 13, 1984, B1; she was quoting Tom McCormack. Comments about the audience reaction are based on my telephone interview of November 11, 1993, with Irene Žemaitaitis, who hosted us for the second production of our play in Stamford.

77. June 8–21, 1991. Both plays were directed by Eimuntas Nekrošius, advertised as one of Eastern Europe's most visionary directors. His New York debut was cosponsored by the Joyce Theater (site of both productions) and Lincoln Center Theater.

78. For this observation I am indebted to a conversation with Professor Algirdas Landsbergis, November 11, 1993. Professor Landsbergis, an American, is no relation to the first post-Soviet Lithuanian parliamentary leader—Vytautas Landsbergis.

79. *New York Times*, February 26, 1990, pp. A1, 10.

80. Bill Keller, "Parliament in Lithuania, 124–0, Declares Nation Independent," in *The Decline and Fall of the Soviet Empire*, edited by Bernard Gwertzman and Michael T. Kaufman (New York: Times Books, 1992), p. 247.

81. *New York Times*, February 10, 1993, late ed., pp. L1, 12.

82. The quotation from Eliot's "The Wasteland" (1922) under "A Cold War Notebook" above points to the ethnic complexity of Lithuanian identity around World War I; Eliot foregrounds German and Russian elements, but many Westerners have noticed the way that Jewish, Polish, and other cultures exert continuing influence on the national character, an influence often denied by Lithuanians themselves. See also Lieven, *The Baltic Revolution*, pp. 52–53.

83. The trial transcripts are ambiguous about whether or not Iešmantas was a party member in 1980; introductory notes indicate that he left the party in 1974, but his quoted testimony belies that fact.

84. In our telephone conversation of November 11, 1993, Professor Algirdas Landsbergis pointed out that whereas most dissidents were religious, Iešmantas was not; thus he was perceived as more liberal than others in post-Soviet Lithuania.

85. According to a letter from the PEN American Center dated February 7, 1986, Miller and Ginsberg were "among a group of 13 prominent American writers visiting the Soviet Union in November 1985, when they raised the issue of human rights and

imprisoned writers in that country." As Miller began to read from a PEN list citing one hundred imprisoned Soviet writers (including Iešmantas), he was stopped by his Soviet host. The PEN letter details Iešmantas's case, indicating that Miller and Ginsberg did not make the trip "intending to embarrass their hosts." Miller's performative protest of USSR policy was made in response to a "catalogue of grievances against the U.S." being recited by members of the Union of Soviet Writers.

It is significant that one of these controversial PEN conferences was held in Lithuania itself, where Arthur Miller among others responded thoughtfully. At that meeting, Miller became the first American to publicly refer to Lithuania as an "occupied country," a move that was harshly attacked by regime writers in Lithuania.

86. This information is from my telephone conversation with Skuodis's wife on December 15, 1993.

87. Joan Sandiford was instrumental in seeing that this play materialized.

88. Mary Pentcheff provided key information needed to write this essay.

89. The official name of this group is the Association of Former Political Prisoners and Exiles, a fact I learned from Rūta Virkutis, Executive Director, Lithuanian Catholic Religious Aid, Brooklyn, telephone conversation, December 20, 1993. Our play dealt with urban intellectuals and bureaucrats, one small segment of Lithuania, a country with shifting borders and many languages and ethnicities. Virkutis told me that country's dominant population of peasants, not represented in our play, was slower to give up the Soviet way of life. Suffering from botched plans to privatize land and farm machinery, these peasants helped bring former communists like Brazauskas back to office.

90. Elaine Scarry, *The Body in Pain* (New York: Oxford University Press, 1987).

91. Trinh T. Minh-ha, *Woman, Native, Other: Writing Postcoloniality and Feminism* (Bloomington: Indiana University Press, 1989), p. 84.

92. Joseph R. Roach, Introduction to "Theater History and Historiography," in *Critical Theory and Performance*, edited by Janelle G. Reinelt and Roach (Ann Arbor: University of Michigan Press, 1992), p. 295.

93. In an epigraph that ironically opens her book, Drakulić (*How We Survived Communism*) quotes György Konrád, who speaks from the position of East Europeans who are "the needy relatives" and "aborigines . . . the ones left behind—the backward, the stunted." In chapter twelve, "A Communist Eye, or What Did I See in New York?" she describes how Western friends say she'll "get used" to seeing beggars on the streets but "One doesn't lose one's third, communist eye that easily" (p. 120).

94. Ibid., p. 119.

95. Ibid., pp. 30–31; see also chap. 5, "On Doing Laundry," pp. 43–54.

96. Czech business and government celebrate this much-visited city in a *New York Times* "ad" ("The Czech Republic," January 7, 1992, p. A13) with a subtitle promising that "Prague, One of Europe's Jewels, Lives Up to Its Mythical Reputation." The article boasts that Prague has "remained remarkably intact through two world wars and more than forty years of communist domination. . . . Central Prague seems untouched by time, apart from the odd modern Soviet-style glass and concrete building. What has been destroyed has been tastefully restored as the original."

97. Marianna Torgovnick, *Gone Primitive: Savage Intellects, Modern Lives* (Chicago: University of Chicago Press, 1990), p. 187.

98. Linda Alcoff, "The Problem of Speaking for Others," *Cultural Critique* (Winter 1991–92): 29.

99. Ofra Bloch, telephone conversation, December 9, 1993.

100. This loss of homeland included genocide; it is estimated by some that about one-third of those living in Lithuania in 1940 were exiled by Soviet authorities and nearly all of them died.

101. See Joan W. Scott, "The Evidence of Experience," p. 795, on the extent to which changes in historical conditions continually alter the "possibilities for thinking the self," making it impossible for any one narrative to account fully for identity.

102. Sąjūdis was the coalition for independent Lithuania that lobbied for secession from the USSR; it included dissidents like Iešmantas.

Notes on the Contributors

Michael S. Bowman is an associate professor in the Department of Speech Communication at Louisiana State University.

Ruth Laurion Bowman is an assistant professor in the Department of Speech Communication at Louisiana State University.

Elizabeth Gray Buck is a doctoral candidate in the Department of Art at the University of North Carolina at Chapel Hill.

Kay Ellen Capo is an associate professor of literature at the State University of New York, Purchase.

David William Cohen is a professor of history and anthropology and director of the International Institute at the University of Michigan.

Tracy C. Davis is a professor of theater, English, and performance studies at Northwestern University.

Kirk W. Fuoss is an associate professor in the Department of Speech and Theater at St. Lawrence University.

Shannon Jackson is an assistant professor in the Department of English and the Committee on Degrees in Literature at Harvard University.

D. Soyini Madison is an associate professor in the Department of Communication Studies at the University of North Carolina at Chapel Hill.

Carol Mavor is an associate professor in the Department of Art at the University of North Carolina at Chapel Hill.

E. S. Atieno Odhiambo is a professor of history at Rice University.

Della Pollock is an associate professor in the Department of Communication Studies at the University of North Carolina at Chapel Hill.

Jeffrey H. Richards is an associate professor of English at Old Dominion University.

Joseph R. Roach is a professor in the Department of English at Tulane University.

Index

evolutionary model of, 271–72; and
resistance, 285
Culler, Jonathon, 144
Cultural politics: and tourism, 146; and
museums, 269; and memory, 333, 335,
339
Cultural production: tourism and,
142–43
Culture, 49, 142
Culture-performance dialectic: 98

Davidson, Kathy N., 239, 245
Deconstruction, 35, 347
Demonstrative performance, 106–7
Desire: homosocial, 57; lesbian, 65–66;
for authenticity, 136; and visuality,
197; and touch, 207; nostalgic, 280;
and ethics, 346
Dialogue, 22–23, 106
Difference: in historicity, 5; and plea-
sure, 38; and surrogation, 58; sexual,
206–7; and sameness, 213; in museum
historiography, 268; and museums,
270; and otherness, 354
Direction of effectivity. See Effectivity
Disruptive performance, 298, 304, 312
Dolan, Jill, 1
Dorst, John, 146
DuBois, Page, 14
Duplicity, 126. See also Ambivalence

Eco, Umberto, 143
École Française d'Extrême Orient, 299,
301
Economies of place, 32
Effectivity, 98, 105
Empowerment: story-telling and, 330
Epidemiology: class and, 172
Eroticism, 207–8, 221
"Essentially Contested Concept"
(ECC), 111–12
Ethnicity: in museums, 270, 273
Everyday life: and performance, 3;
tactical politics of, 18; Fiske on, 30;
slave trade in performance of, 53;
and knowledge, 320

Excess, 8, 33, 193
Exoticization of the South, 143

"Feejee Mermaid," 125
Feldman, Allen, 4, 13
Fernandez, James, 149
Fetish, 206, 213
Fine, Elizabeth, 155
Fiske, John, 4, 30
Flesh, 199; commodification of, 72–73;
theories of. See Theories of the Flesh.
Fliegelman, Jay, 238
Foucault, Michel, 199, 261, 307–8
Freud, Sigmund, 206
Frow, John, 143, 145

Gates, Henry Louis, Jr., 50
Gaze, the: 5, 196; oppositional, 7–8;
sight and, 215; annihilation and, 226;
oppression and, 334
Gaze of the invisible, 196–97, 213, 226
Geertz, Clifford, 343, 345, 351, 355
Gender identity: shame and, 222
Genealogy of performance, 29, 50
Gilroy, Paul, 61, 72
Gitter, Elisabeth G., 219
Gospel tradition, 326–28
Gramsci, Antonio, 262
Gray, Paul, 111
Grotesque, the, 129–30, 133

Habermas, Jürgen, 81
Halttunen, Karen, 123–24, 138
Hamilton, Kristie, 239, 245
Harris, Neil, 123–24
Harrison-Pepper, Sally, 109
Harvey, David, 108–9
Hawthorne, Nathaniel, 31, 121, 126–34
Hegemony, 148, 298, 300
Herskowitz, Richard, 122
Hidden transcript, 288, 299, 311–12
Historical montage, 265
Historical narrative: difference from
narrativity, 12; personal involvement
in, 267–68, 288–89; authenticity in,
283

Musée Victor Hugo, 298, 304
"Museum Effect," 279
Museums, 34–35; as distinct from the-
    ater, 125; and "historical continuity,"
    263; and pedagogy, 263–64; and cul-
    tural diversity, 268; and ethnicity,
    270–73; and objectification, 275; as
    disruptive performance, 298, 304,
    312; and state hegemony, 298; spec-
    tatorship in, 299, 303, 305; and art
    history, 301; theatrical function of,
    301; as metaphor for nation, 302; and
    mimesis, 305; and touch, 310
"Museumification," 34
Myth of objectivity, 5–6

Narrative: truth, 16–18; and ideological
    hegemony, 148; situation, 238–40; of
    nostalgia, 280; authenticity in histori-
    cal, 283; event, 330; journalistic mode,
    352–53. *See also* Historical Narrative
Narratives: public, 29; tour guide, 152;
    of origin, 266–67
Narrativity, 11–13, 24; difference from
    historical narrative, 12
Nation, the: and ambivalence, 24; per-
    formativity of discourse on, 24; and
    discourses of womanhood, 239–45,
    251–54; and performance, 359
Nationalism: and state hegemony, 81;
    and the body, 87; and the metonymic
    function of museums, 302
New Historicism, 30
Nichols, Bill, 135
Nommo, 326–27, 336
Norris, Christopher, 16
Nostalgia, 280

The Octoroon; or, Life in Louisiana (Dion
    Boucicault), 50, 58–66
Odor: social history of, 166; and spatial
    boundaries, 173–74
Oral history, 18; poetic transcription
    approach to, 322–23
Origins: relativization of, 19; and evolu-
    tionary model of museum contextual-

ization, 272; primitivism in search for,
    372
Otherness, 343, 345; and anti-theatrical
    prejudice, 34; and representation,
    137; problem of authority in repre-
    senting, 372–73

Paris Is Burning (Livingston), 135–37
Pedagogy, historical, 274
Péladan, Sar, 294, 303
Performance, 1–2, 4, 22, 28–29; histori-
    ography, 1–2, 291; and history, 2–27;
    and the body, 8; and text, 21–22; per-
    formativity of, 26; and theater, 26–27;
    and culture, 49; displaced transmis-
    sion of, 66–74; as "essentially con-
    tested concept" (ECC), 111–12; and
    humbug, 138; and tourism, 142, 151–
    55; and social reform, 262; and death,
    294; as "occupation," 337; as rhythm,
    337; and theories of the flesh, 338;
    and nationality, 359
—approaches to: in critical theory, 2, 49,
    50, 98; genealogical, 29; demonstra-
    tive, 106–7; remonstrative, 107; ago-
    nistic view of, 114–15; pedagogical,
    264; narrative, 321; poetic transcrip-
    tion, 322–23; *nommo*, 326–27
—politics of, 22, 105, 114–15, 152–53,
    298; and ideological co-option, 272;
    disruptive, 298, 304, 312
"Performative primitives," 146
Performativity, 20–27; Judith Bulter, 2;
    J.L. Austin, 20–21; Mikhail Bakhtin,
    22–23; Homi Bhabha, 23–26; of his-
    tory, 28
Phelan, Peggy, 136–37, 210, 213
Pilgrimage, 149
Poetic transcription approach, 322–23
Postmodern: history, 34; tourism,
    145–46
Poststructuralism, 36
Presence, 26–27, 266, 295, 297;
    rhetorics of, 29; metaphysics of, 262,
    278; in historiography, 278; and per-
    formance historiography, 291

Preziosi, Donald, 301, 302, 304, 305
Price, Sally, 290
Primitivism, 146, 372
Product-producer dialectic, 30, 98
Progressive era, 262, 274; management
  of ambivalence in, 269

Raban, Jonathan, 146
Rabinow, Paul, 137
Reform: of theater sanitation, 162, 172;
  performance-based activities and, 262
Remonstrative performance, 107
Representation: historical, 3–6, 9–16;
  and memory, 10–11; Said on, 13;
  Baudrillard on, 14–16; of the nation,
  24; and theater, 26–27; irony of, 27;
  spatial, 109; of homosexuality, 134–
  37; of race, 134–37; and otherness,
  137, 343; and advertisements, 233;
  and the metaphysics of presence, 278;
  and mimesis, 306; and social relations,
  306
Resiliency, 110
Resistance, 105; laughter as, 130, 288; in
  tour guide performances, 153; and
  museum contextualization, 285; and
  hidden transcripts, 311–12; homeplace as site of, 326; and specialized
  knowledge, 338–39; and theories of
  the flesh, 339; to orthodoxy, 346; and
  a sense of "locale," 351
Rhetorics of presence, 29
Rhythm, 322, 336–37
Ricoeur, Paul, 21
Riggs, Marlon, 134–35, 137
Riviere, Joan, 211
Rosenberg, Howard, 134

Sabean, David, 93
Said, Edward, 13
Sayre, Henry, 26–27
Schechner, Richard, 50, 109
Scholes, Robert, 19
Scott, James, 154, 299, 311
Scott, Joan, 18–19, 261
Searle, John, 21

Seduction, sexual: and American poli-
  tics, 240–43; as narrative situation,
  238–40; and female virtue, 244–45
Senghor, Leopold Sedar, 336
Sentimentalism, 133, 238–239
Sexuality, 199–200; political, 252; and
  hair, 219–21; and hands, 201–7
Shame, 221–22; touristic, 144–45
Sight: and invisibility, 196
Simulacrum, 14–16
Smith-Rosenberg, Carroll, 239, 245
Social drama, 350–51
Soja, Edward, 109
South, the: thearicalization of, 143
Space, 108–11; of performance, 38; and
  representation, 109; as influential and
  latent environments, 110; and odor,
  173–74
Spatialities of life and death, 91
Specialized knowledge, 320–21; and
  counterhegemonic discourse, 338
Spectacle, 59–60
Spectatorship, 33, 299, 303, 305, 310
Speer, Jean Haskell, 155
Spheres of contestation. See Contesta-
  tion, spheres of
Stallybrass, Peter, 199
Stanley, Liz, 199–200
Stewart, Susan, 201, 280
Stories, 16–18, anti-slaveholder, 147;
  anti-Southern, 147; suppression of
  history in, 5; telling as empowerment,
  330–31. See also Narrativity
Strine, Mary S. 111, 115
Surrogation, 58–66
Surveillance, 89–90; and gender, 241

Taussig, Michael, 261, 265, 267
Terdiman, Richard, 105
Text(uality), 21–22; and historiography,
  278; and textualization, 92
Theater: and class differentiation, 172,
  176; as instrument of seduction, 253;
  as interpretive instrument, 343; as
  laboratory for living, 354; and mimesis, 26; and moralism, 243; and the

social history of odor, 170–71; vs. museum, 125; mistrust of. *See* Anti-Theatrical Prejudice

Theatricality, 25–27; and 18th century virtue, 243–49; and humbug, 123; in Nathaniel Hawthorne, 127–33; and American literary/cultural history, 133; and sentimentalism, 238–39; of the South, 143; of the tour, 32

Theories of the Flesh, 319–20, 338–39

Tongues Untied (Riggs), 134–35, 137

Torgovnick, Marianna, 373

Touch, 194–95, 196, 216; and desire, 207; and eroticism, 221; and fetishization, 213; and museum spectatorship, 310; and Victorianism, 219

Tourism, 32, 142–46; and ambivalence, 153, 155; "plantation style," 150; political economy of, 150

Travel, 142, 143

Trickery, 122, 124

Trickster, the, 7–8, 123–24, 130

Trinh Minh-ha, 6, 16–17

"True Womanhood," 334–35

Turner, Victor, 343, 347, 350, 351

Tyler, Stephen, 137

Urry, John, 142

Value: and humbug, 122, 124, 129; and contextualization, 271

Visibility, 193, 277

Visibility politics, 7

Visualism, 5–6, 32; and desire, 197; and tourism, 145

Wallace, Michael, 147

West, Cornel, 328

White, Allon, 199

White, Hayden, 11–13, 261

Womanhood: and the nation, 239–43, 251–54; and virtue, 244–45

Yeazell, Ruth Bernard, 221–22

DATE DUE